Folk Psychology

READINGS IN MIND AND LANGUAGE

1 Understanding Vision: An Interdisciplinary Perspective
   Edited by Glyn W. Humphreys
2 Consciousness: Psychological and Philosophical Essays
   Edited by Martin Davies and Glyn W. Humphreys
3 Folk Psychology: The Theory of Mind Debate
   Edited by Martin Davies and Tony Stone
4 Mental Simulation: Evaluations and Applications
   Edited by Martin Davies and Tony Stone

Folk Psychology

The Theory of Mind Debate

Edited by

Martin Davies and Tony Stone

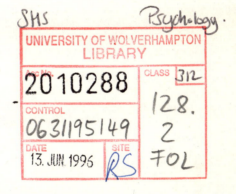

BLACKWELL
Oxford UK & Cambridge USA

Copyright © Blackwell Publishers Ltd, 1995

First published 1995

Blackwell Publishers Ltd
108 Cowley Road
Oxford OX4 1JF
UK

Blackwell Publishers Inc.
238 Main Street
Cambridge, Massachusetts 02142
USA

British Library Cataloguing in Publication Data

A CIP catalogue record for this book is available from the British Library.

Library of Congress Cataloging-in-Publication Data has been applied for.

ISBN 0-631-19514-9; ISBN 0-631-19515-7 (pbk.)

Typeset in 9$^1/_2$ on 11 pt Palatino
by Best-set Typesetter Ltd., Hong Kong
Printed in Great Britain by Hartnolls Ltd., Bodmin, Cornwall

This book is printed on acid-free paper.

Contents

List of Contributors   vii

Acknowledgements   ix

Introduction   1
MARTIN DAVIES AND TONY STONE

1 Replication and Functionalism   45
JANE HEAL

2 Folk Psychology as Simulation   60
ROBERT M. GORDON

3 Interpretation Psychologized   74
ALVIN I. GOLDMAN

4 The Simulation Theory: Objections and Misconceptions   100
ROBERT M. GORDON

5 Folk Psychology: Simulation or Tacit Theory?   123
STEPHEN STICH AND SHAUN NICHOLS

6 'He Thinks He Knows': And More Developmental Evidence
   Against the Simulation (Role-taking) Theory   159
JOSEF PERNER AND DEBORRAH HOWES

7 Reply to Stich and Nichols   174
ROBERT M. GORDON

8 Reply to Perner and Howes   185
   ROBERT M. GORDON

9 In Defense of the Simulation Theory   191
   ALVIN I. GOLDMAN

10 From Simulation to Folk Psychology: The Case for Development   207
    PAUL L. HARRIS

11 Why the Child's Theory of Mind Really *Is* a Theory   232
    ALISON GOPNIK AND HENRY M. WELLMAN

12 Reading the Eyes: Evidence for the Role of Perception in the
    Development of a Theory of Mind   259
    SIMON BARON-COHEN AND PIPPA CROSS

13 Theory, Observation, and Drama   274
    SIMON BLACKBURN

    Index of Authors   291
    Index of Subjects   295

List of Contributors

SIMON BARON-COHEN Departments of Experimental Psychology and Psychiatry, University of Cambridge, Downing Street, Cambridge CB2 3EB, UK

SIMON BLACKBURN Department of Philosophy, University of North Carolina, Chapel Hill, NC 27599, USA

PIPPA CROSS Department of Child Psychiatry, Institute of Psychiatry, De Crespigny Park, London SE5 8AF, UK

MARTIN DAVIES Department of Experimental Psychology, University of Oxford, South Parks Road, Oxford OX1 3UD, UK

ALVIN I. GOLDMAN Department of Philosophy, University of Arizona, Tucson, AZ 85721, USA

ALISON GOPNIK Department of Psychology, University of California, Berkeley, CA 94720, USA

ROBERT M. GORDON Department of Philosophy, University of Missouri – St. Louis, St Louis, Missouri 63121-4499, USA

PAUL L. HARRIS Department of Experimental Psychology, University of Oxford, South Parks Road, Oxford OX1 3UD, UK

JANE HEAL St John's College, Cambridge CB2 1TP, UK

DEBORRAH HOWES Ontario Institute of Studies in Education, 252 Bloor Street West, Toronto, Ontario M5S 1V6, Canada

SHAUN NICHOLS Department of Philosophy, College of Charleston, Charleston, SC 29424, USA

JOSEF PERNER   Institut für Psychologie, Universität Salzburg, Hellbrunnerstrasse 34, A–5020 Salzburg, Austria

STEPHEN STICH   Department of Philosophy, Davison Hall, Rutgers University, New Brunswick, NJ 08903-0270, USA

TONY STONE   School of Science, Technology and Design, King Alfred's College of Higher Education, Sparkford Road, Winchester SO22 4NR, UK

HENRY M. WELLMAN   Center for Human Growth and Development, University of Michigan, Ann Arbor, MI 48109, USA

Acknowledgements

This book, the third in the *Readings in Mind and Language* series, is based upon a Special Issue of *Mind and Language* (volume 7, numbers 1 and 2, spring/ summer 1992). Chapters 4 through 13 are reprinted from that Special Issue, sometimes with modest revisions. Chapters 2 and 3 appeared in earlier numbers of *Mind and Language* (volume, 1, number 2, summer 1986, and volume 4, number 3, autumn 1989, respectively). Chapter 1, 'Replication and Functionalism', by Jane Heal, first appeared in Jeremy Butterfield (ed.), *Language, Mind and Logic* (Cambridge University Press, 1986), and is reprinted with the kind permission of Cambridge University Press.

A companion volume, *Mental Simulation: Evaluations and Applications*, edited by Martin Davies and Tony Stone (Oxford: Blackwell, 1995) contains thirteen further chapters that continue the themes of the present book.

Thanks to Rosalind Barrs for her secretarial assistance.

Introduction

MARTIN DAVIES AND TONY STONE

When David Premack and Guy Woodruff (1978) asked, 'Does the chimpanzee have a theory of mind?', they explained that (1978, p. 515): 'In saying that an individual has a theory of mind we mean that the individual imputes mental states to himself and to others.' This is a rather thin use of the term 'theory of mind'; in this sense, just to attribute mental states is to have a theory of mind. But Premack and Woodruff also used the term 'theory of mind' in a more specifically committed way, when they contrasted the hypothesis that the chimpanzee Sarah has a theory of mind, with the hypothesis that Sarah predicts what an actor will do by engaging in 'empathy' (1978, p. 518):

> The empathy view diverges [from the theory of mind view] only in that
> it does not grant the animal any inferences about another's knowledge.

The idea here is that having a theory of mind is having a body of information about cognition and motivation that is applicable to others, just as much as to oneself. Given such a body of generalizations, one can use premises about what another individual knows or believes, in order to reach conclusions about that individual's actions, for example.

The essays collected in this volume are foundational contributions to a complex interdisciplinary debate about the nature of the theory of mind. On one side of the debate are those philosophers and psychologists who say that the ability to attribute mental states and predict actions is best thought of as resting upon possession of a theory of mind in the more committed sense. On the other side of the debate are those who say that basic theory of mind abilities are better thought of as grounded in a capacity to empathize (or simulate, or identify in imagination with another).

In this Introduction we aim to provide an overview of the debate which will enable the papers that follow to be located within it.

1 The Debate in Outline

It has come to be a standard assumption in philosophy and psychology that normal adult human beings have a rich conceptual repertoire which they deploy to explain, predict and describe the actions of one another and, perhaps, members of closely related species also. As is usual, we shall speak of this rich conceptual repertoire as 'folk psychology' and of its deployment as 'folk-psychological practice'. The conceptual repertoire constituting folk psychology includes, predominantly, the concepts of belief and desire and their kin – intention, hope, fear, and the rest – the so-called propositional attitudes.

If this standard assumption is correct, then we need to begin by asking a very basic question:

> What is the nature, and what are the key characteristics, of normal adult folk psychology and of its deployment?

This question has both philosophical and psychological aspects. We will introduce some of them by considering the celebrated experiment of Heinz Wimmer and Josef Perner (1983).

1.1 The False Belief Task

A puppet show about two characters, Sally and Anne, is performed in front of two groups of children. The younger group has a mean age of around three and a half years; the older group just under five years (the means vary a little between experiments). Sally is shown putting a marble in a basket; she then goes out to play. Whilst she is away, Anne transfers the marble from the basket into a box. Sally then returns and wants to play with her marble. The experimental design ensures that the children understand the story and remember where Sally left her marble. The crucial question, is then asked:

> Where will Sally look for her marble?

Children in the older group have little difficulty in answering this question correctly. They understand that Sally will look for her marble in the place where she left it. They realize that she does not know that the marble has been moved, and so will act upon a false belief. Therefore, they say that Sally will look for the marble in the basket. Children in the younger group, however, fail to answer this question correctly. They say that Sally will look for the marble in the box; that is, they think that Sally will look for the marble where it really is and not where she left it.

This result raises the obvious developmental question:

> Why can five-year-olds get the answer right and three-year-olds not?

Lying behind this question, and the experiment that motivates it, is the assumption that the older children have an understanding of folk psychology that is in key respects identical to the understanding that the mature adult has, whereas the younger children lack some aspects of adult understanding. Given this assumption, the experiment becomes a diagnostic of whether a child has attained the mature state with respect to key components of the conceptual repertoire that comprises our folk psychology.

In order to give any more specific answer to the developmental question raised by Wimmer and Perner's experiment, we need to have some idea of the nature of the adult's folk-psychological ability. That is, in order to answer the developmental question, we must have some answer to the basic question about adults as well. We now set out two approaches to answering the questions about adults and about children.

1.2 The Theory Theory

Here is how a *theory theorist* might begin upon answering the two questions we have put on the table thus far.

(TTa) In order to succeed in the false belief task, a subject must be able to entertain thoughts of the following general form:

(T)   He [some other] believes that *p*

where '*p*' stands in for a proposition which describes some counterfactual state of affairs. In particular, to succeed in the false belief task, a child must be able to entertain the thought:

Sally believes that the marble is in the basket.

even though – as the child knows – the marble is not, in fact, in the basket.

(TTb) To be able to entertain thoughts with this general form a subject needs to have the concept of belief. Having *the concept of belief* is more than just having *beliefs* – more than simply being in belief states. The child who fails the false belief task, whatever his conceptual sophistication, presumably has beliefs. For example, the child believes that the marble is in the box. That is why he says that Sally will look there.

(TTc) In order to have the concept of belief, a subject must possess a body of psychological knowledge: a body of knowledge about psychology that can legitimately be considered a *psychological theory*.

These three steps, leading up to the introduction of the idea of a folk-psychological theory, involve philosophical claims: claims about the necessary conditions for possessing a particular concept. Those philosophical claims are not the immediate focus of psychological research into folk psychology. But the idea of a folk-psychological theory that they introduce frames the theory theorist's answers to the following two clearly empirical questions about normal adult folk-psychological abilities and their development in childhood:

> What psychological processes or mechanisms underpin our mastery of the concept of belief?

> What is the course of development of the child's mastery of the concepts that are deployed in our folk-psychological practice?

The second of these questions demands an answer that is both descriptive and explanatory. We want an accurate and complete description of the developmental stages through which the child passes on the way to adult mastery of folk-psychological concepts. One part of that description will be that children pass through a transition between the ages of three and five. Before the transition, they cannot do the false belief task correctly; afterwards they can. But we also want an illuminating explanatory account of what produces the shifts between the stages so described. The theory theorist says that this is a matter of changes in the available body of psychological knowledge. Thus we have a further cluster of empirical claims:

(TTd) The course of development of folk psychology is a matter of the child gradually adding components to the body of knowledge – the theory – whose completion will constitute full acquisition of the adult concept of belief.

(TTe) These changes in the child's psychological theory can usefully be conceived in terms of the way that scientific theories develop and change. Thus, we can draw an analogy between the development and change of bodies of professional scientific knowledge and the development and change of the child's body of folk-psychological knowledge.

(TTf) In order for a subject to put a body of knowledge to use in folk-psychological practice, various information processing mechanisms are needed. Changes in that practice as a child passes through successive stages of development may be accompanied by, or may even be explained by, changes in underlying information processing mechanisms.

Now, why can five-year-olds in the false belief task experiment get the answer right and three-year-olds not? The theory theorist's answer adverts to both having and using knowledge:

> The child of five succeeds because he meets two conditions. He has a body of knowledge that is sufficient to answer the question correctly, and he has developed the information processing mechanisms that enable that knowledge to be put to use.

> The child of three fails because he does not meet both those conditions. Either he lacks the necessary body of knowledge, or else he lacks the requisite information processing mechanisms for putting that knowledge to use.

Theory theorists differ over whether the three-year-old's crucial deficit is in knowledge about psychology or in mechanisms for using that knowledge.

The six claims (TTa) to (TTf) outline just a hypothetical version of the theory theory – a version motivated by the idea of a link between possession of psychological concepts and knowledge of psychological theory. We shall come to the views of actual theory theorists later. First, we turn to an equally hypothetical version of the simulation alternative.

1.3 The Simulation Theory

One way to introduce the simulation theory is to sketch a philosophical background and then a series of empirical claims parallel to, but of course contrasting with, the theory theorist's (TTa) to (TTf). So, the simulation theorist might make these claims:

(STa) In order to succeed in the false belief task, a subject does not need to entertain thoughts of the form (T), but only thoughts of the form:

I believe that *p*

where the subject *imaginatively identifies* with someone else and imagines a counterfactual situation. Thus, to succeed in the false belief task, a child must be able to imaginatively identify with Sally, imagine the world from Sally's point of view, and then – within the scope of this imaginative identification – entertain the thought:

I [Sally] believe that the marble is in the basket.

even though – as the child knows – the marble is not, in fact, in the basket.

(STb) To be able to entertain thoughts of just that first-person form, a subject does not need to have the full-blown concept of belief. In fact, the 'I believe that' could just as well be deleted. The child identifying with Sally merely needs to entertain the thought: The marble is in the basket. The child does not need to have the concept of belief, but merely to be able to have beliefs. In general, then, what is needed is the ability to entertain thoughts of the form:

(S) *p*

while imaginatively identifying with another.

(STc) Even if having the concept of belief requires a subject to possess a body of knowledge about folk psychology, this is not required in order merely to have beliefs. On the other hand, the ability to have beliefs is not enough, by itself, for success in the false belief task. In addition, the child must be able to simulate another subject whose view on the world is different from her own.

These three claims establish a framework that contrasts sharply with that of the theory theory. Within this alternative framework, the simulation theorist offers his own answers to the empirical questions about normal adult folk-psychological abilities and their development in childhood:

(STd) The course of development of folk psychology is a matter of the child gradually becoming more adept at imaginatively identifying with other people and at imagining counterfactual situations.

(STe) The changes in the child's folk-psychological practice are changes in ability not in knowledge. The appropriate analogy is not the development of scientific theories but rather the development and refining of a skill.

(STf) In order for a subject to engage in these imaginative tasks, various information processing mechanisms are needed. Changes in under-lying mechanisms may accompany, or even explain, developmental transitions.

According to the simulation theory, then, why can five-year-olds in the false belief task experiment get the answer right and three year olds not?

> The child of five succeeds where the child of three fails because the older child has an ability to simulate another whose view upon the world is different from his own. (The child subject saw the marble moved from the basket to the box; Sally in contrast was out of the room, and so quite literally had a different view.)

The simulation theorist's account in terms of ability or skill does not subdivide, in the way that the theory theorist's does, into an account of a body of knowledge plus an account of mechanisms through which the knowledge is put to use. But that must not obscure the fact that the simulation theorist is still interested in psychological mechanisms – information processing mechanisms that underpin the crucial abilities.

One of the most noticeable aspects of this debate is that it is not a matter of simple opposition between two alternatives: it is not just a question of Theory Theory versus Simulation Theory. There are different and competing versions of each of the two major positions, and we shall mention some of those variations in due course. For now, however, our task is to characterize the two theories a little more fully.

2 The Theory Theory

Why would anyone claim that ordinary folk-psychological ability rests upon knowledge of a theory? Our exposition of a version of the theory theory offers some motivation for this claim in the philosophical idea of a link between concept mastery and possession of a body of knowledge. But, still, the claim that folk psychology is a theory will seem to many to pose immediate problems.

Certainly, we need a sense of 'theory' which is robust enough to meet the charge of 'promiscuity' levelled at the theory theorist by Simon Blackburn (this volume, pp. 275). We must use a notion of theory that does not collapse into the idea, merely, that:

> If we are good at something . . . then we can be thought of as making tacit (very tacit) use of some set of principles that could, in principle, provide a description of a device, or possibly a recipe for the construction of a device, that is also good at it.

If our conception of (tacit) knowledge of a theory is as weak as this, then we face the prospect of an early collapse of the debate between the theory theorist and the simulation theorist. For, an advocate of the view that our folk-psychological practice is underpinned by an ability would have little difficulty in agreeing that there can be a theoretical description of a practical ability–just so long as the ability in question has structure to be articulated, which our folk-psychological ability surely does.

So, the claim that folk psychology is a theory must be stronger than the claim that our folk-psychological practice can be given a theoretical description – that is, stronger than the claim that there is a theoretical representation of a practical ability (Dummett, 1976). We must give some thicker sense to the claim that our folk-psychological practice depends upon our being in possession of a body of knowledge. And then we must say what, if anything, it adds if we call the body of knowledge a theory.

In (TTe), we had the theory theorist drawing an analogy between the development and change of bodies of professional scientific knowledge and the development and change of the child's body of folk-psychological knowledge. Philosophers, as well as developmental psychologists, have been happy to make this move explicitly. Indeed, the developmentalists have been following the philosophers here. Paul Churchland (1981, 1991), for example, claims that folk psychology is an empirical theory that is subject to the same canons of empirical evaluation as any other.

However, *prima facie*, folk psychology does not look at all like what we might call 'professional science' – say, quantum physics or the theory of evolution. Folk-psychological practice clearly does not bear the marks of a scientific research programme. If is not, for example, written up in text book form; it is not subject to rigorous empirical investigation; nor does it have to be actively taught.

In what sense, then, is folk psychology a theory? On the one hand, it is not enough to say that it is a theory in the minimal 'promiscuous' sense identified by Blackburn. On the other hand, there seem to be disanalogies between folk-psychological practice and professional scientific research programmes.

Two routes might be taken at this point. The first draws an analogy between folk psychology and linguistics, by making use fo the Chomskyan notion of tacit knowledge. The second route retains elements of the professional science analogy, but does so by drawing some *specific* parallels between the structure and the form of explanations deployed in folk psychology and the structure and form of explanations deployed by science.

2.1 *The Analogy with Linguistics*

Chomskyan linguistics has made a particular explanatory strategy immensely popular within cognitive science. Stephen Stich and Shaun Nichols (this volume) dub it 'the dominant explanatory strategy'. They say (p. 123):

> the dominant explanatory strategy proceeds by positing an internally represented 'knowledge structure' – typically a body of rules or principles or propositions – which serves to guide the execution of the capacity to be explained. These rules or principles or propositions are often described as the agent's 'theory' of the domain in question. In some cases, the theory may be partly accessible to consciousness; the agent can tell us some of the rules or principles he is using. More often, however, the agent has no conscious access to the knowledge guiding his behaviour.

As applied to the case of language, the basic idea is this. Human beings have the ability to produce and understand an indefinite number of sentences of their native language (or idiolect). The linguist wants to explain this capacity, and to explain it in a way which enables the developmental data to be accounted for. Specifically, the explanation of the capacity must be such as to make it feasible for humans to develop the capacity in the way that they do: very quickly, ahead of the development of substantial general intellectual abilities, independently of the development of other symbolic capacities, and without any formal tuition. The explanation provided by the linguist begins with the postulation of a grammar of the language. The grammar postulated by the linguist is such that, were it to be known and deployed by the language user, it would result in the speaker being able to produce and understand just the sentences that she does in fact produce and understand. Up to this point, however, the postulation of the grammar serves a barely descriptive, rather than an explanatory, function.

The application of the 'dominant explanatory strategy' comes when the linguist claims that a person who knows a language does so in virtue of being in possession of the body of knowledge expressed by the grammar. The ordinary language user does not have knowledge of the grammar in the way she might subsequently come to have knowledge of quantum physics, or indeed knowledge of the grammar if she becomes a linguist. The speaker of the language possesses and deploys the body of knowledge tacitly.

Why does this appeal to tacit knowledge not fall to Blackburn's point above? This is a complex and controversial question, but the line of argument of the linguist, and of the cognitive scientist who wishes to use this strategy in other areas of cognitive life, will be something like this. The speaker of the language knows (tacitly) the grammar of the language in that the body of knowledge described by grammar is causally active in the linguistic behaviour of the speaker. It is causally active through being encoded in the mind/brain of the speaker. Much more should be (and indeed has been) said about this strategy, of course. But this tiny sketch is already enough to see that the strategy goes beyond the claim that the principles in the grammar 'could, in principle, provide a description of a device, or possibly a recipe for the construction of a device, that is also good at [doing what we can do]'. Chomsky, of course, has always argued that the claim for the psychological reality of a body of tacit knowledge is just the claim that the attribution of the body of tacit knowledge is correct according to the normal canons of scientific success.

Analogously, then, the theory theorist of folk psychology will want to say that the best explanation of the human ability to predict and explain the actions of others is that humans possess knowledge of the principles of folk psychology. These principles can, like the principles of grammar, be articulated from a third-person viewpoint, and can be said to be possessed and deployed by the human adult. According to the normal canons of scientific success, our grounds for this attribution would be provided by an inference to the best explanation of folk-psychological practice.

2.2 The Analogy with Professional Science

An indication of the theoretical depth of the explanatory strategy followed in linguistics is provided by the rich and sophisticated structure that grammars have had to be given in order to account for the linguistic data. The complexity and idiosyncrasy of the speaker/hearer's task seems to rule out putative alternative explanations, such as explanations in terms of general learning rules. But, in what sense would a folk-psychological theory show comparable richness and sophistication? Here, there seems to be a serious disanalogy with linguistics. For folk psychology is often thought to have a simple and homely content (hence the epithet 'folk'). Once its principles are articulated, they seem to be obvious. (Contrast the principles of a generative grammar.)

The homely nature of folk psychology has not, however, standardly been seen as a problem for the idea that folk psychology is a theory. Indeed, David Lewis (1972) argues that we should see our folk psychology 'as a term-introducing scientific theory, though one invented long before there was any such institution as professional science' (p. 256). The theory is formulated in the following way (ibid.):

> Collect all the platitudes you can think of regarding the causal relations
> of mental states, sensory stimuli and motor responses. . . . Include only

platitudes which are common knowledge among us – everyone knows them, everyone knows that everyone else knows them, and so on.

The general form of these platitudes is said to be (ibid.):

When someone is in so-and-so combination of mental states and receives sensory stimuli of so-and-so kind, he tends with so-and-so probability to be caused thereby to go into so-and-so mental states and produce so-and-so motor responses.

Paul Churchland (1988, pp. 58–9) has given the following concrete examples of these kinds of platitude:

Persons tend to feel pain at points of recent bodily damage

Persons in pain tend to want to relieve that pain

Persons who want that P, and believe that Q would be sufficient to bring about P, and have no conflicting wants or preferred strategies, will try to bring it about that Q.

Furthermore, in line with Lewis's idea that these principles are common knowledge, Churchland speaks of their being learned 'at mother's knee, as we learn our language' (1988, p. 59).

One aspect of the platitudinous nature of these principles is that the concepts that are used in them are not at all remote from the concepts that we ordinarily deploy in our folk-psychological judgements. As we learn to engage in folk-psychological practice, so also we learn the concepts of belief, desire, preference, trying, pain and so on. But, as we learn to engage in linguistic practice – to produce and understand sentences – we do not normally learn the concepts – of phrase structure, head, complement, theta-role, c-command, and so on – that figure in the principles of a generative grammar. Likewise, the platitudinous principles of folk psychology are not difficult to understand or to accept, for someone immersed in the practice. But the principles of a generative grammar are understood only by theoretical linguists, and may be highly unobvious, even to experts.

We said that the theory theory needs to avoid the hopelessly weak notion of tacit theory to which Blackburn draws attention, and also needs to acknowledge the disanalogies between folk psychology and professional science. We suggested two ways forward. One is to pursue an analogy with the use of the 'dominant explanatory strategy' in linguistics. But we have seen that there are disanalogies here too. The other is to pursue a limited analogy with professional science. We have the beginnings of this limited analogy in Lewis's idea of folk psychology as a term-introducing theory.

We can take the limited analogy with professional science a step further by comparing the forms of explanation in folk psychology with the deductive-nomological explanations that are usually regarded as characteristic of science. Explanations in folk psychology are sometimes said to be 'rationalizing' explanations, but the theory theorist says that they are nevertheless a species of 'regularizing' explanations, or explanations by subsumption under generalizations. In his book *Psychosemantics* (1987), Fodor states that common-sense psychological explanation (p. 7):

> exhibit[s] the 'deductive structure' that is so characteristic of explanation in real science. There are two parts to this: the theory's underlying generalizations are defined over unobservables, and they lead to its predictions by iterating and interacting rather than being directly instantiated.

Fodor is saying, then, that folk psychology has the form of a theory because it has the following characteristics:

 (i) it includes nomological generalizations;
(ii) it postulates unobservable entities;
(iii) the unobservable entities play an explanatory role as bearers of causal powers.

In essence, Fodor holds that the structure of folk-psychological explanation is deductive-nomological, and that the generalizations employed are generalizations over unobservable bearers of causal powers. The generalizations Fodor considers to be characteristic of folk psychology are similar to the final one in the list we took from Churchland (1988, p. 59):

> Persons who want that *P*, and believe that *Q* would be sufficient to bring about *P*, and have no conflicting wants or preferred strategies, will try to bring it about that *Q*.

They are generalizations about the role of beliefs and preferences in the causal build-up to decision, intention and action.

2.3 Linguistics, Science and Psychological Concepts

We have been looking at two ways in which the theory theory about folk psychology can avoid the threat of trivialization. One way is to stress the analogy with theoretical linguistics. The other way is to point to a limited analogy with professional science.

Perhaps, though, it is the linguistics analogy that is seen more naturally as a response to the threat that the debate between theory theory and simulation theory might collapse. That threat arises when we start thinking of folk-psychological theory as merely tacit. A tacitly known theory needs to be more than a theoretical description of a practical ability, and so we turn to linguistics and the philosophy of linguistics to fortify the notion of tacit knowledge.

Armed with a more robust notion of tacit knowledge, we then say that the explanatory structures behind our folk-psychological practice comprise a body of tacit knowledge, together with mechanisms for putting that knowledge to use. Not a great deal is added by saying that the body of tacit knowledge is a tacitly known *theory*. In the case of linguistics, the term 'theory' is indicative of the articulation of the body of knowledge into modules of grammar (X-bar theory, theta theory, case theory, binding theory, and so on), and of the complexity of the derivations of structural descriptions for particular sentences from highly general principles. In the case of folk psychology, there is not such evident promise of articulation and complexity.

So, if we start down the road to tacitness, reach for the comparison with linguistics, and then discover that the analogy has limitations, we might turn instead to the analogy with professional science. But a more natural route to that analogy does not take the detour through tacitness at all. Rather, it moves directly from the link between concepts and theories to Lewis's notion of a term-introducing theory.

Our initial account of the theory theory began with the link between concepts and theories – and particularly the link between possession of psychological concepts and knowledge of psychological theory (TTc). To that extent, the initial account sits more happily with the professional science analogy than with the linguistics analogy. For the linguistics analogy does not – at least at first sight – fit so naturally with the link between knowledge of theory and possession of concepts. The reason is that one of the marks of tacit knowledge is that its content does not have to be conceptualized by the subject. Tacit knowledge of principles about theta roles, or case assignment, or c-command does not require the subject who tacitly knows the principles to possess the concepts of theta role, or case, or c-command. So having the tacit knowledge can scarcely constitute grasp of those concepts. Likewise, it is not immediately obvious how a non-conceptualized internal encoding of principles of psychological theory could constitute grasp of psychological concepts.

If we start from the link between concepts and theories, and pursue the science analogy, then we have to face the question as to just how close the analogy between folk psychology and professional science is. As we said earlier (section 2) there do seem to be significant differences. The principles of folk psychology do not seem to be subject to rigorous empirical investigation; folk psychology is not learned by way of explicit formal teaching; nor is it written up in text book form. However, these points need not spoil the analogy. Henry Wellman (1990) draws a helpful distinction between questions about theories – particularly about what he calls 'framework theories' – and questions about theorizing. Framework theories 'define the ontology and basic causal devices for their specific theories' (1990, p. 125). Wellman points to similarities between scientific and common-sense framework theories, while allowing that common-sense theories are not the products of 'rigorous theorizing' (1990, p. 130). In particular (ibid.):

Young children have theories – or at least one theory, a commonsense (framework) theory of mind – but those theories are not the product of scientific theorizing.

It is not at the level of theorizing, but at the level of theory – in point of the 'specification of basic ontological commitments and . . . provision of general causal explanatory frameworks' (1990, p. 127) – that the analogy with professional science is supposed to provide motivation for the theory theory of folk psychology.

We should point out that not all theory theorists opt for a definite commitment to either the linguistics analogy or the science analogy. Stich and Nichols – whose work has done so much to organize and focus the debate – do not lay stress upon the analogy with science. And while they certainly allow tacit knowledge as one way in which the idea of an 'internally represented knowledge structure' might play out, they say no more than that folk psychology is a 'largely tacit psychological theory' (this volume, p. 124). In fact, they prefer to set up the debate using a broad and generic notion of knowledge of theory (Stich and Nichols, 1995, p. 88):

[T]here are lots of domains of common-sense knowledge in which it is rather implausible to suppose that the mentally represented 'knowledge structure' includes theoretical constructs linked together in lawlike ways. Knowledge of cooking or of current affairs are likely candidates here, as is the knowledge that underlies our judgements about what is polite and impolite in our culture. And it is entirely possible that folk-psychological knowledge will turn out to resemble the knowledge structures underlying cooking or politeness judgements rather than the knowledge structures that underlie the scientific predictions and explanations produced by a competent physicist or chemist.

For Stich and Nichols, the defining characteristic of the theory theory of folk psychology is the claim that our folk-psychological practice – principally, our explanations, predictions and descriptions of the actions of others – draws upon a body of psychological knowledge, *however we understand that body of knowledge to be structured.*

They adopt this approach for two reasons. First, they want to allow for versions of the theory theory in which our body of psychological knowledge has a connectionist implementation. So they at least do not want to burden the theory theory with a commitment to sentential encoding of psychological information. Second, they want to define the theory theory sufficiently broadly that it should be plausible that the theory theory and the simulation alternative are the only two candidate positions. Given that set-up, arguments against the one view are *ipso facto* arguments in favour of the other. In contrast, if the theory theory takes on very specific commitments by way of its favoured notion of theory, then an argument against the theory theory so construed is very far from being an argument in favour of simulation. Nor is an argument against the simulation view *ipso facto* an argument in favour of the theory theory so construed.

This hope for a neat debate between two logically exclusive and *de facto* exhaustive alternatives may, in the end, be forlorn, given the possibilities for hybrid views. But it is, of course, possible to follow Stich and Nichols in giving a liberal interpretation of the theory theory, without sharing their reasons. We end this section of the Introduction by returning to the question of the link between concepts and theories, in the context of this generic notion of knowledge of a theory.

The version of the theory theory that lays stress upon the analogy with science goes together well with the view that possession of psychological concepts is constituted by knowledge of a psychological theory embedding those concepts. But this is not an absolutely obligatory combination of views; the two are strictly independent. Either version of the theory theory (the analogy with science or the analogy with linguistics) might be adopted with or without commitment to a close connection between knowledge of theory and concept possession.

On the one hand, someone might favour the version of the theory theory that says that folk-psychological practice rests upon knowledge of a (framework) theory analogous to theories in science, but deny that this knowledge constitutes mastery of mental concepts. This denial might rest upon a suspicion of the whole notion of concept mastery, or upon a conviction that the most basic mastery of psychological concepts is constituted in some other way. On the other hand, we have to acknowledge the possibility that someone might overcome the initial impression that the version of the theory theory that stresses the analogy with linguistics sits uneasily with the idea of possession of psychological concepts as constituted by (tacit) knowledge of psychological theory.

Certainly, then, a neutral version of the theory theory using a generic notion of knowledge of theory could, but need not, go along with the link between knowledge of theory and possession of concepts. We introduced the theory theory via this link, and certainly, for many philosophers, questions about possession of psychological concepts are a prime concern. However, some philosophers and many psychologists will be ready to shift the focus from mastery of folk-psychological concepts to engagement in folk-psychological practice. In that case, the questions about the normal adult state and about childhood development become:

> What psychological processes or mechanisms underpin our normal adult engagement in folk-psychological practice?
>
> What is the course of development of the child's engagement in folk-psychological practice?

The theory theorist's answers to these questions are cast in terms of progress towards an attained state that comprises a body of psychological knowledge. But, given the distinction between having knowledge and using it, a theory

theory also needs to provide an account of the information processing mechanisms that enable that body of knowledge to be put to use.

3 The Simulation Theory

A key claim of the simulation theory is that, in order to succeed in the false belief task, the child needs to be able to entertain thoughts of the form:

> I believe that p

where the child imaginatively identifies with someone else and imagines a counterfactual situation. How does entertaining a thought of this first-person form enable the child to succeed? More generally, how are these first-person judgements supposed to provide a foundation for our folk-psychological practice?

One source of motivation for the simulation theory starts from the recognition that, whilst the prediction of the behaviour of others may be a tricky business, the prediction of our own immediate and near immediate actions is usually a simple and accurate matter.

In 'Folk Psychology as Simulation' (this volume, ch. 2), Robert Gordon provides us with a sample of his own accurate self-predictions. We can easily add our own:

I shall now look up Bob Gordon's examples.
I shall now continue typing this Introduction.
I shall shortly stop typing this Introduction and take a well-earned break.

These first-person statements, if made sincerely, are almost bound to be true. They scarcely have the character of predictions at all, but are reports of decisions that we have just made. They are intuitively quite different from the following predictions:

I am about to sneeze.
When the football match comes on the TV, I shall be unable to continue work.
While I am asleep, I shall keep on breathing.

These are first-person statements, and on the whole they are liable to be correct. Perhaps they are more likely to be correct than corresponding predictions about someone else:

He is about to sneeze.
When the football match comes on the TV, he will be unable to continue work.
While he is asleep, he will continue to breathe.

And perhaps not. But in any case, the difference between the first-person and the third-person case does not seem to run very deep here. It seems to be a matter of degree. In contrast, the predictive statements that issue from my own decisions are distinctively first personal.

Given that these distinctively first-personal, decision based, predictive statements are so accurate, it is tempting to wonder whether the psychological mechanisms that are used in making them might be put at the service of more difficult predictive tasks.

There does seem to be one fairly straightforward extension beyond the first person and his or her actual immediate future. This is the use of decision based methods to predict what I would do in certain specified counterfactual situations. How would I act if I were to be alone in the house and were to hear a sound in the basement? According to Gordon, I can arrive at an answer by employing the very same decision-making processes that I would use were I actually to be alone in the house and to hear a noise in the basement. I simply *pretend* that I am alone and that I have heard a noise and then make a decision – still within the scope of that pretence – about what to do. That decision within the scope of a pretence yields a prediction – not a pretended prediction – as to what I would do in the pretended circumstances (Gordon, this volume, p. 62):

> I imagine, for instance, a lone modification of the actual world: the sound of footsteps in the basement. Then I ask, in effect, 'what shall I do now?' And I answer with a declaration of immediate intention, 'I shall now . . .' This too is only feigned. But it is not feigned on a *tabula rasa*, as if at random: rather, the declaration of immediate intention appears to be formed in the way a *decision* is formed, *constrained* by the (pretended) 'fact' that there is a sound of footsteps from the basement, the (*un*pretended) fact that such a sound would now be unlikely if there weren't an intruder in the basement, the (*un*pretended) awfulness of there being an intruder in the basement, and so forth.

Given the attractiveness of this initial extension, is it possible to extend the first-person decision based methodology to third-person cases? Gordon thinks it is (this volume, p. 63):

> As in the case of hypothetical self-prediction, the methodology essentially involves *deciding what to do*; but, extended to people of 'minds' different from one's own, this is not the same as deciding *what I myself would do*. One tries to make *adjustments for relevant differences*.

To make the extension to the third-person case dramatic, and to bring out more fully the contrast with the theory theory, we can consider an analogy (cf. Heal, this volume, p. 47).

Consider how we might gain an understanding of the effects of a new drug upon the human body. One way would be to deploy the scientific knowledge provided by the disciplines of, *inter alia*, pharmacology and physiology. We could, that is, theoretically work out a hypothesis about the drug's effects by consciously deploying our scientific knowledge. However, there is another method available to us, a method that would often be used in the case of a new drug. We can administer the drug to non-human animals and see what real effects the drug has on those creatures. This method is, of course, fraught with methodological danger. Most obviously, the non-human animals may be biologically very dissimilar from us in important respects. The results of such a trial would, therefore, have to be interpreted in the light of a theoretical understanding of the differences between humans and the other species involved in the trials. In order to be more sure of the effects of the drug, we might, and indeed usually do, run clinical trials with human guinea pigs. In this latter case, no theoretical knowledge about human biology and the chemistry of the drug need be deployed to obtain the result – at least in principle. What is happening is that the bodily organs of human beings are being used in order to discover the effects of the drug.

The human trials have a key advantage over the non-human trials. Human beings have, more or less, identical bodily organs which, to a first approximation at least, behave in the same ways under the same circumstances. There is still the need for methodological care, of course. Imagine I want to find out whether a new substance to be put into food as a preservative is harmful. It seems clear that I have to be sure to get the inputs just right, and I have to be sure that the operation of the body is not affected by any extraneous factors. For example, I will have to make sure that I don't input into the simulation more of the food containing the substance than any one human being could possibly consume in a lifetime. I must also be sure that nothing else is being imbibed that might affect the nature of the reaction. If these sorts of variables can be controlled, things can proceed as we have described.

We can use human bodily organs to make accurate predictions about the effects of a drug. The basic idea of the simulation theory of folk psychology is that, in a similar way, we can use the human mind (the human mental organs) to predict the way in which people will act in actual and counterfactual circumstances. The only assumption that needs to be made – again parallel to the drugs case – is that different human beings have mental organs that are more or less identical in their operations. If that assumption is correct, then the result of a mental simulation should provide accurate information on how someone will or would react in given circumstances.

In his paper 'Interpretation Psychologized' (this volume, ch. 3), Alvin Goldman provides an example that is intended to conform to the simulation theory as we have outlined it. He considers the so-called Tees/Crane experiment. In this experiment, subjects are read a story and then asked a question (Kahneman and Tversky, 1982; Goldman, this volume, p. 83):

> Mr Crane and Mr Tees were scheduled to leave the airport on different flights, at the same time. They travelled from town in the same limousine, were caught in a traffic jam, and arrived at the airport 30 minutes after the scheduled departure time of their flights. Mr Crane is told that

his flight left on time. Mr Tees is told that his was delayed, and just left five minutes ago. Who is more upset?

The result of this experiment was that 96 per cent of subjects said that Tees would be the more upset.

Goldman suggests that this near unanimity cannot be explained by the theory theory, and that it is overwhelmingly plausible that what is happening here is that the subjects in the experiment are simulating. They are, that is, using their own mental apparatus to predict how the two characters in the story would feel. The subjects are feeding into their own minds the inputs that Tees and Crane would have had and just letting their mental organs operate as normal on this input. It is, of course, pretend input that the subjects operate on, and hence a pretend output that emerges – the subjects are not really at an airport, and they do not really find themselves becoming angry or resigned. Their mental organs are, as the simulationists like to say, operating 'off line'.

3.1 Objections and Refinements

Needless to say, the simulation theory has been the subject of a range of objections. Here we briefly consider three.

3.1.1 First objection: Theory-driven or process-driven simulation   An obvious thought – and indeed one that is encouraged by some of the ways in which simulationists have stated their views – is that simulation involves 'putting oneself into somebody else's shoes'. This way of stating the simulation account then lays it open to an objection: that for a simulation to work, the simulator must deploy a body of psychological knowledge. This objection has been forcefully articulated by Daniel Dennett (1987, p. 100):

> How can it work without being a kind of theorizing in the end? For the state I put myself in is not belief but make believe belief. If I make believe I am a suspension bridge and wonder what I will do when the wind blows, what 'comes to me' in my make believe state depends on how sophisticated my knowledge is of the physics and engineering of suspension bridges. Why should my making believe I have your beliefs be any different? In both cases knowledge of the imitated object is needed to drive the make believe 'simulation' and the knowledge must be organized in something rather like a theory.

Goldman answers Dennett's objection by way of a distinction between *theory*-driven and *process*-driven simulation (this volume, p. 85):

> Thus, if one person simulates a sequence of mental states of another, they will wind up in the same (or isomorphic) final states as long as (A) they began in the same (or isomorphic) initial states, and (B) both sequences are driven by the same cognitive process or routine. It is

not necessary that the simulating agent have a theory of what the routine is, or how it works. In short, successful simulation can be *process-driven*.

Goldman agrees that a simulation might be theory driven in the way that Dennett describes. But, the form of simulation needed for a correct account of folk psychology is the process-driven version.

An example of a theory-driven simulation might be provided by a computer simulation of a country's economy. Such a model works because the computer encodes a theory of the working of the economy. When economic data is fed in, the computer deploys the theory on the data – in much the same way that a human economist might. The computer does not go into the same (or isomorphic) states as the economy itself, any more than a human economist does. There is no sense in which the computer goes into a state that is the same as, or isomorphic to, a recession, for example. Such a computer simulation is a case of theory-driven simulation. But that is not the way that mental simulation works. In the case of mental simulation the simulator feeds pretend beliefs and desires into her mental apparatus, and lets the same psychological processes operate as would operate upon real beliefs and desires.

Jane Heal also addresses Dennett's objection, but gives a less cognitive-scientific sounding response than Goldman's. She thinks that Dennett's suspension bridge case is disanalogous to the simulation of persons in that pretending to be a suspension bridge is an alien state for a human (this volume, p. 49). There would be no obvious outcome from deliberating upon it without the assistance of a theory of suspension bridges. But pretending to believe that my flight just left is not alien; it is an everyday activity akin to that of imagining that my flight has just left. When, within the scope of that imagining, I wonder what to do next, there is no need for a theory to drive the deliberation.

3.1.2 Second objection: Getting started   A second objection to the simulation theory as we have so far formulated it is that, even if mental simulation does not need to be driven by a psychological theory, still theory comes in when we try to set the simulation up in the first place.

Recall the example of testing a new drug. The test only gives reliable results if the experimenter takes great methodological care. Especially if non-human subjects are used, the experimenter needs to take into account all the variables that may affect the operation of the drug; and taking those variables into account is a matter of reflecting upon a number of theoretical considerations. Something similar applies in the case of modelling. When we model the behaviour of an aeroplane in a wind tunnel, for example, complex theories of aerodynamics have to be used to ensure that the conditions embodied in the model and the wind tunnel are appropriate.

We noted earlier that, when we simulate another person, we need to make allowances for relevant differences. But which differences are relevant? (Cf.

Does the colour of the model aeroplane matter?) And exactly what allowances have to be made? (Exactly how do we allow for the differences between rats and humans when we use rats to test a new drug?) In order to engage in mental simulation of another whose situation and psychological state are different from my own, I have to decide which pretend beliefs and desires are appropriate inputs. But that, the objector claims, is simply to bring theory in through the back door.

Heal and Gordon both take the view that this second objection 'misdescribes the direction of gaze of the replicator' (Heal, this volume, p. 48). The simulator, they say, should not be regarded as looking at the psychology of the subject of the simulation, but at the environment in which that subject finds herself.

Gordon (this volume, p. 102) gives an example that neatly illustrates this 'direction of gaze' point. He asks us to imagine that we are hiking up a trail with a companion who suddenly turns and retreats back down the path. How can we understand this piece of behaviour? The answer is not to focus narrowly on our companion, but to ask what we would do in his situation – and the emphasis is on being in *his situation*. It is not enough that I should look upon the world from where I am and see whether there is anything out there that would make me think that running away is the thing to do. I need to recognize that our companion's point of view upon the world is different from my own. From my own position, I might see nothing untoward – nothing that would make turning and running an intelligible thing to do. But, moving to where my companion was, and looking in the direction that he was looking, I see a bear up ahead.

The point that Gordon stresses is that my explanation of our companion's behaviour depends upon my looking out to the external world to discover the motive for his action. It does not in any sense depend upon my having a theory of my friend's psychology (this volume, p. 103):

> The issue for you is something like this: 'What is it about these environing rocks, trees, animals, and so forth, that would explain his suddenly turning back?' And the question is understood to presuppose that your friend is *aware* of these very objects, and that whatever it is *about* these objects that constitutes the *explanans* you are seeking is something *known* to him. When you spot the grizzly and think, 'That's it!', . . .

As backing for my explanation, I do not have any psychological generalizations about the tendencies of my friend's behaviour in this kind of environment. Rather, I just see how I would act, given the perceptual input that he was subject to. First, I project myself into his situation, adjusting my own perspective on the world to accord more closely with his, and I make judgements about the world within the scope of that imaginative projection. Then, I allow my decision-taking processes to operate 'off line', carrying me from these (pretend) judgements through to a (pretend) decision to turn and run. (I may also, of course, while coming to understand my companion's sudden withdrawal, form my own real – unpretended – decision to run away.)

The direction-of-gaze point encourages us to think about a range of cases, from *total* projection (where I take the other's situation to be exactly like mine in all respects), through increasingly *'patched'* projections (to use Gordon's phrase). Total projection may be the right method to use when I am already in the other person's shoes, but a small departure from total projection is required when my own shoes are in slightly the wrong place or are pointing in slightly the wrong direction. That is to say, sometimes I can compensate for the only relevant difference between myself and the other by moving or by facing another way. Sometimes, however, I can see the other and the situation around him, but I cannot move to where he is. In such a case '[a] process of recentring the world in imagination is required' (Heal, this volume, p. 48). Basic spatial abilities enable me to imagine how the scene looks from where the other is, and so to imagine being the other in that situation.

As Heal notes, this recentring may have to draw upon some principles, in order to allow for visual occlusion, for example. Perhaps a body of knowledge about the visual world must be drawn upon. That would be an intrusion of theory, to be sure; but it would not be a psychological theory about the way in which people make judgements on the basis of their experiences, nor about the way in which people arrive at decisions given beliefs and desires.

The objector may respond, however, that we have not yet taken full account of what is involved in getting started on a piece of mental simulation. Suppose that our companion thinks that bears are dangerous and finds them terrifying, while I think that bears are friendly and find them cute. In order to understand our companion's behaviour, I need to make allowances for these differences. For if, having recentred my point of view upon the world, I simply use my own decision-taking processes, I shall not arrive at the intention to run away. No amount of fixing my gaze upon our companion's immediate environmental situation will help me here. I need some information about our companion's attitude towards bears. I might arrive at what I need by drawing upon some more general principle – as it might be, that people who have had a certain kind of school education tend to have a fearful attitude towards bears. But that, surely, *is* a piece of psychological theory that plays a crucial role in getting the simulation process started.

Advocates of the simulation theory acknowledge that inductively based generalizations play a role in real-life use of mental simulation (Goldman, this volume, p. 83). They may then proceed in one of two ways. On the one hand, the advocate of the simulation theory may say that, while generalizations are certainly used, they play only a secondary and heuristic role. In principle, if I gazed upon our companion's educational situation – whether in reality or in imagination – I could arrive, within the scope of an imaginative identification with him, at the belief that bears are dangerous and a correspondingly fearful attitude towards them. Use of the inductively based generalization is just a shortcut – and a shortcut whose use is intelligible to me only derivatively upon engagement in mental simulation. This would be a natural way to proceed for someone concerned to defend the view that mental simulation is philosophically fundamental in an account of our folk-psychological concepts.

On the other hand, the friend of simulation may say that psychological theory inevitably does intrude when we need to move from information about a subject's embedding in the world to attribution of perceptual experiences and beliefs. But the simulation theorist may still insist that it is mental simulation that takes us from attributions of beliefs and desires to predictions of action.

The simulation theorist who takes this second option restricts the distinctive claims of the simulation theory to explanation and prediction of decisions given beliefs and desires, and perhaps of beliefs given other beliefs. A concession is made to the theory theory over the explanation and prediction of belief formation in response to the subject's situation.

3.1.3 Third objection: Cognitive penetrability   Stich and Nichols are inclined, in contrast, to make concessions to the simulation theory over the explanation and prediction of belief formation (see their 1995 paper). But they argue strongly for the theory theory as providing a better account of the prediction of behaviour. Their argument hinges on the question of cognitive penetrability.

The term 'cognitive penetrability' can use a little explanation. As originally introduced by Pylyshyn (1984, p. 133), it means: '[t]he rationally explicable alterability of a [processing] component's behavior in response to goals and beliefs'. Cognitive penetrability of the operation of a processing component is thus the opposite of what Fodor (1983) calls 'informational encapsulation'. However, that etymological history does not provide a very good guide to the phenomenon that Stich and Nichols are concerned with. The issue is rather this. If predictions are based upon deployment of a theory, then those predictions are liable to be false if the theory is incorrect in any way. Predictions of decisions, intentions and behaviour may be incorrect if they are based upon a psychological theory that is wrong about some aspects of human psychology. Theory-based predictions are subject to error introduced by misinformation. However, flawed information will obviously have no impact upon predictions that do not draw upon that information. If I have deeply flawed views about what people will decide to do given certain beliefs and desires, but I use mental simulation to generate predictions about what people will do given their beliefs and desires, then the flawed information will introduce no error into those predictions.

We can see this very vividly if we consider my predictions about my own decisions, intentions and behaviour. If I draw upon a body of psychological information and misinformation, then the misinformation is liable to introduce errors into my self-prediction. If I make use of my own decision-taking processes to generate the predictions, then they can hardly be in error unless I fail to feed in the correct inputs.

So, the crucial question is whether people are liable to make false predictions about decisions, intentions and actions. Are they liable to make false predictions even about how they themselves would act in certain circumstances? If they are, then, according to Stich and Nichols, this favours the theory theory. And indeed, there are examples where folk-psychological prediction lets us down.

One of the examples that Stich and Nichols give (this volume, p. 151) is the case of position effects in the rating of the quality of consumer goods. Social-psychological experiments reveal that subjects who are invited to select amongst items all of which are, unknown to them, identical in quality, tend to choose those placed to the right. This is a surprising finding. Few people, if asked to predict what subjects will do when faced with such a choice, hit upon the position effect. The theory theorist can account for this predictive failure by saying that our folk-psychological theory is inadequate to deal with the kind of case represented by the experimental situation. But, Stich and Nichols claim, the simulation theorist faces a problem here. If people make their predictions by employing, in simulation mode, their own decision-taking processes – the very processes that they would use if they were subjects in the experiment – then they should arrive at the correct answer. They should, within the scope of imaginative identification with the subjects, feel the same preference for items placed towards the right.

There are a number of replies that a simulation theorist might make to this kind of example. There would be a relevant difference between the people making the predictions and the subjects in the experiment if the people making the predictions were told that the items offered to the subjects are all identical; for the subjects themselves are not provided with this information. In that case, successful simulation of the subjects would require – what might be virtually impossible – that the predictors set aside this vital piece of information. So, even from the point of view of the simulation theorist, it would be little wonder that the predictors arrive at the wrong answer concerning the subjects' decisions.

There is a general style of response here. The defender of the simulation theory points out that the simulation method will only arrive at correct answers if it begins from the correct inputs. The inputs that the predictors can feed to their decision-making processes (running off line) are very largely determined by the information provided to them about the experimental setup. Quite apart from the fact that the predictors may have information that the subjects lack, the simulation theorist can point to the different format in which the information is presented to the subjects and the predictors. The experimental situation is presented to the subjects visually, but the predictors are told about it verbally.

There is one further point to be made about cognitive penetrability. The simulation theorist will note that there are purely mechanical influences on decision taking which may not be captured by simulation (Harris, this volume, p. 219). We can see this even in the sort of case where Stich and Nichols are inclined to make concessions to the simulation theory. We are able to use our own perceptual abilities and our own inferential abilities in simulation mode in order to arrive at predictions about another's belief formation. But, if we are told that the other has just ingested a certain substance, then we cannot make allowances for that fact by imaginative identification alone. Unless we are prepared to ingest the same substance ourselves, we need to know what effect it has upon the processes of perception and inference. What is needed, then, is a little piece of theory – some information about non-rational influences upon psychological processes. Exactly the same goes for the processes of decision taking. Unless we are ready and able to subject ourselves to the same non-rational influences that affect those whose decisions we seek to predict, we shall need to augment our ability to simulate with some pieces of theory. As Heal says (this volume, p. 48):

> Replication [simulation] theory must allow somewhere for the idea of different personalities, for different styles of thinking and for non-rational influences on thinking.

What the simulation theorist maintains, however, is that the introduction of this element of theory does not undermine the distinction between the simulation theory and the theory theory.

The friend of mental simulation is not, then, totally devoid of a response to what Stich and Nichols regard as the most telling point in favour of the theory theory.

3.2 Simulation and Psychological Concepts

Towards the end of our discussion of the theory theory, we noted that it is possible to separate questions about mastery of folk-psychological concepts from questions about our engagement in folk-psychological practice. We initially introduced the theory theory via the link between possession of concepts and knowledge of theory ((TTa) to (TTc)). But still, someone could in principle defend the theory theory as an account of the underpinnings of our everyday practice of folk-psychological attribution, prediction and explanation, while denying that knowledge of a psychological theory constitutes our most fundamental mastery of psychological concepts.

In a similar way, we should clarify the relationship between questions about concepts and questions about practice, in the context of the simulation theory. We introduced the simulation theory by way of some claims about psychological concepts ((STa) to (STc)). The basic ideas were these. First, success in the false belief task involves only rudimentary self-ascriptions of beliefs, within the scope of imaginative identification with another (STa). Second, this very basic self-ascription does not require possession of the full-blown concept of belief, since the 'I believe that' part of the ascription could be deleted (STb). Third, whatever might or might not be required for mastery of the concept of belief, success on the false belief task fundamentally draws upon the ability simply to have beliefs plus the ability to simulate another (STc). But those claims leave it rather unclear what view of psychological concepts would be most natural for a simulation theorist (supposing that the theorist does not reject the whole notion of concept mastery).

A simulation theorist might take the notion of concept possession to be tied – perhaps definitionally – to knowledge of theory. Against the background of that assumption, the simulation theorist might say that engagement in folk-psychological practice does not require possession of psychological concepts. But the claim that would thereby be made would not really be as dramatic as it would sound.

There is, however, a quite different claim that a simulation theorist might make, using similar words. It might be said that engagement in folk-psychological practice does not require possession of the concept of belief, as that concept is usually conceived to be. On the familiar conception, the logic of the concept of belief is such that expressions of the form:

x believes that p

are predicates. They go together with names of individuals (principally, persons) to form sentences that are true or false according as the named individual does or does not believe that p – is or is not in the state of believing that p. But this familiar conception sometimes seems to be rejected by simulation theorists. Thus, Gordon says (1995, p. 60):

> To ascribe to O a belief that p is to assert that p within the context of a simulation of O.

And the most natural way of taking this is as denying that belief ascriptions are truth evaluable (see Heal, 1995, p. 43; Davies, 1994, pp. 123–4). (These papers by Gordon and Heal are to be found in Davies and Stone, 1995.)

If a simulation theorist does accept the construal of 'believes that p' as a predicate, and also accepts that comprehending engagement in folk-psychological practice requires possession of the concept of belief, then there are still two alternative kinds of view that we need to recognize. On the one hand, the simulation theorist might maintain that the ability to engage in imaginative identification is at the heart of our day-to-day folk-psychological practice, yet deny that the ability to simulate constitutes our most basic mastery of psychological concepts. If the theorist's account of our possession of psychological concepts adverts to knowledge of theory, then, of course, the resulting position is an essentially hybrid one. But other kinds of account – not re-introducing psychological theory – may be possible. Goldman, for example, says (this volume, p. 94):

> It has always seemed plausible . . . that our naïve understanding of mental concepts would prominently involve introspective and not merely causal/relational elements.

And he suggests (1993) that the first-person component of grasp of psychological concepts consists in our ability to recognize our own mental states in virtue of their intrinsic, introspectible properties.

On the other hand, the simulation theorist might try to provide an account of our most basic mastery of psychological concepts by drawing upon the notion of imaginative identification. Since the simulation theory is itself silent about first-person attributions of beliefs, a simulation-based account of the concept of belief would have to draw upon some other resources in order to address the first-person use of that concept. But the idea would be to make use of the notion of simulation in the account of the third-person component of grasp of that concept. However, it has to be said that this idea is problematic in a number of ways, so that it is at best unclear whether the project can be carried through (see Davies, 1994).

If we leave questions about concept mastery to one side, then there remain the questions that we highlighted at the end of section 2:

> What psychological processes or mechanisms underpin our normal adult engagement in folk-psychological practice?

> What is the course of development of the child's engagement in folk-psychological practice?

The theory theorist's answers to these questions were cast in terms of having and using a body of knowledge about psychology. The simulation theorist's answers, in contrast, are in terms of having and employing an ability – the ability to identify with another person in imagination.

Thus far, our account of the debate has been largely driven by the philosophical literature. But the questions at issue are primarily empirical ones, and Stich and Nichols's use of the cognitive penetrability argument, for example, can be seen as their attempt to make the debate empirically tractable. We now turn to look in more detail at the debate, from an empirical psychological perspective.

4 Theory and Simulation in the Psychology of Folk Psychology

Our account of the theory theory began from philosophical, rather than psychological, work. We considered, for example, Churchland's view (1981; 1991) of folk psychology as a theory containing such principles as (1988, p. 59):

> Persons who want that *P*, and believe that *Q* would be sufficient to bring about *P*, and have no conflicting wants or preferred strategies, will try to bring it about that *Q*.

But this view does not give an adequate picture of the range of psychological theories that are included under the 'theory theory' heading. Here we will review three of those theories. The first – which we have already mentioned briefly in the context of the analogy with professional science – is the one that is most closely linked to versions of the theory theory put forward by philosophers such as Churchland.

4.1 *Ontology, Explanation, and Theory Change*

Henry Wellman claims (1990, p. 9) that 'children . . . have a theorylike understanding of the mind by three years of age'. The three-year-old child's theory
of mind is a precursor of the theory which, he says, manifests itself in the
naïve psychology of normal adults. Of the adult theory Wellman says (1990,
pp. 8–9):

> The notions invoked there – thoughts, dreams, beliefs, and desires –
> form an interconnected coherent body of concepts; they rest on, or
> indeed define, basic ontological conceptions; and the theory provides a
> causal-explanatory account of a domain of phenomena: human action
> and thought.

And one aspect of the understanding of three-year-old children is that they
are capable of grasping the fundamental ontological distinction between the
mental and physical worlds. Thus (Wellman, 1993, p. 14):

> For example, if told about one boy who has a dog and another one who
> is thinking about a dog, they correctly judge which 'dog' can be seen,
> touched and petted, and which cannot.

Moreover, Wellman argues that three-year-olds already have a primitive
understanding of belief, and even of the possibility of false belief, but lack
some of the adult theory's explanatory principles linking belief and action.
They 'genuinely understand that persons can have beliefs and at times false
beliefs', but 'do not yet see beliefs as inextricably central to human action'
(ibid., p. 15). What the three-year-olds do see as central to human action is
desire. Wellman says (1993, p. 16):

> Three-year-olds who struggle with false beliefs have little trouble with
> false or unfulfilled desires; three-year-olds who inconsistently evidence
> understanding of how beliefs are involved in emotional reactions
> such as surprise consistently understand how desires are involved in
> emotions such as happiness; three-year-olds who know that two people
> may hold different disires may reject the idea that mental states of belief
> can similarly differ subjectively across people; and in explaining actions,
> three-year-olds who consistently mention the character's desires may
> only rarely, if ever, mention beliefs.

A closely related view (despite some important differences of detail) is developed by Alison Gopnik, who argues that (1993, p. 5):

> there is a quite general shift in the child's concept of the mind at around
> three and a half years. This shift involves central changes in the child's

epistemological concepts, concepts of the relation between mind and world.

Gopnik holds that before the age of four, the child has a radically different theory of the mental world, believing that (ibid., p. 5):

> objects or events are directly apprehended by the mind . . . objects are bullets that leave an indelible trace on any mind that is in their path.

By four or five, however, children have gone through a conceptual revolution. There has been a qualitative change in their body of knowledge (Gopnik, 1993, p. 6):

> Children, at least in our culture, have developed something more like a representational model of the mind. Accordingly, almost all psychological functioning in five-year-olds is mediated by representations. . . . Desires, beliefs, pretences, and images all involve the same basic structure, one sometimes described in terms of propositional attitudes and propositional contents. These mental states all involve representations of reality, rather than direct relations to reality itself . . . the child sees that all mental states involve the same abstract representational structure.

Five-year-old children have thus made major advances in their understanding of the mind. Starting from their appreciation, at age three, that there is an ontology of mental items, they have moved on to understand that these mental states are caused by particular kinds of exposure to the environment and are implicated in the generation of action. They have also come to realize that these mental states have representational properties and that it is the representational properties of the states that explain their role in our mental economy.

Gopnik and Wellman (this volume, ch. 11) are explicit in drawing the analogy between how the child's theoretical knowledge grows and changes and the way in which a scientific theory grows and changes (p. 242):

> [R]ecent evidence suggests that during the period from three to four many children are in a state of transition between the two theories, similar, say, to the fifty years between the publication of *De Revolutionibus* and Kepler's discovery of elliptical orbits.

Indeed their claim is even more bold. For they see significant similarities between the mechanisms of theory change in science and the mechanisms of developmental change in children (this volume, p. 243):

> Recall that we suggested, in the scientific case, that in a transitional period the crucial idea of the new theory may appear as an auxiliary

hypothesis couched in the vocabulary of the original theory, or be used in order to deal with particularly salient types of counter-evidence, but may not be widely applied. There is evidence for both these phenomena in the period from three to four. Children seem to us to initially develop the idea of misrepresentation in familiar contexts like those of desire and perception, without extending the idea more generally. They also initially apply the idea only when they are forced to by counter-evidence.

By propounding the analogy with science in some detail, Gopnik and Wellman do much to meet the challenge that Blackburn posed (see above, section 2) – the challenge, namely, to ensure that the notion of theory used by the theory theorist is not so thin as to vanish into the idea that (Blackburn, this volume, p. 275):

> If we are good at something . . . then we can be thought of as making tacit (very tacit) use of some set of principles that could, in principle, provide a description of a device, or possibly a recipe for the construction of a device, that is also good at it.

But it is fair to note that some critics will have reservations about the explanatory potential of this parallel. To many, the emergence and development of theories in science seems a fairly mysterious affair; and so it may appear that we are being offered an explanation of an obscure matter (child development between the ages of three and five) in terms of one that is even more obscure (the development of science).

4.2 Thinking about Representation

A second account falling under the general 'theory theory' heading is Josef Perner's theory (1991), with its stress upon the notion of meta-representation. We shall introduce Perner's account by contrasting it with the most fully developed version of the simulation theory in the psychological literature, namely that of Paul Harris (1991; this volume). We shall draw the contrast in terms of the two forms of thought – the (T) form and (S) form – that we used in our initial characterization of the debate between the theory theory and the simulation theory.

The theory theory, we said, begins from the claim that, in order to succeed on the false belief task, a subject must be able to entertain thoughts of the form:

(T)   He [some other] believes that p

where 'p' stands in for a proposition describing a counterfactual state of affairs. So, a subject in the Sally-Anne experiment must be able to entertain the thought:

Sally believes that the marble is in the basket.

even though the marble is not, in fact, in the basket. The simulation theory, in the version that we sketched at the outset, focuses instead upon thoughts of the form:

(S)   *p*

entertained within the scope of imaginative identification with another. The experimental subject needs to be able to entertain the thought:

The marble is in the basket.

within the scope of imaginative identification with Sally.

In Perner's terms, the difference between the two forms of thought – (T) and (S) – is that the ability to entertain (T) form thoughts requires that the child be capable of *meta-representational thought*, that is to say, be capable of representing someone else's act of representing the world, whereas entertaining (S) form thoughts merely requires that the child be able to represent some counterfactual state of the world. The latter form of thought only requires the child to be what Perner calls a 'situation theorist' (1991, p. 9). According to Perner, the child is a situation theorist by the age of around two years. The ability to meta-represent, which marks a major shift in the child's conceptual abilities, is not reached until the age of four. It is the occurrence of this shift – from situation theorist to what Perner calls 'representation theorist' – that enables the older child to complete the false belief task successfully.

The theory theory certainly offers one possible explanation of the findings in the false belief task experiment. But, as we indicated at the very outset, those findings do not compel us to go down the theory theory route. For the simulation theorist has an alternative account of the difference in folk-psychological ability between the older and the younger child. It is an account, not in terms of different forms of thought – (S) versus (T) – but in terms of differing uses of thoughts of the form (S). Harris argues (1991; this volume) that the imaginative acts required in order to entertain the *appropriate* thoughts of form (S) can be of greater or lesser degrees of complexity. The complexity here is determined by the extent to which those acts must override 'a background of default settings' (1991, p. 289). Harris describes these default settings as follows (1991, pp. 289–90):

I divide these settings into two classes: states of reality, and Intentional states of the self towards that reality. In daily life, both default settings are normally operative. The child's attention is taken up by some visible or likely target within current reality and by the current Intentional state of the self toward that target. For example, the child sees a cup out of reach and points to it repeatedly, vocalizing at the same time. We describe such an episode quite naturally by saying that the child wants the cup. Here, an Intentional state (a desire) is directed toward a likely target (obtaining the cup).

Harris then suggests that (1991, p. 290):

> to embark on an understanding of mental states, children need to adjust the default setting that specifies their Intentional stance towards current reality, as opposed to the default setting that specifies reality itself. Specifically, they need to imagine a different Intentional stance towards reality from the one that they are adopting.

Beyond this first degree of complexity, there follows the case where 'accurate simulation . . . requires that the child overwrite known reality' (p. 292). Given these two degrees of complexity, a third naturally follows where, in addition to overwriting known reality, the child sets aside 'his or her mental stance toward that non-existent state of affairs and imagine[s] a different stance' (p. 292). According to this kind of account, a child may fail in the false belief task, not because he is unable to meta-represent, but because the simulation task that he needs to undertake in order to get the right answer to the crucial question is simply too complex for him to do.

Thus, in order to entertain in imagination the appropriate first-person thought, I might need to imagine that the world is different from the way I actually take it to be, but not need to adjust my attitudes such as fear, hope or desire. Alternatively, I might have to imagine that my attitudes are different from the way they really are, but not need to imagine the world as different from the way that I really take it to be. Finally, I might have to engage in both kinds of imaginative flexibility at the same time. Of course, in order to simulate succesfully, mere imaginative flexibility is not enough. I not only have to vary the way I take the world to be and vary my attitudinal stance, I have to vary them so that they accord with how the other person stands towards the world as he takes it to be. Some people may present more difficult targets for the imagination than others. Clearly enough, there is a good deal of similarity between Harris's views about kinds and degrees of imaginative flexibility and Gordon's idea of patched projection (see above, section 3.1.2), though there are also important differences.

For Perner, the false belief task is difficult for three-year-old children because they lack the meta-representational ability that would enable them to entertain the (T) form thought: 'Sally believes that the marble is in the basket.' For Harris, on the other hand, the false belief task is difficult for children of three years of age because the complexity of the imaginative task that they face is beyond them. They cannot yet achieve the flexibility of imagination that would enable them to entertain the appropriate (S) form thought: 'The marble is in the basket', where, for Harris, entertaining that thought in imagination requires two things. It requires overwriting current reality (in which the marble is in the box), and adopting the divergent stance towards the world that imaginatively taking on that belief involves.

Both accounts – Perner's and Harris's – can save the data, so far as the false belief task experiments are concerned. In order to make empirical progress, then, what we need are predictions from the meta-representation theory that clearly conflict with the predictions of Harris's simulation theory. We need to be able to distinguish experimentally between, on the one hand, differing degrees of complexity of forms of thought (the favoured explanatory device of the meta-representation theory) and, on the other hand, differing degrees of imaginative use of the (S) form of thought (the favoured explanatory device of the simulation theory).

4.2.1 Experimental findings   In their paper in this volume (ch. 6) Josef Perner and Deborrah Howes report some experimental data, going beyond the basic false belief task findings, by means of which they propose to adjudicate in favour of the meta-representation theory. In their experiment, they presented children with a story about two characters – John and Mary. John tells Mary that he will put a box of chocolates in either the top drawer or the bottom drawer. Mary leaves to go to the library and John puts the chocolates in the top drawer. Then, he goes out to the park. Whilst he is out, his mother moves the chocolates to the bottom drawer.

The children in the experiment were between the ages of four years and ten months and six years and four months; hence, old enough to pass the false belief test. The children were asked the following three questions (Perner and Howes, this volume, p. 164):

Q1. Where does John think the chocolates are?

Q2. What if we go over to the park, and ask John: 'John, do you know where the chocolates are?' What will he say?

Q3. What if we go to the library and ask Mary: 'Mary, does John know where the chocolates are?' What will she say?

Perner and Howes claim that the meta-representation theory and the simulation theory predict different patterns of response to the three questions. The simulation theory predicts that Q1 and Q2 will both be answered equally well and better than Q3; whereas the meta-representation theory predicts that Q1 will be the easiest to answer, but Q2 and Q3 will both be equally hard.

This claim about the pattern of response predicted by the simulation theory relies upon the idea that simulations differ in their complexity, in the following way. If the children were simulating to answer Q1, then the very same act of simulation would provide them with the right answer to Q2. But Q3 would require the more complex act of simulating one person simulating another person: obviously a projection that would need a greater degree of patching. A little more detail may be helpful.

According to the simulation theory, recall, the prediction of another requires that I entertain the thought:

(S) *p*.

In Perner and Howes's experiment, the experimental subject imaginatively identifies with John. Hence, in simulating in order to answer Q1, the subject would have to entertain this thought:

> The chocolates are in the top drawer.

But, if the subject does entertain this thought within the scope of imaginative identification with John, then, Perner and Howes claim, the subject has all that she needs in order to answer the second question correctly also. No further imaginative work needs to be done. But, in order to answer Q3 correctly by way of simulation, the subject has to identify with Mary identifying with John. This second imaginative act would appear to be much more complex than the first.

The predicted pattern of responses according to the meta-representation theory is quite different. In the case of Q1, the subject has to entertain a thought about one of John's thoughts, namely:

> John believes that the chocolates are in the top drawer.

In the case of Q2, the subject has to entertain the following thought:

> John believes that he (John) knows that the chocolates are in the top drawer.

This is a thought about a thought (a meta-level thought), and as such it is more complex than the first thought involved in answering Q1, and no less complex (in point of levels of embedding) than the thought that the subject has to entertain in order to answer Q3, namely:

> Mary believes that John knows that the chocolates are in the top drawer or else in the bottom drawer.

The results that Perner and Howes report are broadly in line with the predictions of the meta-representation theory: children (especially the younger children) found the first question easier than the other two, and the latter two about equally difficult. So, their experiment presents a challenge to the simulation theory. Why do the (younger) children find Q2 more difficult to answer correctly than Q1?

It remains to be seen whether the simulationist can find a response to this challenge. Indeed, if one were of a pessimistic cast of mind, one might wonder whether any test of this kind will enable us to distinguish the theory theory from the simulation theory. For the simulationist can always argue that there are reasons why the subjects may have difficulty with the task. Gordon suggests in his response to Perner and Howes (this volume, ch. 8), that in answering Q2 the subjects are influenced by their understanding that one should not normally claim to know something if one has reason to doubt that it is correct. The idea is that the subjects do have reasons to doubt John's answer to Q1, and that they attribute these reasons to John also. Hence, the (younger) children's answer to Q2 is influenced by their own view as to whether John is in a position to know where the chocolates are. More generally, the intrusion of the concept of knowledge in Q2 inevitably triggers the use of a little piece of theory:

> If it is not the case that p, then John does not know that p

and this may introduce some confusion into any attempt to use simulation to answer Q2.

As optimists, however, we may hope that more subtle experiments of this form will be thought up which will provide a more decisive test of the two theories (see Perner, 1994).

4.2.2 *The course of development*   We have been organizing our discussion around two questions. One is about normal adult engagement in folk-psychological practice; the other is about the course of childhood development, leading up to the normal adult state. Any theory theorist's answer to the question about the attained state will be cast in terms of a body of knowledge (a theory) plus the information processing mechanisms that enable that body of knowledge to be put to use. According to Perner's version of the theory, a crucial component in folk-psychological practice is the ability to have meta-representational thoughts – to think about representations, such as beliefs and other thoughts. As a result, a body of knowledge about representation is part of what underpins normal adult engagement in folk-psychological practice. To say this is to say nothing, yet, about the information processing mechanisms that enable this body of knowledge to be put to use. So, however fully the theory of representation was specified, we would not have a complete answer to the first of our two questions. But even without an account of the information processing that subserves the normal adult practice, we can turn to the second question and ask about the course of childhood development.

As we have seen, Perner considers children of around two years of age to be 'situation theorists'. As situation theorists children are able to construct mental models of the actual world and of counterfactual worlds. But being able to do this, Perner claims, is not enough for children to function as mature folk psychologists. For that, children have to be capable of entertaining meta-representational thoughts; and meta-representational thought, Perner claims, requires possession of the concept of representation. Thus (1991, p. 75):

> It is legitimate to ask, what differentiates the situation theorist from the representation theorist? My answer is that without a proper concept of representation the young situation theorist cannot understand that a picture can be given *different interpretations*, that a picture can have a *sense* and a *referent*, and that pictures can therefore misrepresent.

Perner's use of the Fregean notions of sense and referent deserves more discussion than we can give it here. But, part of the idea seems to be that misrepresentation involves a representation (a picture, for example) which depicts a kind of situation different from the real situation, but which is nevertheless aimed at the real situation. The picture is a misrepresentation of the real situation (which is the (intended) referent), rather than just a representation of a counterfactual situation. Meta-representational thought, as Perner uses the notion, is thought about representations which are conceived of as aiming at the truth about a situation, and as either hitting their mark or missing it.

In any case, this much is clear. On Perner's account, children proceed through two distinct developmental stages. First, they are situation theorists; then they are representation theorists. At the first stage, children can make use of what are, in fact, different representations or models. Thus a child can understand that there can be a picture of Daddy skiing and yet Daddy can be sitting right beside her. The child is capable of forming 'a mental model of Daddy on skis' and can 'also avoid confusion about what Daddy is actually doing' (1991, p. 73). The child does not think of the picture as a representation – nor does the child think of her own thought as a representation. Instead, the child simply thinks of two worldly contexts or situations: for example, the real and the pictured, or the real and the imaginary, or the present and the past.

In the terms we have been using, the child as situation theorist is able to entertain two concurrent thoughts of the (S) form:

> Daddy is skiing

and

> Daddy is sitting beside me

without confusion. For the first thought is a thought about the pictured situation, while the second thought is a thought about the real situation. Similarly, in the case of the false belief task, the child as situation theorist can simultaneously entertain the (S) form thought about the real present situation:

> The chocolates are in the bottom drawer

and the (S) form thought about the situation as John left it before he went to the park:

> The chocolates are in the top drawer.

Furthermore, the situation theorist can entertain both these thoughts without confusion. The two thoughts have different functions within the child's overall cognitive economy. The child's own actions in seeking out the chocolates will be directed by the thought about the real, present situation, and not the thought about the past situation, for example. So, the two thoughts must be flagged or marked in some way, and this flagging or marking might be called a species of 'meta-representation' (1991, p. 175):

> the markers that are necessary to distinguish real from hypothetical (imagined) situations can be called 'meta-representational' in the sense that these markers are not part of the represented situations but are outside comments on the status of these situations.

But flagged internal representations corresponding to (S) form thoughts do not add up to the kind of meta-representation – thought about representation – that is central to the second stage in Perner's account.

The child as situation theorist is unable to entertain the (T) form thought:

> John believes that the chocolates are in the top drawer.

For this is a thought about a belief – a thought about a certain kind of representation that is aimed at the truth about the actual situation. Similarly, the situation theorist child looking at the picture of Daddy skiing does not form a 'mental model representing the picture as a physical object representing, for instance, Daddy' (1991, p. 73). And what is most important here is that it is the (T) form of thought that is crucial, Perner says, for predicting and explaining another person's behaviour (1991, p. 178):

> My argument is that with the ability to interpret certain thinking activities as mental *representation* the child gains new insight into aspects of mental functioning that are nearly impossible to comprehend without a representational theory. One such case is mistaken action, that is, action based on a *misconception* of the world, or *false belief*.

Similarly, in a more recent paper, Perner says (1993, p. 128):

> I have argued that understanding of false belief comes with a new view of representation that is acquired at about four years. At this age children become able to understand things like pictures and the mind *as* representations.

Given the similarity between the child as situation theorist (on Perner's view) and the child using mental simulation (on, say, Harris's view), this is a critical point for Perner's account. Perner needs to characterize the child's transition from situation theorist to representation theorist in such a way that it is clear how this explains the difference between failure and success on the false belief task. We shall not the pursue the question whether Perner fully meets this challenge.

Any theory theorist also faces a more general challenge; namely, he must ensure that the notion of theory in play is not so thin as to be unexplanatory. Earlier (section 2), we discussed two ways in which a theory theorist can avoid the threat of trivialization. One way is to stress the analogy with theoretical linguistics. The other way is to point to a limited analogy with professional science. As we have just seen, Perner sees the child's development of the ability to entertain and deploy meta-representational thoughts as requiring the child to make a conceptual breakthrough. Furthermore, Perner, like Gopnik and Wellman, draws an analogy between the child's conceptual development and the processes of development and change in scientific theories.

However, Perner suggests that the most familiar examples of theory change (like the replacement of Ptolemaic astronomy by Kepler's laws of planetary motion) do not serve the analogy very well (1991, pp. 251–2):

In the most commonly discussed case of theory change the old theory is simply replaced by the new and better theory. . . . Unfortunately, I think the change from a situation theory to a representational theory is not like these examples from the history of science. There is no simple replacement since . . . we stay situation theorists at heart. We resort to a representational theory of mind only when we need to. A better analogy from the history of science may therefore be an instance of *theory extension*: for example, the extension of classical genetics by molecular genetics . . . The representational view does not supplant the situation theory but only amends it for certain problems.

There are delicate issues here. Where on the spectrum from revolution to extension a particular theory change lies is notably difficult to call. But we can note two aspects of Perner's use of the science analogy. On the side of the consequences of the developmental transition, Perner is clear that the earlier situation theory remains in place, while the later representation theory becomes available for dealing with problems that previously could not be solved, such as problems issuing from misrepresentation. On the side of the causes of, or triggers for, the transition, Perner is not quite so explicit (1991, p. 239):

[B]y interpreting statements and determining what they refer to, children are constantly exposed to the process of interpretation and reference. And so, helped by pretence and the observation of correspondences in their attempt to understand these instances of representation, children will eventually hit on the *concept of representation* as their common denominator.

4.4 *Folk Psychology and Information Processing*

Before we move on to the promised third psychological account, let us pause briefly to reflect on the two questions that we have already highlighted on more than one occasion:

What psychological processes or mechanisms underpin our normal adult engagement in folk-psychological practice?

What is the course of development of the child's engagement in folk-psychological practice?

We mentioned (at the beginning of section 4.3.2) that an answer to the first question in terms of a body of knowledge needs to be accompanied by an account of the information processing mechanisms that enable this body of knowledge to be put to use. Something similar could be said about a simulation theorist's answer to the first question. It should give some indication of the mechanisms that underpin the vital imaginative abilities. But the situation is more complex yet. For, when we turn to the course of development, it is surely reasonable to ask for an account of the *changes* in the child's information processing mechanisms that underlie the changes in folk-psychological ability. Indeed, this would be one way of construing the requirement (see above, section 1.2) that the developmental account should be explanatory, and not merely descriptive.

The two psychological accounts that we have taken as versions of the theory theory might seem to be just a little disappointing when looked at from the perspective of information processing psychology. For they seem to make no mention of the cognitive architecture that must underpin the child's successful performance in the false belief task – the task that diagnoses the child's transition to adult competence. Nor correlatively, do we find any mention of the cognitive architecture that must underpin the forms of thought that the child entertains and deploys prior to his transition to the adult state. What we do find in these theories is an empirical investigation of just what the forms of thought are that the child entertains and deploys at various stages of development, and of the conceptual underpinning (the body of knowledge or theory) possession of which, it is claimed, is a prerequisite for being able to entertain and deploy those thoughts.

The same comment can be made about Harris's simulation theory account. Presumably the child's increasing imaginative abilities are underpinned by the development of some information processing mechanisms. Yet Harris does not specify what those mechanisms might be, nor how they might develop.

There are a number of moves that might be made in response to this kind of expression of disappointment. The theory theorists may say that the information processing account can only come after we have a satisfactory account of the body of knowledge that the child must acquire if he is to become a mature folk psychologist. Similarly, Harris might say that an information processing account can only come after we have a satisfactory account of precisely what abilities the child must possess in order to simulate. This would be an eminently reasonable response. After all, we need to know what the information processing account is to be an account of before we can give it. On the other hand, some theorists of folk psychology may have a more daring response to offer. For they might reject the whole idea of subpersonal-level information processing theories.

However this may turn out, it is true that, as things presently stand, the theorists we have discussed so far do not provide an information processing account of what underpins our mature folk-psychological ability, nor of the changes to the child's information processing mechanisms that must occur during the course of development of the ability.

In a series of influential papers (for example, Leslie, 1987; 1988; Leslie and Thaiss, 1992; Leslie and Roth, 1993; Baron-Cohen et al., 1985; 1986) Alan Leslie has developed an account which is explicitly pitched at the information processing level. It is also an account which, as is clear from his contribution to the companion volume (Leslie and German, 1995), is intended to be fully in accord with the 'dominant explanatory strategy' within cognitive science.

To set the scene for Leslie's views, we need to explain the relevance of autism to the development of the theory theory. Autism is a rare condition (about 4 in 10,000 children) which is 'marked mainly by social withdrawal and poor speech development, together with stereotyped behaviour patterns' (Gregory, 1987, p. 65). Although autism is associated with lower than average intelligence, it is characterized by a failure to develop normal social relationships, or to cope with the social environment, even in the cases where intelligence is in the normal range. A particularly suggestive description is that autistic children treat people as if they were objects.

In an influential paper, Simon Baron-Cohen, Alan Leslie and Uta Frith (1985) report an experiment in which they administered the false belief task to a group of autistic children, to a group of children with Down's syndrome and to a group of normal pre-school children. The children in all the groups had a mental age of above four years (as measured by a non-verbal test). Baron-Cohen et al.'s hypothesis was that 'autistic children as a group fail to employ a theory of mind' (1985, p. 43), and the results of the experiment were gratifyingly corroborative. While 86 per cent of the Down's syndrome children and 85 per cent of the normal pre-school children passed the false belief test, 80 per cent of the autistic children were unsuccessful. In a subsequent study, using a different task which also depends upon an understanding of folk psychology, the same pattern of results was found (Baron-Cohen et al., 1986). The good performance of the Down's syndrome children supports the hypothesis that the autistic children's impairment is specifically related to folk psychology and is not simply a matter of a general intellectual deficit. (The mean IQ of the autistic children tested was 82, while the mean IQ for the Down's syndrome children was 64.)

Part of the significance of this result is that autistic children also fail to develop the ability to engage in pretend play. So, there is a powerful suggestion that pretend play and engagement in normal folk-psychological practice are linked. Leslie's theory (1987; 1988) explicitly connects the ability to understand and engage in pretend play, and the ability to understand the mental states (particularly the beliefs) of others. Thus, Leslie summarizes his two main points (1988, p. 20):

> First, that the development of a theory of mind depends on *specific* innate mechanisms, and, second, that these mechanisms are at work very early in life in generating *pretend* play.

Pivotal in Leslie's theory is a similarity between three semantic properties of reports of mental states and three characteristics of pretence (1988, p. 27):

> There is . . . a striking isomorphism between the semantics of mental state reports and the three fundamental forms of pretence.

Pretence involves object substitution, attribution of pretend properties, and imagining objects where none really exist. Reports of mental states are referentially opaque. ('Alan believes that Hesperus is twinkling' may be true, while 'Alan believes that Phosphorus is twinkling' is false.) Their truth value is independent of the truth value of the embedded sentence. And a mental state report may be true, even though a singular term within the embedded sentence fails to have a reference. Leslie remarks (ibid., p. 27):

> I don't think this isomorphism could be coincidental. Instead, I think it reveals that underlying these two seemingly unconnected cognitive phenomena – pretend play and reports of mental states – *there is a common form of internal representation.*

At first glance, it might be thought that Leslie has only pointed to an isomorphism between pretending and believing, or equivalently, between reports of pretending and reports of believing. But, in fact, his overall theory is intended to offer an explanation of the following striking fact (1988, p. 29):

> When the child acquires the ability to pretend herself she simultaneously acquires the ability to understand pretence in others.

Taking that connection into account, we see that Leslie is offering a theory according to which pretence – and understanding of pretence in others – draws upon cognitive resources that are also implicated in our folk-psychological practice of attributing mental states, such as beliefs, to others.

Specifically, Leslie argues that the ability to engage in folk-psychological practice depends upon possession of a domain-specific theory of mind mechanism, or module, (ToMM). This module is, in the normal course of events, an innate endowment of the human species, and begins to develop in infancy. The ToMM is an information processing device which computes data structures called meta-representations. (We need to distinguish Leslie's use of the term 'meta-representation' from Perner's.) Thus (Leslie and Thaiss, 1992, p. 230):

> The metarepresentation makes explicit four kinds of information. These categories of information are:
>
> (1) an informational relation (specifying an attitude – e.g., PRETEND) followed by three arguments which specify, respectively:
> (2) an agent (e.g. mother or self);
> (3) an anchor (e.g. some aspect of the current real situation);
> (4) an imaginary or pretend state.

Thus, in the example:

> Mother PRETENDS (of) this banana (that) 'it is a telephone'

we have (1) an attitude: PRETEND; (2) an agent: Mother; (3) an anchor in the real situation: this banana; and (4) a pretended state: that it is a telephone. We could likewise have (1) an attitude: BELIEVE; (2) an agent: Ralph; (3) an anchor in the real situation: the man in the brown hat; and (4) a believed state: that he is a spy.

Leslie's claim about the autistic syndrome is, then, that the explanation of its central characteristics lies in the absence of, or an abnormality in, the ToMM. In normal children (and in Down's syndrome children), however, the ToMM is present and functioning from an early age, as witness the occurrence of pretence by the age of two years. If this is true, then Leslie needs an account of why, in normal development, the false belief task cannot be successfully completed before the age of four. Leslie's claim is that normal children under the age of four have the ToMM, but are unable to deploy it in performance of the false belief task. They are in possession of the relevant body of knowledge, or competence, but are unable to achieve successful performance because of other cognitive limitations.

Leslie hypothesizes that this performance limitation is to be explained in terms of the younger child having not yet developed a further processing component which he dubs the *Selection Processor* (SP). This component (Leslie and Roth, p. 100):

> co-operates with ToMM and with knowledge of . . . representational artifacts [such as photographs, pictures and maps] to obtain the solution to particular classes of problem. SP is thus a more general mechanism than ToMM.

Leslie's theory thus differs structurally from Perner's. Perner has it that pretence is possible for the situation theorist, while the false belief task requires, in addition, meta-representation (in Perner's sense: a theory of representation). Leslie has it that pretence already draws upon the theory of mind that is implicated in successful performance of the false belief task. Perner has it that the theory of representation deployed in performance of the false belief task is also involved in understanding other kinds of representation. Leslie has it that the false belief task, and tasks with other kinds of representation, both make use of the selection processor (SP), but that the false belief task also draws upon a body of specifically psychological knowledge embodied in the ToMM.

Given this difference, Leslie and Thaiss (1992) argue that it is important to compare the performance of children on the false belief task, and on analogous tasks (using photographs and maps, for example) that test their understanding of representation in general. Autistic children who failed on the false belief task, nevertheless were largely successful on the tests using photographs and maps. This suggests that autism is not the result of a general problem with the concept of representation. Normal children (with a mean mental age of four years and five months, using a verbal test) were mainly successful on both tasks. But to the extent that failures occurred, it was not the case that understanding of false belief lagged behind understanding of other kinds of representation (see also Zaitchik, 1990).

Finally, while Leslie is a theory theorist under the terms of the act, he denies that children undergo a conceptual revolution between the ages of three and five. For Leslie, the conceptual knowledge is present from birth in the normal child, and is already being used by the age of two years.

Leslie's account has occasioned much debate and is as controversial amongst theory theorists as it is amongst those who favour the simulation alternative. However, it is one of the few psychological accounts to provide an explicit information processing account of the underpinning of the developmental course of the normal and abnormal development of folk-psychological practice. There is considerable room for discussion, however, in that the SP has received little independent corroboration, the link between the ability to pretend and the ability to report mental states can be queried (see Currie, 1995, for example), and the claim that our fundamental folk-psychological knowledge is innate will inevitably occasion dissent.

Moreover, although Leslie's theory offers an elegant explanation of the association between absence of pretend play and problems with the false belief task in autistic children, it is also possible to see, at least in outline, how a simulation theorist could give an account of autism. In the simulation theory, the autistic children's inability to pass the false belief test will be regarded as a failure to simulate another person with a different view upon the world. This will be explained in terms of an impairment to the imaginative faculty – the same faculty that is involved in pretend play. Indeed, early presentations of the simulation theory by philosophers (Gordon, this volume; Goldman, this volume) typically cite Baron-Cohen et al.'s finding (1985) as support for the simulation view.

Clearly, in the empirical psychological domain inhabited by the simulation theory (Harris, 1991; this volume), and the various forms of the theory theory (Wellman, 1990; Gopnik and Wellman, this volume; Perner, 1991; Perner and Howes, this volume; Leslie, 1987; 1988; Leslie and Thaiss, 1992; Leslie and German, 1995), there is still work to be done. The theory of mind debate continues.

References

Baron-Cohen, S., Leslie, A. M. and Frith, U. 1985: Does the autistic child have a 'theory of mind'? *Cognition*, 21, 37–46.

Baron-Cohen, S., Leslie, A. M. and Frith, U. 1986: Mechanical, behavioural and intentional understanding of picture stories in autistic children. *British Journal of Developmental Psychology*, 2, 113–25.

Churchland, P. M. 1981: Eliminative materialism and the propositional attitudes. *Journal of Philosophy*, 78, 67–90.

Churchland, P. M. 1988: *Matter and Consciousness* (revised edn). Cambridge, Mass.: MIT Press.

Churchland, P. M. 1991: Folk psychology and the explanation of human behavior. In J. D. Greenwood (ed.), *The Future of Folk Psychology:*

Intentionality and Cognitive Science. Cambridge: Cambridge University Press.

Currie, G. 1995: Imagination and simulation: Aesthetics meets cognitive science. In Davies and Stone, 1995.

Davies, M. 1994: The mental simulation debate. In C. Peacocke (ed.), *Objectivity, Simulation and the Unity of Consciousness. Proceedings of the British Academy*, 83, 99–127.

Davies, M. and Stone, T. (eds) 1995: *Mental Simulation: Evaluations and Applications.* Oxford: Blackwell Publishers.

Dennett, D. C. 1987: Making sense of ourselves. In *The Intentional Stance.* Cambridge, Mass.: MIT Press.

Dummett, M. 1976: What is a theory of meaning? (II). In G. Evans and J. McDowell (eds), *Truth and Meaning: Essays in Semantics.* Oxford: Oxford University Press.

Fodor, J. 1983: *The Modularity of Mind.* Cambridge, Mass.: MIT Press.

Fodor, J. 1987: *Psychosemantics.* Cambridge, Mass.: MIT Press.

Goldman, A. I. 1993: The psychology of folk psychology. *Behavioral and Brain Sciences*, 16, 15–28.

Gopnik, A. 1993: How we know our own minds: The illusion of first-person knowledge of intentionality. *Behavioral and Brain Sciences*, 16, 1–14.

Gordon, R. M. 1995: Simulation without introspection or inference from me to you. In Davies and Stone, 1995.

Gregory, R. L. 1987: *The Oxford Companion to the Mind.* Oxford: Oxford University Press.

Harris, P. L. 1991: The work of the imagination. In A. Whiten (ed.), *Natural Theories of Mind: Evolution, Development and Simulation of Everyday Mindreading.* Oxford: Blackwell Publishers.

Heal, J. 1995: How to think about thinking. In Davies and Stone, 1995.

Kahneman, D. and Tversky, A. 1982: The simulation heuristic. In D. Kahneman, P. Slovic and A. Tversky (eds), *Judgment Under Uncertainty.* Cambridge: Cambridge University Press.

Leslie, A. M. 1987: Pretense and representation: The origins of 'theory of mind'. *Psychological Review*, 94, 412–26.

Leslie, A. M. 1988: Some implications of pretence for mechanisms underlying the child's theory of mind. In J. W. Astington, P. L. Harris and D. R. Olson (eds), *Developing Theories of Mind.* Cambridge: Cambridge University Press.

Leslie, A. M. and German, T. P. 1995: Knowledge and ability in 'theory of mind': One-eyed overview of a debate. In Davies and Stone, 1995.

Leslie, A. M. and Roth, D. 1993: What autism teaches us about metarepresentation. In S. Baron-Cohen, H. Tager-Flusberg and D. Cohen (eds), *Understanding Other Minds: Perspectives from Autism.* Oxford: Oxford University Press.

Leslie, A. M. and Thaiss, L. 1992: Domain specificity in conceptual development: Neuropsychological evidence from autism. *Cognition*, 43, 225–51.

Lewis, D. 1972: Psychophysical and theoretical identifications. *Australasian*

Journal of Philosophy, 50, 249–58. Repr. in N. Block (ed.), *Readings in Philosophy of Psychology, Volume 1*. London: Methuen, 1980.

Perner, J. 1991: *Understanding the Representational Mind*. Cambridge, MA: MIT Press.

Perner, J. 1993: The theory of mind deficit in autism: Rethinking the metarepresentation theory. In S. Baron-Cohen, H. Tager-Flusberg and D. Cohen (eds), *Understanding Other Minds: Perspectives from Autism*. Oxford: Oxford University Press.

Perner, J. 1994: The necessity and impossibility of simulation. In C. Peacocke (ed.), *Objectivity, Simulation and the Unity of Consciousness*. *Proceedings of the British Academy*, 83, 145–54.

Premack, D. and Woodruff, G. 1978: Does the chimpanzee have a theory of mind? *Behavioral and Brain Sciences*, 4, 515–26.

Pylyshyn, Z. 1984: *Computation and Cognition*. Cambridge, MA: MIT Press.

Stich, S. and Nichols, S. 1995: Second thoughts on simulation. In Davies and Stone, 1995.

Wellman, H. M. 1990: *The Child's Theory of Mind*. Cambridge, MA: MIT Press.

Wellman, H. M. 1993: Early understanding of mind: The normal case. In S. Baron-Cohen, H. Tager-Flusberg and D. Cohen (eds), *Understanding Other Minds: Perspectives from Autism*. Oxford: Oxford University Press.

Wimmer, H. and Perner, J. 1983: Beliefs about beliefs: Representation and constraining function of wrong beliefs in young children's understanding of deception. *Cognition*, 13, 103–28.

Zaitchik, D. 1990: When representations conflict with reality: The preschooler's problem with false belief and 'false' photographs. *Cognition*, 35, 41–68.

1
Replication and Functionalism

JANE HEAL

1 The Functional Strategy versus the Replicative Strategy

In this paper I want to examine two contrasted models of what we do when we try to get insight into other people's thoughts and behaviour by citing their beliefs, desires, fears, hopes, etc. On one model we are using what I shall call the *functional strategy* and on the other we use what I label the *replicative strategy*. I shall argue that the view that we use the replicative strategy is much more plausible than the view that we use the functionalist strategy. But the two strategies issue in different styles of explanation and call upon different ranges of concepts. So at the end of the paper I shall make some brief remarks about these contrasts.

The core of the functionalist strategy is the assumption that explanation of action or mental state through mention of beliefs, desires, emotions, etc. is causal. The approach is resolutely third personal. The Cartesian introspectionist error – the idea that from some direct confrontation with psychological items in our own case we learn their nature – is repudiated. We are said to view other people as we view stars, clouds or geological formations. People are just complex objects in our environment whose behaviour we wish to anticipate but whose causal innards we cannot perceive. We therefore proceed by observing the intricacies of their external behaviour and formulating some hypotheses about how the insides are structured. The hypotheses are typically of this form: 'The innards are like this. There is some thing or state which is usually caused by so and so in the environment (let us call this state "X") and another caused by such and such else (let us call this "Y"); together these cause another, "Z", which, if so and so is present, probably leads on to . . .' And so on. It is in some such way as this that terms like 'belief' and 'desire' are introduced. Our views about the causes, interactions and outcomes of inner states are sometimes said to be summed up in 'folk psychology' (Stich, 1982a, p. 153ff). Scientific psychology is in the business of pursuing the same sort of programme as folk psychology but in more detail and with more statistical accuracy. On this view a psychological statement is an existential claim – that something with so-and-so causes and effects is occurring in a person (Lewis, 1972). The philosophical advantages, in contrast with dualism and earlier materialisms such as behaviourism and type–type identity theory, are familiar. It is via these contrasts and in virtue of these merits that the theory emerged. See Putnam (1967) for a classic statement.

This is a broad outline. But how is psychological explanation supposed to work in particular instances? What actual concepts are employed and how, in particular, are we to accommodate our pre-theoretical idea that people have immense numbers of different beliefs and desires, whose contents interrelate?

Functionalists would generally agree that there is no hope of defining the idea of a particular psychological state, like believing that it is raining, in isolation from other psychological notions. Such notions come as a package, full understanding of any member of which requires a grip on its role in the system as a whole (Harman, 1973). This is true of any interesting functional concepts, even, for example, in explaining functionally something as comparatively simple as a car. If we try to build up some picture of the insides of a car, knowing nothing of mechanics and observing only the effects of pushing various pedals and levers and inserting various liquids, we might well come up with ideas like 'engine', 'fuel store', 'transmission', etc. But explanation of any one of these would clearly require mention of the others. Similarly we cannot say what a desire is except by mentioning that it is the sort of thing which conjoins with beliefs (and other states) to lead to behaviour.

But something more important than this is that the number of different psychological states (and hence their possibilities of interaction) are vastly greater than for the car. There is no clear upper bound on the number of different beliefs or desires that a person may have. And, worse, we cannot lay down in advance that for a given state these and only these others could be relevant to what its originating conditions or outcome are. This 'holism of the mental' (Quine, 1960, Davidson, 1970) which is here only roughly sketched, will turn out to be of crucial significance and we shall return to it. But for the moment let us ask how the functionalist can accommodate the fact that, finite creatures as we are, we have this immensely flexible and seemingly open-ended competence with psychological understanding and explanation. A model lies to hand here in the notions of axioms and theorems. We have understanding of hitherto unencountered situations because we (in some sense) know some basic principles concerning the ingredients and modes of interaction of the elements from which the new situations are composed.

What can the elements be? Not individual beliefs and desires because, as we have seen, there are too many of them. Hence the view that having an individual belief or desire must be, functionally conceived, a composite state. This is one powerful reason why the idea of the having of beliefs and desires as relations to inner sentences seems attractive (Field, 1978, pp. 24–36). The functional psychologist hopes that, with a limited number of elements (inner words), together with principles of construction and principles of interaction (modelled on the syntactic transformations of formalized logic), the complexity of intra-subjective psychological interactions can be encapsulated in a theory of manageable proportions.

But, however elegantly the theory is axiomatized the fact remains that it is going to be enormously complex. Moreover we certainly cannot now formulate it explicitly. There should therefore be some reluctance to credit ourselves with knowing it (even if only implicitly) unless there is no alternative account of how psychological explanation could work. But there is an alternative. It is the replicating strategy to which I now turn.

On the replicating view psychological understanding works like this. I can think about the world. I do so in the interests of taking my own decisions and forming my own opinions. The future is complex and unclear. In order to deal with it I need to and can envisage possible but perhaps non-actual states of affairs. I can imagine how my tastes, aims and opinions might change, and work out what would be sensible to do or believe in the circumstances. My ability to do these things makes possible a certain sort of understanding of other people. I can harness all my complex theoretical knowledge about the world and my ability to imagine to yield an insight into other people *without any further elaborate theorizing about them.* Only one simple assumption is needed: that they are like me in being thinkers, that they possess the same fundamental cognitive capacities and propensities that I do.

The method works like this. Suppose I am interested in predicting someone's action. (I take this case only as an example, not intending thereby to endorse any close link between understanding and prediction in the psychological case. Similar methods would apply with other aspects of understanding, for example, working out what someone was thinking, feeling or intending in the past.) What I endeavour to do is to replicate or recreate his thinking. I place myself in what I take to be his initial state by imagining the world as it would appear from his point of view and I then deliberate, reason and reflect to see what decision emerges.

Psychological states are not alone in being amenable to this approach. I might try to find out how someone else is reacting or will react to a certain drug by taking a dose of it myself. There is thus a quite general method of finding out what will or did happen to things similar to myself in given circumstances, namely ensuring that I myself am in those circumstances and waiting to see what occurs. To get good results from the method I require only that I have the ability to get myself into the same state as the person I wish to know about and that he and I are in fact relevantly similar.

As so far described the method yields us 'understanding' of another person in the sense of particular judgements about what he or she feels, thinks or does, which may facilitate interaction on particular occasions. We may also get from this method 'understanding' in the sense of some sort of answer to a why-question. If I am capable of describing the initial conditions which I replicated then I can cite them. But the method does not yet yield any hint of theoretical apparatus. No answer is forthcoming to the question 'Certain states are experimentally found to be thus linked – but why? What principles operate here?' We will return in section 3 to consider what concepts and principles of connection the replication method turns out to presuppose. Could they for example be identical with those the functional strategy calls upon?

But I would first like to discuss in section 2 three direct lines of attack upon my claim that replication is, at least in its method of delivering particular judgements, a real and conceptually economical alternative to the functional approach, that is, an alternative which avoids the need to credit ourselves with knowledge of complex theories about each other.

2 Three Arguments Against the Replicative Strategy

The first line of attack concentrates on how I am supposed to get myself into the correct replicating state. One might argue as follows; the replication method demands that I be able, on the basis of looking at someone else, to know what psychological state he or she is in, so that I can put myself in the same state; but to do this I must, perhaps at some inexplicit level, be in possession of a theory about the interrelations of psychological states and behaviour; but this will just be the functionalist theory all over again.

Two lines of defence against this attack are available. First, we may object that the attack presupposes that knowledge of another's psychological state must always be inferentially based and rest upon observation of behaviour, conceived of as something neutrally describable. But we need not buy this premiss and may propose instead some more direct model of how we come to knowledge of others' feelings and so forth (McDowell, 1982).

Secondly (and this is the more important line of defence) the attack misdescribes the direction of gaze of the replicator. He is not looking at the subject to be understood but at the world around that subject. It is what the world makes the replicator think which is the basis for the beliefs he attributes to the subject. The process, of course, does not work with complete simplicity and directness. The replicator does not attribute to someone else belief in every state of affairs which he can see to obtain in the other's vicinity. A process of recentring the world in imagination is required. And this must involve the operation of some principles about what it is possible to perceive. Visual occlusion is the obvious example. But a theory about what one can know about the world from what viewpoint is not the same thing as a theory about how psychological states interact with each other or about what behaviour they produce.

It is worth remarking here that we need not saddle the replication theory with a commitment to the absurd idea that we are all quite indistinguishable in our psychological reactions – that any two persons with the same history are bound to respond to a given situation in the same way. Replication theory must allow somewhere for the idea of different personalities, for different styles of thinking and for non-rational influences on thinking. It is not clear what shape such additions to the core replication process would take. But there is no reason to suppose that they would take the form of the reimportation of the proposed functionalist-style theory.

Someone might try to press or to reformulate the objection by conceding that looking at the world rather than the subject might be a good heuristic device for suggesting hypotheses about his or her beliefs, but insisting that, nevertheless, we must employ (implicitly or explicitly) some criteria for the correctness of these hypotheses. What shows me that I am thinking of the world in the same way as the person I seek to understand? I must have some theory about what constitutes sameness of psychological state, and this theory, it will be suggested, could well, or indeed must, take a functionalist form.

But why should we accept the foundationalist epistemological presuppositions of this argument? Is it not enough for us to credit ourselves with the concept of 'same psychological state' that we should, first, be able to make generally agreed judgements using the notion and, secondly, that when our expectations are falsified we are usually able to detect some source of error when we cast around for further features of the situation, and hence to restore coherence among our own views and between our views and those of others?

We touch here on large issues in epistemology. But at the weakest we could say this, that there is not in this area any quick knock-down argument in favour of functionalism as against a claimed economical replication view.

Let us turn to a second reason for supposing that replication cannot be more economical than functionalism. Dennett (commenting on something similar to the replication view which he finds hinted at by Stich (1982b)) writes:

> How can it [the idea of using myself as an analogue computer] work without being a kind of theorising in the end? For the state I put myself in is not belief but make believe belief. If I make believe I am a suspension bridge and wonder what I will do when the wind blows, what 'comes to me' in my make believe state depends on how sophisticated my knowledge is of the physics and engineering of suspension bridges. Why should my making believe I have your beliefs be any different? In both cases knowledge of the imitated object is needed to drive the make believe 'simulation' and the knowledge must be organised in something rather like a theory. (Dennett, 1982, p. 79)

Of course Dennett is quite right that the psychological case as I have sketched it is not one of strict replication, unlike the drug case. It would clearly be absurd to suppose that in order to anticipate what someone else will do I have actually to believe what he or she believes. But Dennett is wrong in thinking that what he calls 'make believe belief' is as alien a state – and hence as demanding of theoretical underpinning – as making believe to be a suspension bridge. Make-believe belief is imagining. And we do this already on our own behalf. The sequence of thought connections from imagined state of affairs to imagined decision parallels that from real belief to real decision. If it did not we could not use the technique of contemplating possibilities and seeing what it would be sensible to do if . . . as part of our own decision making. So to make the replication method work I do not require the theory which Dennett mentions. I require only the ability to distinguish real belief from entertaining a possibility and the ability to attribute to another person as belief what I have actualized in myself as imagining.

The third attempt to show that replication and functionalism coincide takes a bolder line. The replicator supposes that some working out is to be done in order to find out what it would be sensible to do in the situation the other person envisages. Similarly the functionalist also supposes that working out is to be done; it is from a knowledge of particular states together with general principles or laws that a judgement on this case is to be reached. Why should we not suppose that the working out involved in the two cases is, contrary to superficial appearances, the same? The description of the replication method given so far suggests that sequences of thought states occur in me without mediation of any further thought, just as the sequences of reactions to drugs do. But perhaps this is a misleading picture; perhaps transitions from one thought to another occur in virtue of my awareness of some principle or law requiring the occurrence of the one after the other. Doing the actual thinking, which the replicator represents as something *toto caelo* different from functionalist-style thinking about thinking, is not in fact fundamentally different. Making up my own mind is just the first-person version of what in third-person cases is functional-style causal prediction. ·

But this will not do at all. For a start, an infinite regress threatens. If any transition from thought to thought is to be underpinned by some further thought about links, how are we to explain the occurrence of the relevant thought about links without invoking some third level and so on? But let us waive this objection. More substantial difficulties await.

It is indeed tempting to suppose that whenever I draw a conclusion, that is, base one judgement on another, I must implicitly know or have in mind some general principle which links the two. But whether or not we think it right to yield to this temptation, the only sense in which the claim is plausible is one in which the principle in question is a normative one ('one ought to believe so-and-so if one believes such-and-such') or relatedly a semantic one ('the belief that so-and-so would be true if the belief that such-and-such were true'). In neither case is the principle in question a causal law, such as the supposed axioms of the functionalist theory are to be. The terminology I used above in arguing my opponents' case (a 'principle' or 'law' by which the occurrence of one belief 'requires' the occurrence of another) is designed to obscure this vital difference. If we try to restate the proposal being quite explicit that the connections in question are causal, we arrive at the most bizarre results. It amounts to supposing that it makes no difference whether a thinker asks himself or herself the question 'What ought I to think next?' or the question 'What will I, as a matter of fact, think next?' On the proposed view, these are just different wordings of the same question.

Suppose then that I do infer that q on the basis that p and that my knowledge that belief that p causes belief that q is integral to the process. We seem to have the following choice. Either we could say that the inference that *q* is based not just on the premiss that *p* (as *prima facie* but misleading appearance has it) but also on the (implicit) premiss that belief that *p* causes belief that *q*. This amounts to endorsing the principle of inference 'I will be caused to believe that *p*, therefore *p'*. Alternatively we could suppose that drawing the inference just is making the prediction. And this amounts to identifying belief that *p* with belief that one is being made to think that *p*.

Clearly none of this will do. It makes judgements about the world collapse into or rest upon judgements about me; and moreover they are judgements about me which have quite disparate truth conditions and roles in thought from the judgements about the world they are required to stand in for.

There are certain conditions under which the assimilation would appear less ludicrous. These are that I could isolate causal factors constitutive of my rational thinking from interfering ones; that I am a perfect thinker (that is, I rely on no confused concepts or plausible but unreliable rules of inference) and that I know that I am a perfect thinker. In other words, if I knew that physiologically I embodied a logical system and I knew the meta-theory for my own system, then causal-syntactic knowledge about myself would have semantic equivalents. The discussion of fallibility below will indicate some of the reasons why this is unacceptable.

So far I have been examining attempts to show that the replication strategy cannot be a real alternative to the functionalist one. And I maintain that none of them has undermined the plausibility of the original claim that the two approaches are different and that the former is more economical than the latter.

3 The Autonomy of Replication

I turn now to a different line of thought, one which concedes the above claim but argues that nevertheless a replicative style of psychological understanding is compatible with a functionalist style. The use of the one does not preclude the other. A functionalist theory could develop out of and dovetail smoothly with use of the replicating strategy. Perhaps it is already doing so; or perhaps it will, when cognitive science is more advanced.

In the case of reaction to drugs something like this is clearly possible. At one stage of the development of knowledge I may be unable to anticipate others' reactions except via the replication method and unable to conceptualize them except through ideas appropriate to that method. For example, I ask of another person 'Why was she sick?' An initial answer might muster all the relevant information I have like this:'I was sick; she took the same drug as I did and she is like me.' Or we might express it more naturally: 'She is like me and she took the drug which made me sick.' But this is not a stopping point. When I become reflective I shall ask 'In what respects is she relevantly similar to me?' and 'What feature of the drug connects with this feature of us to make us sick?' There is no reason in this case why the answers should not be ones the finding of which precisely does amount to my finding a causal theory which will emancipate me, wholly or partially, from the need to replicate. The key feature here is that the relevant similarity will probably turn out to be something about body chemistry. When I have these physiological concepts to hand I can specify directly what sort of creatures will be affected by some drug without mention of myself as a standard of similarity. And I can describe directly what the drug does to them instead of pointing to myself and saying 'It makes you like this.'

Now why should this not also be the case with psychological replication? Perhaps replication is a method by which primates unreflectively facilitate their social interactions. But we, it might be said, are in the process of emancipating ourselves from this primitive approach. (This is a view suggested to me by some remarks of Andrew Woodfield (1982, pp. 281–2).) So when one unreflectively attributes a thought to another creature one may replicate that thought, and at the first attempts one may be unable to characterize the state in question in any other way than by pointing to oneself and saying 'Well, it is like what I am doing now.' And one will be unable to anticipate others except by recreating and attempting to rethink their thoughts because on has no access to the nature of the thought as it is in itself or the respects in which the other subject and oneself are relevantly similar. Nevertheless, reflection shows us that there is such a thing as the nature of the thought in itself, some intrinsic character that it has, and some non-demonstrative specification of relevant similarity. So when we use psychological terminology reflectively it is to these things that we intend to refer. And cognitive science is about to fill in the actual detail of what they are.

But I want now to argue that this will not do. When we reflect on the notion of 'relevant similarity', as it needs to be used in psychological explanation, we discover an insuperable bar to imagining it being superseded by the sort of physiological or structural description which functionalism requires. And relatedly we find that we cannot get at the nature of the thought as it is in itself but continue to have access to it only in an indirect and demonstrative fashion.

The difference between psychological explanation and explanation in the natural sciences is that in giving a psychological explanation we render the thought or behaviour of the other intelligible, we exhibit them as having some point, some reasons to be cited in their defence. Another way of putting this truism is to say that we see them as exercises of cognitive competence or rationality. (I intend these terms to be interchangeable and to be understood very broadly to mean what is exercised in the formation of intention and desire as well as belief.)

This is a feature of psychological explanation which the replication method puts at the centre of the stage. When I start reflecting upon the replication method and trying to put the particular judgements and connections it indicates in a theoretical context, it is the notion of cognitive competence, of the subject struggling to get things right, which must present itself as the respect in which I and the other are relevantly similar.

But what further account can we give of rationality? Could it be discovered to be identical with and replaceable by something which would suit the functionalist programme? Initial thoughts about rationality or cognitive competence suggest that it surely has something to do with the ability to achieve success in judgement (that is, truth for belief and whatever the analogous property or properties are for desires, intentions, etc.). But the nature of the link is difficult to capture. Is rationality something which guarantees the actual success of judgement in particular cases? Arguably not, since the question 'But have I got this right?' can always be raised. We must recognize ourselves to be thoroughly fallible. This is one important implication of the extreme complexity of interaction of psychological states which our earlier discussion did not bring out. In our earlier remarks about functionalism the complexity served merely as a spur to thinking of psychological states as molecular rather than atomic. That move was needed because we could not specify in advance what beliefs might be relevant to any other – as premises or conclusions. Thus given enough background of the right sort any belief could bear upon the truth of any other. It is this which prevents the individuation of beliefs as atomic units by their placement in some specifiable pattern of a limited number of other psychological states. But a further implication of this (as Quine constantly stresses) is that we cannot pick upon any belief or beliefs as immune to any possible influence from future information.

So cognitive competence is not the claim that for at least some sorts of judgement success is guaranteed. Could it be defined, then, in terms of inference rules relied on or judgement-forming procedures, for example, by mention of specific rules like *modus tollens* or inductive generalization or, more non-committally, via the idea of inference rules which are generally reliable? This again will not do and its failure is crucial to the incompatibility between replication and functionalism. I can fail to follow simple and reliable inference rules and can adopt some most unreliable ones, and recognize later that this was what I was doing, quite compatibly with continued trust in my then and present cognitive competence. The only constraint is that I should be able to make intelligible to myself why I failed to notice so-and-so or seemed to assume such-and-such. And, as with the case of individual judgements, enough scene setting can do the trick. This is not to say that I can make sense of my past self – or of someone else – even where I can find no overlap at all between my present judgements and inference procedures and those of the other. Rather my claim is that we cannot arrange inference procedures (or judgements) in some clear hierarchy and identify some as basic or constitutive of rationality.

We may have models or partial views of what constitutes rationality (in logic, decision theory and so forth) but thinking in accordance with the rules or standards there specified cannot be definitive of or exhaust the notion of rationality. This is not only because our current views on these matters may be wrong but for another reason also. If rationality were thus definable then the claim that I myself am rational would acquire some specific empirical content, would become just one proposition among all the others which form my view of the world. It would thus be potentially up for grabs as something falsifiable by enough evidence of the right character. But, notoriously, any attempted demonstration to me by myself that I am a non-thinker must be absurd because self-undermining. Hence any account of what it is to be a thinker which seems to make such a demonstration possible must be at fault.

How does all this bear upon the idea that as we gain more knowledge and conceptual sophistication some primitive replication method could gracefully give way to a more scientific functional understanding? It is relevant because this idea does require exactly the assumption that rationality can be given a complete formal definition in terms of syntactically specifiable inference rules. It is only if this is the case that the replicating assumption of relevant similarity – 'they are like me in being cognitively competent' – can be replaced by the functional assumption – 'they are like me in being systems with inner states structured and interacting according to so-and-so principles'.

I have used as a premiss a strong version of fallibilism which some may find implausible. Surely, one might protest, some propositions (that I exist, that this is a desk, that here is a hand) are in some sense unassailable, as are also some rules of inference. Am I seriously suggesting that the law of non-contradiction or universal instantiation might be overthrown?

Suppose we concede the force of these remarks; does it then become defensible again to maintain that functionalism will turn out to be compatible with the replication approach and will ultimately replace it? It does not. As long as we admit that there are any parts of our implicit inferential practices which may be muddled – that is, as long as we admit (as we surely must) that the world has some funny surprises in store for us as a result of which we shall recognize our earlier thinking patterns as muddled and inadequate, then we must also admit that our formal grip on rationality is not complete.

It is position within the network defined by the supposed formal account of rationality which is to provide the functionalist account of what a thought is in itself. Thoughts are, for functionalists, identified and individuated by causal-explanatory role. So a corollary of the non-existence of a formal account of rationality is the non-availability of that mode of characterizing thoughts which functionalism counts on – a mode imagined to be independent of our entertaining or rethinking those thoughts.

4 *Content and Explanation*

I turn finally to some sketchy and programmatic remarks about the concepts and modes of explanation which will be called on under the two strategies – replicating and functionalist.

Recent writings in the functionalist school have produced powerful arguments to show that according to their approach, the semantic properties of psychological states, that is, their referential relations to particular objects or sorts of stuff in the world, are not directly relevant to their explanatory roles. We think of psychological states (they say) both as things which are true or false in virtue of semantic connections with the world, and also as things which are explanatory of behaviour. But these two ways of thinking about them are in some sense independent. So that-clauses are systematically ambiguous; sometimes we use them to ascribe truth conditions and sometimes to ascribe causal-explanatory role (Fodor, 1980; McGinn, 1982; Field, 1978).

I shall not fully rehearse the arguments for this view here. The nub of the matter is just this, that admission of the referential as explanatory in the functionalists' causal framework would amount to admitting a very mysterious action at a distance which goes against all our causal assumptions. Distant objects exert their causal influence over us via chains of intermediate events, where these events could occur from other causes even if the distant object did not exist. The functionalist views as explanatory a state which could exist even if the supposed referent did not; and thus he claims to unite economically, in one form of account, actions guided by true beliefs (i.e. ones which are referentially well grounded) and also actions which are based on illusion. The functionalist claims that we have a concept of what is common to referentially well-based cognition and illusory cognition, a concept which is specifiable without mention of referential success; and that referential success is thus a conjunctive notion (cf. McDowell, 1982).

But what is this something else, this non-referential content which we sometimes use that-clauses to ascribe? One thing which is clear is that in attributing non-referential content to someone's thought I do not commit myself to the existence of any particular thing (or natural kind) outside him. I merely characterize him as he is intrinsically.

But obscurities remain. One of these has been noted (Bach, 1982). Non-referential content could be something thought of merely syntactically – that is, to be labelled 'content' only in an exceedingly stretched sense. On the other hand the notion of non-referential content could be recognizably a notion of meaning in some sense. In reporting it we report the subject's 'mode of representing the world' – but without commitment to the existence of anything outside him.

But within the latter option there is also an important further obscurity. Is non-referential content strongly conceptually independent of reference and truth, in that someone could have the former idea without the others so much as having crossed his mind? Or are they only weakly conceptually independent in that ascription of non-referential content does not commit one to an actual referent or truth conditions but does commit one to some disposition concerning reference and truth? On the second view, in thinking of something as having non-referential content we are thinking of it precisely as something which in a certain context or under certain other conditions would have such-and-such referent and truth conditions.

There are thus three options. Non-referential content is:

(a) a merely syntactic notion;
(b) a notion of meaning strongly independent of truth and reference;
(c) a notion of meaning only weakly independent of truth and reference.

Which of these do the functionalists propose?

It is claimed that classification of beliefs as explanatory and classification of them as truth bearers are 'independent' because such classifications can, cross cut (e.g. in the case of indexicals or Twin Earth situations: cf. Fodor, 1980, pp. 66–8; McGinn, 1982, pp. 208–10). And in the discussion of why we are interested in reference at all, it seems to be assumed that this 'cross-cutting classification' argument has established (a) or (b) – that is, has established 'independence' in a strong sense of complete conceptual detachment. These discussions proceed on the assumption that grip on the non-referential notion of content has provided no foothold at all for truth and our interest in it has to be motivated totally *ab initio* (Field, 1978, pp. 44–9; McGinn, 1982, pp. 225–8). But in fact the cross-cutting classification point does not establish this. Consider 'fragile' and 'broken': these classifications cross cut. But this would hardly show that we could understand 'fragile' without understanding 'breaks' or that our interest in breakage needed to be motivated independently of our interest in fragility.

On the other hand the notion of non-referential content is sometimes elucidated in terms of notions like subjective probability, inference, Fregean sense, or Kaplanesque 'character' (Field, 1977; McGinn, 1982). And these notions are ones which *prima facie* have conceptual links with reference and truth. Thus Kaplan's notion of the character of an indexical utterance or belief is precisely the notion of something which, placed in a certain context, determines a referent and hence a truth value.

Whichever of these options the functionalist takes there will be difficulties. On (a) and (b) it turns out that a view which I earlier offered as a truism, namely that in psychological explanation we exhibit the explanandum having a point or being at least in part justified, is false. The explanatory notions postulated in (a) and (b) are ones which provide no foothold for talk of justification or point. So, if presented as a view about everyday psychological talk and explanation, this philosophical theory has the problem of explaining where the semantic and related justificatory aspects of the practices fit in and why they seem to loom so large for us. I do not say that this cannot be done, only that attempts so far have not been convincing.[1] On the other hand, if the theory is presented not as an account of notions we now employ but as a blueprint for a future, highly abstract version of neurophysiology, then it is not faced with that problem but its relevance for philosophical accounts of current practice is non-existent.

If the functionalist adopts (c) as his account of non-referential content then his problems are different. This content notion is one in which two elements are linked – namely the idea of a 'a mode of representing the world' and the idea of a 'causal-explanatory role'; moreover they are linked in such a way that the one 'is constitutive of' the other (McGinn, 1982, p. 210). The mode of representing notion now invoked has enough link with truth for notions like justification and seeing the point to get a grip. So it would not be absurd to offer this as an account of part of what we are ordinarily doing with psychological statements. But, if the arguments centring on fallibilism in the earlier part of the paper were persuasive, the difficulty will be to show convincingly how there *can* be a notion which dovetails this 'mode of representing' idea with the 'causal–explanatory role' idea. Grip on a causal–explanatory role is grip on some pattern, thought of as fixed and where the *relata* are known. But grip on a justificatory content is confidence in my power to see the point, to understand arguments and justifications involving this notion when I am called upon to do so, without supposing that I *now* know that those other related thoughts are. That such a functionalist notion, that is, one in which the two elements are dovetailed, is called for by a plausible version of functionalism is not an argument for its coherence, unless functionalism itself is unassailable.

In summary, then, in this section I have been arguing that much work needs to be done to clarify the notion of non-referential content which functionalists ought to espouse and to demonstrate that such a notion is coherent.

What will be the theoretical apparatus and modes of explanation which the replication account calls for? In stressing that one is only in position to understand another psychologically by rethinking his or her thoughts, I am putting the idea of 'doing the same thing oneself' in a prominent place. And it may thus seem that Cartesian introspectionism is reappearing on the scene. But this is not so. And the crucial difference is that, on the view I maintain, one has no more access to the intrinsic nature of one's own thoughts than one does to the intrinsic nature of others'. Thinking about my own thoughts is not, on my model, direct and intimate confrontation with something about whose nature I cannot be deceived. It is, in my own case as for others, to replicate – that is, putting on a certain sort of performance, rather than being in possession of a certain kind of knowledge. Psychological ascriptions – the use of that-clauses – might better be called re-expression than description. I do not by saying this mean to outlaw the phrases 'psychological knowledge' or 'psychological description' but rather to put us on our guard against a certain way of conceiving of such knowledge or descriptions. We may agree that a person knows of himself or herself what he or she is thinking more easily than he or she knows this of others. In one's own case one does not have the complexities of recentring to deal with, so replication comes very easily. But the technique for doing it, namely looking at the world, and the outcome, namely placing oneself in a position to put on a certain sort of performance, are just the same whether one thinks of oneself or another. And the emphasis on fallibilism shows that my easy replication of my own thought gives me no privileged position *vis-à-vis* claims to understand it, see what follows from it or the like.

I have argued that the notion of rationality or cognitive competence is central on the replication account. But equally I have argued that no substantive definition of it can be given. It is not that rationality has no conceptual connections with other notions. The idea of cognitive competence must have something to do with the idea of attaining success in cognition, that is, truth for beliefs and whatever the analogous properties are for other intentional states. Hence the idea that semantic notions such as truth have no importance in psychological explanation will clearly be mistaken on the replication view.

Rationality cannot be understood without a grip on the semantic notions which define success or failure in cognition.

But one might still wonder about the point or usefulness of deploying the notion of rationality. If I affirm of myself that I am rational what point can my action have if I am not offering something with a testable content, a description of the world? I conjecture that we have here one of those items at the limits of our conceptual scheme which present themselves sometimes as statements but at other times rather as programmes of action or announcements of a stance. One thing that I might be doing in affirming myself to be rational is acknowledging the necessity of taking success as the norm in my cognitive enterprises, that is, taking success as what is to be expected unless evidence of mistake appears. I suspect that pursuit of this clue might lead to a more illuminating picture of what psychological explanation is than attempts to elaborate a functionalist account. But that is a topic for another paper.

Notes

1   Field suggests (1978, pp. 44–9) that we attribute reference and truth conditions to the inner states of others because we find it useful to 'calibrate' them; we can then use facts about their inner states, in conjunction with some reliability theory, to gain information about the world for ourselves. McGinn (1982, pp. 225–6) objects to this that it makes assignment of reference to others' beliefs and utterances too contingent. On Field's account we would not bother to do it if we thought the other person, through limitations of his knowledge or his unreliability, had nothing to teach us. Yet surely we might assign reference even in these circumstances. So McGinn proposes (1982, pp. 226–8) that we need the notion of reference in characterizing the practice of communication. 'A hearer understands a speech act as an assertion just if he interprets it as performed with a certain point or intention – viz. to convey information about the world.' But this, on McGinn's own earlier showing, will hardly do. The phrase 'about the world' is itself subject to the bifurcation of role which McGinn claims to find in all that-clauses or content ascribers. When I ascribe to another an intention to 'convey information about the world' on McGinn's account I may understand this attribution of content to his or her intention in either of two ways – first as ascribing an inner explanatory state, grasp of the nature of which requires no semantic concepts, or secondly as ascribing an inner state with semantic relations. And only the former is needed for psychological explanation and understanding of communicative behaviour. So, failing some further account of 'characterising the activity of communication' (an account which shows it to be other than psychological explanation of it), we are no further forward.

What is odd about both these accounts, Field's in particular, is that they take for granted that we want true beliefs for ourselves. But once this is acknowledged the attempt to anchor the notion of truth and our interest in it by pointing to some complex of causal facts and correlations observable in third-person cases seems strange. The interest in truth is already anchored as soon as a person comes to express reflectively his or her own beliefs and to ask 'But is that right?'

References

Bach, K. 1982: De re belief and methodological solipsism, in *Thought and Object*, ed. A. Woodfield. Oxford: Clarendon Press.

Davidson, D. 1970: Mental events, in *Experience and Theory*, eds L. Foster and J. W. Swanson. Cambridge, Mass.: University of Massachusetts Press.

Dennett, D. C. 1982: Making sense of ourselves, in *Mind, Brain and Function*, ed. J. I. Biro and R. W. Shahan. Brighton: Harvester Press.

Field, H. 1977: Logic, meaning and conceptual role. *Journal of Philosophy*, 74, 379–409.

Field, H. 1978: Mental representation. *Erkenntnis*, 13, 9–61.

Fodor, J. A. 1980: Methodological solipsism considered as a research strategy in cognitive psychology. *Behavioral and Brain Sciences*, 3, 63–73.

Harman, G. 1973: *Thought*. Princeton, NJ: Princeton University Press.

Lewis, D. 1972: Psychological and theoretical identifications. *Australasian Journal of Philosophy*, 50, 249–58.

McDowell, J. 1982: Criteria, defeasibility and knowledge. *Proceedings of the British Academy*, 68, 455–79.

McGinn, C. 1982: The structure of content, in *Thought and Object*, ed. A. Woodfield. Oxford: Clarendon Press.

Putnam, H. 1967: The nature of mental states. First published as Psychological predicates, in *Art, Mind and Religion*, eds W. H. Capitan and D. D. Merrill. Pittsburgh: University of Pittsburgh Press. Reprinted in H. Putnam, *Mind, Language and Reality: Philosophical Papers*, vol. 2. Cambridge: Cambridge University Press, 1975.

Quine, W. V. O. 1960: *Word and Object*. Cambridge, Mass.: MIT Press.

Stich, S. 1982a. On the ascription of content, in *Thought and Object*, ed. A. Woodfield. Oxford: Clarendon Press.

Stich, S. 1982b: Dennett on intentional systems, in *Mind, Brain and Function*, ed. J. I. Biro and R. W. Shahan. Brighton: Harvester Press.

Woodfield, A. 1982: On specifying the contents of thoughts, in *Thought and Object*, ed. A. Woodfield. Oxford: Clarendon Press.

2
Folk Psychology as Simulation

ROBERT M. GORDON

Recently I made a series of predictions of human behavior, using the meager resources allotted to a non-scientist. Having nothing to rely on but 'common-sense' or 'folk' psychology and being well forewarned of the infirmities of that so-called theory, I had reason to anticipate at best a very modest rate of success.

These were the predictions:

I shall now pour some coffee.
I shall now pick up the cup.
I shall now drink the coffee.
I shall now switch on the word processor.
I shall now draft the opening paragraphs of a paper on folk psychology.

My predictions, as I think no one will be surprised to learn, proved true in every instance. Should anyone doubt this, I recommend spending a few minutes predicting from one moment to another what you are 'about to do'. Such predictions, if not quite as reliable as 'night will follow day' or 'this chair will hold my weight', are at least among the most reliable one is likely to make. Of course, one would have to allow for unforeseen interventions by 'nature' (sudden paralysis, a coffee cup glued to the table) and for ignorance (the stuff you pour and drink isn't coffee). But that seems a realistic limitation on any *psychological* basis for prediction.

This paper offers an account of the nature of folk psychology. Sections 1 and 2 focus on the prediction of behavior, beginning with reflections on my little experiment in prediction. Section 3 concerns the interaction of explanation and prediction in what I call hypothetico-practical reasoning. Finally, a new account of belief attribution is proposed and briefly defended in section 4.

1 Predicting One's Own Behavior

At least one lesson can be drawn from my prediction experiment. Discussions of the nature of 'folk psychology' and of its own adequacy, particularly as a basis for predictions of overt human behavior, ought to begin by dividing the question: *one's own* behavior or *another's*; behavior in the *immediate* or in the *distant* future; behavior under *existing* conditions or under specified *hypothetical* conditions? For such a division uncovers a little-known and unappreciated success story: our prodigious ability to foretell what we ourselves are 'about to do' in the (actual) immediate future. We have in this department a success rate that surely would be the envy of any behavioral or neurobehavioral science.

The trick, of course, is not to predict until one has 'made up one's mind' what to do: then one simply declares what one 'intends' to do. We display our confidence in the *predictive reliability* of these declarations by the way we formulate them: one typically says, not 'I intend now to . . .', but simply 'I shall now . . .' or 'I will now . . .' Somehow, in learning to 'express our (immediate) intention' we learn to utter sentences that, construed as statements about our own future behavior, prove to be extremely reliable.[1] (Normally, apart from the conditions mentioned earlier, the only errors occur when something 'makes us change our mind': the telephone rings before we have poured the coffee, we see that the stuff isn't coffee, and so on.) A plausible explanation of this reliability is that our declarations of immediate intention are causally tied to some actual precursor of behavior: perhaps tapping into the brain's updated behavioral 'plans' or into 'executive commands' that are about to guide the relevant motor sequences.[2] In any case, these everyday predictions of behavior seem to have an anchor in psychological reality.

One might have thought all predictions of human behavior to be inferences from theoretical premises about beliefs, desires, and emotions, together with laws connecting these with behavior: laws of the form: 'if A is in states S1, S2, S3, etc., and conditions C1, C2, C3 obtain, then A will (or will probably) do X'. Thus one would have a *deductive-nomological* or *inductive-nomological* basis for prediction. This is plainly not so: declarations of immediate intention – 'I shall now X' – are not products of inference from such premises.

Moreover, if they were, one could not account for either their predictive reliability or our *confidence* in their predictive reliability. We are not self-omniscient: we do not keep tabs on all of the relevant beliefs and attitudes, and *a fortiori* we do not keep a *reliable* inventory of these. But even if we knew all the relevant beliefs and attitudes, our predictions would at best be qualified and chancy. Folk psychology, on most accounts, doesn't specify a deterministic system; it specifies only the probable or 'typical' effects of mental states. Using it as my basis I should have to qualify my predictions by saying, e.g. '*Typically*, I would now pick up the cup.' And actions that are *atypical*, *exceptional*, or *out of character* – my wearing a tie to class, or my heckling the commencement speaker – would defy prediction altogether, even seconds before I take action. Whereas in fact I feel confident that I can predict what I am about to do now, whether the act is typical or not; and my confidence seems well-founded: I predict imminent atypical actions about as reliably as any others.

Although they are not based on nomological reasoning, declarations of immediate intention – these ultra-reliable predictors of behavior – are often products of *practical* reasoning: reasoning that provides the basis for a decision *to do* something.[3] 'I shall now write a letter' may express a decision based on certain salient facts (a student asked me to write a letter of recommendation), salient norms and values (I have a duty to write letters for good students who request letters, and she's a good student), and a background of other facts, norms, and values that I am unable to list exhaustively. The important point is that declarations of the form: 'I shall now do X' offer a bridge between such practical reasoning and prediction.

This bridge introduces a very interesting possibility: that of using *simulated* practical reasoning as a *predictive* device. First of all, it is easy to see how, by simulating the appropriate practical reasoning, we can extend our capacity for self-prediction in a way that would enable us to predict *our own behavior in hypothetical situations*. Thus I might predict, for example, what I would do if, right now, the screen of the word processor I am working on were to go blank; or what I would do if I were now to hear footsteps coming from the basement.

To simulate the appropriate practical reasoning I can engage in a kind of *pretend-play*: pretend that the indicated conditions *actually obtain*, with all other conditions remaining (so far as is logically possible and physically probable) as they presently stand; then – continuing the make-believe – try to 'make up my mind' what to do given these (modified) conditions. I imagine, for instance a lone modification of the actual world: the sound of footsteps from the basement.[4] Then I ask, in effect, 'what shall I do now?' And I answer with a declaration of immediate intention, 'I shall now . . .' This too is only feigned. But it is not feigned on a *tabula rasa*, as if at random: rather, the declaration of immediate intention appears to be formed in the way a *decision* is formed, *constrained* by the (pretended) 'fact' that there is the sound of footsteps from the basement, the (*un*pretended) fact that such a sound would now be unlikely if there weren't an intruder in the basement, the (*un*pretended) awfulness of there being an intruder in the basement, and so forth.

What I have performed is a kind of *practical simulation*, a simulated deciding *what to do*. Some simulated decisions in hypothetical situations include acting out: e.g. rehearsals and drills. The kind I am interested in, however, suppress the behavioral output. One reports the simulated decision as a *hypothetical prediction*: a prediction of what I would do in the specified hypothetical circumstances, other things being as they are. For example: if I were now to hear footsteps from the basement, (probably) I would reach for the telephone and call an emergency number.[5]

I noted earlier that one could not account for either the *confidence* or the *reliability* with which I predict what I am about to do now, if such predictions were based on attributions of beliefs, desires, etc., together with laws. The same holds for *hypothetical* self-predictions. Once again I don't know enough about my beliefs and desires; and the laws would at best yield only the *typical* effects of those states, anyway.[6] In real life we sometimes surprise ourselves with *atypical* responses: 'I certainly wouldn't have thought I'd react that way!' Practical simulation imitates real life in this respect, giving us the capacity to surprise ourselves *before* we confront the actual situation. If I pretend *realistically* that there is an intruder in the house I *might* find myself surprisingly brave – or cowardly.[7]

2 Predicting the Behavior of Others

In one type of hypothetical *self*-prediction the hypothetical situation is one that some *other* person has actually been in, or at least is described as having been in. The task is to answer the question, 'What would *I* do in *that* person's situation?' For example, chess players report that, playing against a human opponent or even against a computer, they visualize the board from the other side, taking the opposing pieces for their own and vice versa. Further, they pretend that their *reasons for action* have shifted accordingly: whereas previously the fact that a move would make White's Queen vulnerable would constitute a reason *for* making the move, it now becomes a reason *against*; and so on. Thus transported in imagination, they 'make up their mind what to do.' *That*, they conclude, is what *I* would do (have done). They are 'putting themselves in the other's shoes' in one sense of that expression: that is, they project themselves into the other's *situation*, but without any attempt to project themselves into, as we say, the other's 'mind'.

A prediction of how I would act in the other's situation is not, of course, a prediction of how the other will act – unless, of course, the other should happen to be, in causally relevant respects, a *replica* of me. But people claim also that by 'putting themselves in the other's shoes', in a somewhat different sense of that expression, they can predict the *other's* behavior. As in the case of hypothetical self-prediction, the methodology essentially involves *deciding what to do*; but, extended to people of 'minds' different from one's own, this is not the same as deciding *what I myself would do*. One tries to make *adjustments for relevant differences*. In chess, for example, a player would make not only the imaginative shifts required for predicting 'what *I* would do in his shoes', but the further shifts required for predicting what *he* will do in his shoes. To this purpose the player might, e.g. simulate a lower level of play, trade one set of idiosyncrasies for another, and above all pretend ignorance of *his own* (actual) intentions. Army generals, salespeople, and detectives claim to do this sort of thing. Sherlock Holmes expresses the point with characteristic modesty:

> You know my methods in such cases, Watson. I put myself in the man's place, and, having first gauged his intelligence, I try to imagine how I should myself have proceeded under the same circumstances. In this

case the matter was simplified by Brunton's intelligence being quite first-rate, so that it was unnecessary to make any allowance for the personal equation, as the astronomers have dubbed it. (Doyle, 1894)

The procedure serves cooperative as well as competitive ends: not to go far afield, bridge players claim they can project themselves into their *partner's* shoes.

Several earlier philosophers claimed that interpersonal understanding depends on a procedure resembling what I call simulation. Precursors of simulation include historical reenactment (Collingwood, 1946) and *Verstehen* or 'empathetic understanding' (Schutz, 1962, 1967; von Wright, 1971, ch. 1).[8] But little attention has been given to prediction. Nor have these authors appreciated the methodological importance of hypothesis-testing and experimentation in practical simulation: the fact that at its heart is a type of reasoning I characterize as *hypothetico-practical*. Finally, they have not tried to explain the very concept of belief in terms of practical simulation, as I shall.

3 Hypothetico-practical Reasoning

Let me illustrate with an extended example of hypothetico-practical reasoning. A friend and I have sat down at a table in a fashionable international restaurant in New York. The waiter approaches. He greets me effusively in what strikes me as a Slavic language. He says nothing to my friend. I do not speak any Slavic language.

I wish to understand the waiter's behavior. I wish also to predict his future behavior, given various responses I might make to his greeting. As a first step, I shift spatiotemporal perspectives – I am standing over there now, where the waiter is, not sitting here. In some cases, shifting spatiotemporal perspectives might be enough: e.g. for predicting, or explaining, the behavior of a person I see in the path of an oncoming car. This would be woefully inadequate for the restaurant example, of course. As a further experiment, I might switch institutional roles. I suppose (and perhaps imagine) myself to be a waiter, waiting on a customer sitting here in this restaurant. Such counterfactual suppositions raise difficult questions: for example, shall I suppose myself to be a waiter who has read Quine (as I have)? Shall I suppose the *customer* to have read Quine?[9] Fortunately, I do not ordinarily have to ask these questions, since they would make no difference in my behavior in this situation; and when they do make a difference, the situation is likely to alert me to their relevance.

Donning my waiter's uniform is clearly not enough: to have what I see as a basis for greeting the customer in a Slavic language, supposing I could, I shall have to alter other facts. As a first stab, I might see myself as an *emigré* from a Slavic country, working as a waiter. I seem to recognize the customer: he is a countryman of mine who used to eat at the restaurant many years ago. It pleases him, as I recall, to be greeted in our native tongue. That would be a reason for doing so. There being no reason not to, that is what I shall do.

Other modifications of the world would lead to the same decision. Suppose that, before the restaurant episode, I had read a cheap spy thriller. Under its corrosive influence I hypothesize as follows: I am a counterintelligence agent posing as a waiter. The customer I am waiting on is a known spy from a Slavic country, and there is good reason to get him to reveal that he knows the language of this country. One way to do this is to watch his reaction as I address him in the language of his country. Given this background, I would indeed address him in that language, if I could.

To choose between the two hypotheses would require further tests. Suppose that in my real role of customer, I look puzzled and respond: 'I don't understand that language. You must be making a mistake.' On the country-man hypothesis, the waiter will probably apologize – in English – and explain that he had mistaken me for someone else. On the counterspy hypothesis, he may either persist in speaking in the foreign tongue or turn to more subtle devices for getting the customer to reveal his knowledge of the language. If in fact the waiter apologizes, then the counterspy hypothesis will have suffered one perhaps small defeat.

Ideally, the hypothesis-testing would continue until the subject appeared to be, as it were, *the puppet of my (simulated) intentions*. In actuality, when I persist in my effort to find a pretend-world in which the other's behavior would accord with my intentions, I usually find myself, after a number of errors, 'tracking' the other person fairly well, forming a fairly stable pretend-world for that person. Of course, I cannot predict or anticipate exactly what he will do, to any fine-grained description. But, by and large, I will not be very much surprised very often, at least in matters that are important to interpersonal coordination.

No matter how long I go on testing hypotheses, I will not have tried out all candidate explanations of the waiter's behavior. Perhaps some of the unexamined candidates would have done at least as well as the one I settle for, if I settle: perhaps indefinitely many of them would have. But these would be 'far-fetched', I say intuitively. Therein I exhibit my inertial bias: the less 'fetching' (or 'stretching', as actors say) I have to do to track the other's behavior, the better. I tend to *feign* only when necessary, only when something in the other's behavior doesn't fit. This inertial bias may be thought of as a 'least effort' principle: the 'principle of least pretending'. It explains why, other things being equal, I will prefer the less radical departure from the 'real' world – i.e. from what I myself take to be the world.

Within a close-knit community, where people have a vast common fund of 'facts' as well as shared norms and values, only a minimum of pretending would be called for. (In the limit case – a replica – the distinction noted earlier between 'what I would do in the other's situation' and 'what *the other will* do in his situation' would indeed vanish, except as a formal or conceptual distinction: what *I would* do and what *the other will* do would invariably coincide.) A person transplanted into an alien culture might have to do a great deal of pretending to explain and predict the behavior of those around him. Indeed, one might eventually learn to *begin* all attempts at explanation and prediction with a stereotypic set of adjustments: pretending that dancing causes rain, that grasshoppers taste better than beefsteak, that blue-eyed should never marry brown-eyed, and so on. This 'default' set of world-modifications might be said to constitute one's 'generalizations' about the alien culture.

Whether or not practical simulation begins with such stereotypes, it does not essentially involve (as one might think) an implicit *comparison to oneself*. Although it does essentially involve *deciding what to do*, that, as I have noted, is not the same as deciding *what I myself would do*. To predict another's behavior I may have to pretend that there is an Aryan race, that it is meta-physically the master race, and that I belong to it; finally, that I was born in Germany of German stock between 1900 and 1920. To make decisions within such a pretend-world is not to decide what *I myself* would do, much less to reliably know what *I myself* would do 'in that situation'. First, it is not possible for *me* to be in that situation, if indeed it is a *possible* situation (for anyone); second, it is not possible for me even to *believe* myself to be in that situation – not, at least, without such vast changes in my beliefs and attitudes as to make all prediction unreliable. Hence in such a case I cannot be making an implicit *comparison to myself.*[10]

4 Attributions of Beliefs

I do not deny that explanations are often couched in terms of *beliefs, desires,* and other propositional attitudes; or that predictions, particularly predictions of the behavior of others, are often made on the basis of attributions of such states. Moreover, as functionalist accounts of folk psychology have empha-sized, common discourse about beliefs and other mental states presupposes that they enter into a multitude of causal and nomological relations. I don't want to deny this either. A particular instance or 'token' of belief, such as Smith's belief that Dewey won the election, may be (given a background of other beliefs, desires, etc.) *a cause of* Smith's doing something (joining the Republican party) or undergoing something (being glad, being upset); it may have been *caused by* his reading in the newspapers that Dewey won and his believing that newspapers are reliable in such matters, or by his having taken a hallucinogenic drug.

There are in addition certain formally describable regularities that might be formulated as laws of typical causation: e.g. a belief that p and a belief that (if p then q) will typically cause a belief that q; a desire that p and a belief that (p if and only if I bring it about that q) will typically cause a desire to bring it about that q. And there are more specific regularities that obtain for particular individuals, classes, communities, or cultures: e.g. when some tennis players believe their opponents aren't playing at their best they typically get angry; when members of a certain tribe see a cloud they think inhabited by an animal spirit they typically prepare for the hunt. Sometimes it helps to remember such regularities when predicting or explaining behavior – even one's own.

One mustn't apply such generalizations too mechanically, however. For there are indefinitely many circumstances, not exhaustively specifiable in advance, in which these general or specific regularities fail to hold. Those generalizations that do not explicitly concern only 'typical' instances should be understood to contain implicit *ceteris paribus* clauses. (This point is developed, along with much else that is congenial, in Putnam, 1978, lecture VI.) How does one know how to recognize atypical situations or to expand the *ceteris paribus* clause? An answer is ready at hand. As long as one applies these generalizations *in the context of practical simulation*, the unspecifiable constraints on *one's own* practical reasoning would enable one to delimit the application of these rules. This gives one something to start with: as one learns more about others, of course, one learns how to modify these constraints in applying generalizations to them.

Moreover, the *interpretation* of such generalizations, as indeed of all common discourse about beliefs and other mental states, remains open to question. In the remainder of this paper I sketch and at least begin to defend a way of interpreting ordinary discourse about beliefs in terms of pretend play and practical simulation. The idea isn't wholly new. In *Word and Object*, Quine explained indirect quotation and the ascription of propositional attitudes in terms of what he called 'an essentially dramatic act':

> We project ourselves into what, from his remarks and other indications, we imagine the speaker's state of mind to have been, and then we say what, in our language, is natural and relevant for us in the state thus feigned. (1960, p. 92)

That is, we first try to simulate, by a sort of pretending, another's state of mind; then we just 'speak our mind'. In Quine's view, this is essentially an exercise in translation and heir to all its problems. Stephen Stich develops the idea further, using a device introduced by Davidson: in saying, e.g. 'Smith believes that Dewey won', one utters the content sentence 'Dewey won', pretending to be asserting it oneself, as if performing a little skit (Stich, 1983). To ascribe such a belief to Smith is to say that he is in a state *similar* to the one that might typically be expected to underlie that utterance – had it not been produced by way of play-acting.

As Stich portrays the play-acting device, it is merely a device for producing a specimen utterance which in turn is used to specify a particular theoretical state. The attribution of such a state is supposed to play a role in nomological reasoning roughly analogous to that of attributions of theoretical states in the physical sciences, and in that role to serve in the tasks of explaining and predicting the object's behavior.[11] Rather than treating the observer as an *agent* in his own right, as one who might form intentions to *act* on the basis of pretend inputs, it calls upon him merely to *speak* as he would given those inputs.

Stich's assumption that the methodological context for such attributions is nomological reasoning leads him, I believe, to misrepresent the role of pretending in folk psychology. I shall sketch very briefly a different role for pretending in belief attribution. On this account, the methodological context for such attributions is not nomological reasoning but practical simulation.

A chess player who visualizes the board from his opponent's point of view might find it helpful to *verbalize* from that point of view – to assert, for example, 'my Queen is in danger.' Stepping into Smith's shoes I might say: 'Dewey won the election.' Such assertions may then be used as premises of simulated practical inference. But wouldn't it be a great advantage to us practical simulators if we could *pool our resources*? We'll simulate Smith *together*, cooperatively, advising one another as to what premises or inputs to practical reasoning would work best for a simulation of Smith. That is, give the best predictions and the most stable explanations, explanations that won't have to be revised in the light of new evidence. Of course, I couldn't come *straight out* with the utterance: 'Dewey won.' I need to flag the utterance as one that is being uttered *from within a Smith-simulation mode* and addressed to *your* Smith-simulation mode. I might do this by saying something like the following:

1   Let's do a Smith simulation. Ready? *Dewey won the election.*

The same task might be accomplished by saying:

2   *Smith believes that* Dewey won the election.

My suggestion is that (2) be read as saying the same thing as (1), though less explicitly.

It is worth noting that unlike Stich I am not characterizing belief as a relation to any linguistic entity or speech act, e.g. a sentence or an assertion. Nor, as far as I can see, does my suggestion involve explicating the contents of belief in terms of possible worlds. Rather than specifying *in a standard non-pretending mode of speech* a set of possible worlds, one says something about the *actual* world, albeit *in a non-standard, pretending mode of speech*. Needless to say, the exposition and defense of this account of belief are much in need of further development. But it is interesting to note that, given the 'principle of least pretending' mentioned earlier, our belief attributions would be in accord with something like the 'principle of charity' put forward by Quine and Davidson: roughly, that one should prefer a translation that maximizes truth and rationality. More precisely, our attributions would conform to an improved version of this principle: Grandy's more general 'principle of humanity' according to which one should prefer a translation on which 'the imputed pattern of relations among beliefs, desires, and the world be as similar to our own as possible' (Grandy, 1973, p. 443).

If I am right, to attribute a belief to another person is to make an assertion, to state something as a fact, *within the context of practical simulation*. Acquisition of the capacity to attribute beliefs is acquisition of the capacity to make assertions in such a context. There is some experimental support for this view. Very young children give verbal expression to predictions and explanations of the behavior of others. Yet up to about the age of four they evidently lack the concept of belief, or at least the capacity to make allowances for false or differing beliefs. Evidence of this can be teased out by presenting children with stories and dramatizations that involve dramatic irony: where we the audience know something important the protagonist doesn't know (Wimmer and Perner, 1983).[12]

In one such story (illustrated with puppets) the puppet-child Maxi puts his chocolate in the box and goes out to play. While he is out, his mother transfers the chocolate to the cupboard. Where will Maxi look for the chocolate when he comes back? In the box, says the five-year-old, pointing to the miniature box on the puppet stage: a good prediction of a sort we ordinarily take for granted. (That is, after all, where the chocolate had been before it was, without Maxi's knowledge, transferred to the cupboard.) But the child of three to four years has a different response: verbally or by pointing the child indicates the cupboard. (That is, after all, where the chocolate is to be found, isn't it?) Suppose Maxi wants to mislead his gluttonous big brother to the *wrong* place, where will he lead him? The five-year-old indicates the cupboard, where (unbeknownst to Maxi) the chocolate actually is; often accompanying the response with what is described as 'an ironical smile'. The *younger* child indicates, incorrectly, the box.[13]

From this and other experiments it appears that normal children around age four or five vastly increase their capacity to predict the behavior of others. The child develops the ability to make allowances for what the other isn't in a position to know. She can predict behavioral failures, e.g. failure to look in the right place, failure to mislead another to the wrong place, that result from *cognitive* failures, i.e. *false beliefs*. At an earlier age she makes all predictions in an egocentric way, basing them all on *the actual facts*, i.e. the facts as she herself sees them. She either lacks the concept of belief altogether or at least lacks the ability to employ it in the prediction of behavior. One may even say that the young child attributes knowledge – by default – before she has learned to attribute belief.

It is the position of many philosophers that common-sense terms such as 'believes' are *theoretical* terms, the meanings of which are fixed in the same way as theoretical terms in general: by the set of laws and generalizations in which they figure. This view is widely (but not universally) assumed in functionalist accounts of folk psychology. (It is the offspring of the dispositional theories that were popular in the days of philosophical behaviorism.) Presumably, mastery of the concept of belief would then be a matter of internalizing a sufficiently large number of laws or generalizations in which the term 'belief' (and related verb forms) occurs. The term 'belief' would be used in something like the way biologists used the term 'gene' before the discovery of DNA.[14]

But suppose that mastery of the concept of belief did consist in learning or in some manner internalizing a system of laws and generalizations concerning belief. One would in that case expect that *before* internalizing this system, the child would simply be unable to predict or explain human action. And *after* internalizing the system the child could deal indifferently with actions caused by *true* beliefs and actions caused by *false* beliefs. It is hard to see how the semantical question could be relevant.

Suppose on the other hand that the child of four develops the ability to make assertions, to state something as fact, *within the context of practical simulation*. That would give her the capacity to overcome an initial egocentric limitation to the *actual facts* (i.e. as *she* sees them). One would *expect* a change of just the sort we find in these experiments.

There is further evidence. Practical simulation involves the capacity for a certain kind of systematic pretending. It is well known that *autistic* children suffer a striking deficit in the capacity for pretend play. In addition they are often said to 'treat people and objects alike'; they fail to treat others as subjects, as having 'points of view' distinct from their own. This failure is confirmed by their performance in prediction tests like the one I have just described. A version of the Wimmer–Perner test was administered to autistic children of ages *six to sixteen* by a team of psychologists (Baron-Cohen, Leslie, and Frith, 1985). *Almost all* these children gave the wrong answer, the three-year-old's answer. This indicates a highly specific deficit, not one in general intelligence. Although many autistic children are also mentally retarded, those tested were mostly in the average or borderline IQ range. Yet children with Down's syndrome, with IQ levels substantially below that range, suffered no deficit: almost all gave the right answer. My account of belief would predict that only those children who can engage in pretend play can master the concept of belief.[15] It is worth noting that autistic children do at least as well as normals in their comprehension of *mechanical* operations – a distinct blow to any functionalists who might think mastery of the concept of belief to consist in the acquisition of a theory of the functional organization of a mechanism.

I suspect that, once acquired, the capacity for practical simulation operates primarily at a sub-verbal level, enabling us to *anticipate* in our own actions the behavior of others, though we are unable to say *what* it is that we anticipate or *why*. The *self-reported* pretending I have described would then only be the tip of the iceberg. Something like it may happen quite regularly and without our knowledge: our decision-making or practical reasoning system gets partially disengaged from its 'natural' inputs and fed instead with suppositions and images (or their 'subpersonal' or 'subdoxastic' counterparts). Given these artificial pretend inputs the system then 'makes up its mind' what to do. Since the system is being run off-line, as it were, disengaged also from its natural output systems, its 'decision' isn't actually executed but rather ends up as an anticipation, perhaps just an unconscious *motor* anticipation, of the other's behavior.

One interesting possibility is that the readiness for practical simulation is a prepackaged 'module' called upon automatically in the perception of other human beings. One might even speculate that such a module makes its first appearance in the useful tendency many mammals have of turning their eyes toward the target of another's gaze. Thus the very sight of human eyes might *require* us to simulate at least their spatial perspective – and to this extent, at least, to put ourselves in the other's shoes. This would give substance to the notion that we perceive one another primarily as *subjects*: as world-centers rather than as objects in the world. It is pleasant to speculate that the phenomenology of *the Other* – particularly the Sartrean idea that consciousness of the Other robs us of our own perspective – might have such humble beginnings.

It remains the prevailing view of philosophers and cognitive scientists that mental states, as conceived by naïve folk psychology, are constructs belonging to a pre-scientific theory of the inner workings of the human behavior control system housed, as we now know, in the brain. One problem with this conception of folk psychology is that mastery of its concepts would seem to demand a highly developed theoretical intellect and a methodological sophistication rivaling that of modern-day cognitive scientists. That is an awful lot to impute to the four-year-old, or to our savage ancestors. It is also uncanny that folk psychology hasn't changed very much over the millennia. Paul Churchland writes:

> The [folk psychology] of the Greeks is essentially the [folk psychology] we use today, and we are negligibly better at explaining human behavior in its terms than was Sophocles. That is a very long period of stagnation and infertility for any theory to display. (1981, p. 75)

Churchland thinks this a sign that folk psychology is a bad theory; but it could be sign that it is no theory at all, not, at least, in the accepted sense of (roughly) a system of laws implicitly defining a set of terms. Instead it might be just the capacity for practical reasoning, supplemented by a special use of a childish and primitive capacity for pretend play. I hope that I have shown that to be a plausible and refreshing alternative.[16]

Notes

1   The qualifying phrase is added because I am concerned with *assertive* reliability, not *commissive* reliability: that of predictions, rather than that of promises, vows, and expressions of intention. Construing 'I shall now X' as a mere expression of intention, if the speaker does not X he will have 'failed to carry out' his intention: his *action* would in a (non-moral) sense be 'at fault'. Construing it as a mere prediction, on the other hand, it would be the *prediction* that is 'at fault', not the *action*. To use Seale's distinction (derived from Anscombe), declarations of intention have a world-to-word 'direction of fit', whereas predictions and other 'assertive' speech acts have a word-to-world direction of fit (Searle, 1983). This distinction does not affect the essential point being made here.

2   A further possibility is that a degree of normative commitment is added by the *declaration* of an intention, even if it is announced only to oneself: one is then motivated to *mold* one's behavior to the declared intention. This was suggested to me by Brian McLaughlin.

3   More precisely, *what is expressed* by these declarations are often products of practical reasoning.

4   Imagery is not always needed in such simulations. For example, I need no imagery to simulate having a million dollars in the bank. Mere *supposition* would be enough.

5   Contrast, 'I would (if such a situation were now to arise) reach for the telephone and dial an emergency number' uttered as a declaration of *conditional intention*. The difference can be partially explicated in terms of 'direction of fit'.

6   Granted, if one were to do some of the pretending out loud, one might say, e.g. 'I believe someone has broken into the house.' But such a verbalization has a role in practical not nomological reasoning: one is articulating a possible basis for action, not giving a state description that is to be plugged into laws that bridge between internal states and behavior.

7   Needless to say, like any attempt to explain or predict one's own behavior, this may be corrupted by prejudice or self-deception.

8   Closer to my own view is Morton (1980, ch. 3) on the uses of imagination in understanding another's behavior.

9   As Quine has noted: 'Casting our real selves thus in unreal roles, we do not generally know how much reality to hold constant' (1960, p. 92).

10 Nozick seems to miss this point in his account of *Verstehen* as 'a special form of inference by analogy, in that I am the thing to which he is analogous'. He argues that the inferences depends on two empirical correlations: 'that he acts as I would, and that I would as I (on the basis of imaginative projection) think I would' (1981, p. 636). Nozick's mistake is to think it relevant to ask, and indeed essential as the inferential link, how I would *in fact* behave in the other's shoes.

11 To do *this* job properly, it would have to meet certain standards of objectivity. And Stich argues with considerable force that it cannot. For it never frees itself fully from the subjectivity it necessarily begins with, the speaker-relativity that is built into the ascription of content.

12 The psychologists who conducted this study credit three philosophers (J. Bennett, D. Dennett, and G. Harman) with suggesting the experimental paradigm, each independently, in commentaries published with Premack and Woodruff, 1978).

13 My account simplifies the experiment and the results; but not, I think, unconscionably.

14 But a functionalist might wish to say that, whereas the correct *explication* of the concept requires that one cite such laws, *mastery* of the concept, i.e. capacity to *use* it, does not require that one have internalized such laws. Thus some functionalists might even be prepared to embrace something like my account of belief attributions. This possibility (or something close to it) was pointed out to me independently by Larry Davis and Sydney Shoemaker. I am inclined to think that this would be an uneasy alliance, but I confess I don't (as yet) have the arguments to persuade anybody who might think otherwise.

15 My account is close in many respects to the theory the investigators were themselves testing in the autism experiment. This is presented in Leslie, 1987.
16 I have benefited enormously from the advice and criticism of Stephen Stich, in correspondence and conversation. I am indebted to Fred Adams and Larry Davis for much help in seeing through the murk, and have benefited further from comments by Robert Audi, John Barker, Hartry Field, Brain McLaughlin, Sydney Shoemaker, Raimo Tuomela, and (no doubt) others.

References

Baron-Cohen, S., Leslie, A. M., and Frith, U. 1985: Does the autistic child have a 'theory of mind'? *Cognition*, 21, 37–46.
Churchland, P. M. 1981: Eliminative materialism and the propositional attitudes. *Journal of Philosophy*, 78, 67–90.
Collingwood, R. G. 1946: *The Idea of History*. New York: Oxford University Press.
Doyle, A. Conan 1894: The Musgrave Ritual. In *The Memoirs of Sherlock Holmes*. New York: Harper Bros.
Grandy, R. 1973: Reference, meaning, and belief. *Journal of Philosophy*, 70, 439–52.
Leslie, A. M. 1987: Pretense and representation: The origins of 'theory of mind'. *Psychological Review*, 94, 412–26.
Morton, A. 1980: *Frames of Mind*. Oxford: Oxford University Press.
Nozick, R. 1981: *Philosophical Explanations*. Cambridge, Mass.: Harvard University Press.
Premack, D. and Woodruff, G. 1978: Does the chimpanzee have a theory of mind? *Behavioral and Brain Sciences*, 1, 515–26.
Putnam, H. 1978: *Meaning and The Moral Sciences*. Boston: Routledge & Kegan Paul.
Quine, W. V. O. 1960: *Word and Object*. Cambridge, Mass.: MIT Press.
Schutz, A. 1962: *Collected Papers*. The Hague: Nijhoff.
Schutz, A. 1967: *Phenomenology and the Social World*. Evanston, Ill.: Northwestern University Press.
Searle, J. R. 1983: *Intentionality*. Cambridge: Cambridge University Press.
Stich, S. 1983: *From Folk Psychology to Cognitive Science: The Case Against Belief*. Cambridge, Mass.: MIT Press.
Wimmer, H. and Perner, J. 1983: Beliefs about beliefs: Representation and constraining function of wrong beliefs in young children's understanding of deception. *Cognition*, 13, 103–28.
Von Wright, G. H. 1971: *Explanation and Understanding*. Ithaca: Cornell University Press.

3

Interpretation Psychologized

ALVIN I. GOLDMAN

1 Introduction

A central problem of philosophy of mind is the nature of mental states, or the truth-conditions for the ascription of such states. Especially problematic are the propositional attitudes: beliefs, desires, and so forth. One popular strategy for attacking these problems is to examine the practice of speakers in ascribing these states, especially to others. What principles or procedures guide or underlie the ascriber's activity? In identifying such principles or procedures, one hopes to glean the criteria or satisfaction conditions of the mentalistic predicates (or something like this). Now the ascription of the attitudes involves the assignment of some sort of 'content' or 'meaning' to the mind, which can be seen as a kind of 'interpretation' of the agent or his behavior. (It is also related, on many theories, to the interpretation of the agent's utterances.) Thus, ascription of mental states, especially the attitudes, can be thought of as a matter of interpretation; and the strategy of studying the interpreter, in order to extract the conditions of mentality, or propositional attitudehood, may be called the *interpretation strategy*. I do not assume here that this strategy will or can succeed. Nonetheless, its popularity, if nothing else, makes it worthy of investigation.

The aim of this paper, then, is to study interpretation, specifically, to work toward an account of interpretation that seems descriptively and explanatorily correct. No account of interpretation can be philosophically helpful, I submit, if it is incompatible with a correct account of what people actually do when they interpret others. My question, then, is: how does the (naïve) interpreter arrive at his/her judgments about the mental attitudes of others? Philosophers who have addressed this question have not, in my view, been sufficiently psychological, or cognitivist, even those who are otherwise psychologically inclined. I shall defend some proposals about the activity of interpretation that are, I believe, psychologically more realistic than their chief competitors.

In the very posing of my question – how does the interpreter arrive at attributions of propositional attitudes (and other mental state) – I assume that the attributor herself has contentful states, at least beliefs. Since I am not trying to prove (to the skeptic) that there is content, this is not circular or question-begging. I assume as background that the interpreter has beliefs, and I inquire into a distinctive subset of them, viz., beliefs concerning mental states. It is conceivable, of course, that a proper theory of interpretation, together with certain ontological assumptions, would undermine the onto-logical legitimacy of beliefs. This is a prospect to which we should, in prin-ciple, stay alert, though it is not one that will actively concern me here. I shall proceed on the premise that the interpreter has beliefs. Indeed, it is hard to see how to investigate the problem without that assumption.

Since I am prepared to explain the interpreter's activity in terms of contentful states, I am obviously not attempting to give a purely 'naturalistic' theory of interpretation, i.e., a theory that makes no appeal to semantical notions. Interpretation theorists standardly hope to extract naturalistic truth-conditions for the presence of content. I take it to be an open question, however, whether the interpretation strategy can yield such fruit.

I structure the discussion in terms of three types of interpretation theories. Two of these have tended to dominate the field: (1) rationality, or charity, theories, and (2) folk-theory theories. According to the first approach, an attributor A operates on the assumption that the agent in question, S, is rational, i.e. conforms to an ideal or normative model of proper inference and choice. The attributor seeks to assign to S a set of contentful states that fits such a normative model. According to the second approach, the attributor somehow acquires a common-sense or folk-psychological theory of the men-tal, containing nomological generalizations that relate stimulus inputs to cer-tain mental states, mental states to other mental states, and some mental states to behavioral outputs. She then uses this theory to infer, from stimulus inputs and behavioral outputs, what states S is in. The related doctrine of analytical functionalism asserts that our common-sense mentalistic predicates are im-plicitly *defined* in terms of this common-sense psychological theory.[1] The third approach, which I shall defend, is the simulation theory. This approach has been placed in the field but has not received sustained development, and is not yet sufficiently appreciated.[2]

2 The Rationality Approach

The most widely discussed version of the charity approach is that of Donald Davidson (1980, 1984). Actually, Davidson's approach to interpretation in-volves three strands. First, there is a compositional postulate for assigning meanings to the agent's whole utterances as a function of the meanings of their parts. Second, there is a charity principle that enjoins the interpreter (*ceteris paribus*) to assign belief states to the agent so as to maximize (or optimize) the proportion of truths in the agent's belief set. Third, there is the rationality principle that enjoins the interpreter (*ceteris paribus*) to assign beliefs and desires so as to maximize the agent's rationality. Another prominent specimen of the rationality approach is that of Daniel Dennett (1971, 1987a). Dennett's 'intentional stance' is a method of attributing intentional states by first postulating ideal rationality on the part of the target system, and then trying to predict and/or explain the system's behavior in terms of such rationality.

I shall say nothing here about Davidson's compositional postulate. But a brief comment on his truthfulness principle is in order before turning to more extended discussion of rationality. Davidson holds that one constraint on interpretation precludes the possibility of ascribing 'massive' or 'preponderant' error (by the interpreter's lights) to the interpretee. In an early essay he writes: 'A theory of interpretation cannot be correct that makes a man assent to very many false sentences: it must generally be the case that a sentence is true when a speaker holds it to be' (Davidson, 1984, p. 168). And in a more recent essay he says: 'Once we agree to the general method of interpretation I have sketched, it becomes impossible correctly to hold that anyone could be mostly wrong about how things are' (Davidson, 1986, p. 317). These contentions, however, are dubious. Along with Colin McGinn (1977) I have presented examples of possible cases in which it seems natural to ascribe to an agent a set of beliefs that are largely, in fact predominantly, false (Goldman, 1986, pp. 175–6). Furthermore, if Davidson were right in this matter, one could dismiss the intelligibility of radical skepticism out of hand; but it seems implausible that principles of interpretation should have this result (see McGinn, 1986). There are at least two sorts of context in which an attributor, *A*, will assign beliefs to an agent, *S*, which are false by *A*'s lights: first, where *S* is exposed to misleading evidence, and second, where *S* uses poor inductive methods such as hasty generalization, or inferential maxims such as 'Believe whatever your cult leader tells you'. These points are stressed by David Lewis in his own theory of interpretation (Lewis, 1983a).

Let us turn to the rationality component of Davidson's charity approach, a component common to many writers. For the rationality principle to have substance, there must be some specification of the norms of rationality. While few writers say precisely how these norms are to be chosen or fixed, there seems to be wide agreement that they are derived from a priori models of ideal rationality, models inspired by formal logic, by the calculus of probability, and/or by Bayesian decision theory (or its ilk). Even so, there is room for stronger and weaker norms. Dennett often imputes to the intentional stance the component of deductive closure. Davidson usually illustrates rationality with the weaker norm of logical consistency. Let us test the rationality approach by reference to logical consistency and probabilistic coherence. Do interpreters impose these norms in making interpretations? I shall argue in the negative.

Consider a paradox-of-the-preface example. My friend Hannah has just completed a book manuscript. She says that although she is fully confident of each sentence in her book, taken singly, she is also convinced of her own fallibility, and so believes that at least one of her claims is false. At least this is how she *reports* her beliefs to me. But if these were indeed Hannah's beliefs, she would be guilty of believing each of a logically inconsistent set of propositions. Now if the consistency norm were part of our ordinary interpretation procedure, an interpreter would try, other things equal, to avoid ascribing to Hannah all the beliefs she ostensibly avows. Understood as a description of interpretive practice, the rationality approach 'predicts' that interpreters confronted with Hannah's avowals will try to find a way to assign a slightly different set of beliefs than Hannah seems to endorse. Interpreters will feel some 'pressure', some prima facie reason, to revise their belief imputation to be charitable to Hannah. Of course, as Davidson admits, other constraints on interpretation, e.g., the compositional meaning constraint, might make a revision too costly. So an interpreter might settle for imputing inconsistency after all. But some vector will be exerted to avoid the imputation.

Does this approach accord with the facts? Speaking as one interpreter, I would feel no temptation to avoid ascribing the inconsistent belief set to Hannah. And I submit that other everyday interpreters would similarly feel no such temptation. Admittedly, if Hannah said that she recognized she was being inconsistent, but still believed all these things anyway, many people might feel something is amiss. Recognition of inconsistency can be expected to breed caution. But let us suppose that Hannah shows no sign of recognizing the inconsistency. Surely, an ordinary interpreter would have no qualms in attributing an inconsistent belief set to her.

An analogous example is readily produced for the norm of probabilistic coherence. Suppose my friend Jeremy has just been the subject of a probability experiment by the psychologists Amos Tversky and Daniel Kahneman (1983). In this experiment, Jeremy is given a thumbnail sketch of someone called 'Linda', who is described as having majored in philosophy in college, as having been concerned with issues of social justice, and having participated in an anti-nuclear demonstration. Subjects are then asked to rate the probabilities that Linda is now involved in certain vocations or avocations. Like so many other subjects, Jeremy rates the probability of Linda being both a bank teller and a feminist higher than he rates the probability of Linda being a bank teller. But these comparative probability judgments violate the probability calculus: it is impossible for any conjunctive event A and B to be more probable than either of its conjuncts. So if I accept the coherent probabilities norm of interpretation, my duty is to try to reassign contents so as to avoid the indicated imputations to Jeremy.[3]

Again, as one interpreter, I report feeling no such duty. There seems nothing even prima facie wrong about attributing to Jeremy this set of probability assignments, despite their incoherence. I feel no reason to seek a revised interpretation. So this norm must not in fact play its alleged role in interpretation.[4]

Perhaps the rationality approach should be weakened, so that it no longer imposes ideal rationality as the norm for attitude attribution. Christopher Cherniak (1986, p. 10) suggests that a better rationality condition is that an agent must display minimal deductive ability; he must make *some*, but not necessarily all, of the sound inferences from his belief set. As a condition for attitude attribution, this is certainly an improvement over an ideal deductive requirement. But Cherniak's purely existential requirement is too vague. It cannot yield any definite predictive or explanatory inferences that an interpreter would make about an agent's beliefs.

Another variant of the rationality approach might say that interpreters expect agents to make 'obvious' inferences. But obvious to whom? To the interpreter? What is obvious to one interpreter is not necessarily obvious to another. So the rationality approach could no longer maintain that a single set of rationality principles constrain the ascription of the attitudes. Alternatively, there might be an attempt to derive obviousness from pure logic. But this is unpromising; obviousness is a psychological, not a logical, notion. Perhaps the rationality theorist should abandon any attempt to distill norms of rationality from logic, probability theory, decision theory, and the like. Perhaps the norms should be distilled from actual human practices of inference and choice (see Cohen, 1981; Pollock, 1986).

There are two problems with this approach. Experimental findings strongly suggest that human agents think in ways that contravene widely accepted norms. They often commit the so-called gambler's fallacy; in making choices, they commonly flout the 'sure-thing' principle (as Allais's paradox shows); and when it comes to deductive inference, they display a number of failings.[5] It is doubtful, therefore, whether actual practice can establish norms of rationality. Secondly, it is dubious that the naïve interpreter has an accurate reflective grasp of actual practice. But it is precisely the interpretive practice of naïve agents that we seek to illuminate.

Assuming that correct norms of rationality can somehow be identified, is it psychologically plausible to suppose that ordinary interpreters appeal to such norms in making (or constraining) their interpretations? Untrained adults are not generally acquainted with abstract principles like maximizing expected utility, or the sure-thing principle, or probabilistic coherence. Furthermore, we should bear in mind that children display interpretive skills quite early, at least by age four, five, or six. It stretches credulity to suppose that such children employ any of the abstract precepts that rationality theorists commonly adduce. Thus, if we seek to extract principles of interpretation from the psychological determinants of ordinary interpretive practice, norms of rationality do not look promising.

It may be replied that although children lack any explicitly formulated concept of rationality, or any articulated principles of reasoning, they do have *de facto* patterns of reasoning that govern their own cognitive behavior. Perhaps they simply apply those same tacit patterns in interpreting others. This indeed strikes me as a plausible hypothesis. But it is, in effect, a statement of the simulation approach that I shall be advocating shortly.

3 The Folk-theory Approach

I turn next to the folk-theory approach to interpretation. Here again one must wonder whether naïve interpreters, including children, really possess the sorts of principles or common-sense nomological generalizations that this approach postulates, and whether such principles are indeed applied in (all) their interpretive practice.

At least three sorts of problems face the theory theory: vagueness, inaccuracy, and non-universality. When philosophers try to formulate the laws, their examples are typically larded with *ceteris paribus* clauses. This vagueness is a problem because it is hard to see how an interpreter could draw any reasonably definite interpretive conclusion using laws so vague. How could they tell when the *ceteris paribus* clauses are satisfied? Yet interpreters frequently do manage to make quite definite assignments of desires and beliefs. The second problem, the problem of accuracy, arises as follows. It is important for analytical functionalism that the laws be reasonably accurate. If the names of mental states work like theoretical terms, especially in the Ramsey-sentence account of theoretical terms, they do not name anything unless the theory (the cluster of laws) in which they appear is more or less *true* (see Lewis, 1983b and 1972). It is doubtful, however, that ordinary interpreters do possess laws that are true. Third, the standard version of this approach assumes that a single set of laws or platitudes is shared by all competent users of mentalistic vocabulary. But this universality assumption is very dubious.

As Stephen Schiffer (1987, ch. 2) argues, perceptual input conditions may be in the worst shape on these scores. If people really possess laws that relate perceptual input conditions to perceptual beliefs, there must be some way of filling out a schema like 'If there is a red block in front of x and . . . , then x will believe that there is a red block in front of x'; and it must be filled out so that it is true and really possessed by all competent speakers. But it is unlikely that this requirement is satisfied. Can *any* ordinary speaker complete this schema so that it yields a truth? (Notice that the gap has to be filled with conditions entailing that x is 'well enough' sighted, is not colorblind, is sober and undrugged, etc.) It is doubtful, moreover, that *all* speakers who possess the concept of belief share the *same* perceptual input laws. A blind person, for example, may grasp the concept of belief perfectly well, but not possess the same laws of visual input as sighted people.

The accuracy problem also looms large for internal functional laws, including laws that putatively link certain desires and beliefs with further desires. One of the favorite sorts of platitudes offered by philosophers is something like 'If x believes "p only if q" and x desires p, then x desires q'. But the relationship formulated by this 'platitude' simply does not systematically obtain. It ignores the fact that merely dispositional, unactivated desires and beliefs do not have the same inference-inducing powers as activated desires and beliefs (see Goldman, 1986, section 10.1, and Goldman, 1970, ch. 4). If x's belief in 'p only if q' is stored in memory and fails to get retrieved or activated, it does not influence x's practical reasoning. The problem, of course, is not merely that philosophers neglect these differences, but that it is unlikely that common folk have any firm grasp of these relationships, at least in any 'theoretical' fashion.

Perhaps the functionalist will reply that although the 'folk' do have (more or less) true laws in their possession, philosophers have simply failed to articulate those laws correctly. But why, one wonders, should it be so difficult to articulate laws if we appeal to them all the time in our interpretive practice? Admittedly, they may be merely tacit generalizations, and tacit representations are characteristically difficult to reconstruct. A skeptic is entitled to suspect, however, that what goes on when philosophers proffer mentalistic platitudes is not the extraction of pre-existing representations in the minds of the 'folk', but the fresh creation of laws designed to accommodate philosophical preconceptions about the character of 'theoretical' terms.[6]

Still more grounds for doubt center on the problem of acquisition. Recall the point that children seem to display interpretive skills by the age of four, five, or six. If interpretation is indeed guided by laws of folk psychology, the latter must be known (or believed) by this age. Are such children sophisticated enough to represent such principles? And how, exactly, would they acquire them? One possible mode of acquisition is cultural transmission (e.g. being taught them explicitly by their elders). This is clearly out of the question, though, since only philosophers have even tried to articulate the laws, and most children have no exposure to philosophers. Another possible mode of acquisition is private construction. Each child constructs the generalizations for herself, perhaps taking clues from verbal explanations of behavior that she hears. But if this construction is supposed to occur along the lines of familiar modes of scientific theory construction, some anomalous things must take place. For one thing, all children miraculously construct the same nomological principles. This is what the (folk-) theory theory ostensibly implies, since it imputes a single folk psychology to everyone. In normal cases of hypothesis construction, however, different scientists come up with different theories. This is especially natural if they do not communicate their hypotheses, which is what obtains in the present case where the hypotheses are presumed to be tacit and unformulated. It is also surprising that the theory should stay fixed in each cognizer once it is acquired, as functionalism apparently assumes. This too contrasts with normal scientific practice, where theories are commonly amended at least to some degree with the accumulation of new data.

Jerry Fodor, a staunch defender of the theory theory, endorses the hypothesis that the folk theory is *innate* (Fodor, 1987, pp. 132–3). He cites three pieces of 'evidence' for this: (1) intentional explanation appears to be a cultural universal; (2) a rudimentary awareness of the mental world is present in toddlers and preschoolers; and (3) there are no (plausible) suggestions about how a child might acquire the apparatus of intentional explanation 'from experience'. I agree with Fodor on these points. Indeed, I have just been stressing how hard it is to swallow the supposition that toddlers and preschoolers acquire functional laws by induction or theory construction. Thus, *if* a grasp of the mental world and intentional explanation involves laws, there is credibility in the hypothesis that these laws are possessed innately. But why accept the antecedent? Fodor simply ignores the possibility that the apparatus of intentional explanation may involve no theory at all. By contrast, I submit that intentional explanation and prediction can be accounted for without positing any large-scale theory or set of functional generalizations. This is what I now proceed to argue, apropos of the attribution of intentional states (and mental states generally) to others. The full story may well feature innate components: perhaps an innate propensity to identify mental categories within oneself (analogous to some innate propensities for individuating material bodies), and an innate propensity to project such categories on others. But it need not feature innate possession of *laws*.

4 The Simulation Approach

The account I favor may be introduced by reference to a proposal of Richard Grandy (1973). Grandy proposes to replace charity principles with what he calls the 'humanity principle'. This is the constraint imposed on translations that the imputed pattern of relations among beliefs, desires, and the world be as similar to our own as possible. This conforms, says, Grandy, with our actual practice of predicting people's behavior based on our attitudinal attributions. We do not use mathematical decision theory (i.e. expected utility theory) to make predictions; rather, we consider what *we* should do if we had the relevant beliefs and desires. Now I do not think that naïve interpreters advert to Grandy's humanity principle as an abstract precept. Rather, they ascribe mental states to others by pretending or imagining themselves to be in the other's shoes, constructing or generating the (further) state that they would then be in, and ascribing that state to the other. In short, we *simulate* the situation of others, and interpret them accordingly. This idea has been explicitly put forward by Robert Gordon (1986, reprinted as ch. 2 in this volume; also Gordon, 1987, ch. 7), and something like it has been endorsed by Adam Morton (1980). The idea has been a dominant motif in the *Verstehen* and hermeneutic traditions, and earlier precursors include the eighteenth-century Scottish philosophers.[7]

Several writers on interpretation put forward somewhat analogous views in discussing belief ascriptions. W. V. Quine explains indirect quotation in terms of an 'essentially dramatic act' in which we project ourselves into the speaker's mind (Quine, 1960, p. 219). Similarly, drawing on Davidson's paratactic account of indirect discourse, Stephen Stich proposes that when I say 'Andrea believes that lead floats on mercury', I am performing a little skit: I am saying that Andrea is in a belief state content-identical to one that would lead me to assert the sentence which follows the 'that'-clause (Stich, 1983, p. 84). However, these writers do not explicitly develop the simulation approach; nor do I mean to endorse the proposed paraphrase of belief-state ascriptions.

The simulation idea has obvious initial attractions. Introspectively, it seems as if we often try to predict others' behavior – or predict their (mental) choices – by imagining ourselves in their shoes and determining what we would choose to do. To use one of Gordon's examples, if we are playing chess, I may try to anticipate your next move by imagining myself in your situation and deciding what I would choose to do. Similarly, if we agree to meet for lunch tomorrow, I (mentally) 'predict' that you will expect me at roughly the appointed time and place. I ascribe this expectation to you because this is the expectation I would form if I were in your (presumed) situation. The simulation procedure can also be used for explanatory, or 'retrodictive', assignment of mental states. (Indeed, this is the more central type of case for the theme of 'interpretation'.) If you make a surprising chess move, I may infer a new strategy on your part, one that might have led me, if I were in your situation, to the observed move. To assure the plausibility of this being your strategy, I would see whether I could simulate both (a) arriving at this strategy from your presumed antecedent states, and (b) choosing the observed move given this strategy. Ascriptions of intent that lie behind observed behavior would, on the simulation theory, commonly take this second, explanatory from.

In all of these examples, my inference to a new state of yours draws on assumptions about your prior mental states. Does this not threaten a regress? How do I get any initial entrée into your mental world? Can that be explained by simulation?[8] Yes. The regress presumably stops at perceptual cases, and at basic likings or cravings. From your perceptual situation, I infer that you have certain perceptual experiences or beliefs, the same ones I would have in your situation. I may also assume (pending information to the contrary) that you have the same basic likings that I have: for food, love, warmth, and so on.

Simulation is also relevant in inferring *actions* from mental states, not just mental states from other mental states. For ordinary 'basic' actions, I expect your 'choice' of an action to issue in its production because my own choice would so issue. In more problematic cases, such as uttering a tongue-twister, simulation might lead me to doubt that you will succeed. Morton (1980) points out that 'analysis-by-synthesis' accounts of speech perception invoke a (tacit) simulation of motor activity. According to this approach, in trying to categorize a speaker's acoustic sequence as one or another phonemic string, the perceiver constrains the choice of interpretation by 'running a model' of how his own vocal apparatus might articulate those sounds.

It would be a mistake, of course, to use the simulation procedure too simplistically, without adequate attention to individual differences. If I am a chess novice and you are a master, or vice versa, it would be foolish to assume that your analysis would match mine. To optimize use of the simulation procedure, I must not only imagine myself in possession of your goals and beliefs about the board configuration, but also in possession of your level of chess sophistication. People may not always take such factors into account; and frequently they lack information to make such adjustments accurately. In any case, there is no assumption here that people are always successful or optimal simulators. What I do conjecture is that simulation – whether explicit or implicit – is the fundamental method used for arriving at mental ascriptions to others. (A more complex variant of the simulation theme will be briefly sketched in section 5.)

I am not saying, it should be emphasized, that simulation is the *only* method used for interpersonal mental ascriptions, or for the prediction of behavior. Clearly, there are regularities about behavior and individual differences that can be learned purely inductively. If Jones always greets people with a smile whereas Brown greets them with a grunt, their acquaintances can form appropriate expectations without deploying simulation. If people who enter a car in the driver's seat regularly proceed to start it, this is the basis for future expectations that need not appeal to simulation. The suggestion, then, is that simulation is an intensively used heuristic, and one on which interpretation fundamentally rests. Inductive or nomological information is not wholly absent, but it is sparser than the folk-theory approach alleges.

Does the simulation approach accommodate the problems confronting the rational norms approach? Very straightforwardly. The mere fact that the 'preface' belief ('at least one of my claims is false') produces inconsistency does not tempt me to withhold attribution of this belief to Hannah. This is just the belief I too would form, especially if I were unaware of the inconsistency (a similar point is made by Stich, 1985). Similarly, the mere fact that Jeremy's probability assignments violate the probability calculus does not make me shrink from attributing them; for I too can feel their intuitive pull.

The merits of the simulation approach are further demonstrated by seeing how easily it handles a number of cases that the rival approaches cannot handle, or can handle only with difficulty. In an experiment by Daniel Kahneman and Amos Tversky (1982), subjects were given the following example:

> Mr. Crane and Mr. Tees were scheduled to leave the airport on different flights, at the same time. They traveled from town in the same limousine, were caught in a traffic jam, and arrived at the airport 30 minutes after the scheduled departure time of their flights. Mr. Crane is told that his flight left on time. Mr. Tees is told that his was delayed, and just left five minutes ago. Who is more upset?

Surely people do not possess a tacit folk-psychological *theory* that warrants any particular answer to this question. But 96 percent of the subjects in the experiment said that Mr Tees would be more upset. How did they severally arrive at the same answer? Clearly, by simulation. They imagined how *they* would feel in Mr Crane's and Mr Tees's shoes, and responded accordingly.

More evidence in a similar vein comes from the domain of verbal communication. Verbal communicators commonly make assumptions – often correct

– about the contextual information accessible to their audience and likely to be used in the comprehension process. For example, inspired by the landscape, Mary says to Peter, 'It's the sort of scene that would have made Marianne Dashwood swoon.' This allusion to Austen's *Sense and Sensibility* is based on Mary's expectation that this utterance will act as a prompt, making Peter recall parts of the book that he had previously forgotten, and construct the assumptions needed to understand the allusion. My question is: How does a communicator proceed to estimate what pieces of information will be marshalled, or made salient, in the mind of the audience, in short, which pieces of information are 'calculable'?

Dan Sperber and Deirdre Wilson (1986), from whom the preceding example was borrowed, have an interesting theory of the hearer, which postulates a variety of pertinent cognitive traits. For example, they postulate that cognizers have a number of rules of deductive inference, but these are all *elimination* rules (e.g. from '*P and Q*' you may infer '*Q*') and not *introduction* rules (e.g. from '*P*' you may infer '*P or Q*'). Now assume that this piece of cognitive psychology is correct. Clearly, it is not known or believed by the naïve speaker. The speaker cannot appeal to any such *theoretical* knowledge to make predictions of what is likely to be derived or calculated by the hearer. Nonetheless, speakers are evidently pretty good at making such predictions; more precisely, at predicting what kinds of 'implicatures' will be appreciated by an audience. How do they do that? Again, I suggest, by simulation. They can simulate in themselves the states that result from the inference rules, without knowing what those rules are. Hence, they can project, with fairly substantial reliability, what hearers will be able to infer and understand.

A related point concerns people's intuitive grasp of what others will find *funny*.[9] Again it seems far-fetched to suppose that my ability to gauge what will amuse you is based on a theory of humor (of what amuses people). I do not possess any general theory of this sort. More plausibly, I gauge *your* probable reaction to a joke by projecting my own. (There can be adjustments here for factual information about interpersonal differences, but this is just a corrective to the basic tactic of simulation.) There are (arguably) two states of yours that I judge or anticipate through simulation. I estimate by simulation that you will grasp the intended point of the joke: a cognitive state. I also judge by simulation that you will be amused by it: not a purely cognitive state.

Apropos of non-cognitive states, it is worth stressing that a virtue of the simulation theory is its capacity to provide a uniform account of all mental state attributions, not only of propositional attitudes but of non-propositional mental states like pains and tickles. This contrasts with the rationality approach, which has no resources for explaining the latter. No principle of *rationality* dictates when a person should feel pain, or what one should do when in pain. Similarly for tickles. Thus, a rationality (or charity) approach to propositional attitude interpretation would have to be supplemented by an entirely different element to account for attributions of sensations, and perhaps emotions as well. Such bifurcation has less appeal than the unified account offered by the simulation approach.

In a brief discussion of the simulation idea, Dennett (1987b) finds it very puzzling. How can it work, he asks, without being a kind of theorizing? If I make believe I am a suspension bridge and wonder what I will do when the wind blows, what comes to mind depends on how sophisticated my *knowledge* is of the physics and engineering of suspension bridges. Why should making believe that I have your beliefs be any different? Why should it too not require theoretical knowledge?

To answer this question, we need to say more about the general idea of simulation. For a device to simulate a system is for the former to behave in a way that 'models', or maintains some relevant isomorphism to, the behavior of the latter. This is the sense in which a computer might simulate a weather system or an economy. Now if a person seeks to simulate the weather or the economy, in the sense of mentally constructing or anticipating an actual (or genuinely feasible) sequence of its states, she is very unlikely to be accurate unless she has a good theory of the system. A successful simulation of this kind must be *theory-driven*, let us say. This is Dennett's point. But must all mental simulations be theory-driven in order to succeed? I think not. A simulation of some target systems might be accurate even if the agent lacks such a theory. This can happen if (1) the *process* that drives the simulation is the same as (or relevantly similar to) the process that drives the system, and (2) the initial states of the simulating agent are the same as, or relevantly similar to, those of the target system. Thus, if one person simulates a sequence of mental states of another, they will wind up in the same (or isomorphic) final states as long as (A) they begin in the same (or isomorphic) initial states, and (B) both sequences are driven by the same cognitive process or routine. It is not necessary that the simulating agent have a theory of what the routine is, or how it works. In short, successful simulation can be *process-driven*.

Now, in central cases of interpretation, the interpreter is not actually in the very same initial states as the interpretee. While there may be overlap in beliefs and goals, there are typically relevant differences as well. So how can the interpreter succeed via simulation? The critical move, of course, is that the interpreter tries to imagine, or 'feign', the same initial states as the interpretee. She 'pretends' or 'makes believe' she has the relevant initial states, and then performs reasoning operations (or other cognitive operations) to generate successive states in herself. But are these 'pretend' states – the pseudo-beliefs, pseudo-desires, and so forth – relevantly similar to the genuine beliefs and desires that they model? Is it plausible that imagined beliefs and actual beliefs would yield the same, or analogous, outputs when operated upon by the same cognitive operations?[10]

It *is* plausible, I submit. Consider hypothetical, or subjunctive, reasoning. I ask myself, 'Suppose I did action *A* – what would be the result?' How do I proceed to answer this question? It seems that what I do is imagine myself believing the proposition 'I do *A*', and then draw causal inferences from that pseudo-belief together with (certain) antecedent genuine beliefs. Furthermore, it seems that I use the very same inference processes as those I would use on a set of wholly genuine belief inputs. (The output, though, is only a belief in the same hypothetical mood, not a genuine belief.) Similarly, I make contingency plans by executing practical reasoning operations on feigned beliefs in certain contingencies; and these are the same planning operations that I would apply to genuine beliefs in those contingencies. So it seems that 'pretend' belief states *are* relevantly similar to belief states; there are significant isomorphisms. The possibility of isomorphisms between 'genuine' states and imaginatively, or artificially, generated 'copies' is further illustrated in the imagery domain. Roger Shepard, Stephen Kosslyn, and their respective colleagues have produced striking evidence to support the claim that visual images are similar in important respects to genuine visual perceptions (Shepard and Cooper, 1982; Kosslyn, 1980). To determine the congruence or non-congruence of two shapes, forming a mental image of one being rotated into alignment with the other can be almost as reliable as actually seeing the results of this rotation. This would hardly be possible if imagery were not relevantly similar to genuine perception.[11]

5 Simulation and Psychology

Let us explore the psychological defensibility of the simulation approach in more detail. We may first note that several cognitive scientists have recently endorsed the idea of mental simulation as one cognitive heuristic, although these researchers stress its use for knowledge in general, not specifically knowledge of others' mental states. Kahneman and Tversky (1982) propose that people often try to answer questions about the world by an operation that resembles the running of a simulation model. The starting conditions for a 'run', they say, can either be left at realistic default values or modified to assume some special contingency. Similarly, Rumelhart, Smolensky, McClelland and Hinton (1986) describe the importance of 'mental models' of the world, in particular, models that simulate how the world would respond to one's hypothetical actions. They first apply this idea to actual and imagined conversations, and later describe a PDP (parallel distributed processing) network for playing tic-tac-toe, a network that embodies 'simulations' of the world's (i.e. the opponent's) response to the agent's possible moves.

Since part of my argument rests on the superior plausibility of the simulation approach in accounting for children's interpretational ability, let us next look at recent work by developmental psychologists that bears on this point. The most striking findings are those by Heinz Wimmer and Josef Perner, conjoined with a follow-up study by Simon Baron-Cohen, Alan Leslie, and Uta Frith. Various experimental studies had previously shown that as early as two and a half years, children use a substantial vocabulary about perception, volition, major emotions, and knowledge. But experiments by Wimmer and Perner (1983) strongly indicate that around the ages of four to six, an ability to clearly distinguish between someone else's belief state and reality becomes firmly established. In their study, children between three and nine years of age observed a sketch in which a protagonist put an object into a location X. The children then witnessed that, in the absence of the protagonist, the object was transferred from X to location Y. Since this transfer came as a surprise, they should assume that the protagonist still believed that the object was in X. Subjects were then required to indicate where the protagonist will look for the object on his return. None of the three- to four-year-olds, 57 percent of the four- to six-year olds, and 86 percent of the six- to nine-year-olds pointed correctly to location X. In their related study, Baron-Cohen, Leslie and Frith (1985) studied the ability of autistic children to perform this sort of task. Of critical relevance here are two facts about autistic children. First, the main symptom of autism is impairment in verbal and non-verbal communication. Second, autistic children show a striking poverty of pretend play. Baron-Cohen et al.'s experiment showed that when the tested children were asked where the doll protagonist would look for her marble, 85 percent of the normal children answered correctly, but only 20 percent of the autistic children (with a mean age close to 12 and a relatively high mean IQ of 82) answered *correctly*. Especially striking was the fact that the test also included a pool of Down's syndrome children, 86 percent of whom answered the crucial question correctly. This suggests that the failure of the autistic children is not due to general mental retardation, a trait shared by Down's syndrome children. Rather it is a specific cognitive deficit. Baron-Cohen et al. hypothesize that autistic children as a group fail to acquire a 'theory of mind', i.e. an ability to impute beliefs to others and therefore predict their behavior correctly. This would account for their social and communicational impairment. It might also be related to their lack of pretend play. Perhaps, as Gordon (this volume, ch. 2) suggests, all this points to a prepackaged 'module' for simulation directed at other human beings, a module that is impaired in autism.

One of the co-authors of the autism study, Alan Leslie, has sketched a theory that interrelates pretend play and the representation of mental states (Leslie, 1987). He points out that pretending is in some ways an odd practice. From an evolutionary point of view, one might expect a high premium on maintaining an accurate and objective view of the world. A child who acts as if dolls have genuine feelings is scarcely acting upon a veridical picture of the world. Yet pretend play emerges at an early age, and becomes more elaborate during development. It is not implausible to conjecture that pretend play is a preliminary exercise of a mechanism the primary function of which is the simulation of real people's mental states. Roughly this theme is articulated both by Leslie and by Paul Harris (1989). Such a mechanism, on the present theory, underlies interpersonal interpretation, prediction, and perhaps communication as well.

Whatever the force of these findings and speculations, there is a straightforward challenge to the psychological plausibility of the simulation approach. It is far from obvious, introspectively, that we regularly place ourselves in another person's shoes and vividly envision what we would do in his circumstances. This is a natural thing to do while watching a tennis match, perhaps, or while listening to someone relating their tragic life story. But the simulation approach ostensibly makes this empathic attitude the standard mode of interpretation. Is that not difficult to accept?

Two replies should be made. First, simulation need not be an introspectively vivid affair. The approach can certainly insist that most simulation is semi-automatic, with relatively little salient phenomenology. It is a psychological commonplace that highly developed skills become automatized, and there is no reason why interpersonal simulation should not share this characteristic. (On the issue of conscious awareness, the simulation theory is no worse off than its competitors. Neither the rationality approach nor the folk-theory theory is at all credible if it claims that appeals to its putative principles are introspectively prominent aspects of interpretation.)

A second point might be that many cases of rapid, effortless interpretation may be devoid of even automatized simulation. When a mature cognizer has constructed, by simulation, many similar instances of certain action-interpretation patterns, she may develop generalizations or other inductively formed representations (schemas, scripts, and so forth) that can trigger analogous interpretations by application of those 'knowledge structures' alone, *sans* simulation. I have, of course, already acknowledged the role of inductively based predictions of behavior and the need for standard empirical information to make adjustments for individual differences. The present point is a slightly larger concession. It agrees that in many cases the interpreter relies solely (at the time of interpretation) on inductively acquired information. But this information, it suggests, is historically derived from earlier simulations. If this story is right, then simulation remains the fundamental source of interpretation, though not the essence of every act (or even most acts) of interpretation. We might call this the complex variant of the simulation approach. It converges somewhat toward the folk-theory theory (though the exact degree of convergence depends on the nature of the inductively based knowledge structures it posits). It still remains distinct, however, (A) because the folk-theory theory makes no allowance for simulation, and (B) because the complex variant postulates simulation as the originating source of (most) interpretation.

Commenting in part on an earlier version of this paper, Paul Churchland (1989) poses two difficulties for the simulation theory. First, he says, simulation is not necessary for understanding others. People who are congenitally deaf, or blind, are quite capable of understanding normal people, and people who have never themselves felt profound grief or rejection, can nevertheless provide appropriate interpretations of others who are so afflicted. In general, understanding goes beyond what one has personally experienced. I have already granted, however, that straightforwardly empirical information is required to accommodate individual differences, and these examples are just more extreme illustrations of the point. We must certainly allow for the human capacity to extrapolate from one's own case, to project types of sensory or emotional sensibility that one does not oneself instantiate. This concession does not undermine the point that interpretation primarily starts from the home base of one's own experience.

Churchland further objects that while simulation may account for the prediction of others' behavior, it does not provide for *explanation*. The simulation theory makes the understanding of others depend crucially on having an initial understanding of oneself. But it leaves mysterious, he says, the nature of first-person understanding. More specifically, *explanatory* understanding requires appreciation of the *general patterns* that comprehend individual events in both cases. This requires a *theory*, which the simulation approach spurns. In my opinion, however, explanation can consist of telling a story that eliminates various alternative hypotheses about how the event in question came about, or could have come about. This can effectively answer a 'Why'-question, which is the essence of explanation (see van Fraassen, 1980, ch. 5). In the case of interpretive explanation this is done by citing a specific set of goals and beliefs, which implicitly rules out the indefinitely many alternative desire-and-belief sets that might have led to the action.

Churchland rejects the deductive nomological theory of explanation on the grounds that it presupposes a sentential, or propositional-attitude, account of knowledge representation. He proposes to replace this picture of cognition with a prototype-based picture, especially one that is elaborated within a connectionist framework. He still wishes to count human cognition as significantly *theoretical*, but theory possession is apparently no longer associated with nomologicality. Churchland is welcome to use the term 'theory' in this neological fashion; but it cannot resuscitate the standard version of the folk-theory approach to interpretation. It is only in the usual, nomological construal of theories that I am addressing (and rejecting) that approach. I am pleased to see Churchland also reject that approach, but it seems to have ramifications for his other views that I shall mention below.

6 Simulation and Similarity

Considering the complexity of the human organism, it may well be considered remarkable that we are able to predict human behavior as well as we do. Is this impressive success fully accounted for by the simulation theory? Only, I think, with an added assumption, viz., that the other people, whose behavior we predict, are psychologically very similar to ourselves. Just as the child readily learns a grammar of a natural language because its native grammar-learning structures mirror those of its language-creating mates, so a person can successfully simulate the internal operations of others because they are largely homologous to her own. The fuller picture, then, has strong affinities to Noam Chomsky's emphasis on the role of species-specific traits in mental activity.

Although I view this theme as Chomskyesque, it is also similar to one made by Quine (1969). Quine asks how the language learner manages to learn the law of English verbal behavior connected with 'yellow'. The answer, he says, is that the learner's quality spacing is enough like his neighbor's that such learning is almost a foregone conclusion: he is making his induction in a 'friendly world'. He is playing a game of chance with favorably loaded dice. Similarly, I am suggesting, people's predictions of other people's behavior, based heavily on attributions of content, are so successful because people operate with the same set of fundamental cognitive constraints. (Notice, I need not say that people are successful at assigning correct contents to people's mental states; that would assume that there is an independent fact of the matter about content, prior to the activity of interpretation. Since some interpretation theorists would reject this thesis, I can confine my claim to successful prediction of *behavior*.)

The constraints I have in mind must be constraints on the specific contents assigned to an agent's propositional attitudes. Without positing such constraints, it is hard to account for the definiteness and interpersonal uniformity in content attributions. There would seem to be too much 'play', too much looseness, in the sorts of abstract constraints that a theorist like Davidson, for example, imposes. Assuming the interpretations of the interpreter to be given, we need to explain why she makes those rather than the innumerable other conceivable interpretations.

In a similar (though not identical) context, Lewis (1983c) worries whether enough constraints on content are imposed by his theory to exclude preposterous and perverse misinterpretations. To exclude perverse interpretations, Lewis says we need a priori presumptions about just what sorts of things are apt to be believed or desired. These presumptions should be thought of as built into our interpretation procedures. Adopting a suggestion of Gary Merrill, Lewis proposes that natural kinds are more eligible for content attributions than non-natural kinds. Taking naturalness to be a graded affair, more natural kinds have greater eligibility for content inclusion than less natural kinds. Principles of content possession should therefore impute a bias toward believing that things are green rather than grue, toward having a basic desire for long life rather than for long-life-unless-one-was-born-on-Monday-and-in-that-case-life-for-an-even-number-of-weeks.

I agree with Lewis that to get things right, i.e. to conform to our actual content attributions, account must be taken of what is 'natural' and 'unnatural'. But only if this means 'natural for us': congenial to human psychology. This is not what Lewis means. By 'natural' Lewis means properties Nature herself deems natural, those categories that are objectively, independently, non-anthropocentrically natural. This is not very plausible. Granted that the kind 'a mass of molecules' is more of a natural kind than, say, 'table', it is still less plausible to attribute beliefs about masses of molecules to scientifically untutored people than beliefs about tables. Or take the hue yellow. From an objective, non-anthropocentric viewpoint, yellow is less natural than other possible spectral or reflectancy categorizations. Nonetheless, it is more plausible to attribute contents involving yellow than more objective categorizations of light frequency. Clearly, it is concepts that are humanly more natural, i.e. psychologically congenial, that are more eligible for content.[12]

What I am suggesting, then, is that uniformity in cross-personal interpretations should be partly explained by psychological preferences for certain modes of categorization and 'entification', or more basically, by operations that generate categorial and entificational preferences. The precise nature of these operations and/or preferences remains to be spelled out by cognitive science. But let me give some examples of what I mean.

Our entification practices include propensities to group together, or unify, certain sets of elements rather than others in a perceptual display. The Gestalt principles of similarity, proximity, closedness, and good continuation are attempts to systematize the mental operations that underpin these unificational practices. The Gestalt principles apply not only in the visual domain, but in the temporal domain as well. Thus, presented with the opening passage of Mozart's fortieth symphony, principles of temporal proximity (and so forth) make it natural to segment the passage into three distinct phrases (I oversimplify here). Other conceivable segmentations are highly unnatural. It is plausible to conjecture that the same Gestalt principles are at work in fixing our conceptual (as opposed to perceptual) intuitions of identity, or unity, of objects through time (see Goldman, 1987).

Another set of categorial preferences feature what Eleanor Rosch calls the 'basic level' of categories (Rosch, 1975, 1978). Language (and presumably thought) is full of category hierarchies such as *poodle, dog, mammal, animal, physical object*. Experiments show that the categories in the middle of such hierarchies, in the present case *dog* rather than *poodle* or *physical object*, have a definite psychological primacy.

How do entitative and categorial preferences of the interpreter get deployed in the interpretation process? Two slightly different hypotheses are possible. First, the preferences may be registered directly; that is, the interpreter uses her own categorial preferences to assign content to the interpretee. Second, they might be used in conjunction with the simulation heuristic. In assigning reference and meaning, the interpreter imagines what the agent's concept-forming or proposition-forming devices might generate in the present context, and this imaginative act is structured by the interpreter's own concept-forming and judgment-forming operations.

In either case, the hypotheses I am advancing would account for a substantial degree of uniformity in specific content attributions. It would also mesh with Davidson's theme of belief similarity among interpreters and interpretees, but only subject to important qualifications. The simulation hypothesis assumes that the interpreter tends to impute to the interpretee the same fundamental categories as her own, or at least the same basic category-forming (and proposition-forming) operations. She also tends to project the same basic belief-forming processes. But these practices still leave room for wide divergence in belief content. The simulation procedure can take account of differences in the agent's evidential exposures, and in the special inferential habits, algorithms, and heuristics that he has learned or acquired.[13] Differences along these dimensions can ramify into substantial differences in belief sets.

My emphasis on conspecific psychological traits may suggest the possibility that only other *people* are interpretable by us. That is not a claim I endorse. On the contrary, we certainly think of ourselves as interpreting other animals; and although we may partly deceive ourselves with misplaced anthropomorphism, we do have moderate predictive success. Of course, the use of straightforward inductively gathered information is prominent here. But, as indicated earlier, we also use our own psychology as a home base, and make conservative revisions from that starting point. Perhaps this is why it is more difficult to construct right-seeming interpretations of heterospecifics than conspecifics. Dolphins seem to be highly intelligent and to communicate among themselves, yet no human has constructed a plausible interpretation of their language.

Although my discussion centers on the psychological dimensions involved in content attributions, it by no means precludes an important role for the external world, especially causal relations with the external world, in the choice of semantic assignments to thoughts. In deciding what is the *referent* of an imputed thought, in particular, it seems clear that the interpreter takes into account the thought's causal history. Similarly, it is plausible to suppose that imputation of other semantic dimensions of thought involves mind–world connections. These are plausibly part of the conceptual background with which the interpreter operates. Although I am not addressing these issues, which lie at the heart of much current debate, they are complementary to the themes I am pursuing.

7 *Philosophical Ramifications*

In this final section I briefly address several possible philosophical ramifications of the simulation approach, including the interpretation strategy with which I began.

Does the simulation approach imply a sharp divide between explanations of the mental and the physical? If so, it would vindicate the claim of the hermeneutic tradition, which contrasts understanding of human action with understanding of physical phenomena. No sharp contrast necessarily follows from the simulation theory. For one thing, we have already noted that simulation or mental modeling is sometimes postulated as a cognitive heuristic for representing physical phenomena as well as mental states. Admittedly, this realization of the simulation heuristic would presumably be theory-driven rather than process-driven. Still, this already admits an important parallel. Furthermore, proponents of interpretational simulation need not maintain that nomological explanation of human phenomena is impossible. They just maintain that *common-sense* explanations and predictions of the mental do not (in the main) invoke laws.

A second philosophical issue raised by the simulation theory is the epistemology of other minds. Ostensibly, the theory is a version of the 'analogical' theory of mental state ascription. It seems to impute to interpreters inferences of roughly the following form: 'If he is psychologically like me, he must be in mental state *M*; he is psychologically like me; therefore, he is in mental state *M*.' But there is a long-standing suspicion of such arguments from analogy, centering on the second premise. How can the interpreter know (or believe justifiably) that the agent is psychologically like her? Can physical and behavioral similarity support this premise? Is not an analogy based on a single case a thin reed on which to rest?

The best line of reply, I think, is to deny that interpreters must believe the second premise. Many beliefs are formed by mechanisms, or routines, that are built into the cognitive architecture. Although these mechanisms might be described in terms of 'rules' or 'principles', it would be misleading to say that the cognizers believe those rules or principles. For example, it is plausible to say that people form perceptual beliefs (or representations) in accord with Gestalt rules, but implausible to say that they literally believe those rules. They represent certain partly occluded figures as being single, unitary objects when there is sufficient 'continuity' between their perceived parts, but they do not believe the continuity principle itself. In our case, cognizers make interpretations in accordance with a routine that could be formulated by the principle, 'Other people are psychologically like me'. But this is not really a believed 'premise' on which they inferentially base their interpretations.

Could a belief that is produced by such a routine qualify as justified, or as a piece of knowledge, if the rule is not believed? Reliabilism is one species of epistemology that would be congenial to this result. If the routine, or process, is a generally reliable one, then reliabilism (in certain forms) may be prepared to count its output beliefs as justified (see Goldman, 1986). So there is at least one type of epistemology that promises to resolve the epistemic challenge to the simulation theory.[14]

A third noteworthy philosophical point concerns the ramification of abandoning the folk-theory theory. This theory has been a salient premise in the argument for eliminativism about propositional attitudes. Eliminativists standardly begin by emphasizing that the attitudes – and all our common-sense mentalistic notions – are part of a folk-psychological theory. They then point to the bleak history of past folk scientific theories, suggesting that the same scenario is in store for folk psychology (see Churchland, 1981). Since folk psychology will ultimately prove to have poorer predictive value than scientific psychology, its constructs will need to be replaced or eliminated, just like the constructs of, say, alchemy. However, if it turns out that there is no folk theory, in the sense of a set of common-sense generalizations that define the mental terms, then an important premise for eliminativism is no longer available. (This point has been made by Gordon.)

Let me turn now to what is probably the most pressing philosophical issue posed by the simulation theory. What is the relation, it may be asked, between the simulation approach and what it is for mental ascriptions to be *correct*? The simulation theory purports to give an account of the procedure used in ascribing mental states to others. What light does this shed, however, on the conditions that are *constitutive* of mental state possession (especially possession of the attitudes)? The interpretation strategist hopes to extract from the interpretation procedure some criteria of correctness for mentalistic ascriptions. Certainly the rationality and functionalist theories would generate answers to this question. (Whether or not the answers they generate are correct is another matter. Functionalist definitions, for example, have many familiar problems.) But the simulation theory looks distinctly unpromising on this score. Since simulation is such a fallible procedure, there is little hope of treating '*M* is ascribed (or ascribable) to *S* on the basis of simulation' as constitutive of '*S* is in *M*'. Furthermore, simulation assumes a prior understanding of what state it is that the interpreter ascribes to *S*. This just re-raises the same question: what state is it that the interpreter is imputing to the agent when she ascribes state *M*? What does her understanding of the *M*-concept consist in?

As far as the interpretation strategy is concerned, it indeed appears that if the simulation theory is correct, the interpretation strategy is fruitless. One cannot extract criteria of mentalistic ascription from the practice of interpersonal interpretation if that practice rests on a prior and independent understanding of mentalistic notions. As far as the interpretation strategy goes, then, the moral of the simulation theory is essentially a negative one. It should be recalled, however, that I warned from the outset that the hope of the interpretation strategy may not be well founded.

Since the simulation theory is only a theory of interpretation, a theory of how people apply mental terms to others, it is officially neutral about the *meaning* of these terms. It is even compatible with, say, a functionalist account of their meaning! It is conceivable that what people mean by mental terms is given by functionalism, yet they use simulation as a heuristic procedure for ascertaining or inferring the mental states of others. Although this is compatible with the simulation theory, we have already given independent reasons for concluding that the central presupposition of (common-sense) functionalism, viz., the existence of a folk theory, is not satisfied. Furthermore, other well-known difficulties with functionalism, such as absent qualia problems and (other) threats of liberalism and chauvinism, render its prospects quite bleak (see Block, 1980). The time is ripe to reconsider the prospects of the first-person approach to the understanding of mental concepts. It has always seemed plausible, prior to philosophical theorizing, that our naïve understanding of mental concepts should prominently involve introspective and not merely causal/relational elements. Some such approach to the concept of the mental would nicely complement the simulation theory of interpretation. However, this topic cannot be pursued here.[15]

Whether or not I have mounted a successful defense of the simulation theory, I hope I have at least persuaded the reader of the importance of getting the descriptive story of interpretive activity right. Although I think that the evidence in favor of the simulation account is substantial, I am even more convinced of the thesis that philosophers (as well as cognitive scientists) must pay closer attention to the psychology of the interpreter. Making that point has been the principal aim of this paper.

Notes

Earlier versions of this paper were presented to the philosophy of mind seminar of the Centre National de la Recherche Scientifique in Paris, a conference on the Chomskyan turn in Jerusalem, the Oxford Philosophical Society, the Society for Philosophy and Psychology, and the philosophy departments

at King's College, London and Rutgers University. Commentator and audience comments on all of these occasions were most helpful. I am particularly
indebted to Michael Ayers, Michael Bratman, Pascal Engel, Jerry Fodor, Eliza-
beth Fricker, Samuel Guttenplan, J. Christopher Maloney, Christopher
Peacocke, Stephen Schiffer, and Robert van Gulick. Special thanks are due to
Holly Smith, who read and commented on several previous drafts.

1 Functionalism, or the folk-theory theory, has not usually been presented
   under the 'interpretation' label. Nonetheless, I believe it causes no distor-
   tion, and indeed provides illumination, to view it in this guise.
2 Not all theories of content are discussed here. Many of these theories are
   not conveniently formulated as theories of interpretation, i.e. as accounts
   of the interpreter. For example, the causal, covariational, or information-
   theoretic approach (Fodor, 1987; Dretske, 1981) is normally stated directly as a theory of content, not in terms of the methods or constraints
   employed by an interpreter. The same holds of the evolutionary,
   'selectionist', or learning historical, approaches to content (Millikan, 1984;
   Dennett, 1987c; Dretske, 1988). Furthermore, some of these approaches
   (especially in their pure forms) do not seem promising as full theories of
   content ascription unless they are supplemented by one of the three
   approaches I discuss. The covariational approach seems best suited to
   handle only beliefs, and indeed only that fraction of beliefs under 'direct'
   causal control of their referents. To handle all types of beliefs, and the
   other attitudes, the approach probably needs to be incorporated into a
   larger, functional framework (or another such framework). Even Fodor,
   for example, who defends a covariational theory of content, also endorses
   a functional account of the attitude types (Fodor, 1987, pp. 69–70); and he
   acknowledges that the content of certain mental representations, viz., the
   logical vocabulary, should be handled in terms of their functional roles
   (Fodor, 1990, pp. 110–11). Furthermore, many of the foregoing theories
   would be extremely dubious accounts of how we *ordinarily* understand
   and ascribe contentful states, which is our present topic. A person can
   grasp and apply the concept of belief, for example, without any knowledge of, or any commitment to, either evolutionary theory or operant
   conditioning.
3 Hartry Field (1977) appeals to probabilistic coherence in the context of a
   theory of content.
4 It may be argued that Jeremy's judgments are not expressions of 'probability' judgments, but merely degrees of inductive support, which need
   not obey the probability calculus (see Levi, 1985). However, even if the
   Linda-style case does not make the point at hand, other cases involving
   genuine probabilities could do so.
5 A convenient set of readings on the sure-thing principle appears in
   Gärdenfors and Sahlin, 1988, part III. For a survey of deductive failings,
   see Anderson, 1985, ch. 10. For empirically based misgivings about the
   charity approach, similar to those expressed here, see Thagard and
   Nisbett, 1983.

6   Putnam, 1988 contains some new difficulties for functionalism. But this critique does not challenge the use of functional-style generalizations by interpreters.

7   A classical statement of the *Verstehen* approach is Collingwood (1946). Other recent writers who find the simulation approach congenial include Heal (1986, reprinted as ch. 1 in this volume), Ripstein (1987), Putnam (1978, lecture VI), Nozick (1981, pp. 637–8), Montgomery (1987), and Johnson (1988). Heal and Ripstein, in particular, anticipate a number of points made here. Unfortunately, those papers came to my attention only after this one was complete.

8   The threat of a regress was pointed out by Stephen Schiffer.

9   Here I am indebted to Michael Ayers.

10 This question is raised by Dennett (1987b), and its importance was impressed upon me by J. Christopher Maloney. For helpful discussion, see Ripstein, 1987.

11 I am indebted here to Christopher Peacocke. Notice that I am not assuming any sort of 'pictorial' theory of imagery, only the 'perception-similitude' thesis about imagery (see Goldman, 1986, ch. 12).

12 This answer would admittedly not serve Lewis's purposes, since he wants (roughly) purely 'physicalistic' constraints. This is implied by his own formulation of the problem of radical interpretation (in his paper of that title), as well as by the fact that he is trying to meet Hilary Putnam's challenge to resolve problems of content indeterminacy from an 'externalist' perspective. Although my answer would not serve Lewis's purposes, the crucial point of my argument is that his own answer just is not satisfactory.

13 Here I place significant weight on my distinction between basic 'processes' and acquired 'methods' in Goldman, 1986. It is assumed that the interpreter spontaneously uses the same *processes* as the interpretee, but may differ in the *methods* she deploys.

14 Another variant of the problem of other minds is presented by Wittgenstein and reconstructed by Kripke (1982). According to this problem, if the primary concept of a mental state is derived from my own case, I cannot coherently form even a conception of another person's being in that state. For a good reply to this problem, see Loar, 1990.

15 For a first-person, or subjective, rendering of mental content, see Loar, 1987. Interestingly, Loar couples his internalist account of content with a 'projective', or simulational, account of understanding others.

References

Anderson, J. 1985: *Cognitive Psychology and Its Implications*, 2nd edn. New York: W. H. Freeman.

Baron-Cohen, S., Leslie, A. and Frith, U. 1985: Does the autistic child have a 'theory of mind'? *Cognition*, 21, 37–46.

Block, N. 1980: Troubles with functionalism. In N. Block (ed.), *Readings in Philosophy of Psychology*, vol. 1. Cambridge, Mass.: Harvard University Press.

Cherniak, C. 1986: *Minimal Rationality*. Cambridge, Mass.: MIT Press.

Churchland, P. 1981: Eliminative materialism and the propositional attitudes. *Journal of Philosophy*, 78, 67–90.

Churchland, P. 1989: Folk psychology and the explanation of human behavior. In *The Neurocomputational Perspective*. Cambridge, Mass.: MIT Press.

Cohen, L. J. 1981: Can human irrationality be experimentally demonstrated? *Behavioral and Brain Sciences*, 4, 317–31.

Collingwood, R. 1946: *The Idea of History*. Oxford: Clarendon Press.

Davidson, D. 1980: *Essays on Actions and Events*. Oxford: Oxford University Press.

Davidson, D. 1984: *Inquiries into Truth and Interpretation*. Oxford: Oxford University Press.

Davidson, D. 1986: A coherence theory of truth and knowledge. In E. LePore (ed.), *Truth and Interpretation*. Oxford: Blackwell.

Dennett, D. 1971: Intentional systems. *Journal of Philosophy*, 68, 87–106.

Dennett, D. 1987a: True believers. In *The Intentional Stance*. Cambridge, Mass.: MIT Press.

Dennett, D. 1987b: Making sense of ourselves. In *The Intentional Stance*. Cambridge, Mass.: MIT Press.

Dennett, D. 1987c: Evolution, error, and intentionality. In *The Intentional Stance*. Cambridge, Mass.: MIT Press.

Dretske, F. 1981: *Knowledge and the Flow of Information*. Cambridge, Mass.: MIT Press.

Dretske, F. 1988: *Explaining Behavior*. Cambridge, Mass.: MIT Press.

Field, H. 1977: Logic, meaning, and conceptual role. *Journal of Philosophy*, 74, 379–409.

Fodor, J. 1987: *Psychosemantics*. Cambridge, Mass.: MIT Press.

Fodor, J. 1990: *A Theory of Content and Other Essays*. Cambridge, Mass.: MIT Press.

Gärdenfors, P. and Sahlin, N. E. (eds) 1988: *Decision, Probability, and Utility*. Cambridge: Cambridge University Press.

Goldman, A. 1970: *A Theory of Human Action*. Englewood Cliffs, NJ: Prentice Hall.

Goldman, A. 1986: *Epistemology and Cognition*. Cambridge, Mass.: Harvard University Press.

Goldman, A. 1987: Cognitive Science and Metaphysics. *Journal of Philosophy*, 84, 537–44.

Gordon, R. 1986: Folk psychology as simulation. *Mind and Language*, 1, 158–71. Reprinted as ch. 2 in this volume.

Gordon, R. 1987: *The Structure of Emotions*. Cambridge: Cambridge University Press.

Grandy, R. 1973: Reference, meaning, and belief. *Journal of Philosophy*, 70, 439–52.

Harris, P. 1989: *Children and Emotion: The Development of Psychological Understanding*. Oxford: Blackwell.

Heal, J. 1986: Replication and functionalism. In Butterfield, J. (ed.), *Language, Mind and Logic*. Cambridge: Cambridge University Press. Reprinted as ch. 1 in this volume.

Johnson, C. N. 1988: Theory of mind and the structure of conscious experience. In J. Astington, P. Harris, and D. Olson (eds), *Developing Theories of Mind*. Cambridge: Cambridge University Press.

Kahneman, D. and Tversky, A. 1982: The simulation heuristic. In D. Kahneman, P. Slovic and A. Tversky (eds), *Judgment under Uncertainty*. Cambridge: Cambridge University Press.

Kosslyn, S. 1980: *Image and Mind*. Cambridge, Mass.: Harvard University Press.

Kripke, S. 1982: *Wittgenstein on Rules and Private Language*. Cambridge, Mass.: Harvard University Press.

LePore, E. (ed.) 1986: *Truth and Interpretation*. Oxford: Blackwell.

Leslie, A. 1987: Pretense and representation: The origins of 'theory of mind'. *Psychological Review*, 94, 412–26.

Levi, I. 1985: Illusions about uncertainty. *British Journal for the Philosophy of Science*, 36, 331–40.

Lewis, D. 1972: Psychophysical and theoretical identifications. *Australasian Journal of Philosophy*, 61, 249–58.

Lewis, D. 1983a: Radical interpretation. In *Philosophical Papers*, vol. 1. New York: Oxford University Press.

Lewis, D. 1983b: How to define theoretical terms. In *Philosophical Papers*, vol. 1. New York: Oxford University Press.

Lewis, D. 1983c: New work for a theory of universals. *Australasian Journal of Philosophy*, 50, 343–77.

Loar, B. 1987: Subjective intentionality. *Philosophical Topics*, 15, 89–124.

Loar, B. 1990: Phenomenal states. In J. E. Tomberlin (ed.), *Philosophical Perspectives, 4: Action Theory and Philosophy of Mind*. Atascadero, Calif.: Ridgeview.

McGinn, C. 1977: Charity, interpretation, and belief. *Journal of Philosophy*, 74, 521–35.

McGinn, C. 1986: Radical interpretation and epistemology. In LePore, 1986.

Millikan, R. 1984: *Language, Thought, and Other Biological Categories*. Cambridge, Mass.: MIT Press.

Montgomery, R. 1987: Psychologism, folk psychology and one's own case. *Journal for the Theory of Social Behavior*, 17, 195–218.

Morton, A. 1980: *Frames of Mind*. Oxford: Oxford University Press.

Nozick, R. 1981: *Philosophical Explanations*. Cambridge, Mass.: Harvard University Press.

Pollock, J. 1986: *Contemporary Theories of Knowledge*. Totowa, NJ: Rowman & Littlefield.

Putnam, H. 1978: *Meaning and the Moral Sciences*. London: Routledge and Kegan Paul.

Putnam, H. 1988: *Representation and Reality*. Cambridge, Mass.: MIT Press.

Quine, W. V. 1960: *Word and Object*. Cambridge, Mass.: MIT Press.

Quine, W. V. 1969: Natural kinds. In *Ontological Relativity and Other Essays*. New York: Columbia University Press.

Ripstein, A. 1987: Explanation and empathy. *Review of Metaphysics*, 40, 465–82.

Rosch, E. 1975: Cognitive representations of semantic categories. *Journal of Experimental Psychology: General*, 104, 192–233.

Rosch, E. 1978: Principles of categorization. In E. Rosch and B. Lloyd (eds), *Cognition and Categorization*. Hillsdale, NJ: Lawrence Erlbaum.

Rumelhart, D., Smolensky, P., McClelland, J. and Hinton, G. 1986: Schemata and sequential thought processes in PDP models. In J. McClelland, D. Rumelhart, and the PDP Research Group, *Parallel Distributed Processing*, vol. 2. Cambridge, Mass.: MIT Press.

Schiffer, S. 1987: *Remnants of Meaning*. Cambridge, Mass.: MIT Press.

Shepard, R. and Cooper, L. 1982: *Mental Images and Their Transformations*. Cambridge, Mass.: MIT Press.

Sperber, D. and Wilson, D. 1986: *Relevance*. Oxford: Blackwell.

Stich, S. 1983: *From Folk Psychology to Cognitive Science: The Case Against Belief*. Cambridge, Mass.: MIT Press.

Stich, S. 1985: Could man be an irrational animal? In H. Kornblith (ed.), *Naturalizing Epistemology*. Cambridge, Mass.: MIT Press.

Thagard, P. and Nisbett, R. 1983: Rationality and charity. *Philosophy of Science*, 50, 250–67.

Tversky, A. and Kahneman, D. 1983: Extensional versus intuitive reasoning: the conjunction fallacy in probability judgment. *Psychological Review*, 90, 293–315.

Van Fraassen, B. 1980: *The Scientific Image*. New York: Oxford University Press.

Wimmer, H. and Perner, J. 1983: Beliefs about beliefs: Representation and constraining function of wrong beliefs in young children's understanding of deception. *Cognition*, 13, 103–28.

4

The Simulation Theory: Objections and Misconceptions

ROBERT M. GORDON

In an earlier paper (Gordon, 1986a, reprinted as ch. 2 in this volume)[1] I argued that human competence in predicting and explaining behavior depends chiefly on a capacity for mental simulation, particularly for decision-making within a pretend context. The paper explained how simulated practical reasoning would work as a device for predicting one's own behavior in hypothetical situations and, with the aid of 'hypothetico-practical' reasoning, for predicting the actual behavior of others. It was suggested that the Simulation Theory (ST) competes with the so-called 'Theory' Theory (TT), the view that a common-sense psychological theory, a 'folk psychology', underlies human competence in explaining and predicting behavior and implicitly defines our concepts of the various mental states.

The present paper has two main purposes. One is to correct some common misconceptions of simulation: for example, that to simulate another is just to *'put yourself in her place'*, or that it is to *use oneself as a model* of the other. (Here I cannot speak for all proponents of ST, as Alvin Goldman (1989) and Paul Harris (1989) evidently accept the 'model' model of simulation. What I shall be calling 'ST' is therefore just my own version of the Simulation Theory.[2])

The *second* purpose is to answer some objections to ST, particularly objections that rest on misconceptions of simulation. For example, some philosophers have objected that ST doesn't really compete with TT, because simulation requires a background theory or at least cannot be *justified* except in terms of a theory. I shall try to show that these arguments are based on misconceptions. It has also been objected that

> simulations, even if they motivate predictions about others, do not by themselves provide any explanatory understanding of the behavior of others. (Churchland, 1989, p. 234)

In response I shall show, not just that simulation does provide an adequate basis for explanation, but also that ST makes clear the great practical (and biological) importance of *getting our explanations right* – unlike TT, which usually views these explanations as a kind of theoretical speculation that we can get wrong with impunity, as long as the *predictions* come out right.

1 Putting Oneself in the Other's Place

It is tempting to explain simulation in terms of the familiar notion of 'putting oneself in the other's place'. This would pose a problem for ST, however. We often explain and predict another's behavior *without* putting ourselves in the other's place – or so it would appear. So it would follow that we often explain and predict another's behavior without *simulating* the other. How then could human competence in predicting and explaining behavior depend chiefly on a capacity for simulation?

In defense of ST one *might* try to respond to this by stealing a trick from the Theory Theorist's bag. TT typically extends the notion of having and using a theory, to allow *unconscious* theorizing, where the theorizer is unaware of applying or even having the theory. Likewise, ST may extend the notion of putting oneself in another's place, by allowing it to go on unconsciously. Also, TT may further extend the notion of having and using a theory to include a kind of information processing in the brain, a computational operation on quantified sentences in a so-called language of thought. It is conceivable that such theorizing goes on in me even when it wouldn't be correct to say that *I* am doing it, even unconsciously. So ST may hypothesize that when I put myself in another's place – at least, when I do so *successfully* or *correctly* – my own brain actually begins to function like the other's brain, to resemble it *functionally* and perhaps *computationally*, at least up to a point. Again, such functional simulation may conceivably go on even when it wouldn't be correct to say that *I* am *doing* it, even unconsciously.

These ways of extending the notion of putting oneself in another's place are interesting in their own right, but I won't develop them here. Rather, I want to *agree* with the premise of the objection: putting ourselves in the other's place is *not* something we – or our brains – regularly do in predicting or explaining another's behavior. As a family therapist remarked to me, if her clients did regularly put themselves in the place of others, they would have far less need for her services. And as Daniel Dennett pointed out to me, if people did this routinely, we wouldn't have to *say* to them, 'Put yourself in her place'.

Here is the fundamental problem with equating simulating another with putting oneself in the other's place. '*Put* yourself in her place' presupposes that you are not *already* in her 'place'. You are being asked to make imaginative adjustments for relevant *differences* between her situation and psychology, and your own: for example, differences in upbringing, education, social role, values, temperament, or epistemic situation. When you are asked to 'put yourself in someone's place', what is the implied contrasting condition: what is it that you are implicitly being asked *not* to do? I think it is clear that the contrast is not with taking an *external* or *'third-person'* view of the other person, the sort of stance a *theorist* might be expected to take. Rather, what is implied is that you shouldn't just *project your own* situation and psychology on the other. But 'just projecting', without making adjustments, is itself a kind of simulation, as I will try to show in the following section. If this is correct, then I can fully agree with the therapist: people would indeed understand each other better if they made the necessary adjustments, as opposed to simulation of the kind we call 'just projecting'. And I can agree with Dennett that people often have to be told to put themselves in the other's place, as opposed to just projecting. Because 'just projecting' is simulation, too, the points raised by the therapist and by Dennett cannot be counted objections to ST.

2 The Primacy of Total Projection

It is true that simulating often does require imaginatively 'putting' oneself in the other's place, at least in the literal sense of 'place': that is, transporting oneself in imagination to the other's spatial or temporal location. But with like-minded individuals in close spatiotemporal proximity, we often get by with 'just projecting', that is, with *total*, as opposed to merely *partial*, projection, without even an adjustment for spatial or temporal differences. Such *total* projection is simply the *default mode* of simulation, the mode one is in if one makes no adjustments. Or, to express the point with *projection* as the primitive term, simulation is total or partial projection, that is, projection with or without adjustments in imagination.

Consider the following example. You and a friend are hiking up a mountain trail, talking. Suddenly, in mid-sentence, you friend stops in his tracks, blurts out, 'Go back!' then turns and walks quietly and quickly back down the trail. You are puzzled. You follow him, looking over your shoulder to *search the environment* for an explanation. Initially, at least, you search the common environment, making no compensation for the three-meter distance or the five-second interval that separate you now from your friend at the time he stopped in his tracks. You look for salient features in the middle distance, particularly *for menacing, frightening* things further up the trail, of a sort that might show up on mountain trails in the region. (Less plausibly, you might also look for *attractive* things back *down* the trail, especially if your friend was looking back down when he stopped. And you might wonder, too, about internal causes such as pain).

Then you spot it: above you, at the next switchback, something startling, menacing, and frightening – a large bear, and it's a grizzly! So *that's* why he suddenly turned back: because there's a grizzly – *that grizzly there* – up ahead. (There may of course be more than one plausible candidate. This possibility raises Davidson's problem (Davidson, 1963). What distinguishes the one *because of which* the agent acted? I'll say a little about this problem below.)

In searching the environment for an explanation of your friend's action, you are projecting your own beliefs about the environment onto your friend. The field of search consists in a subset of those features you yourself believe (after looking around) to comprise the actual world. And the objects within that field are fixed by your own ways of 'entifying' and categorizing the world (Goldman, this volume, pp. 90–1). The issue for you is something like this: 'What is it about these environing rocks, trees, animals, and so forth, that would explain his suddenly turning back?' And the question is understood to presuppose that your friend is *aware* of these very objects, and that whatever it is *about* these objects that constitutes the *explanans* you are seeking is something *known* to him. When you spot the grizzly and think, 'That's *it!*', the presupposition is that he is aware of, or at least knows about, *that* grizzly *there*. If the fact *that it is a grizzly* is part of the explanation, then it is presupposed that he knows *that it is a grizzly*. Thus, implicitly you are projecting on to your friend your own belief, and presumed knowledge, that there's a grizzly up ahead, and even your *de re* belief that it's *that* grizzly *there*.

But this may seem hasty. Just because you *don't suspend* your own beliefs as you seek an explanation, it surely doesn't follow that you are *projecting* these. After all, we don't ordinarily suspend our own beliefs when searching for a naturalistic, non-animistic explanation of a physical phenomenon. Suppose you notice that a particular tree in the forest was split, and you wonder how it got to be that way. In searching for an explanation, you wouldn't lay aside your own beliefs about the environment, for these beliefs are to be the *basis* (or part of the basis) for your explanation. Yet you are certainly not projecting your beliefs about the tree's environment *onto the tree*.

The difference lies in the way the beliefs about the environment are *used*. To explain why a particular tree in the forest is split, one would typically search the environment for features that are theoretically relevant to the phenomenon to be explained. If the tree were charred – especially, if it were charred just in the vicinity of the split – one might be led to believe that lightning had split the tree. For we believe that lightning often both splits trees and chars them near the split, and that nothing else commonly does this. By contrast, in seeking an explanation of your friend's action, you were looking for features of the environment (features you believed it to possess) that were *menacing, frightening, attractive*, and the like. This is not a matter of looking dispassionately for features believed to produce certain characteristic actions or emotions. Rather, it is a search that essentially engages your own practical and emotional responses. This is an indication that the procedure is *projective*, unlike the search for a naturalistic, non-animistic explanation of a physical phenomenon. The search, one might say, is not for *theoretically* relevant features but for *practically* or *emotionally* relevant features.

(The point is not that one's own responses are engaged, but that one's *practical* or *emotional* responses are engaged – responses that dispose one to particular types of behavior and thus enable one to explain or predict the other's behavior. A search for a particular color or other 'secondary' quality would likewise engage one's own 'responses', broadly construed. Yet such engagement would not be an indication that the procedure is projective. When I see a car stop at an intersection, I have a ready explanation if the light is red. Here indeed I am projecting to the driver. But there are also naturalistic explanations in terms of color: Because the light is red, it doesn't fog the photographic paper in the developing tray. Here I am *not* projecting to the paper.)

But to speak here of practically or emotionally *relevant* features may be misleading. For the normative force of the term 'relevant' may suggest that the search is limited to features of the environment that constitute *good reasons*, say, to turn back, or to be frightened. This would imply that you would reject as an explanans of your friend's action a feature of the environment that moved you to turn back, but did so in a way that you judged *irrational*. For example, suppose that instead of a grizzly you had spotted an animal that intellectually but not emotionally you knew to be perfectly harmless, and that you felt compelled to turn back 'in spite of yourself'. Were your search for an explanans a search for *good reasons* for turning back, it would turn a blind eye to such irrational responses. But it seems implausible that someone would do this, unless he had some special reason to think his own irrationality atypical. (As Goldman (this volume, pp. 76–8 and p. 83) argues, ST predicts – correctly – that we will sometimes attribute irrationality to others, something that would not be readily predicted by what he calls the 'rational norms' approach. ST even predicts – again correctly, it would appear – just *when* we are most likely to do so: namely, when we are most prone to such irrationality ourselves.) When we look to the environment to explain another's surprising action, we are not in general trying to find good reasons, whether they move us or not; rather we are seeking to be moved, whether rationally or not. In fact our search response seems much like the typical response of apes and monkeys to alarm calls: namely, to retreat to safety and then to search the environment for the cause or trigger of the alarm, usually a predator. The search ends, it would appear, when the responding animal finds in the environment something that it too would ordinarily have been 'alarmed' by, something that would have moved it to retreat to safety even in the absence of an alarm call – indeed, something that might have caused it to issue an alarm call itself.[3]

A point worth adding is that it isn't only when we are puzzled or surprised by another's behavior that we project. We are ordinarily *not* puzzled or surprised by the behavior of others. For example, your friend, hiking up the trail a few paces ahead, occasionally interrupts his straightforward progress with a series of turns left and right, and occasionally breaks his regular gait by stopping, raising his leg unaccustomedly high, and shifting his weight to the high leg. Peculiar! But not at all puzzling. You aren't puzzled when you see your fellow hiker turn sharply to the right, provided he does so when *the trail* turns sharply to the right. You aren't at all puzzled when he raises his leg high, provided he does so when there is an obstacle to step over. Philosophers concerned to give an adequate account of the common-sense explanation of behavior need to ask why. ST's account is simple: When we are aware of others – that is, aware of them *as* others – we are constantly, automatically projecting onto them our own beliefs about the environment.

3 *The Place of Behavioral Laws*

Some Theory Theorists might suggest that your lack of surprise or puzzlement is due to your acceptance of a number of laws of typical behavior, generalizations that correlate external circumstances with behavior, such as the following: 'Hikers follow trails (and thus turn right when the trail turns right, etc.)'. As to the 'grizzly' example, it might be suggested that you were just applying the law that 'People move away from approaching dangerous things'. Nisbett and Ross (1980, p. 211) claim that even first person explanations are standardly just applications of such laws of typical behavior: 'A person who answers a telephone and asserts that he did so "because it was ringing" is surely right. . . . A person who asserts that he opened the refrigerator door because he was hungry is usually right. But we have theories about why we answer telephones . . . and why we open refrigerators, and these theories are usually correct.' I find this implausible; but even if it were true, it would not be telling, as I argue in the remainder of this section.

Some people clearly do find it useful to write down reminders of the idiosyncrasies of acquaintances they don't know very well: one might write a note in one's address book, or warn someone else, that Joe 'always' drinks a martini before dinner, that the Jones's 'always' go to sleep at 9 o'clock, that Bill 'always' drops his coat on a particular chair when he comes in the door. Travel guides are full of generalizations about alien cultures: for example, that a Japanese host 'always' waits in the doorway until the departing guest is out of sight. But such generalizations, as I suggested in this volume (ch. 2) and shall argue here at greater length, are not mechanically interpreted and applied, but rather interpreted and applied within the context of a simulation.

Suppose your friend, call him Bill, has just come in the door. You know what happens next: he'll throw his coat on a particular chair. It might be thought that your competence in predicting Bill's action depends only on the following behavioral generalization, call it G, which you believe on the basis of past observation: 'Whenever Bill enters the house he drops his coat on that chair.' But G, mechanically applied, is an extremely simple, insensitive predictive device, and *you* are not: by and large, you would know when *not* to use G.

For one thing, G is to be interpreted as if from Bill's 'point of view'. In circumstances in which you could not project onto Bill your belief that the antecedent is satisfied, that is, that Bill is now entering the house, you would not be led to expect Bill to throw his coat on the chair. Suppose Bill intended to be breaking into your neighbor's house, but it's dark outside and he winds up breaking into your house, but he doesn't know that, because it's also dark *inside*. As far as Bill is concerned, he has entered *your neighbor's* house, not *yours*. But *G* applies only to *your* house. If you had an inkling of what was going on, you would know better than to apply *G* in this instance.

Further, a generalization like *G* must be taken with an indefinitely expandable grain of *ceteris paribus*. If a large bowl of fruit punch were sitting on your chair, you probably wouldn't expect Bill to throw his coat there. Nor would you if the chair were on fire, or (depending on the sort of person Bill is) if you had just asked Bill to kindly hang his coat in the closet. One way in which you are a better predictor than your generalization *G* is that *you* can, at least for a start, use your own continually updated knowledge of the actual environment (including the full punch bowl), together with your own reactions to throwing your own coat on the chair in such circumstances. (Of course, we may learn that with regard to coat-dropping, Bill acts 'blindly' and inflexibly; but we *start* with our own human-like proclivities, not insect-like fixed-action tendencies.) Another advantage you have over generalizations like *G* is game-theoretic: were others to learn that you were relying on a mechanically applied generalization about them, they could alter their policy or habit in order to outfox you.

In short, even where we do make use of generalizations that correlate external circumstances with behavior, it is not the generalizations themselves, that is, the generalizations mechanically applied, that explain our predictive or explanatory competence: it is our skill at using the generalizations as heuristics or rules of thumb as we simulate others. (Some philosophers would rather say that we know when to make exceptions because we ascribe propositional attitudes to others in accordance with a normative principle of charity or rationality. But in any case our competence in predicting Bill's action depends on more than the generalizations themselves.) It should be remarked that Theory Theorists typically do not make much of *behavioral* generalizations: the generalizations they bank on are highly abstract generalizations about mental states, such as the *modus ponens* law that if *A* believes *p* and *A* believes if *p* then *q*, then *A* believes q (Fodor, 1987). But even generalizations like the *modus ponens* law lack predictive power unless one has a basis for deciding whether *A* will come to believe *q* or give up believing at least one of the premises. Although a case might be made that by using other laws as well one could assign *degrees* of belief, a more plausible account is that we use simulation to make such determinations (Gordon, unpublished).

4 Patching Total Projection

Total projection, it is obvious, is unreliable under some conditions. Under these conditions, we need an alternative basis for explanation and prediction. Two kinds of alternatives seem possible, one conservative, the other radical. The conservative alternative: where total projection is unreliable, modify, adjust, or patch it so as to restore reliability. The radical alternative: where total projection is unreliable, scrap projection altogether and start all over with a fundamentally *non-projective* basis for explanation and prediction.

I take TT (Theory Theory) to be an elaboration of the radical alternative. According to TT, we (ordinary folk) regard other human beings as 'black boxes'. To explain or predict the behavior of the black boxes, we apply a theory – innate, acquired, or hybrid – of the general goings-on in their behavior control centers. Details vary, but most current versions of TT would agree that the theory we apply endows the control centers with states occupying representational and functional roles that bridge between sensory input and behavior. So in searching for an explanation of the hiking companion's startling and turning back, you *disregard* the startling, dangerous, or attractive aspects of the environment and take a completely 'external' or non-projective view of him. At most, you might regard these emotive qualities of the environment as *evidence* of the current internal states of your own control center, and then hypothesize that, with perhaps some exceptions, your own control center is a good model of your friend's. (Some people seem to think that this is what *simulation* amounts to. It isn't, as I hope to make clear in this paper.)

Consider some conditions under which total projection would be unreliable: first, a situation in which the *spatial disparity* between yourself and the other is relevant. Suppose that when you saw your fellow hiker startle and then go back, you followed out the path of his gaze and found nothing startling and frightening from where you stand. Total projection fails to explain his behavior. As a next step you might walk over to where *he* was, putting yourself in his place (literally) so as to occupy his vantage point, and then resume scanning the environment. This is a way of patching total projection that would in some cases *restore reliability*. However, because a 'fix' like this *takes time*, it will not restore reliability unless one adjusts in imagination for the *temporal* difference, picturing the scene as it looked when *he* occupied the vantage point. Instead of mentally adjusting for the temporal difference, why not simply adjust for the *spatial* difference, thereby avoiding the time-consuming and sometimes effortful or dangerous *physical* change of place? That is, why not put yourself in the other's *place* (literally) by transporting yourself in imagination? You are already equipped to perform imaginative shifts of perspective, it would seem, if you have the capacity to anticipate and integrate changes of perspective as you yourself move past an object.

Probably the most important use of this capacity to put oneself in the other's (spatial) place is to reveal, not *what* the other perceives, but *how* he perceives it. For example, the grizzly that is approaching, not you, but your friend, who is some distance away, must be seen as an *approaching grizzly*: that is, one you might describe as 'approaching *me*'. (But, as I shall insist later, the referent of the personal pronoun is not *you*, the particular individual doing the simulating: it shifts, within the context of the simulation, to *your friend* over there. If 'me' were to retain its standard reference, then you would be imagining something that is false, namely that the grizzly is moving toward *you*. But if 'me', as used within the context of the simulation, comes to refer to your friend, then you are *not* imagining something that is false.)

In general terms, what you are doing is shifting the locations and vectors of environmental features on your egocentric map – that is, the mental map in which things and events are represented in relation to yourself, here, and now – so as properly to engage your location-specific or vector-specific tendencies to action or emotion. Many of our emotion-tendencies and action-tendencies are specially keyed to egocentric locations and vectors. For example, actions such as retreating, fleeing to cover (climbing a tree, for example) and freezing in place are specially triggered by *approaching* dangerous animals. By using imagination to shift on one's egocentric map the grizzly's vector so as to represent it as 'approaching', as coming closer to 'here' and to 'oneself', one can engage these special tendencies – though in 'off-line' mode, inhibited from their normal overt expression. Such an adjustment would enable you to explain why the other hiker retreats, even though you yourself, confronted with no *approaching* grizzly, have no present tendency to do likewise. Had you been locked into total projection, unable to shift the grizzly's vector to make it an 'approaching' grizzly, you would have found it hard to explain why your companion is retreating. Or if a second animal, a snarling dog, happened to be approaching you and causing you to retreat (or at least be so inclined) at the very time your companion was approached by the grizzly, total projection would have led you to think that he, like you, was retreating because of the dog. By shifting the vectors of the two animals, you escape from the egocentrism that would have led you to this mistaken explanation. Thus the adjustment in imagination allows you to *regain reliability* under conditions in which total projection would be unreliable.

If I am right that the starting point or default is total projection, then it is implausible to suppose that where total projection fails, we forfeit its benefits altogether and start from scratch, with a theory of the human behavior control center: so that, for example, if the grizzly that had been approaching both of you now approaches only the other hiker, you now must deduce from a theory what you had previously determined by projection, that it is the grizzly that causes him to retreat. It is far more plausible that, instead of forcing us to theorize, nature simply enhances the reliability of the projective method by exploiting our capacity to shift spatial perspectives – a capacity needed, as I suggested, for other purposes – so that we 'put ourselves in the other's place'. Thus we explain behavior, just as in the unproblematic cases, by looking for environmental features that are salient, alarming, frightening, and so on; only now we do so after we have made the necessary changes in the egocentric locations and vectors of environmental features.

One may further extend the explanatory and predictive reliability of projection by other imaginative adjustments. Besides shifting spatial perspectives, one may adjust what is attractive, or frightening, or repelling: that is, what types of environmental feature, and more generally what types of fact, are 'moving', and what types of actions or emotions they move one to. For example, you see a grizzly and you start to turn back; but you see your hiking companion, an intrepid naturalist, take out her pencil and notebook instead. Here total projection would have failed you in explanation as well as prediction. Your companion's action takes you by surprise, and you probably have no plausible explanation available. But these lapses could be avoided if, in imagination even if not in reality, you were to *imitate* or *model yourself* on your companion, on the basis of your prior knowledge that she is a naturalist. If you were to 'prep' yourself with the appropriate intrepid naturalist attitudes and desires, you should then be able to project with greater reliability, so that even if the sight of the grizzly alarms you and moves you to turn back, you will not be surprised to see your companion take out her pencil and notebook. And the explanation will be readily available to you: she's doing it because there's a grizzly up ahead.

Consider an example in which both spatial and attitudinal adjustments are made. I read that Linda Ronstadt will be coming to St Louis to give a concert next Saturday. I remember that Fred, who lives a two-hour drive from St Louis, has all of Ronstadt's albums, that he sends her fan mail, that he once paid a hundred dollars for a ticket to one of her concerts, and so forth. I'm not a Ronstadt fan. To explain Fred's 'deviant' behavior, I pretend to myself that Ronstadt's singing is the most exquisite I have ever heard, and that the opportunity to see and hear her in person is a reason for making great sacrifices. Pretending all that, I am ready to pack my bag and go. And, checking as I would *in propria persona* for reasons *not* to go, I find no evidence that Fred is seriously ill or incapacitated, and so forth; though there might of course be reasons I am unaware of. Nor do I find evidence of a non-rational deterrent, such as sloth or depression. So, within the context of this Fred-simulation, there is nothing to stop me. Returning to my own person: Since Fred will probably be coming to St Louis next Saturday, why not call and try to arrange to meet him when he's in town? Or suppose Fred phones me first, to tell me he's coming to town. I have an explanation ready at hand: 'I'll bet I know one reason you're coming', I tell him, just a little smugly.

Attitudinal adjustments present a special problem. I may find it difficult or impossible even to *pretend* that Ronstadt's singing is the most exquisite I have ever heard, and that the opportunity to see and hear her in person is a reason for making great sacrifices. Being exquisite and being worthy of sacrifice are *supervenient* qualities and not easily detachable from those 'descriptive' qualities on which they supervene. So in order to imagine Ronstadt's singing to be exquisite, and so forth, I might first have to imagine her singing to have quite different sound qualities from those it has.[4] And, given my own limitations (let us say), I might even have to imagine it to be singing of a different genre altogether – Wagnerian opera – or not singing at all but conducting, lecturing on philosophy, or basketball-playing. And of course it would not be Linda Ronstadt's conducting or basketball-playing. Like a method actor of the Stanislavsky–Strasberg school, I would conjure up some nearly comparable idol of my own: say, Bernstein doing Mahler in a St Louis-like city two hundred miles from here.

But how do I know that Ronstadt is to Fred as Bernstein is to me? How, in general, is one to pick out an *equivalent* replacement? Wouldn't this require a *theory*? It would, indeed, according to Josef Perner, who discusses a different example (Perner, 1991, p. 268):

> Assume you learn that your colleague's mother-in-law has just died. How does he feel? It will not do to imagine that your mother-in-law has just died. . . . because your relationship . . . may be quite different from your colleague's. . . . Your simulation must be informed by some 'theory' about which personal relationships are emotionally relevant. If you love your mother-in-law but your colleague hated his, then your simulation will be more accurate if you imagine the death of one of your foes.

It is true that your simulation must be informed by *evidence* regarding your colleague's personal relationships. But why a *theory*? In the Ronstadt example, I surmised that Fred's reaction to the news that the singer was coming to St Louis would probably be different from my own, on the basis of evidence concerning Fred's past behavior: that he had all of Ronstadt's albums, sent her fan mail, and so forth. How did I get that prediction out of this evidence? Not by plugging the evidence into a general theory of the organization of the human behavior control system, but by trying to motivate similar behavior within the context of a simulation. To motivate such behavior required a change of some sort: pretending Ronstadt's singing to be quite different from what it is, or perhaps even substituting Bernstein's conducting Mahler. (There are indefinitely many other possible changes that would motivate such behavior – making Fred a masochist, for example (apologies again to Ms. Ronstadt).) But a 'principle of least pretending' seems to guide our simulations (this volume, p. 65).) Given such a change, the news that Ronstadt was coming to St Louis evoked a different response (within the context of the simulation) from the one it actually evoked in me.

By a similar use of evidence concerning your colleague's past behavior (*vis-à-vis* his mother-in-law, or his wife, or his relatives in general, or perhaps just people in general), you could learn whether the standard move – substituting one's own mother-in-law – is likely to work in this instance. There is thus no need for *theoretical* input. So Perner's example doesn't yield the conclusion he wants. It does, however, call our attention to an interesting fact about kinship relations: that they create not only individual *differences* in attitudes and behavior but also, in most cases, remarkable *analogies* in attitudes and behavior across individuals. On the one hand, the other person's attitudes and behavior regarding his child, his mother, or his mother-in-law, are likely to be very different from one's own regarding *his* child, *his* mother, or *his* mother-in-law. Yet on the other hand, simulation will *typically* – though of course, as Perner notes, not always – yield fairly accurate predictions if one substitutes, for his child, mother, or mother-in-law, an individual who stands in the *same kinship relation to oneself*: one's own child, mother, or mother-in-law.

(Kinship-preserving substitutions are generally so successful that they may play an important role as a stepping stone in conceptual development. For example: you are two years old (more or less) and the little girl playing next to you loses her balloon and sees it fly off into the sky. You empathize, until you see her run, crying, not to *Mommy* (the one who gives comfort when things go bad) but to a *different woman*. That part of her behavior eludes empathetic explanation – you just can't get yourself to run to *that* woman – until, perhaps experimenting with various fantasies, you mentally replace the strange woman with *Mommy*. That proves to be the key that fits the lock, making it *all* make sense. You have taken your first step toward a general concept of 'mommy' (the-one-to-go-to-when-things-go-bad, etc.) as a two-place predicate: one individual is mommy to *me*, another individual is mommy *to her*, and so forth. Moreover, in learning that for other children a different individual fills the bill, you have begun to see the 'moving' (action- and emotion-inciting) qualities of various individuals and environmental features as *agent-relative* qualities. The would be a major step, I submit, in developing the concepts of attitude and desire.)

There are many twists and turns that need to be considered in a full account of the simulation of attitudes, desires, and emotions, and the brevity of this discussion should not be taken to belittle these complications. (A relevant distinction among desires is discussed, though without attention to simulation, in Gordon, 1986b and 1986c.)

But the most philosophically problematic adjustments to projection are adjustments, not in spatial or temporal perspective or in attitude, and thus in the 'moving' powers of various facts, but in the facts themselves. In discussing the hiker example, I suggested that if the field within which you seek the explanation for his action is the actual environment (or more generally the actual facts), then you are in effect projecting to him your own awareness of the environment and your presumed knowledge of these facts. But this would lead to errors in explanation and prediction if the hiker were, at least for the moment, *epistemically handicapped*, barred from access to some of these facts or environmental features: if, say, he had severe uncorrected myopia. If you see him gazing in the direction of the grizzly, total projection wrongly leads you to expect him to react. If the hiker does in fact startle and turn back, total projection wrongly leads you to think he does so because there is a grizzly up ahead. But if in predicting and explaining his behavior by simulation you were to *visualize everything beyond ten feet as a blur*, you would probably avoid these errors. Upon sighting a (quiet) grizzly, you would know you had to *inform* your companion of it. Were your companion to startle and turn back *before* you had informed him, you would know better than to think he did so because of the grizzly: perhaps something else is wrong, too. The adjustment in imagination allows you to explain and predict with relative reliability under conditions in which total projection would be quite unreliable.

Consider, however, what appears to be a problematic example. At the next switchback is a very large dog. You recognize it as a Newfoundland, which you believe to be a friendly breed, and you have no inclination to avoid it. Your hiking companion spots the animal, startles, and turns back. You may be able to motivate such behavior by 'blanking out' the fact that the animal belongs to a friendly breed of dog, thus allowing your more primitive responses to its large size to gain ascendance. Or you may pretend that *grizzlies* look quite a bit like that, and that there are said to be many grizzlies in this area, and few dogs. But how could it *improve one's reliability* in explaining another's behavior to 'blank out' some of the facts or even to pretend something to be so that one knows isn't so?

My answer is that in cases like this, there is a lapse in knowledge, a failure to know, a bit of ignorance on the other's part, that accounts for his acting differently from you. By adjusting the facts as you simulate the other, you are able *to pinpoint the relevant ignorance*. On the first hypothesis stated above, what accounted for your companion's turning back when you didn't was his failure to know that that dog, the Newfoundland at the switchback, belongs to a species that is not at all vicious. On the second hypothesis stated above, what accounted for his turning back was his failure to know that the dog *wasn't in fact a grizzly bear*. This failure in turn was due to his failure to know that grizzlies do *not* look Newfoundlandish, and also his failure to know that there are *not* lots of grizzlies and few dogs in the area. What we have then is an explanation, not in terms of fact, but in terms of ignorance of fact.

Such explanations are useful in a number of ways. Perhaps most important, they tell us how to correct the behavior of others, particularly children. They pick out the facts we have somehow to impart to the child. For example, you belong to a group of hunter-gatherers. You see your child running away from an animal and you laugh, because the animal he is running away from is *prey*, not *predator*. Pretending it to be a predator, you can explain his running, as well as perhaps other behavior of his. Your task is clear: to teach him that it isn't a predator, and also, perhaps, that it is prey. You see your child climb a tree and pick some fruit, and to account for that behavior you have to pretend that the fruit isn't (as you know it *is*) poisonous. It is clear what lesson you will have to impart in order to correct this dangerous behavior.

As these examples suggest, it is not correct to think (as many philosophers do) that it is exclusively or primarily the *predictive* employment of common-sense psychology that our lives, and more precisely, our inclusive fitness, depend on; and that *explanatory* success makes little or no contribution to fitness except insofar as it affects our predictions. *Explanatory* reliability is clearly important in its own right, both in explanations that cite environmental features or facts on which the behavior depends, and in explanations that cite the ignorance on which the behavior depends. It is often extremely important to be right about the environmental cause of another's action or emotion, and likewise to be right about what another, particularly a child, needs to know. Theory theorists tend to miss this point. Although they like to stress that folk psychology is much concerned with the *causes* that *explain* behavior, they also tend to identify these causes with obscure goings-on inside the black box; which leaves one to wonder why it would be of any practical consequence whether common folk get these explanations right or wrong, particularly where the wrong explanations can serve as adequate guides to correct *predictions*.

5 Imitative Mechanisms

ST (simulation theory) encourages an approach to human cognition that attends to contingent features of mammalian, more especially primate, and most especially human biology. For one thing, much of the work of simulation appears to be carried out by relatively superficial imitative mechanisms. An example is the automatic and often subliminal muscular mimicry of the bodily postures and especially the facial expressions of others, beginning with the infant's smiling response to smiles. Feedback from such 'motor mimicry' appears to be an important factor in the recognition of emotions in others. Other imitative mechanisms would seem to play an important role in ascribing *content* to the other's expressive behavior. One such mechanism is mimicry of perceptual orientation, especially gaze mimicry: When conspecifics are seen gazing intently in a particular direction, especially with a display of emotion, human beings – like other primates, apparently, and many other mammals – tend to look in the same direction, where 'same direction' may have to be determined by triangulation. By getting us to see 'through the other's eyes', this imitative mechanism facilitates identifying the situational cause or 'object' of the other's action or emotion: 'Ah, there's something moving through the bushes, *that's* why he's running', 'Ah, strange object in the sky, *that's* what startled him', 'Ah, something that looks like food over there, *that's* what she must be excited about'. The existence of such automatic aids suggests that the readiness for simulation is a prepackaged 'module' called upon automatically in the perception of conspecifics and perhaps members of other species.

The existence of such imitative mechanisms suggests a response to critics of ST who argue that one could not simulate a type of mental state such as fear unless one already had the *concept* of that state. Perhaps they will grant that *total* projection may not demand that one conceptualize what one projects, for total projection doesn't require that you take introspective note of each of your beliefs and fears and then imaginatively transfer them to the other. You transfer your beliefs in one fell swoop simply in searching the actual world for an explanation, and you project your fears by making no adjustment in what is fearful. But what of simulating a mental state *different* from your own: for example, fear, when you yourself are not afraid; or lack of fear, when you are afraid?

Part of the answer, at least, is that we have imitative mechanisms that work without such concepts. If an infant is with her mother in a strange situation, her response tends to be a copy of her mother's response: anxious or frightened if the mother displays anxiety or fright, unruffled if the mother appears calm. This well-established phenomenon clearly predates the capacity to *attribute* fear to others, as well as the capacity to fine tune the attribution to one of 'anxiety' or 'fright'. Why then should such capacities be required where the imitation is limited to the *imagination*? The ability to confine emotional contagion to the imagination may demand sophistication that comes only with greater maturity, but I see no reason to think it introduces a need for *conceptual* sophistication, as if one had to chart the contagion. Interest, as well as emotion, is contagious at a very young age. Long before the child is able to attribute to herself or another an *interest* in something, she will turn her eyes to what the other is gazing at; and at a later stage, pull up alongside another child who is studying an object on the floor. So an adult needn't use the concept of interest, in order to simulate the naturalist's interest in the behavior of wild animals, nor the concept of fear in order to simulate her lack of fear in the proximity of the grizzly. There are more complex cases (e.g. where the person one is simulating doesn't believe one way or the other), but I believe these pose no problem.

6 Using Oneself as a Model

I said earlier that some have objected that the process of simulating another person requires that the simulator himself have a theory, just the sort of theory that TT ascribes to people.[5] Some, as I noted, think the simulator himself must have a theory because they think that in order to project one's mental states, or at least in order to make imaginative *adjustments* in one's states, one first has to discriminate them, and this requires that one already have the relevant *concepts*. Paul Churchland (1989) offers a different reason for thinking the simulator himself must have a theory. Replying to my claim that simulation removes the need for a folk theory, he argues that even if simulation might successfully be used to predict another's behavior, it couldn't provide any *explanatory understanding* in the absence of a theoretical background.[6] The reason is that to use a model to explain the behavior of something else, one must be able to explain the behavior of the model itself. Thus in order to explain another's behavior by simulating the other, one must be able to discern the causes of *one's own* behavior, whether under actual or simulated conditions. But Churchland thinks this demands a framework of laws, or at least 'a moderately general *theory*'. He offers the analogy of a miniature model of the physical universe that could be manipulated to simulate real situations and thus predict and retrodict the behavior of the real universe:

> Even if my miniature unfailingly provided accurate simulations of the outcomes of real physical processes, I would still be no further ahead on the business of *explaining the behavior* of the real world. In fact, I would then have two universes, both in need of explanation. (Churchland, 1989, p. 234)

Obviously, an explanation of some phenomenon in the actual universe isn't provided simply by saying, 'It's the same as whatever explains the counterpart event in my miniature universe'. One must at least go on to *explain* the counterpart event. So, too, to use oneself as a model of another, one must be able to explain one's own behavior. And Churchland thinks that this demands a nomic framework, or at least 'a moderately general *theory*', that permits 'an appreciation of the *general patterns* that comprehend the individual events' (1989, p. 234).

The first point to be made is that Churchland appears to overlook the advantage gained by having a *manipulable* model such as his miniature universe. A manipulable model can be used to *model counterfactual conditions*. Suppose we want to find out why the Earth has so much more oxygen in its atmosphere than its immediate neighbors: More specifically, is it largely because of the presence of oxygen-emitting organisms such as plants and certain bacteria? To test this, we modify the miniature universe so that the mini-Earth does not develop such organisms: then we check the content of its atmosphere. (The test would have to be more sophisticated than this, of course. For one thing, if the high oxygen content is causally overdetermined, then this simple test might not reveal the influence of oxygen-emitting organisms. For another, it matters *how* we prevent the emergence of such organisms in our miniature: we don't want to introduce conditions that would of themselves lower the oxygen content. But any methodology for explanation would have to contend with these complications.)

We might need a theory to understand the terms used in framing the question: for example, 'oxygen' and 'organisms'. But, given the model, we don't need a theory powerful enough to *answer* the question: to tell us whether without oxygen-emitting organisms the Earth would have had a surplus of oxygen – either in the actual universe or in the model. Similarly, wind tunnel models can be used to explain as well as to predict the behavior of airplanes. To predict what the plane will do under certain conditions one observes what the model does under similar conditions. And to test competing *explanations* why the actual plane behaved as it did on some occasion, one tries to simulate the conditions and then vary them, using Mill's methods. For example, if a plane has stalled, we can simulate the stall conditions in the wind tunnel. Then, we simulate a variety of counterfactual conditions – different control configurations and wing designs, for example – using Mill's Methods, essentially, to find out how these factors affect the model's behavior. And we don't need aerodynamic theory to find this out. Thus a manipulable model, because it can be used to model counterfactual conditions, permits us to say what causes or causal factors account for the behavior of the model and thus, if we can extrapolate, permits us to say what causes or causal factors account for the behavior of whatever it is a model of. *Contra* Churchland, this task does not appear to demand a grasp of laws or a general theory comprehending the individual events. So, too, in explaining one's own behavior, it would seem that one can – without invoking or using laws or theory – simulate *in imagination* various counterfactual conditions and test their influence by methods akin to Mill's: for example, 'Imagining the animal to be a brown bear instead of a grizzly: shall I turn back?'[7] And one can perform such thought experiments not just in one's own case but also within the context of a simulation of another.

But is there perhaps an important ingredient in an adequate explanation that such counterfactual-testing alone could not provide, even if it is adequate to pick out causes or causal factors? An argument implicit in Churchland (1989) and explicit in Horgan and Tiensen (1990) is that explanation involves not only picking out causes or causal factors but 'seeing the connection' between cause and effect, understanding *why* the cause has the effect it does.

> One can know that certain facts 'made a difference' – i.e. that if those facts had not obtained, then the phenomenon being explained would not have occurred – even if one has no inkling *why* the facts made a difference . . . Explanatory understanding requires the latter kind of knowledge, not just the former. (Horgan and Tiensen, 1990, p. 276)

And for such explanatory understanding, they argue, one needs to invoke a connecting *law* or *generalization* (or at least, Churchland might add, a 'moderately general theory').

Where model airplanes and model universes are in question, Horgan and Tiensen may have a point. Even granting that we don't need aerodynamic theory to tell us that the airplane stalled because it was climbing at low throttle, such a theory may be required if we are to understand why this condition would have caused the plane to stall. (If instead one were to cite some further 'side-condition', then the theory would be needed to explain why, *given* this side-condition, the cause has the effect it has.) But just what *sort* of 'connection' between explanans and explanandum are we looking for when we want to understand why a person acted as she did? I don't think it is a nomological connection.

Consider a would-be explanation likely to cause people to complain that they 'fail to see the connection'. Your hiking companion later informs you that what had alarmed him was seeing *a tree with a rope tied around it.* You fail to see the connection: how could the fact that there was a tree there with a rope around it have made a difference, how could his turning back have depended on that? I submit that a nomological connection would be neither sufficient nor necessary for the kind of explanatory understanding you are lacking. Suppose we were to learn that turning back is *just the sort of thing all blue-eyed people do* when they see a rope around a tree: that it is just a brute-fact law of human psychology that they do this, and that it has nothing to do with the *significance* of roped trees. I for one would still be perplexed – perhaps even more than before, for now it is not just one person but many people who act in a way that I fail to comprehend.

For explanatory understanding, what one would want is background information, for example, about the significance or meaning of a roped tree: that it indicates (conventionally or as a natural sign) extreme danger, say. For if it indicated extreme danger, then the presence of a roped tree would make turning back an *attractive* option (imagined *in situ*, back there on the trail). More precisely, there being a roped tree would be a part (an *indispensable* part) of a condition sufficient in context to make turning back at least as attractive as (or less repulsive than) the available alternatives, or in any case as attractive as any that a hiker is likely to have considered at the time. It gives the act of turning back *the sort of relative attractiveness we generally see in our own actions at the time we act*. The explanatory understanding that had eluded you before is thus *empathetic* understanding.

This view is in fact much in agreement with Davidson's account of 'reason' explanations (Davidson, 1963 and elsewhere). An explanation in terms of the agent's reasons for acting should enable one to understand what features of the world made the action attractive to the agent. This requires that we see the world, and the agent's situation in it, as if through the agent's eyes.[8] The empathetic method gives us all the explanatory understanding we want; it (not a law) enables us to see the connection between explanans and explanandum. What the empathetic method does *not* furnish, according to Davidson, is what Horgan and Tiensen allow that it *does* furnish: the causal component in a 'reason' explanation, or (roughly) the stipulation that the reason 'made a difference'. Suppose the agent finds the action attractive for a number of reasons: there is always the further matter of which (one or more) of these considerations *actually* moved her to action. One wants to know not only that the agent saw something – some fact, or at least something she believed to be fact – as a reason, but also that she acted *because* of that fact. And for Davidson *this* is where laws enter in: if the 'because' is understood to indicate a causal relation, then it purports that some unspecified law or laws connect the cause with the effect under some description.

(I believe that Davidson, too, is mistaken. Just as by experimenting on a wind tunnel model one can pick out which of several conditions was actually a factor in the plane's stall, so by counterfactual testing in imagination one can (as I suggested earlier) pick out which of several candidate factors actually influenced one's action – and similarly for the actions of others, if the counterfactual testing is carried out within the context of a simulation. The generality implicit in these explanations is furnished by a counterfactual supporting rule or 'maxim' (in the Kantian sense) rather than by a law. (Such rules regulate with respect to 'content', so there is no problem of explaining how content can 'make a difference'.) I am inclined to say that the 'because' in reason explanations indicates a 'causal' relation, but not *in the same sense as* in a naturalistic explanation of, say, the tree's being split. Rather, the relation is 'causal' in the original 'primitive' sense of 'cause', as Collingwood (1946) and Strawson (1985) have urged. But I leave this complex and difficult issue to another paper.)

If I am right, then seeing the connection between explanans and explanandum in 'reason' explanations is not like seeing the connection between the airplane's climbing at low throttle and the airplane's stalling. This is one respect in which the use of models to explain and predict the behavior of an airplane or a hurricane or the universe is a poor analogue to the use of imaginative simulation to explain and predict the behavior of other agents. There are other reasons why I believe the Simulation Theory must staunchly reject the convenient '*Model*' Model of simulation, that is, the view that the simulator, whether aware of it or not, is actually using himself as an analogue or model of the other, much as one might use a wind tunnel model to simulate a real airplane or a computer model to simulate a hurricane. For the Model Model invites the objection that even if one may use a manipulable model as a device for producing explanations without using a theory, one couldn't *validate* the simulation except in terms of such a theory. The theory theorist can argue that to *justify* reliance on a model *M* in predicting and especially in explaining the behavior of a system *S*, one must assume that *M* and *S* are similar in all relevant respects, and that it takes a theory to tell us whether they are. For example, a wind tunnel model is typically built on a smaller scale than the airplane it models. It is therefore important to know whether differences in scale may affect airfoil behavior. For this purpose one needs to know a bit of aerodynamic theory. *If* mental simulation of other agents is a species of modeling similar in its essentials to the use of engineering models for purposes of prediction or explanation, then it too stands on a premise of similarity in theoretically relevant respects. Reasoning along lines similar to these, Daniel Dennett (1987, p. 101) and Paul Churchland (1989) have held that simulating in imagination presupposes a common-sense theory, and thus that the Simulation Theory isn't really a competitor to the Theory Theory. In this way the Model Model of simulation appears to support the Theory Theory of common-sense explanation and prediction.

Some defenders of a simulation account may think extrapolation from a model needn't presuppose a theory. Maybe they are right, but in any case I think the Model Model of simulation is faulty and misleading. Although no one has to my knowledge presented a clear and explicit account of the Model Model of simulation, Robert Nozick (1981, pp. 636–8) provides a clear exposition of what amounts to a Model Model of *Verstehen*, or empathetic understanding, as a method employed by the social sciences. He argues that *Verstehen* is 'a special form of inference by analogy, in that I am the thing to which [the other agent] is analogous'. One is using a model, but instead of actually manipulating conditions and seeing how the model behaves, as one might with an engineering model, one conducts a kind of thought experiment, testing in imagination how the model – oneself – would behave in the other's situation. Then one makes an inference from one's own case to the other's case. The inference thus depends on two empirical correlations, according to Nozick: 'that [the other agent] acts as I would, and that I would as I (on the basis of imaginative projection) think I would' (1981, p. 636). In short, Nozick thinks *Verstehen* is a simulation of *oneself* under counterfactual conditons, followed by an extrapolation to the other.

Nozick's clear account exposes what is wrong with the Model Model of simulating others. It is true that one does sometimes reason by analogy, letting oneself stand in for another. One asks, 'What would I do, or feel, in Jill's situation?', presuming that Jill will do or feel the same. But at those times one is not *simulating the other*. One is just identifying in imagination with *oneself* in counterfactual circumstances and then making an inference to Jill, rather than simply identifying in imagination with *Jill*. That indeed is using oneself as a model of the other. But it isn't *Verstehen*: not if *Verstehen* is a form of imaginative simulation *of another*. Nozick evidently thinks that the pronoun 'I' is a rigid designator even in pretend contexts: to imagine being in a situation is necessarily to imagine *oneself*, the particular individual, doing the simulating, in that situation. Thus in our farthest flights of vicarious imagination we can't really get outside ourselves. This can't be right. The question of how *I – this distinct individual RMG* – would actually behave in the other's situation and mental state – is not relevant. When I simulate Napoleon at Waterloo and try to explain or 'predict' his actions, the pattern of inference is not, 'This is what *RMG* would have done if *he* had been Napoleon, so probably this is what *Napoleon* did when *he* was being Napoleon.' There is no intermediate judgment about what one individual *RMG* would have done had *he actually* been a different individual, *Napoleon* – if that is even intelligible. Or suppose I imagine, not being Napoleon, but merely being Napoleonic – that is, *just like* Napoleon in personality, outlook, mental capacities, memories, and so forth. Even here, the reliability of the simulation doesn't depend on my being able to say how *RMG* would have acted had *he actually* been just like Napoleon – whatever that might mean. What *is* relevant is to ask, within a pretend context in which I simulate being Napoleon or being Napoleonic, 'What shall I do now?' The crucial difference is that in such a context 'I' and 'now' do not have their ordinary references: they do not refer, respectively, to the distinct individual doing the simulating and the distinct time he is doing it. As I suggested earlier, what remains constant is not the reference of personal pronouns (or other 'essential indexicals'), but rather the special ties they have because our perceptions, memories, actions, and emotions are keyed to our egocentric map. Thus, within the context of the simulation, the realization that *now* is the time to rout Wellington spurs me to action. And the special motivational role of *self*-concern is indexed to another self: What moves me is the fact that *I, Napoleon*, am the one to whom the insulting communiqué was addressed.

(A similar point, that to imagine being Napoleon is not to imagine an identity between two distinct individuals, is made by Zeno Vendler (1984). Unfortunately, Vendler assumes, as Nozick does, that 'I' is a rigid designator even in pretend contexts: that the term must retain the reference it has outside the pretend context, in the real world. This leads him to an extravagant conclusion: that the 'I' that gets identified with Napoleon must refer, not to the particular individual, Vendler, but to what he calls (disclaiming fidelity to Kant) a *transcendental* self: a neutral *tertium quid* that is identical with neither the simulator (Vendler) nor Napoleon. Individual subjects are, according to Vendler, nothing but *states* of the one transcendental self: the state of *being Vendler*, the state of *being Napoleon*, and so forth. This move is easily parodied, for the same issue arises with temporal and spatial indexicals in pretend contexts. For example, on November 1st I imagine it to be Christmas, and thus that 'today' is December 25th. Reasoning similar to Vendler's would force one to speak of a transcendental *time*: the 'ultimate now', neither November 1st nor December 25th. Likewise, one can be led to postulate a transcendental *place* (the 'ultimate here'). I take this to be a *reductio ad absurdum*. In any case,

Vendler's position rests on the implausible assumption that 'I' is a rigid designator in pretend contexts.)

If I am right, the simulator is not using one individual, himself, as a model of another, and there is no implicit inference of any sort from oneself to the other. The argument that a theory is needed to *justify* the (alleged) inference from oneself to the other is therefore based on a misconception. ST does really compete with TT. Or rather the two theories compete, provided *TT* is capable of standing on its own – which is dubious if, as was argued above, we must use our own decision-making system to fill in the *ceteris paribus* clause in behavioral and psychological generalizations.

The Model Model of simulation is one of the misconceptions I tried to correct in this paper. Another is that simulation is just 'putting oneself in the other's place'. I agreed that we often do not put ourselves in the other's place when we explain or predict behavior: but that isn't to say we are not simulating. When we seek to explain another's actions or emotions by searching the actual environment for salient and moving features, without imaginative adjustments, we are projecting, and projection (*total* projection) is just the default mode of simulation. I further argued that when we *depart* from total projection, we don't turn to a fundamentally non-projective basis for explanation and prediction, but rather make such adjustments in imagination as are needed to restore reliability. And I argued that ST not only accounts for the explanation of behavior, but also shows explanatory reliability to be practically important in its own right, not just as providing a basis for correct prediction.

Notes

Research for this paper was supported by a fellowship from the National Endowment for the Humanities. I thank Martin Davies and anonymous other editors and readers for helpful queries and suggestions.

1   Also, with some additional material pertaining to knowledge and the emotions, in the final chapter of Gordon (1987).

2   Adam Morton (1980), Jane Heal (1986, reprinted as ch. 1 in this volume), and Arthur Ripstein (1987) have independently made suggestions along congenial lines, though again I do not think we are in full agreement.

3   See the discussions of alarm cries in Cheney and Seyfarth (1990) and also in Wilson (1975). The hypothesis that the environmental search ends when the animal finds something that would have independently evoked an alarm response is my own. Although primatologists and primate keepers I have spoken with find it consistent with their observations, the hypothesis has not been tested.

4   Apologies to Ms Ronstadt. The example is fictional.

5   Among others, Dennett (1987) and Churchland (1989).

6   Churchland offers other, narrower objections to ST, but the one I discuss

appears to be his major objection. I should mention that since I wrote this paper Churchland has become much more sympathetic to ST, as he told me in a recent conversation.

7   I am not claiming, of course, that this method gives us a direct introspective window on one's motivation, much less that it furnishes us with infallible self-knowledge.

8   Davidson (1963) appears to assume that if x makes the action y attractive to an agent z, then x constitutes a *reason* (or a part of a reason) of z's for performing y; whereas I would allow it as a possibility that, even if z would not have performed y unless something had made y *attractive* to z or *moved* z to perform y, z performed y for no reason at all.

References

Cheney, D. L. and Seyfarth, R. M. 1990: *How Monkeys See the World*. Chicago: University of Chicago Press.

Churchland, P. M. 1989: Folk psychology and the explanation of human behaviour. In J. E. Tomberlin (ed.), *Philosophical Perspectives, Volume 3: Philosophy of Mind and Action Theory*. Atascadero, CA: Ridgeview Publishing Co. Repr. in R. Bogdan (ed.), *Mind and Common Sense*. New York: Cambridge University Press, 1989.

Collingwood, R. G. 1946: *The Idea of History*. New York: Oxford University Press.

Davidson, D. 1963: Actions, reasons, and causes. *Journal of Philosophy*, 60, 685–700.

Dennett, D. C. 1987: *The Intentional Stance*. Cambridge, Mass.: MIT Press.

Fodor, J. A. 1987: *Psychosemantics: The Problem of Meaning in the Philosophy of Mind*. Cambridge, Mass.: MIT Press.

Goldman, A. I. 1989: Interpretation psychologized. *Mind and Language*, 4, 161–85. Reprinted as ch. 3 in this volume.

Gordon, R. M. 1986a: Folk psychology as simulation. *Mind and Language*, 1, 158–71. Reprinted as ch. 2 in this volume.

Gordon, R. M. 1986b: Desire and self-intervention. *Noûs*, 20, 221–38.

Gordon, R. M. 1986c: The circle of desire. In J. Martin (ed.), *The Ways of Desire*. Chicago: Precedent, 101–14.

Gordon, R. M. 1987: *The Structure of Emotions: Investigations in Cognitive Philosophy*. Cambridge: Cambridge University Press.

Gordon, R. M. Unpublished: Fodor's intentional realism and the simulation theory.

Harris, P. 1989: *Children and Emotion: The Development of Psychological Understanding*. New York: Blackwell.

Heal, J. 1986: Replication and functionalism. In J. Butterfield (ed.), *Language, Mind, and Logic*. Cambridge: Cambridge University Press. Reprinted as ch. 1 in this volume.

Horgan, T. and Tiensen, J. 1990: Soft laws. In P. A. French, T. E. Uehling and

H. K. Wettstein (eds), *Midwest Studies in Philosophy, 15: Philosophy of the Human Sciences*, 256–79.

Morton, A. 1980: *Frames of Mind*. Oxford: Oxford University Press.

Nisbett, R. E. and Ross, L. 1980: *Human Inference: Strategies and Shortcomings of Social Judgment*. Englewood Cliffs: Prentice-Hall.

Nozick, R. 1981: *Philosophical Explanations*. Cambridge, Mass.: Harvard University Press.

Perner, J. 1991: *Understanding the Representational Mind*. Cambridge, Mass.: MIT Press.

Ripstein, A. 1987: Explanation and empathy. *Review of Metaphysics*, 40, 465–82.

Stich, S. 1983: *From Folk Psychology to Cognitive Science: The Case Against Belief*. Cambridge, Mass.: MIT Press.

Strawson, P. F. 1985: Causation and explanation. In B. Vermazen and M. B. Hintikka (eds), *Essays on Davidson: Actions and Events*. Oxford: Oxford University Press, 115–35.

Vendler, Z. 1984: *The Matter of Minds*. Oxford: Oxford University Press.

Wilson, E. O. 1975: *Sociobiology*. Cambridge, Mass.: Harvard University Press.

5
Folk Psychology: Simulation or Tacit Theory?

STEPHEN STICH AND SHAUN NICHOLS

1 Introduction

A central goal of contemporary cognitive science is the explanation of cognitive abilities or capacities (Cummins, 1983). During the last three decades a wide range of cognitive capacities have been subjected to careful empirical scrutiny. The adult's ability to produce and comprehend natural language sentences and the child's capacity to acquire a natural language were among the first to be explored (Chomsky, 1965; Fodor, Bever and Garrett, 1974; Pinker, 1989). There is also a rich literature on the ability to solve mathematical problems (Greeno, 1983), the ability to recognize objects visually (Rock, 1983; Gregory, 1970; Marr, 1982), the ability to manipulate and predict the behavior of middle-sized physical objects (McClosky, 1983; Hayes, 1985), and a host of others.

In all of this work, the dominant explanatory strategy proceeds by positing an internally represented 'knowledge structure' – typically a body of rules or principles or propositions – which serves to guide the execution of the capacity to be explained. These rules or principles or propositions are often described as the agent's 'theory' of the domain in question. In some cases, the theory may be partly accessible to consciousness; the agent can tell us some of the rules or principles he is using. More often, however, the agent has no conscious access to the knowledge guiding his behavior. The theory is 'tacit' (Chomsky, 1965) or 'sub-doxastic' (Stich, 1978). Perhaps the earliest philosophical account of this explanatory strategy is set out in Jerry Fodor's paper, 'The Appeal to Tacit Knowledge in Psychological Explanation' (Fodor, 1968). Since then, the idea has been elaborated by Dennett (1978a), Lycan (1981; 1988), and a host of others.

Among the many cognitive capacities that people manifest, there is one cluster that holds a particular fascination for philosophers. Included in this cluster is the ability to *describe* people and their behavior (including their linguistic behavior) *in intentional terms* – or to 'interpret' them, as philosophers sometimes say. We exercise this ability when we describe John as *believing that the mail has come*, or when we say that Anna *wants to go to the library*. By exploiting these intentional descriptions, people are able to offer explanations of each other's behavior (Susan left the building *because* she believed that it was on fire) and to *predict* each other's behavior, often with impressive accuracy. Since the dominant strategy for explaining any cognitive capacity is to posit an internally represented theory, it is not surprising that in this area, too, it is generally assumed that a theory is being invoked (Churchland, 1981, 1989; Fodor, 1987; Sellars, 1963; see also Olson et al., 1988). The term 'folk psychology' has been widely used as a label for the largely tacit psychological theory that underlies these abilities. During the last decade or so there has been a fair amount of empirical work aimed at describing or modeling folk psychology and tracking its emergence and development in the child (D'Andrade, 1987; Leslie, 1987; Astington et al., 1988).

Recently, however, Robert Gordon, Alvin Goldman and a number of other philosophers have offered a bold challenge to the received view about the cognitive mechanisms underlying our ability to describe, predict and explain people's behavior (Goldman, 1989; Gordon, 1986; unpublished; Montgomery, 1987; Ripstein, 1987; Heal, 1986).[1] Though they differ on the details, these philosophers agree in denying that an internally represented folk-psychological theory plays a central role in the exercise of these abilities. They also agree that a special sort of mental *simulation* in which we use ourselves as a model for the person we are describing or predicting, will play an important role in the correct account of the mechanisms subserving these abilities. In this paper, although we will occasionally mention the view of other advocates of simulation, our principal focus will be on Gordon and Goldman.

If these philosophers are right, two enormously important consequences will follow. First, of course, the dominant explanatory strategy in cognitive science, the strategy that appeals to internally represented knowledge structures, will be shown to be mistaken in at least one crucial corner of our mental lives. And if it is mistaken there, then perhaps theorists exploring other cognitive capacities can no longer simply take the strategy for granted.

To explain the second consequence we will need a quick review of one of the central debates in recent philosophy of mind. The issue in the debate is the very existence of the intentional mental states that are appealed to in our ordinary explanations of behavior – states like believing, desiring, thinking, hoping, and the rest. *Eliminativists* maintain that there really are no such things. Beliefs and desires are like phlogiston, caloric and witches; they are the mistaken posits of a radically false theory. The theory in question is 'folk psychology' – the collection of psychological principles and generalizations which, according to eliminativists (and most of their opponents) underlies our everyday explanations of behavior. The central premise in the eliminativist's argument is that neuroscience (or connectionism or cognitive science) is on the verge of demonstrating persuasively that folk psychology is false. But if Gordon and Goldman are right, they will have pulled the rug out from under the eliminativists. For if what underlies our ordinary explanatory practice is not a theory at all, then obviously it cannot be a radically false theory. There is a certain delightful irony in the Gordon/Goldman attack on eliminativism. Indeed, one might almost view it as attempting a bit of philosophical ju-jitsu. The eliminativists claim that there are no such things as beliefs and desires because the folk psychology that posits them is a radically false theory. Gordon and Goldman claim that the theory which posits a tacitly known folk psychology is *itself* radically false, since there are much better ways of explaining people's abilities to interpret and predict behavior. Thus, if Gordon and Goldman are right, *there is no such thing as folk psychology!* (Gordon, ch. 2, p. 71; Goldman, ch. 3, p. 93.)

There can be no doubt that if Gordon and Goldman are right, then the impact on both cognitive science and the philosophy of mind will be considerable. But it is a lot easier to doubt that their views about mental simulation are defensible. The remainder of this paper will be devoted to developing these doubts. Here's the game plan for the pages to follow. In sections 2 and 3, we will try to get as clear as we can on what the simulation theorists claim. We'll begin, in section 2, with an account of the special sort of simulation that lies at the heart of the Gordon/Goldman proposal. In that section our focus will be on the way that simulation might be used in the *prediction* of behavior. In section 3, we'll explore the ways in which mental simulation might be used to explain the other two cognitive capacities that have been of special interest to philosophers: *explaining* behavior and producing *intentional descriptions* or *interpretations*. We'll also consider the possibility that simulation might be used in explaining the *meaning* of intentional terms like 'believes', and 'desires'. Since the accounts of simulation that Gordon and Goldman have offered have been a bit sketchy, there will be a lot of filling in to do in sections 2 and 3. But throughout both sections, our goal will be sympathetic interpretation; we've tried hard not to build straw men. In the following two sections, our stance turns critical. In section 4, we will do our best to assemble all the arguments offered by Gordon and Goldman in support of their simulation theory, and to explain why none of them are convincing. In section 5 we will offer two arguments of our own, aimed at showing why, in light of currently available evidence, the simulation theory is very implausible indeed. Section 6 is a brief conclusion.

2 Predicting Behavior: Theory, Simulation and Imagination

Suppose that you are an aeronautical engineer and that you want to predict how a newly built plane will behave at a certain speed. There are two rather different ways in which you might proceed. One way is to sit down with pencil and paper, a detailed set of specifications of the plane, and a state of the art textbook on aerodynamic theory, and try to calculate what the theory entails about the behavior of the plane. Alternatively, you could build a model of the plane, put it in a wind tunnel, and observe how it behaves. You have to use a bit of theory in this second strategy, of course, since you have to have some idea which properties of the plane you want to duplicate in your model. But there is a clear sense in which a theory is playing the central role in the first prediction and a model or simulation is playing a central role in the second.[2]

Much the same story could be told if what you want to do is predict the behavior of a person. Suppose, for example, you want to predict what a certain rising young political figure would do if someone in authority tells him to administer painful electric shocks to a person strapped in a chair in the next room. One approach is to gather as much data as you can about the history and personality of the politician and then consult the best theory available on the determinants of behavior under such circumstances. Another approach is to set up a Milgram-style experiment and observe how some other people behave. Naturally, it would be a good idea to find experimental subjects who are psychologically similar to the political figure whose behavior you are trying to predict. Here, as before, theory plays a central role in the first prediction, while a simulation plays a central role in the second.

In both the aeronautical case and the psychological case, we have been supposing that much of the predicting process is carried on outside the predictor. You do your calculations on a piece of paper; your simulations are done in wind tunnels or laboratories. But, of course, it will often be possible to internalize this process. The case is clearest when a theory is being used. Rather than looking in a textbook, you could memorize the theory, and rather than doing the calculations on a piece of paper, you could do them in your head. Moreover, it seems entirely possible that you could learn the theory so well that you are hardly conscious of using it or of doing any explicit calculation or reasoning. Indeed, this, near enough, is the standard story about a wide variety of cognitive capacities.

A parallel story might be told for predictions using simulations. Rather than building a model and putting it in a wind tunnel, you could *imagine* the model in the wind tunnel and see how your imaginary model behaves. Similarly, you could *imagine* putting someone in a Milgram-style laboratory and see how your imaginary subject behaves. But obviously there is a problem lurking here. For while it is certainly possible to imagine a plane in a wind tunnel, it is not at all clear how you could successfully imagine the behavior of the plane unless you had a fair amount of detailed information about the behavior of planes in situations like this one. When the simulation uses a real model plane, the world tells you how the model will behave. You just have to look and see. But when you are only imagining the simulation, there is no real model for you to look at. So it seems that you must have an internalized knowledge structure to guide your imagination. The theory or knowledge structure that you are exploiting may, of course, be a tacit one, and you may be quite unaware that you are using it. But unless we suppose your imagination is guided by some systematic body of information about the behavior of planes in situations like this one, the success of your prediction would be magic.

When you are imagining the behavior of a person, however, there are various ways in which the underlying system might work. One possibility is that imagining the behavior of a person is entirely parallel to imagining the behavior of a plane. In both cases your imagination is guided by a largely tacit theory or knowledge structure. But there is also a very different mechanism that might be used. In the plane case, you don't have a real plane to observe, so you have to rely on some stored information about planes. You do, however, have a real, human cognitive system to observe – your own. Here's a plausible, though obviously over-simplified, story about how that system normally works:

> At any given time you have a large store of beliefs and desires. Some of the beliefs are derived from perception, others from inference. Some of the desires (like the desire to get a drink) arise from systems monitoring bodily states, others (like the desire to go into the kitchen) are 'sub-goals' generated by the decision-making (or 'practical reasoning') system. The decision-making system, which takes your beliefs and desires as input, does more than generate sub-goals, it also somehow or other comes up with a decision about what to do. That decision is then passed on to the 'action controllers' – the mental mechanisms responsible for sequencing and coordinating the behavior necessary to carry out the decision. (Rendered boxologically, the account just sketched appears in figure 5.1.)

Now suppose that it is possible to take the decision making system 'off-line' by disengaging the connection between the system and the action controllers. You might then use it to generate decisions that you are not about to act on. Suppose further that in this off-line mode, you can feed the decision-making system some hypothetical or 'pretend' beliefs and desires – beliefs and desires that you do not actually have, but that the person whose behavior you're trying to predict does. If all this were possible, you could then sit back and let the system generate a decision. Moreover, if your decision-making system is similar to the one in the person whose behavior you're trying to predict, and if the hypothetical beliefs and desires you've fed into your system off-line are close to the ones that he has, then the decision that your system generates will often be similar to the one that his system generates. There is no need for a special internalized knowledge structure here; no tacit folk-psychological theory is being used. Rather, you are using (part of) your own cognitive mechanism as a model for (part of) his. Moreover, just as in the case where the prediction exploits a theory, this whole process may be largely unconscious. It may be that all you are aware of is the prediction itself. Alternatively, if you consciously imagine what the target of your prediction will do, it could well be the case that your imagination is guided by this simulation rather than by some internally represented psychological theory.

We now have at least the outline of an account of how mental simulation might be used in predicting another person's behavior. An entirely parallel

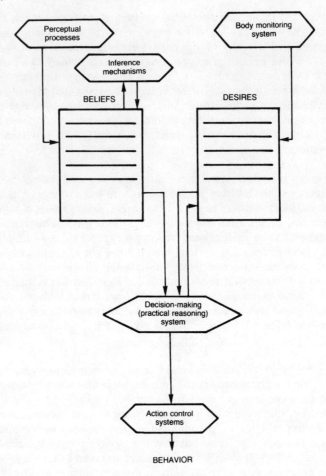

Figure 5.1

story can be told about predicting our own behavior under counterfactual circumstances. If, for example, I want to know what I would do if I believed that there was a burglar in the basement, I can simply take my decision-making system off-line and provide it with the pretend belief that there is a burglar in the basement.[3]

In the next section we'll try to get clear on how this process of simulation might be used in explaining various other cognitive capacities. But before attending to that task, we would do well to assemble a few quotes to confirm our claim that the story we've told is very close to the one that those we'll be criticizing have in mind. Gordon is much more explicit than Goldman on the use of simulation in prediction. Here's a passage from his 1986 paper (this volume, p. 70):

> [O]ur decision-making or practical reasoning system gets partially disengaged from its 'natural' inputs and fed instead with suppositions and images (or their 'subpersonal' or 'sub-doxastic' counterparts). Given these artificial pretend inputs the system then 'makes up its mind' what to do. Since the system is being run off-line, as it were, disengaged also from its natural output systems, its 'decision' isn't actually executed but rather ends up as an anticipation . . . of the other's behavior.

And another, this time from an unpublished manuscript contrasting his view to Fodor's:

> The Simulation Theory as I present it holds that we explain and predict behavior not by applying a theory but simply by exercising a skill that has two components: the capacity for practical reasoning – roughly, for making decisions on the basis of facts and values – and the capacity to introduce 'pretend' facts and values into one's decision-making typically to adjust for relevant differences in situation and past behavior. One predicts what the other will decide to do by making a decision oneself – a 'pretend' decision, of course, made only in imagination – after making such adjustments. (Gordon, unpublished, p. 3)

Gordon later suggests that the capacity to simulate in this way may be largely innate:

> [Evidence] suggests that the readiness for simulation is a prepackaged 'module' called upon automatically in the perception of other human beings.[4] It suggests also that supporting and complementing the conscious, reportable procedure we call putting ourselves in the other's place, those neural systems that are responsible for the formation of emotions and intentions are, often without our knowledge, allowed to run off-line: They are partially disengaged from their 'natural' inputs from perception and memory and fed artificial pretend inputs; uncoupled also from their natural output systems, they terminate not as intentions and emotions but as anticipations of, or perhaps just unconscious motor adjustments to, the other's intentions, emotions, behavior. (Gordon, unpublished, p. 5)

3 Other Uses for Simulation: Explanation, Interpretation and the Meaning of Intentional Terms

Let's turn, now, to people's ability to offer *intentional explanations* of other people's actions. How might mental simulation be used to account for that ability? Consider, for example, a case similar to one proposed by Gordon.[5] We are seated at a restaurant and someone comes up to us and starts speaking to us in a foreign language. How might simulation be exploited in producing an intentional explanation for that behavior?

One proposal, endorsed by both Gordon and Goldman, begins with the fact that simulations can be used in predictions, and goes on to suggest that intentional explanations can be generated by invoking something akin to the strategy of analysis-by-synthesis. In using simulations to predict behavior, hypothetical beliefs and desires are fed into our own decision-making system (being used 'off-line' of course), and we predict that the agent would do what we would decide to do, given those beliefs and desires. A first step in *explaining* a behavioral episode that has already occurred is to see if we can find some hypothetical beliefs and desires which, when fed into our decision mechanism, will produce a decision to perform the behavior we want to explain.

Generally, of course, there will be *lots* of hypothetical beliefs and desires that might lead us to the behavior in question. Here are just a few:

(a) If we believe someone only speaks a certain foreign language and we want to ask him something, then we would decide to speak to him in that language.
(b) If we want to impress someone and we believe that speaking in a foreign language will impress him, then we will decide to speak to him in that language.
(c) If we believe that speaking to someone in a foreign language will make him laugh, and if we want to make him laugh, then we will decide to speak to him in that language.

And so on. Each of these simulation-based predictions provides the kernel for a possible explanation of the behavior we are trying to explain. To decide among these alternative explanations, we must determine which of the input belief/desire pairs is most plausibly attributed to the agent. Some belief/desire pairs will be easy to exclude. Perhaps the agent is a dour fellow; he never wants to make anyone laugh. If we believe this to be the case, then (c) won't be very plausible. In other cases we can use information about the agent's perceptual situation to assess the likelihood of various beliefs. If Mary has just made a rude gesture directly in front of the agent, then it is likely the agent will believe that Mary has insulted him. If the rude gesture was made behind the agent's back, then it is not likely he will believe that she has insulted him. In still other cases, we may have some pre-existing knowledge of the agent's beliefs and desires. But, as both Goldman and Gordon note, it will often be the case that there are lots of alternative explanations that can't be excluded on the basis of evidence about the agent's circumstances or his history. In these cases, Goldman maintains, we simply assume that the agent is psychologically similar to us – we attribute beliefs that are 'natural for us' (Goldman, this volume, p. 90) and reject (or perhaps do not even consider) hypotheses attributing beliefs that we consider to be less natural (pp. 90–1). Gordon tells much the same story (this volume, p. 65):[6]

> No matter how long I go on testing hypotheses, I will not have tried out *all* candidate explanations of the [agent's] behavior. Perhaps some of the unexamined candidates would have done at least as well as the one I settle for, if I settle: perhaps indefinitely many of them would have. But these would be 'far fetched', I say intuitively. Therein I exhibit my inertial bias. The less 'fetching' (or 'stretching', as actors say) I have to do to track the other's behavior, the better. I tend to *feign* only when necessary, only when something in the other's behavior doesn't fit. This inertial bias may be thought of as a 'least effort' principle: the 'principle of least pretending'. It explains why, other things being equal, I will prefer the less radical departure from the 'real' world – i.e. from what I myself take to be the world.[6]

Though the views endorsed by Gordon and Goldman are generally very similar, the two writers do differ in their emphasis. For Gordon, prediction and explanation loom large, while for Goldman, the capacity to *interpret* people, or to describe them in intentional terms, is given pride of place. Part of the story Goldman tells about simulation-based intentional description relies on the account of simulation-based explanation that we have just sketched. One of the ways we determine which beliefs and desires to attribute to people is by observing their behavior and then attributing the intentional states that best explain their behavior. A second simulation-based strategy for determining which beliefs and desires to attribute focuses on the agent's perceptual situation and on his or her 'basic likings or cravings' (Goldman, this volume, p. 82):

> From your perceptual situation, I infer that you have certain perceptual experiences or beliefs, the same ones I would have in your situation. I may also assume (pending information to the contrary) that you have the same basic likings that I have: for food, love, warmth, and so on.

As we read them, there is only one important point on which Gordon and Goldman actually *dis*agree. The accounts of simulation-based prediction, explanation and interpretation that we have sketched all seem to require that the person doing the simulating must already understand intentional notions like belief and desire. A person can't pretend he believes that the cookies are in the cookie jar unless he understands what it is to believe that the cookies are in the cookie jar; nor can a person imagine that she wants to make her friend laugh unless she understands what it is to want to make someone laugh. Moreover, as Goldman notes, when simulation is used to attribute intentional states to agents, it 'assumes a prior understanding of what state it is that the interpreter attributes to [the agent]' (Goldman, this volume, p. 94). Can the process of simulation somehow be used to explain the meaning or truth conditions of locutions like '*S* believes that *p*' and '*S* desires that *q*'? Goldman is skeptical, and tells us that 'the simulation theory looks distinctly unpromising on this score' (this volume, p. 93). But Gordon is much more sanguine. Building on earlier suggestions by Quine, Davidson and Stich, he proposes the following account (Gordon, this volume, p. 68):

> My suggestion is that
>   (2) [*Smith believes that* Dewey won the election]
> to be read as saying the same thing as
>   (1) [Let's do a Smith simulation. Ready? *Dewey won the election*]
> though less explicitly.

We are not at all sure we understand this proposal, and Gordon himself concedes that 'the exposition and defense of this account of belief are much in need of further development' (this volume, p. 68). But no matter. We think we do understand the simulation-based accounts of prediction, explanation and interpretation that Gordon and Goldman both endorse. We're also pretty certain that none of these accounts is correct. In the sections that follow, we will try to say why.

4 Arguments in Support of Simulation-based Accounts

In this section we propose to assemble all the arguments we've been able to find in favor of simulation-based accounts and say why we don't think any of them is persuasive. Then, in the following section, we will go on to offer some arguments of our own aimed at showing that there is lots of evidence that simulation-based accounts cannot easily accommodate, though more traditional theory-based accounts can. Before turning to the arguments, however, we would do well to get a bit clearer about the questions that the arguments are (and are not) intended to answer.

The central idea in the accounts offered by Gordon and Goldman is that in predicting, explaining or interpreting other people we simulate them by using part of *our own* cognitive systems 'off-line'. There might, of course, be other kinds of simulation in which we do not exploit our own decision-making system in order to model the person we are simulating. But these other sorts of simulation are not our current concern. To avoid confusion, we will henceforth use the term *off-line simulation* for the sort of simulation that Gordon and Goldman propose. The question in dispute, then, is whether off-line simulation plays a central role in predicting, explaining or interpreting other people. Gordon and Goldman say yes; we say no.

It would appear that the only serious alternatives to the off-line simulation story are various versions of the 'theory-theory' which maintain that prediction, explanation and interpretation exploit an internally represented theory or knowledge structure – a tacitly known 'folk psychology'. So if an advocate of off-line simulation can mount convincing arguments against the theory-theory, then he can reasonably claim to have made his case. The theory-theory is not the only game in town, but it is the only *other* game in town. It is not surprising, then, that in defending off-line simulation Gordon and Goldman spend a fair amount of time raising objections to the theory-theory.

There are, however, some important distinctions to be drawn among different types of theory-theories. Until fairly recently, most models that aimed at explaining cognitive capacities posited internally represented knowledge structures that invoked explicit rules or explicit sentence-like principles. But during the last decade there has been a growing dissatisfaction with sentence-based and rule-based knowledge structures, and a variety of alternatives have been explored. Perhaps the most widely discussed alternatives are connectionist models in which the knowledge used in making predictions is stored in the connection strengths between the nodes of a network. In many of these systems it is difficult or impossible to view the network as encoding a set of sentences or rules (Ramsey, Stich and Garon, 1990). Other theorists have proposed quite different ways in which non-sentential and non-rule-like strategies could be used to encode information. (See, for example, Johnson-Laird, 1983.)

Unfortunately, there is no terminological consensus in this domain. Some writers prefer to reserve the term 'theory' for sentence-like or rule-based systems. For these writers, most connectionist models do not invoke what they would call an internally represented theory. Other writers are more liberal in their use of 'theory', and are prepared to count just about any internally stored body of information about a given domain as an internally represented theory of that domain. For these writers, connectionist models and other non-sentential models do encode a tacit theory. We don't think there is any substantive issue at stake here. But the terminological disagreements can generate a certain amount of confusion. Thus, for example, someone who used 'theory' in the more restrictive way might well conclude that if a connectionist (or some other non-sentence-based) account of our ability to predict other people's behavior turns out to be the right one, then the theory-theory is mistaken. So far, so good. But it is important to see that the falsity of the theory-theory (narrowly construed) is no comfort at all to the off-line simulation theorist. The choice between off-line simulation theories and theory-theories is plausibly viewed as exhaustive only when 'theory' is used in the *wide* rather than the restrictive way. For the remainder of this paper, we propose to adopt the wide interpretation of 'theory'. Using this terminology, the geography of the options confronting us is represented in figure 5.2.[7] In the pages that follow, we will be defending option (A) in answer to Question (I). We take no stand at all on Question (II). So much for getting clear on the questions. Now let's turn to the arguments.

Argument 1: No one has been able to state the principles of the internally represented folk-psychological theory posited by the theory-theory.

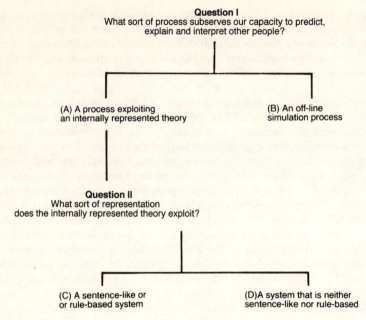

Figure 5.2

Both Goldman and Gordon go on at some length about the fact that it has proven very difficult to state the principles or laws of the folk psychological theory that, according to the theory-theorist, guide our interpretations and predictions (Goldman, 1989, p. 167 of original version):

> [A]ttempts by philosophers to articulate the putative laws or 'platitudes' that comprise our folk theory have been notably weak. Actual illustrations of such laws are sparse in number; and when examples are adduced, they commonly suffer from one of two defects: vagueness and inaccuracy . . . But why, one wonders, should it be so difficult to articulate laws if we appeal to them all the time in our interpretative practice? (See also Gordon, this volume, p. 67; and unpublished, sec. 3.7.)

Reply: Goldman is certainly right about one thing. It is indeed very difficult to articulate the principles of folk psychology precisely and accurately. But it is hard to see why this fact should be of any comfort to advocates of the off-line simulation theory. For much the same could be said about the knowledge structures underlying all sorts of cognitive capacities. It has proven enormously difficult to state the principles underlying a speaker's capacity to judge the grammaticality of sentences in his language. Indeed, after three decades of sustained effort, we don't have a good grammar for even a single natural language. Nor do we have a good account of the principles underlying people's everyday judgements about the behavior of middle-sized physical objects, or about their ability to solve mathematical problems, or about their ability to play chess, etc. But, of course, in all of these domains, the theory-theory really is the only game in town. The off-line simulation story makes no sense as an account of our ability to judge grammaticality, or of our ability to predict the behavior of projectiles.

The difficulties encountered by those who have sought to describe the rules or principles underlying our grammatical (or mathematical or physical) abilities have convinced a growing number of theorists that our knowledge in these domains is not stored in the form of rules or principles. That conviction has been an important motive for the development of connectionist and other sorts of non-sentential and non-rule-based models. But none of this should encourage an advocate of the off-line simulation theory. The dispute between connectionist models and rule-based models is the dispute between (C) and (D) in figure 5.2. And that is a dispute *among theory-theorists*. Of course on a narrow interpretation of 'theory', on which only rule-based and sentence-based models count as theories, the success of connectionism would indeed show that the 'theory-theory' is mistaken. But, as we have taken pains to note, a refutation of the theory-theory will support the off-line simulation account only when 'theory' is interpreted broadly.

Argument 2: Mental simulation models have been used with some success by a number of cognitive scientists.

Here's how Goldman makes the point (this volume, p. 86):

> [S]everal cognitive scientists have recently endorsed the idea of mental simulation as one cognitive heuristic, although these researchers stress its use for knowledge in general, not specifically knowledge of others' mental states. Kahneman and Tversky (1982) propose that people often try to answer questions about the world by an operation that resembles the running of a simulation model. The starting condition for a 'run', they say, can either be left at realistic default values or modified to assume some special contingency. Similarly, Rumelhart [et al.] describe the importance of 'mental models' of the world, in particular, models that simulate how the world would respond to one's hypothetical actions.

Reply: Here, again, it is our suspicion that ambiguity between the two interpretations of 'theory' is lurking in the background and leading to mischief. The 'simulation' models that Goldman cites are the sort that would be classified under (D) in figure 5.2. If they are used in the best explanation of a given cognitive capacity, then that capacity is subserved by a tacit theory, and *not* by an off-line simulation. Of course when 'theory' is read narrowly, this sort of simulation will not count as a tacit theory. But, as already noted, on the narrow reading of 'theory' the falsity of internalized theory accounts lends no support at all to the off-line simulation theory.

Argument 3: 'To apply the alleged common-sense theory would demand anomalous precocity.'

What we've just quoted is a section heading in one of Gordon's unpublished papers.[8] He goes on to note that recent studies have shown children as young as two and a half 'already see behavior as dependent on belief and desire'. It is, he suggests, more than a bit implausible that children this young could acquire and use 'a theory as complex and sophisticated' as the one that the theory-theory attributes to them. Goldman elaborates the argument as follows (this volume, p. 80):

> [C]hildren seem to display interpretive skills by the age of four, five or six. If interpretation is indeed guided by laws of folk psychology, the latter must be known (or believed) by this age. Are such children sophisticated enough to represent such principles? And how, exactly, would they acquire them? One possible mode of acquisition is cultural transmission (e.g. being taught them explicitly by their elders). This is clearly out of the question, though, since only philosophers have even tried to articulate the laws, and most children have no exposure to philosophers. Another possible mode of acquisition is private construction. Each child constructs the generalizations for herself, perhaps taking clues from verbal explanations of behavior which she hears. But if this construction is supposed to occur along the lines of familiar modes of scientific theory construction, some anomalous things must take place. For one thing, all children miraculously construct the same nomological principles. This is what the (folk-) theory theory ostensibly implies, since it imputes a single folk psychology to everyone. In normal cases of hypothesis construction, however, different scientists come up with different theories.

Reply: There is no doubt that if the theory-theory is right, then the child's feat is indeed an impressive one. Moreover, it is implausible to suppose that the swift acquisition of folk psychology is subserved by the same learning mechanism that the child uses to learn history or chemistry or astronomy. But, once again, we find it hard to see how this can be taken as an argument against the theory-theory and in favor of the off-line simulation theory. For there are other cases in which the child's accomplishment is comparably impressive and comparably swift. If contemporary generative grammar is even *close* to being right, the knowledge structures that underlie a child's linguistic ability are enormously complex. Yet children seem to acquire the relevant knowledge structures even more quickly than they acquire their knowledge of folk psychology. Moreover, children in the same linguistic community all acquire much the same grammar, despite being exposed to significantly different samples of what will become their native language. Less is known about the knowledge structures underlying children's abilities to anticipate the behavior of middle-sized physical objects. But there is every reason to suppose that this 'folk physics' is at least as complex as folk psychology, and that it is acquired with comparable speed. Given the importance of all three knowledge domains, it is plausible to suppose that natural selection has provided the child with lots of help – either in the form of innate knowledge structures or in the form of special-purpose learning mechanisms. But whatever the right story about acquisition turns out to be, it is perfectly clear that in the case of grammar, and in the case of folk physics, what is acquired must be some sort of internally represented theory. Off-line simulation could not possibly account for our skills in those domains. Since the speed of language acquisition and the complexity of the knowledge acquired do not (indeed, could not) support an off-line simulation account of linguistic ability, we fail to see why Gordon and Goldman think that considerations of speed and complexity lend any support at all to the off-line simulation account for our skills in predicting, explaining and interpreting behavior.

Argument 4: The off-line simulation theory is much simpler than the theory-theory.

Other things being equal, we should surely prefer a simple theory to a more complex one. And on Gordon's view (unpublished, sec. 3, p. 7):

> the simulation alternative makes [the theory-theory] strikingly unparsimonious. Insofar as the store of causal generalizations posited by [the theory-theory] mirrors the set of rules *our own* thinking typically conforms to, the Simulation Theory renders it altogether otiose. For whatever rules our own thinking typically conforms to, our thinking continues to conform to them within the context of simulation . . . In the light of this far simpler alternative, the hypothesis that people must be endowed with a special stock of laws corresponding to rules of logic and reasoning is unmotivated and unparsimonious.

Reply: When comparing the simplicity of a pair of theories, it is important to look at the whole theory in both cases, not just at isolated parts. It is our contention that if one takes this broader perspective, the greater parsimony of the simulation theory simply disappears. To see the point, note that for both the theory-theory and the simulation theory the mechanism subserving our predictions of other people's behavior must have two components. One of these may be thought of as a data base that somehow stores or embodies information about how people behave. The other component is a mechanism which applies that information to the case at hand – it extracts the relevant facts from the data base. Now if we look only at the data base, it does indeed seem that the theory-theory is 'strikingly unparsimonious' since it must posit an elaborate system of internally represented generalizations or rules – or perhaps some other format for encoding the regularities of folk psychology. The simulation theory, by contrast, uses the mind's decision-making system as its 'data base', and that decision-making system would have to be there on any theory, because it explains how we make real, 'on-line' decisions. So the off-line simulation theory gets its data base for free.

But now let's consider the other component of the competing theories. Merely *having* a decision-making system will not enable us to make predictions about other people's behavior. We also need the capacity to take that system 'off-line', feed it 'pretend' inputs and interpret its outputs as predictions about how someone else would behave. When we add the required cognitive apparatus, the picture of the mind that emerges is sketched in figure 5.3. Getting this 'control mechanism' to work smoothly is sure to be a *very* non-trivial task. How do things look in the case of the theory-theory? Well, no matter how we go about making predictions about other people, it is clear that in making predictions about physical systems we can't use the off-line simulation strategy; we have to use some sort of internalized theory (though, of course, it need not be a sentence-like or rule-based theory). Thus we know that the mind is going to have to have some mechanism for extracting information from internalized theories and applying it to particular cases. (In figure 5.1 we have assumed that this mechanism is housed along with the other 'inference mechanisms' that are used to extract information from pre-existing beliefs.) If such a mechanism will work for an internally represented folk physics, it is plausible to suppose that, with minor modifications, it will also work for an internally represented folk psychology. So while the simulation theorist gets the data base for free, it looks like the theory-theorist gets the 'control mechanism' for free. All of this is a bit fast and loose, of course. But we don't think either side of this argument can get much more precise until we are presented with up-and-running models to compare. Until then, neither side can gain much advantage by appealing to simplicity.

Argument 5: When we introspect about our predictions of other people's behavior, it sometimes seems that we proceed by imagining how we would behave in their situation.

Here is how Goldman makes the point (this volume, p. 82):

> The simulation idea has obvious initial attractions. Introspectively, it seems as if we often try to predict others' behavior – or predict their (mental) choices – by imagining ourselves in their shoes and determining what we would choose to do.

And here is Gordon (this volume, p. 63):

> [C]hess players report that, playing against a human opponent or even against a computer, they visualize the board from the other side, taking the opposing pieces for their own and vice versa. Further, they pretend

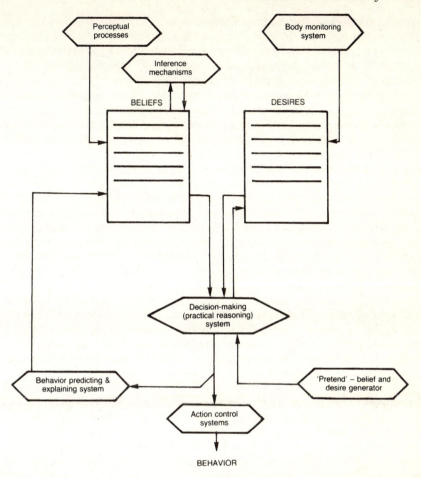

Figure 5.3

that their reasons for action have shifted accordingly ... Thus transported in imagination, they 'make up their mind what to do'.

Both authors are aware that appeal to introspection can be a two-edged sword, since it also often happens that we predict other people's behavior *without* introspecting any imaginary behavior (Goldman, this volume, p. 87):

[T]here is a straightforward challenge to the psychological plausibility of the simulation approach. It is far from obvious, introspectively, that we regularly place ourselves in another person's shoes, and vividly envision what we would do in his circumstances.

And (Gordon, this volume, p. 72 n. 4):

> Imagery is not always needed in such simulations. For example, I need
> no imagery to simulate having a million dollars in the bank.

To deal with this 'challenge', Goldman proposes a pair of replies. First, simulation need not always be introspectively vivid. It can often be 'semi-automatic, with relatively little salient phenomenology'. Second, not all
interpretations rely on simulation. In many cases interpreters rely solely on
'inductively acquired information' though the information is 'historically derived from earlier simulations' (this volume, pp. 87–8).

Reply: We don't propose to make any fuss at all about the frequent absence of
'salient phenomenology'. For it is our contention that when the issue at hand
is the nature of the cognitive mechanism subserving our capacity to interpret
and predict other people's behavior, the entire issue of introspective imagination is a red herring. Indeed, it is *two* red herrings. To see the first of them,
consider one of the standard examples used to illustrate the role of imagery in
thought. Suppose we ask you: 'How many windows are there in your house?'
How do you go about answering? Almost everyone reports that they *imagine*
themselves walking from room to room, counting the windows as they go.
What follows from this about the cognitive mechanism that they are exploiting? Well, one thing that surely *does not* follow is that off-line simulation is
involved. The *only* way that people could possibly answer the question accurately is to tap into some internally represented store of knowledge about
their house; it simply makes no sense to suppose that off-line simulation is
being used here. So even if a cognitive process is *always* accompanied by vivid
imagery, that is no reason at all to suppose that the process exploits off-line
simulation. From this we draw the obvious conclusion. The fact that prediction and interpretation *sometimes* involve imagining oneself in the other
person's shoes is less than no reason at all to suppose that off-line simulation
is involved.

It might be suggested that, though imagery provides no support for the off-
line simulation hypothesis, it does challenge the theory-theory when 'theory'
is interpreted narrowly. For it shows that some of the information we are
exploiting in interpretation and prediction is not stored in the form of sentences or rules. But even this is far from obvious. There is a lively debate in the
imagery literature in which 'descriptionalists', like Pylyshyn and Dennett,
maintain that the mechanisms underlying mental imagery exploit language-
like representations, while 'pictorialists', like Kosslyn and Fodor, argue that
images are subserved by a separate, non-linguistic sort of representation
(Pylyshyn, 1981; Dennett 1969, 1978b; Fodor, 1975; Kosslyn, 1981). We don't
propose to take sides in this dispute. For present purposes it is sufficient to
note that, unless it is supplemented by a persuasive argument in favor of
pictorialism and against descriptionism, the introspective evidence does not
even challenge the theory-theory *construed narrowly*.

Argument 6: The off-line simulation account is supported by recent experimental studies focusing on children's acquisition of the ability to interpret and predict other people.

On our view, this is far and away the most interesting argument that has been offered in favor of the off-line simulation theory. To see exactly what the experimental studies do, and do not, support, we'll have to look at both the evidence and the argument with considerable care. Gordon does a good job of describing one important set of experiments (this volume, pp. 68–9):

> Very young children give verbal expression to predictions and explanations of the behavior of others. Yet up to about the age of four they evidently lack the concept of belief, or at least the capacity to make allowances for false or differing beliefs. Evidence of this can be teased out by presenting children with stories and dramatizations that involve dramatic irony: where we the audience know something important the protagonist doesn't know . . .
>
> In one such story (illustrated with puppets) the puppet-child Maxi puts his chocolate in the box and goes out to play. While he is out, his mother transfers the chocolate to the cupboard. Where will Maxi look for the chocolate when he comes back? In the box, says the five-year-old, pointing to the miniature box on the puppet stage: a good prediction of a sort we ordinarily take for granted . . . But the child of three to four years has a different response: verbally or by pointing, the child indicates the cupboard. (That is, after all, where the chocolate is to be found, isn't it?) Suppose Maxi wants to mislead his gluttonous big brother to the *wrong* place, where will he lead him? The five-year-old indicates the cupboard, where (unbeknownst to Maxi) the chocolate actually is . . . The *younger* child indicates, incorrectly, the box.

These results, Gordon maintains, are hard to square with the theory-theory. For if the theory-theory is correct, then (pp. 69–70):

> before internalizing [the laws and generalizations of folk psychology] the child would simply be unable to predict or explain human action. And *after* internalizing the system, the child could deal indifferently with actions caused by *true* beliefs and actions caused by *false* beliefs. If is hard to see how the semantical question could be relevant.

But, according to Gordon, these data are just what we should expect, if the off-line simulation theory is correct (Gordon, unpublished, sec. 3.6, p. 11):

> The Simulation Theory [predicts that] prior to developing the capacity to simulate others for purposes of prediction and explanation, a child will make *egocentric errors* in predicting and explaining the actions of others. She will predict and explain as if whatever she herself counts as

'fact' were also fact to the other; which is to say, she fails to make allowances in her predictions and explanations for false beliefs or for what the other isn't in a position to know.

Reply: According to Gordon, the theory-theory can't easily explain the results of the 'Maxi' experiment, though the off-line simulation theory predicts those results. We're not convinced on either score. Let's look first at just what the off-line simulation story would lead us to expect.

Presumably by the time any of these experiments can be conducted, the child has developed a more or less intact decision-making system like the one depicted in figure 5.1. That system makes 'on-line' decisions and thus determines the child's actions on the basis of her actual beliefs and desires. But by itself it provides the child with no way of predicting Maxi's behavior or anyone else's. If the off-line simulation theory is right, then in order to make predictions about other people's behavior two things must happen. First, the child must acquire the ability to take the output of the decision-making system off-line – treating its decisions as predictions or expectations, rather than simply feeding them into the action controlling system. Second, the child must acquire the ability to provide the system with input other than her own actual beliefs and desires. She must be able to supply the system with 'pretend' input so that she can predict the behavior of someone whose beliefs and desires are different from her own. (These are the two capacities that are represented in figure 5.3 and absent in figure 5.1.) There is, of course, no a priori reason to suppose that these two steps happen at different times, nor that the one we've listed first will occur first. But if they do occur in that order, then we might expect there to be a period when the child could predict her own behavior (or the behavior of someone whose beliefs and desires are the same as hers), though she could not predict the behavior of people whose beliefs or desires are different from hers. It is less clear what to expect if the steps occur in the opposite order. Perhaps the result would be some sort of pretending or play-acting – behaving in a way that someone with different beliefs or desires would behave. Though until the child develops the capacity to take the output of the decision-making system off-line, she will not be able to predict other people's behavior or her own. So it looks like the off-line simulation story makes room for three possible developmental scenarios.

(1) The child acquires both abilities at the same time. In this case we would expect to see two developmental stages. In the first the child can make no predictions. In the second she can make a full range of predictions about people whose beliefs and desires are different from her own.
(2) The child first acquires the ability to take the output off-line, and then acquires the ability to provide the system with pretend input. In this case we would expect three developmental stages. In the first, the child can make no predictions. In the second, she can only make predictions about her own behavior or about the behavior of people whose beliefs and

desires are identical to hers. In the third, she can make the full range of predictions.

(3) The child first acquires the ability to provide the system with pretend inputs, and then acquires the ability to take the output off-line. In this case, too, we would expect three developmental stages. The first and last stages are the same as those in (2), but in the middle stage the child can play-act but not make predictions.

Now let's return to the Maxi experiment. Which of these developmental scenarios do the children in these experiments exhibit? At first blush, it might be thought that the pattern Gordon reports is much the same as the one set out in scenario (2). But that would be a mistake. The younger children – those who are giving the wrong answers – are not predicting that Maxi would do what someone with their own beliefs and desires would do. For they have no desire to get the chocolate, nor to deceive the gluttonous brother. Those are *Maxi's* desires, not *theirs*. If anything, it would appear that these children are half-way between the second and third stages of scenario (2): they can feed 'pre-tend' desires into the decision-making system, but not 'pretend' beliefs. Of course none of this shows that the off-line simulation theory is false. It is perfectly compatible with the theory to suppose that development proceeds as in (2), *and* that the transition from the second to the third stage proceeds in two sub-stages – desires first, and then beliefs. (This pattern is sketched in figure 5.4.) But it is, to say the least, something of an exaggeration to say that the off-line simulation theory 'predicts' the experimental results. The most that can be said is that the theory is compatible with the observed develop-mental pattern, and with lots of other patterns as well.[9]

For the results that Gordon describes to be at all relevant to the dispute between the off-line simulation theory and the theory-theory, it would have to be the case that the latter theory is *in*compatible with the reported develop-mental pattern. But that is patently not the case. To see why, we should first note that the theory-theory is not committed to the claim that folk psychology is acquired all in one fell swoop. Indeed, one would expect just the opposite. If children really are acquiring a tacit theory of the mind, they probably acquire it a bit at a time. Thus it might be the case that, at a given stage in development, children have mastered the part of the theory that specifies how beliefs and desires lead to behavior, though they have not mastered the entire story about how beliefs are caused. At this stage, they might simply assume that beliefs are caused by the way the world is; they might adopt the strategy of attributing to everyone the very same beliefs that they have. A child who has acquired this much of folk psychology would (incorrectly) attribute to Maxi the belief that the chocolate is in the cupboard. She would then go on to make just the predictions that Gordon reports. Of course, the theory-theory is also compatible with lots of other hypotheses about which bits of folk psy-chology are acquired first. Thus, like the off-line simulation theory, it is compatible with (but does not entail) lots of possible developmental patterns.

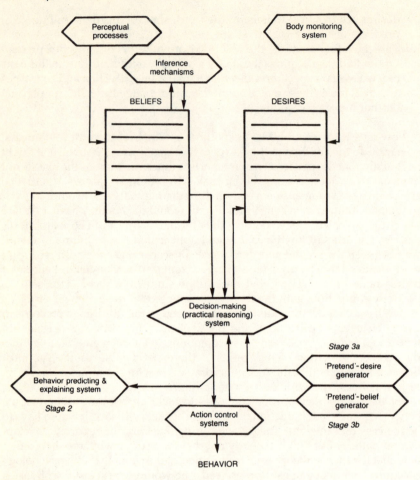

Figure 5.4

So it looks like the developmental studies that Gordon and Goldman cite can't be used to support one theory over the other.

Argument 7: Autistic children are highly deficient in their ability to engage in pretend play. These children are also frequently unable to impute beliefs to others or to predict other people's behavior correctly.

Here's how Gordon sets out the argument (this volume, p. 70):

Practical simulation involves the capacity for a certain kind of system-atic pretending. It is will known that *autistic* children suffer a striking deficit in the capacity for pretend play. In addition, they are often said to 'treat people and objects alike'; they fail to treat others as subjects, as having 'points of view' distinct from their own. This failure is confirmed by their performance in prediction tests like the [Wimmer–Perner 'Maxi' experiment] I have just described. A version of the Wimmer–Perner test was administered to autistic children of ages *six to sixteen* by a team of psychologists . . . *Almost all* these children gave the wrong answer, the 3-year-old's answer. This indicates a highly specific deficit, not one in general intelligence. Although many autistic children are also mentally retarded, those tested were mostly in the average or border-line IQ range. Yet children with Down's syndrome, with IQ levels sub-stantially below that range, suffered no deficit: almost all gave the right answer. My account of belief would predict that only those children who can engage in pretend play can master the concept of belief.

Goldman is rather more tentative. He claims only that the inability of austistic children 'to impute beliefs to others and therefore predict their behavior correctly . . . might . . . be related to their lack of pretend play' (this volume, p. 87).

Reply: The fact that autistic children are both incapable of pretend play and unable to predict the behavior of other people in Wimmer–Perner tests is very intriguing. Moreover, Gordon is certainly right in suggesting that the off-line simulation theory provides a possible explanation for these facts. If the off-line simulation theory is right, predicting the behavior of people whose beliefs differ from our own requires an ability to provide our own decision-making system with pretend input. And it is plausible to assume that this ability would also play a central role in pretend play. So if we hypothesize that autistic children lack the ability to provide the decision-making system with pretend input, we could explain both their performance on the Wimmer–Perner test and their failure to engage in pretend play. But, of course, this will not count as an argument for the off-line simulation theory and against the theory-theory if the latter account can offer an equally plausible explanation of the facts. And it will require no creativity on our part to produce such an alternative explanation since one of the investigators who discovered the fact that autistic children do poorly in Wimmer–Perner tests has offered one himself.

Leslie (1988) takes as an assumption 'the hypothesis that human cognition involves *symbolic computations* in the sense discussed . . . by Newell (1980) and particularly by Fodor' (Leslie, 1988, p. 21). He also assumes that an internal-ized theory of mind underlies the normal adult's ability to predict other people's behavior. An important theme in Leslie's work is that developmental studies with both normal and autistic children can help to illuminate the expressive resources of the 'language of thought' in which our theory of mind is encoded. According to Leslie, the notion of a 'meta-representation' is central in understanding how our theory of mind develops. Roughly speaking, a meta-representation is a mental representation about some other representational state or process. We exploit meta-representations when we think that

Maxi believes that the chocolate is in the box

or that

Maxi's brother wants the chocolate

or that

Mommy is pretending that the banana is a telephone.

On Leslie's view, 'autistic children do not develop a theory of mind normally' (Leslie, 1988, p. 39). And while 'it is far too soon to say with any confidence what *is* wrong' with these children, he speculates that at the root of the problem may be an inability to use meta-representations. If this were true, it would explain both their difficulty with pretend play and their failure on the Wimmer–Perner test.

Though we find Leslie's speculation interesting and important, it is no part of our current project to defend it. To make our case we need only insist that, on currently available evidence, Leslie's hypothesis is no less plausible than Gordon's. Since Leslie's speculation presupposes that normal children acquire and exploit a theory of mind that is encoded in a language of thought, the evidence from studies of autistic children gives us no reason to prefer the off-line simulation account over the theory-theory.[10]

Our theme, in this reply and in the previous one, has been that the empirical evidence cited by Gordon and Goldman, while compatible with the off-line simulation theory, is also compatible with the theory-theory, and thus does not support one theory over the other. But there are other studies in the recent literature that *can* be used to support one theory over the other. These studies report results that are comfortably compatible with the theory-theory though not with the off-line simulation account. Before we sketch those results, however, it is time to start a new section. In this section we've tried to show that none of the arguments in favor of the off-line simulation theory is persuasive. In the next one we'll set out a positive case for the theory-theory.

5   *In Defense of the Theory-Theory*

Argument 1: There are developmental data that are easily accommodated by the theory-theory, but very hard to explain if the off-line simulation account is correct.

Let's start with a description of the experimental setup, and a quick overview of the data.

The setup of the task in these experiments was rather simple. Two children were placed facing each other on opposite sides of a table. In each trial one child served as subject and had access to the other child's knowledge and his or her own knowledge of the content of a closed box. The box was placed in the middle of the table between the two children. The outside of it was neutral and not suggestive of its content. In each box was a familiar object like a pencil, a comb, a piece of chocolate, and so on. The specific questions were: 'Does (name of other child) know what is in the box or does she not know that?' and 'Do you know what is in the box or do you not know that?' . . .

Before the knowledge-questions were asked, either the other or the subject had access to the content of the box. One kind of access was visual perception. In this case either the other child or the subject had a chance to look into the box. The other kind of access was verbal information. Here the experimenter looked into the box and then informed one of the children by whispering the name of the content object into the child's ear. Because the two children were facing each other the subject was fully aware of the information conditions the other child was exposed to, that is, of whether the other child did or did not look into the box and of whether the other was or was not informed. (Wimmer et al., 1988, p. 175)

The results of this experiment were quite striking. The older children (five-year-olds) gave uniformly correct answers. But younger children (three- and four-year-olds) did not.

The most frequent error was denial of the other child's knowledge when the other child had looked into the box or was informed by the experimenter.

Most 3-year-olds and some 4-year-olds said that the other did not know what was in the box. This kind of error was nearly absent in children's assessment of their own knowledge. When subjects themselves had looked into the box or were informed, then they claimed to know and they could, of course, tell what was in the box. (Wimmer et al., 1988, pp. 175–6)

In another experiment, designed to be sure that the younger children were aware the other child had looked in the box, the subjects were asked both whether the other child had looked in the box and whether the other child knew what was in the box. 'The children consistently responded affirmatively to the look-question but again quite frequently responded negatively to the knowledge question' (Wimmer et al., 1988, p. 176).

What is going on here? The explanation offered by the experimenters is that younger children are using quite different mental processes in assessing what they know and in assessing what the other child knows. To answer the question, 'Do you know what is in the box?' the children use what the experimenters call the 'answer check procedure'. They simply check to see whether they have an answer to the embedded question in their knowledge base, and if they do they respond affirmatively. To answer the question about the other child's knowledge, the older children used what the experimenters call a 'direct access check procedure'. In effect, they ask themselves whether the other child looked in the box or was told about its contents. If so, they respond affirmatively. If not, they respond negatively. However, the three-year-olds did not use this procedure. They simply checked whether the other child had uttered a correct statement about the box's contents. If she had not, the subject said the other did not know. A very natural way to describe the situation is that while the younger children know that people who say *that p* typically believe or know *that p*, these children have not yet learned that people will come to know *that p* by seeing or being told *that p*. The younger children have acquired a fragment of folk psychology, while the older children have acquired a more substantial piece of the theory.[11] The older children have not, however, entirely mastered the theory, as indicated by another series of experiments.

These experiments focused on the role of *inference* in the acquisition of knowledge or belief. What they show is that 'four- and five-year olds relied on inference in their own acquisition of knowledge but denied that the other person might know via inference' (Wimmer et al., 1988, p. 179):

> Inferential access was realized in these experiments in a very simple and concrete way. In a first step the child and the other person together inspected the content of a container and agreed that only sweets of a certain kind, for example, black chocolate nuts, were in the container. In a second step the other person or the subject was prevented from seeing how one choconut was transferred from the container into an opaque bag. However, this person was explicitly informed by the experimenter about this transfer, for example, 'I've just taken one of the things out of this box and put it in the bag'.
>
> The condition where knowledge could be acquired via simple inference was contrasted with a condition where knowledge depended on actually seeing the critical object's transfer. In this latter condition two kinds of sweets were in the original container, and thus one could only know what the content of the critical bag was by having seen the transfer from container to bag.

Once again, the results were quite striking. In most cases the older children (six-year-olds, in this case) generally gave the right answers both about their own knowledge and about the other child's knowledge. But although the four-year-olds used inference in forming their own beliefs, a substantial majority of them exhibited a pattern that the experimenters called 'inference neglect'.

> The response pattern 'inference neglect' means that the other person was assessed according to perceptual access: When the other person

saw the object's transfer to the bag, 4-year-olds attributed knowledge; when the other did not see this transfer, ignorance was attributed even when the other person in fact knew via inference. (Wimmer et al., 1988, p. 179)

One plausible way of accounting for these results is to hypothesize that the older children had mastered yet another part of the adult folk psychology. They had learned that knowledge and beliefs can be caused by inference as well as by direct perceptual access. And, indeed, this is just the interpretation that the experimenters suggest.

In contrast to the 3-year-olds discussed in the previous [experiment], the 4-year-olds and 5-year-olds in the present experiments understood quite well that one has to consider the other person's informational conditions when one is questioned about the other person's knowledge. Their only problem was their limited understanding of informational conditions. They understood only direct visual access as a source of knowledge and this led them to mistaken but systematic ignorance attributions in the case of inferential access. (Wimmer et al., 1988, p. 181)

Let's now ask what conclusions can be drawn from these experiments that will be relevant to the choice between the off-line simulation theory and the theory-theory. A first obvious fact is that the data are all comfortably compatible with the theory-theory. Indeed, the explanation of the data offered by the experimenters is one that presupposes the correctness of the theory-theory. What appears to be happening is that as children get older, they master more and more of the principles of folk psychology. By itself, of course, the theory-theory would not enable us to predict the data, since the theory-theory does not tell us anything about the order in which the principles of folk psychology are acquired. But the pattern of results described certainly poses no problem for the theory-theory.

The same cannot be said for the off-line simulation theory. It is clear that even the younger children in these studies form beliefs as the result of perception, verbally provided information, and inference. So there is nothing about their decision making system, when it is being used on-line, that will help to explain the results. To make predictions about other people, the off-line simulation theory maintains, children must acquire the capacity to take the decision-making system off-line and provide it with some pretend inputs. But there is no obvious way in which this process could produce the pattern of results that has been reported. The difficulty is particularly clear in the case of inference. If the subject has seen that the box contains only chocolate nuts, and if she is told that one of the items in the box has been put in the bag, she comes to believe that there is a chocolate nut in the bag. But if she knows the other child has also seen what is in the box, and that the other child has been told that one of the items in the box has been put in the bag, she insists that the other child does not know what is in the bag. The problem can't be that the subject doesn't realize that the other child knows what is in the box. Children of this age do a good job of attributing belief on the basis of perception. Nor can it be that the subject doesn't believe that the other child believes the transfer has been made. For children of this age are also adept at attributing beliefs on the basis of verbally communicated information. So it looks like the subject has all the information needed for a successful simulation. But the answer she comes up with is *not* the one that she herself would come up with, were she in the subject's place. There are, of course, endlessly many ways in which a resolute defender of the off-line simulation theory might try to accommodate these data. But all the ones we've been able to think of are obviously implausible and *ad hoc*.

Argument 2: Our predictions and explanations of behavior are 'cognitively penetrable'.

One virtue of using a simulation to predict the behavior of a system is that you need have no serious idea about the principles governing the behavior of the target system. You just run the simulation and watch what happens. Sometimes, of course, a simulation will do something that was utterly unexpected. But no matter. If the simulation really was similar to the target system, then the prediction it provides will be a good one. In predictions based on simulations, what you don't know won't hurt you. All of this applies to the off-line simulation theory, of course. If there is some quirk in the human decision-making system, something quite unknown to most people that leads the system to behave in an unexpected way under certain circumstances, the accuracy of predictions based on simulations should not be adversely affected. If you provide the system with the right pretend input, it should simulate (and thus predict) the unexpected output. Adapting a term from Pylyshyn, we might describe this by saying that simulation-based predictions are not 'cognitively penetrable'.[12]

Just the opposite is true for predictions that rely on a theory. If we are making predictions on the basis of a set of laws or principles, and if there are some unexpected aspects of the system's behavior that are not captured by our principles, then our predictions about those aspects of the system's behavior should be less accurate. Theory based predictions are sensitive to what we know and don't know about the laws that govern the system; they *are* cognitively penetrable. This contrast provides a useful way of testing the two theories. If we can find cases in which ignorance about the workings of one's own psychology leads people to make mistakes in predicting what they, or other similarly situated people, would do, it will provide yet another reason to think that the off-line simulation theory is untenable. And, as it happens, cases illustrating cognitive penetrability in the prediction of behavior are not all that hard to find. The literature in cognitive social psychology is full of them. We'll illustrate the point with three examples, but it would be easy to add three dozen more.

First Example: Suppose you are walking through the local shopping mall, and encounter what looks to be yet another consumer product opinion survey. In this one a polite, well-dressed man invites you to examine an array of familiar products – nightgowns, perhaps, or pantyhose – and to rate their quality. A small reward is offered for your participation – you can keep the garment you select. On examining the products, you find no really significant differences among them. (You couldn't, because, unbeknownst to you they are identical.) What would you do? Confronted with this question, most of us think we would report that the garments looked to be very similar, and then choose one randomly. However, when the experiment was actually tried, this turned out to be mistaken. 'There was a pronounced position effect on evaluations, such that the right-most garments were heavily preferred to the left-most garments.' But it was clear that few of the subjects had any awareness at all of the effect of position on their decision. Indeed, 'when questioned about the effect of the garments' position on their choices, virtually all subjects denied such an influence (usually with a tone of annoyance or of concern for the experimenter's sanity)' (Nisbett and Ross, 1980, p. 207).

This sort of case poses real problems for the off-line simulation theory. Most people have no trouble imagining themselves in the situation described. They can supply their decision-making system with vivid 'pretend' input. But few people who have not heard of the experiment predict that they would behave in the way that the subjects behaved. The natural interpretation of the experiment is that people's predictions about their own behavior (and the subjects' explanations of their own choice) are guided by an incomplete or inaccurate theory, one which includes no information about these so-called 'position effects'.

Second Example: Here's another case to run through your own simulator. Suppose someone in the office is selling $1.00 tickets for the office lottery. In some cases, when a person agrees to buy a ticket, he or she is simply handed one. In other cases, after agreeing to buy a ticket, the buyer is allowed to choose a ticket from several that the seller has available. On the morning of the lottery, the seller approaches each purchaser and attempts to buy back the ticket. Now imagine yourself in both roles – first as a person who had been handed the ticket, second as a person who had been given a choice. What price would you ask in each case? Would there be any difference between the two cases? On several occasions one of us (Stich) has asked large undergraduate classes to predict what they would do. Almost no one predicts that they would behave the way that people actually do behave. Almost everyone is surprised to hear the actual results.

Ah, yes, the results; we haven't yet told *you* what they are. When the experiment was actually done, 'no-choice subjects sold their tickets back for an average of $1.96. Choice subjects, who had personally selected their tickets, held out for an average of $8.67!' (Nisbett and Ross, 1980, p. 136). If, like Stich's students, you find this surprising and unexpected, it counts as yet another difficulty for the off-line simulation theory.

Third Example: In the psychology laboratory, and in everyday life, it sometimes happens that people are presented with fairly persuasive evidence that they have some hitherto unexpected trait. In the light of that evidence people form the belief that they have the trait. What will happen to that belief if, shortly after this, people are presented with a convincing case discrediting the first body of evidence? Suppose, for example, they are convinced that the test results were actually someone else's, or that no real test was conducted at all. Most people expect that the undermined belief will simply be discarded. If until recently I never had reason to think I had a certain trait, and if the evidence I just acquired has been soundly discredited, then surely it would be silly of me to go away thinking that I *do* have the trait. That seems to be what most people think. And the view was shared by a generation of social psychologists who duped subjects into believing all sorts of things about themselves, observed their reactions, and then 'debriefed' the subjects by explaining the ruse. The assumption was that no enduring harm could be done because once the ruse was explained the induced belief would be discarded. But in a widely discussed series of experiments, Ross and his coworkers have demonstrated that this is simply not the case. Once a subject has been convinced that she is very good at telling real from fake suicide notes, for example, showing her that the evidence was completely phony does not succeed in eliminating the belief. Moreover, third-person observers of the experiment exhibit even stronger 'belief perseverance'. If an observer subject watches a participant subject being duped and then debriefed, the observer, too, will continue to believe that the participant is particularly good at detecting real suicide notes (Nisbett and Ross, 1980, pp. 175–9).

Neither of these results should have been at all surprising to anyone if we predict each other's beliefs and behavior in the way that the off-line simulation theory suggests. But clearly the results *were* both surprising and disturbing. We can't simply ask ourselves what we would do in these circumstances and expect to come up with the right answer. For the theory-theorist, this fact poses no particular problem. When our folk psychology is wrong, it is to be expected that our predictions will be wrong too. It is simply another illustration of cognitive penetrability in predicting and explaining behavior. The theory-theory, unlike the off-line simulation theory, predicts that people's predictions and explanations of behavior will be cognitively penetrable through and through. If it is agreed that these experiments confirm cognitive penetrability, the off-line simulation theory is in serious trouble.

6 Conclusion

Our paper has been long but our conclusion will be brief. The off-line simulation theory poses an intriguing challenge to the dominant paradigm in contemporary cognitive science. Moreover, if it were correct the off-line simulation account of psychological prediction and explanation would largely undermine *both* sides in the eliminativism dispute. But it has been our contention that the prospects for the off-line simulation theory are not very bright. None of the arguments that have been offered in defense of the theory are at all persuasive. And there is lots of experimental evidence that would be very hard to explain if the off-line simulation account were correct. We don't claim to have provided a knock-down refutation of the off-line simulation theory. Knock-down arguments are hard to come by in cognitive science. But we do claim to have assembled a pretty serious case against the simulation theory. Pending a detailed response, we don't think the off-line simulation theory is one that cognitive scientists or philosophers should take seriously.

Notes

We are grateful to Jerry Fodor for his helpful comments on an earlier version of this paper. Thanks are also due to Joseph Franchi for help in preparing the figures.

1   We are grateful to Professor Gordon for providing us with copies of his unpublished papers, and for allowing us to quote from them at some length. Goldman (1989) is reprinted as ch. 3 in this volume. Gordon (1986) is reprinted as ch. 2; see also ch. 4. Heal (1986) is reprinted as ch. 1.
2   The wind tunnel analogy is suggested by Ripstein (1987, p. 475ff). Gordon also mentions the analogy in ch. 4 in this volume, but he puts it to a rather different use.
3   The burglar in the basement example is borrowed from Gordon, this volume, p. 62.
4   The evidence Gordon cites includes the tendency to mimic other people's facial expressions and overt bodily movements, and the tendency in both humans and other animals to direct one's eyes to the target of a conspecific's gaze.
5   Gordon, this volume, pp. 64 ff.
6   Ripstein's account of the role of simulation in intentional exlanation is quite similar.

> I wish to defend the claim that imagining what it would be like to be in 'someone else's shoes' can serve to explain that person's actions . . . I shall argue that imagining oneself in someone else's situation . . . allows actions to be explained without recourse to a theory of human behavior. (Ripstein, 1987, p. 465)

> [T]he same sort of modeling [that engineers use when they study bridges in wind tunnels] is important to commonsense psychology: I can use my personality to model yours by 'trying on' various combinations of beliefs, desires and character traits. In following an explanation of what you do, I use my personality to determine that the factors mentioned would produce the result in question . . . I do not need to know how you work because I can rely on the fact that I work in a similar way. My model . . . underwrites the explanation by demonstating that particular beliefs and character traits would

lead to particular actions under normal circumstances. (Ripstein, 1987, pp. 476–7)

7   As Jerry Fodor has pointed out to us, the logical geography is actually a bit more complex than figure 5.2 suggests. To see the point, consider the box labeled 'Decision-making (practical reasoning) system' in figure 5.1. Gordon and Goldman tell us relatively little about the contents of this box. They provide no account of how the practical reasoning system goes about the job of producing decisions from beliefs and desires. However, there are some theorists – Fodor assures us that he is one – who believe that the practical reasoning system goes about its business by exploiting an internally represented decision theory. If this is right, then we exploit a tacit theory each time we make a decision based on our beliefs and desires. But now if we make predictions about other people's behavior by taking our own practical reasoning system off-line, then we also exploit a tacit theory when we make these predictions. Thus, contrary to the suggestion in figure 5.2, off-line simulation processes and processes exploiting an internally represented theory are not mutually exclusive, since some off-line simulation processes may also exploit a tacit theory.

In the pages that follow, we propose to be as accommodating as possible to our opponents and to make things as hard as possible for ourselves. It is our contention that prediction, explanation and interpretation of the sorts we have discussed do not use an off-line simulation process, *period*. So if it turns out that Fodor is right (because the practical reasoning system embodies an internally represented theory) *and* that Gordon and Goldman are right (because we predict and explain by taking this system off-line), then we lose, and they win. Also, of course, if Fodor is wrong about how the practical reasoning system works but Gordon and Goldman are right about prediction, explanation and interpretation, again we lose and they win. So as we construe the controversy, it pits those who advocate any version of the off-line simulation account against those who think that prediction, explanation and interpretation are subserved by a tacit theory *stored somewhere other than in the practical reasoning system*. But do keep in mind that we interpret 'theory' broadly. So, for example, if it turns out that there is some non-sentence-like, non-rule-based module which stores the information that is essential to folk-psychological prediction and explanation, and if this module is not used at all in ordinary 'on-line' practical reasoning and decision-making, then we win and they lose.

It might be protested that in drawing the battle lines as we propose to draw them, we are conceding to the opposition a position that they never intended to occupy. As we have already noted, Gordon and Goldman expend a fair amount of effort arguing that a tacit theory is not exploited in folk-psychological prediction and explanation. Since they think that the practical reasoning system *is* exploited in folk-psychological prediction and explanation, presumably they would deny that the practical reasoning system uses an internally represented decision theory. So it is a bit odd to say that *they* win if Fodor is right about the practical reasoning system and they are right abut off-line simulation. This is a point we happily concede. It is a bit odd to draw the battle lines in this way. But in doing so, we are only making things more difficult for ourselves. For we must argue that *however the practical reasoning system works* we do not predict and explain other people's behavior by taking the system off-line.

8   Gordon (unpublished), sec. 3.5.

9   Actually, the developmental facts are rather more complicated than Gordon suggests. For, as Leslie (1988) emphasizes, children are typically able to appreciate and engage in pretend play by the time they are two and a half years old – long before they can handle questions about Maxi and his false beliefs. It is not at all clear how the off-line simulation theory can explain both the early appearance of the ability to pretend and the relatively late appearance of the ability to predict the behavior of people whose beliefs and desires differ from one's own.

10 It's worth noting that both Gordon's account and Leslie's 'predict that only those children who can engage in pretend play can master the concept of belief' (Gordon, this volume, p. 70). This may prove a troublesome implication for both theorists, however. For it is not the case that *all* autistic children do poorly on the Wimmer–Perner test. In the original study reported by Baron–Cohen, Leslie and Frith (1985), only 16 out of 20 autistic subjects failed the Wimmer–Perner test. The other 4 answered correctly. The investigators predicted that these children 'would also show evidence of an ability to pretend play' (p. 43). Unfortunately, no data was reported on the pretend play ability of these subjects. If it should turn out that some autistic children do well on the Wimmer–Perner test *and* lack the ability for pretend play, both Gordon's explanation and Leslie's would be in trouble. If the facts do turn out this way, advocates of the theory-theory will have a variety of other explanations available. But it is much less clear that the off-line simulation account could explain the data, if some autistic children can't pretend but can predict the behavior of people with false beliefs.

11 Another experiment reported by Perner et al. (1987) provides some additional evidence for this conclusion. In the first part of the experiment children were shown a box of Smarties (a type of candy), and asked what they thought was in the box. All of them answered that the box contained Smarties. They were then shown that the box contained a pencil, and no Smarties. After this the children were asked three questions:

(i)   What is in the box?
(ii)   What did you think was in the box when you first saw it?
(iii) What would a friend, waiting outside, think was in the box if he saw it as it is now?

Most of the younger children answered (iii) incorrectly; they failed to predict their friend's false belief. But more than half of those who got (iii) wrong answered (ii) correctly. They were able to tell the experimenter that they had thought the box contained Smarties, and that they were wrong. In commenting on this experiment, Leslie notes that

[d]espite the ability to *report* their false belief, these 3-year-olds could not understand where that false belief had come from . . . Despite the fact that they themselves had just undergone the process of getting that false belief, the children were quite unable to understand and reconstruct that process, and thus unable, minutes later, to predict what would happen to their friend. (Leslie, 1988, pp. 33–4)

12   Pylyshyn, 1981, 1984. It is perhaps worth noting that we are using the term 'cognitively penetrable' a bit more loosely than Pylyshyn does. But in the present context the difference is not important.

References

Astington, J., Harris, P. and Olson, D. (eds) 1988: *Developing Theories of Mind.* Cambridge: Cambridge University Press.
Baron-Cohen, S., Leslie, A. and Frith, U. 1985: Does the autistic child have a 'theory of mind'? *Cognition*, 21, 37–46.
Chomsky, N. 1965: *Aspects of the Theory of Syntax*. Cambridge, MA: MIT Press.
Churchland, P. 1981: Eliminative materialism and the propositional attitudes. *Journal of Philosophy*, 78, 67–90.
Churchland, P. 1989: Folk psychology and the explanation of human behavior. In *A Neurocomputational Perspective*. Cambridge, MA: MIT Press.
Cummins, R. 1983: *The Nature of Psychological Explanation*. Cambridge, MA: MIT Press.
D'Andrade, R. 1987: A folk model of the mind. In D. Holland and N. Quinn (eds), *Cultural Models in Language and Thought*. Cambridge: Cambridge University Press.
Dennett, D. 1969: *Content and Consciousness*. London: Routledge and Kegan Paul.
Dennett, D. 1978a: Artificial intelligence as philosophy and psychology. In *Brainstorms*. Cambridge, MA: MIT Press.
Dennett, D. 1978b: Two approaches to mental images. In *Brainstorms*. Cambridge, MA: MIT Press.
Fodor, J. 1968: The appeal to tacit knowledge in psychological explanation. *Journal of Philosophy*, 65, 627–40.
Fodor, J. 1975: *The Language of Thought*. New York: Thomas Crowell.
Fodor, J. 1981: *Representations*. Cambridge, MA: MIT Press.

Fodor, J, 1987: *Psychosemantics*. Cambridge, MA: MIT Press.

Fodor, J., Bever, T. and Garrett, M. 1974: *The Psychology of Language: An Introduction to Psycholinguistics and Generative Grammar*. New York: McGraw-Hill.

Goldman, A. I. 1989: Interpretation psychologized. *Mind and Language*, 4, 161–85. Reprinted as ch. 3 in this volume.

Gordon, R. M. 1986: Folk psychology as simulation. *Mind and Language*, 1, 158–71. Reprinted as ch. 2 in this volume.

Gordon, R. M. Unpublished: Fodor's intentional realism and the simulation theory. MS dated 2/90.

Gregory, R. 1970: *The Intelligent Eye*. New York: McGraw-Hill.

Greeno, J. 1983: Conceptual entities. In D. Gentner and A. Stevens (eds), *Mental Models*. Hillsdale, NJ: Erlbaum.

Hayes, P. 1985: The second naive physics manifesto. In J. Hobbs and R. Moore (eds), *Formal Theories of the Commonsense World*. Norwood, NJ: Ablex, 1–36.

Heal, J. 1986: Replication and functionalism. In J. Butterfield (ed.), *Language, Mind and Logic*. Cambridge: Cambridge University Press. Reprinted as ch. 1 in this volume.

Johnson-Laird, P. 1983: *Mental Models: Towards a Cognitive Science of Language, Inference and Consciousness*. Cambridge, MA: Harvard University Press.

Kahneman, D. and Tversky, A. 1982: The simulation heuristic. In D. Kahneman, P. Slovic and A. Tversky (eds), *Judgment Under Uncertainty*. Cambridge: Cambridge University Press.

Kosslyn, S. 1981: The medium and the message in mental imagery: A theory. In N. Block (ed.), *Imagery*. Cambridge, MA: MIT Press.

Leslie, A. 1987: Pretense and representation: The origins of 'theory of mind'. *Psychological Review*, 94, 412–26.

Leslie, A. 1988: Some implications of pretense for mechanisms underlying the child's theory of mind. In J. Astington, P. Harris and D. Olson (eds), *Developing Theories of Mind*. Cambridge: Cambridge University Press.

Lycan, W. 1981: Form, function and feel. *Journal of Philosophy*, 78, 24–50.

Lycan, W. 1988: Toward a homuncular theory of believing. In *Judgement and Justification*. Cambridge: Cambridge University Press.

Marr, D. 1982: *Vision*. San Francisco: Freeman.

McCloskey, M. 1983: Naive theories of motion. In D. Gentner and A. Stevens (eds), *Mental Models*. Hillsdale, NJ: Erlbaum.

Montgomery, R. 1987: Psychologism, folk psychology and one's own case. *Journal for the Theory of Social Behavior*, 17, 195–218.

Newell, A. 1980: Physical symbol systems. *Cognitive Science*, 4, 135–83.

Nisbett, R. and Ross, L. 1980: *Human Inference*. Englewood Cliffs, NJ: Prentice-Hall.

Olson, D., Astington, J. and Harris, P. 1988: Introduction. In J. Astington, P. Harris and D. Olson (eds), *Developing Theories of Mind*. Cambridge: Cambridge University Press.

Perner, J., Leekam, S. and Wimmer, H. 1987: Three-year-olds' difficulty with false belief: The case for a conceptual deficit. *British Journal of Developmental Psychology*, 5, 125–37.

Pinker, S. 1989: *Learnability and Cognition*. Cambridge, MA: MIT Press.

Pylyshyn, Z. 1981: The imagery debate: Analog media versus tacit knowledge. In N. Block (ed.), *Imagery*. Cambridge, MA: MIT Press.

Pylyshyn, Z. 1984: *Computation and Cognition*. Cambridge, MA: MIT Press.

Ramsey, W., Stich, S. and Garon, J. 1990: Connectionism, eliminativism and the future of folk psychology. *Philosophical Perspectives*, 4, 499–533.

Ripstein, A. 1987: Explanation and empathy. *Review of Metaphysics*, 40, 465–82.

Rock, I. 1983: *The Logic of Perception*. Cambridge, MA: MIT Press.

Rumelhart, D., Smolensky, P., McClelland, J. and Hinton, G. 1986: Schemata and sequential thought processes in PDP models. In J. McClelland, D. Rumelhart and the PDP Research Group, *Parallel Distributed Processing*, vol. 2. Cambridge, MA: MIT Press.

Sellars, W. 1963: Empiricism and the philosophy of mind. In *Science, Perception and Reality*. London: Routledge and Kegan Paul.

Stich, S. 1978: Beliefs and subdoxastic states. *Philosophy of Science*, 45, 499–518.

Wimmer, H., Hogrefe, J. and Sodian, B. 1988: A second state in children's conception of mental life: Understanding informational access as origins of knowledge and belief. In J. Astington, P. Harris and D. Olson (eds), *Developing Theories of Mind*. Cambridge; Cambridge University Press.

6

'He Thinks He Knows': And More Developmental Evidence Against the Simulation (Role-taking) Theory

JOSEF PERNER AND DEBORRAH HOWES

1 Introduction

How do children come to understand the mind? There are many different answers in the offing from philosophy of mind. For present purposes we want to focus on the suggestion that children understand the mind by putting themselves in the particular mental state in question by off-line simulation. In developmental circles this is an old idea known under the names of 'role-taking' or 'perspective-taking', which was thought to be the method by which the young child overcomes his egocentric attitude which encourages him to accept his own view as the only one possible (Piaget and Inhelder, 1948/1956, p. 194). This is achieved – as the saying goes – by 'putting himself into the other person's shoes', which, presumably, means experiencing in simulation what the other person experiences for real.

Although simulation is suggested by the the terms 'role-' and 'perspective-taking', it has not been worked out as a systematic theoretical position. John Flavell (personal communication), who has used 'role taking' in the title of one of his books (Flavell et al., 1968), assured us that he had not intended to take any particular theoretical position, but used the term purely as the then usual label for the development of social cognition.

Gordon (1986, reprinted as ch. 2 in this volume) and Goldman (1989, reprinted as ch. 3 in this volume) proposed this idea as a systematic position in the philosophy of mind, and Harris (1989, 1991; see also ch. 10 in this volume) turned it into a developmental alternative to the predominant view that children acquire a 'theory of mind'. To see the distinguishing feature of the simulation theory let us consider the following two examples.

Assume you are designing an obstacle course and you are not quite sure whether your wall is the right size. It should be a challenge for climbing it but not too dangerous for jumping down from it. You can find out by simulating this bit of the course on your own body. You climb up and jump down. If you barely manage but don't hurt yourself then it's just right. This is off-line simulation, because you are not seriously in the race. You just recreate the initial conditions for a certain section of the whole course for yourself. The initial conditions are recreated in – in some sense – hypothetical fashion only, since they are only approximations to the real conditions pertaining in the real race; for instance, you are not as exhausted as you would be at this point in the real race. The actual climb and jump are, however, really executed.

Mental simulation is in essential parts the same. Assume you want to find out how people (or yourself) would feel and react if a seedy looking character were to follow them along a dark street. You try to find out on your way home at night by *imagining* that a seedy looking character is following you. As a result you may detect a certain feeling cropping up and your pace quickening. Again this is off-line simulation because there is no real person following you. Rather you (hypothetically) recreate in your imagination the perceptual conditions that would pertain if a real person were following you. And this imagined situation provides the initial conditions for a simulation involving *real* emotional and (in this case) behavioral reactions. To obtain these reactions you engage your real mental mechanism, as you engaged your real body in the physical simulation of the obstacle course.

What makes these two examples cases of simulation is that you try to figure out an answer to your question by observing the reaction of your own body or mind to some initial (hypothetical) conditions which are set as closely as possible to how they would be in the real case. What makes it hypothetical is that the initial conditions are only approximations to real conditions. Otherwise, however, you are using your body as a real wall-climbing and jumping mechanism, and your mind as a real emotion-producing and pace-quickening mechanism.

In contrast to simulation the defining feature of a non-simulation attempt to find an answer to your question is that you cannot use your body or mind as real mechanisms. Instead you need a mental representation (knowledge) of those mechanisms, or at least of what results these mechanisms yield when put into the initial conditions. So, in the case of the obstacle course the difference is very clear. Instead of using your body, you use knowledge about bodies which is stored in your mind to arrive at the answers.

In the case of the mental simulation this difference may be more difficult to see since you are using your mind in both instances.[1] However, the difference is there. Where you use your mind as an emotion-producing mechanism in simulation, without simulation you have to use your mind to produce a description of that mechanism or its functioning. It is another question whether this description (knowledge) takes the form of a 'folk theory' (children are seen as acquiring a 'theory of mind'), or whether – as theorists in the Wittgenstein–Ryle tradition would prefer – it takes the form of attributing (inner) states that are perceptually transparent from people's conduct-in-context (e.g. Coulter, 1979, ch. 2).

We present developmental data which – we think – pose a problem for the simulation theory, and which we explain in terms of the complexity of the descriptions (mental representations) of the mental states that need to be attributed to story characters. We need not commit ourselves whether these descriptions are of perceptual origin or of a theoretical nature.

Before considering the developmental evidence against the simulation theory we should ask what this theory claims that children acquire through simulation. The strongest claim is perhaps that simulation is sufficient for providing children with intentional concepts like belief, knowledge, desire, etc. Gordon seemed to make this strong claim when he said (this volume, p. 68):

1. Let's do a Smith simulation. Ready? *Dewey won the election....*
2. *Smith believes that* Dewey won the election.

My suggestion is that (2) be read as saying the same thing as (1), though less explicitly.

Also Harris (1989, 1991) is a proponent of this strong claim, insofar as he presents simulation as an alternative to other explanations of how children develop mentalistic concepts, since an explanation of how such concepts are acquired is of central concern to all research under the label of 'children's theory of mind'.

This strong claim is often referred to as 'Cartesian', because Descartes (1954) thought that the mind was transparent to itself (Churchland, 1984, p. 75). That is, when the mind is in a certain state (through simulation, for instance) then the mind knows what state it is in (i.e. must have the concept of what kind of state it is). The developmental evidence presented by Wimmer and Hartl (1991) was directed at this claim inherent in the strong version of the simulation theory.

A considerably more cautious claim is that simulation is at best necessary (but not sufficient) for the acquisition of intentional concepts. In other words, in whatever process of concept acquisition children are engaged in, simulation provides a useful (perhaps necessary) source of data for this process, but does not in itself constitute understanding of these concepts.

An even weaker claim has been suggested by Goldman (this volume, p. 94), namely that simulation depends on ready formed intentional concepts: '[S]imulation assumes a prior understanding of what state it is that the interpreter [the child] ascribes to S [another person or herself].' In this case, simulation would play a relatively minor role in development. It would only help children acquire knowledge (or the theory) about the connections between different mental states, environmental conditions and behavioral reactions. Our experimental evidence speaks even against this weakest version of the simulation theory.

We told children stories of the following kind. John and Mary unpack their swagbag. As Mary has to leave, it is left to John to store away the chocolate. He tells Mary that he will put it into one of the two drawers and later decides which one. While he is playing in the park their mother unexpectedly transfers the chocolate to the other drawer. As a consequence, John mistakenly thinks that the chocolate is still in the original drawer. Children's understanding of John's belief and of his and Mary's reflections on it was investigated by three critical questions. The first assessed their understanding of the content of John's mistake, 'Where does John think the chocolate is?'[2] The second investigated their understanding of John's self-reflection, 'If we ask John: "Do you know where the chocolate is?", what will John say?' And the last one assessed their understanding of another person's reflection on John's knowledge, 'If we ask Mary: "Does John know where the chocolate is?", what will Mary say?'

Now let us see how children might fare on these three questions if they work by simulation. To answer the questions about John, the child has to imagine herself in John's situation, in particular, imagine herself not having seen mother transfer the chocolate to the new location. Once this hypothetical position has been taken the simulating child will find herself in a simulated false belief about where the chocolate is and in position to answer both our questions about John by assuming they were asked about herself in her simulated mental state. Hence when asked, 'Where do you think the chocolate is?', the child can answer, 'In the old location.' When asked, 'Do you know where the chocolate is?' the child can answer: 'Yes.' In other words, both questions about John should be of comparable difficulty and be successfully answered at the same age.

In contrast, the question about Mary should pose a much greater problem for the simulating child than the questions about John, because it requires simulation of John's state of mind within the simulation of Mary's mind. Such a second-order simulation should be considerably more difficult than ordinary simulations. Or, in Harris's (1991) terminology, a simulation of a simulation requires two levels of changes in default settings, whereas the simulation of John's mind requires but one such level of changes. This prediction does justice to what we already know about children's development, namely that they find it much easier to answer the question about where John thinks the chocolate is than about what Mary would say about John's knowledge of where the chocolate is (e.g. Perner and Wimmer, 1985).

In summary, if children use simulation to answer these questions, then the two questions about John (where he thinks the chocolate is and what he will say when asked whether he knows where it is) should be equally easy, whereas the question about what Mary will say about John's knowledge should be relatively difficult.

In contrast, if children do not simulate John and Mary's mental states on their own mind in order to figure out what these characters will answer to the questions about their knowledge, the children have to mentally represent these characters' mental states. We know from existing research (Perner and Wimmer, 1985) that children become able to mentally represent a person's first-order mental state (e.g. 'John thinks the chocolate is in the original location') much earlier (about four years) than second-order mental states (e.g. 'Mary thinks that John knows where the chocolate is'; at about five to eight

Table 6.1   Prediction of relative difficulty

| | Theory | |
| | Simulation (role-taking) | Representing mental states |
Questions		
John think?	easy	easy
John say John knows?	easy	difficult
Mary say John knows?	difficult	difficult

years or even later: Eliot et al., 1979; Miller et al., 1970; Shultz and Cloghesy, 1981). However, this developmental lag can also be explained by simulation theory, since understanding of a person's second-order belief about another person's knowledge requires embedded simulation, which is plausibly more difficult than a simple simulation.

The critical question that differentiates between the theories is the one about how John would respond to the question about his own knowledge. As discussed above, this should pose no special problem for a person successfully simulating John's belief, since it is part and parcel of a belief to be convinced that one knows where the object is. In contrast, if children have to mentally represent John's mental state a quite different prediction follows, because explicit representation of John's subjective conviction requires formulation of a second-order state: 'John *thinks* he *knows* where the chocolate is.' This should be of comparable difficulty to representing Mary's second-order belief about John's knowledge, which we know to be substantially more difficult than representation of John's belief about the chocolate's location.

Thus we have the differential predictions of relative difficulties for our three critical questions shown in table 6.1.

2 Method

Subjects. Thirty-two children (18 boys and 14 girls) from two public schools in Metropolitan Toronto participated in this study. Their ages ranged from 4 years 10 months to 6 years 4 months.

Materials and Procedure. Three dolls were used in both conditions to represent John, Mary, and John's mother. In one condition the critical object was a box of chocolates which was transferred from the top drawer to the bottom drawer of a chest. In the other condition a set of wooden blocks was transferred from a white plastic bag to a blue bag.

Table 6.2 gives the text for the story with the chocolate in the drawers. In the experimental condition John's mother transfers the chocolate, unbeknownst to John, to the other drawer. As a consequence, John doesn't known where the

Table 6.2   Chocolate-in-drawer stories

John and Mary return home from the store with a box of chocolates. The children have been told that they have to put the chocolates away until after dinner.

Mary remembers that she has to go to the library and she asks John where he will put the chocolates. John tells her that he will put them in either the TOP drawer or the BOTTOM drawer. Mary then leaves.

John decides to put the chocolates in the TOP drawer and he goes off to play in the park.

Control Question 1: Does Mary know where the chocolates are?
    Correct answer: 'no'

TRANSFER EPISODE (omitted in control condition):
While John and Mary are away their mother takes the chocolates from the TOP drawer and moves them to the BOTTOM drawer.

Control Question 2: Does John know where the chocolates are?
        Correct answer for experimental condition: 'no'
                              control condition: 'yes'

TEST QUESTIONS (in counterbalanced order):
1. Think Question: Where does John think the chocolates are?
    Correct answer: 'TOP'
2. Self-Reflection Question: What if we go over to the park and ask John: 'John, do you know where the chocolates are?' What will he say?
    Correct answer: 'yes'
3. Other-Reflection Question: What if we go to the library and ask Mary: 'Mary, does John know where the chocolates are?' What will she say?
    Correct answer: 'yes'

---

chocolate really is but he thinks be knows. In the control condition John knows where it really is. The story is essentially the same as in the experimental condition except that the episode of mother's unforeseen interference is omitted. The objective of this condition was to demonstrate that children who give wrong answers in the experimental condition did not do so because of difficulties interpreting the test questions.

For half the children the chocolate-in-the-drawers scenario was used for the experimental condition and the blocks-in-bags story for the control condition, for the other half this assignment was reversed. Children were taken individually from their classroom to a quiet room in the school for testing. They were introduced to the three dolls and then they were told the two stories in counterbalanced order. Also the three test questions (see table 6.2) were asked

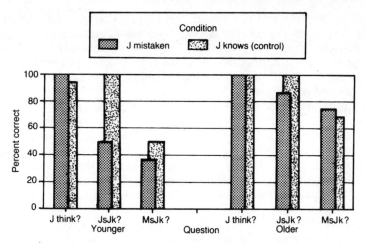

Figure 6.1   *Percentage of children giving correct answers*

in four different orders, 1-2-3, 2-1-3, 3-1-2 and 3-2-1. One of these sequences was assigned at random to each subject to be used for both stories.

3 Results

Children had no difficulty following the basic events in the stories since all of them (with the exception of one six-year-old in the experimental condition) gave correct answers in both conditions to the two control questions about whether John and Mary knew where the chocolate was. Also, all children responded correctly to the think-question about where John thinks the chocolate was. This was expected from previous research on this age group. The only exception was a child of 5 years and 7 months who answered 'don't know' to this question in the control condition.

Substantial numbers of errors were committed only on the reflection questions assessing children's appreciation of John's self-reflection on his own knowledge and Mary's reflection on John's knowledge. The percentage of correct responses on these questions was first subjected to a preliminary analysis of between-subject factors. This was done by logistic regressions (sex (2) × age (interval) × task-order (2) × question-order (4)), a different one for each question in each condition. There were no significant main or interaction effects in any of the four analyses except for an age difference in the experimental condition on the self-reflective question: χ^2 (1, d.f. = 28) < 0.05 (in the control condition all children gave correct answers to this question) and the question about Mary's reflection on John's knowledge in the experimental condition: χ^2 (1, d.f. = 28) < 0.05, but not in the control condition: χ^2 (1, d.f. = 28) > 0.60.

To display these age differences graphically, the left half of figure 6.1 shows the percent correct answers to all three test questions for the younger 16 children (four years ten months to five years eight months) and the right half for the older group. With the help of figure 6.1 we can now look at the theoretically more interesting within-subject comparison of different questions and conditions.

The most important result is that there is a substantial gap between children's ability to answer the question about what John thinks and their ability to answer the self-reflection question about what he thinks about his knowledge. As figure 6.1 shows this gap is particularly marked for the younger group, all of whom gave correct answers to the think-question but only half of them to the self-reflection question: McNemar's χ^2 $(1, N = 8) = 8.0$, $p < 0.001$ (also significant for both groups combined: χ^2 $(1, N = 10) = 10.0$, $p < 0.01$).

Figure 6.1 also shows that children's problems with the self-reflection question in the experimental condition were not caused by the linguistic complexity of this question since all children gave correct answers to the very same question in the control condition: McNemar's χ^2 $(1, N = 8) = 8.0$, $p < 0.01$.

The other side of this finding is that children's performance on the self-reflection question closely matches their performance on the other-reflection question (what Mary thinks about John's knowledge). The slight difference that there was (figure 6.1) is not statistically significant (Binomial test: $x = 1$, $N = 6$, $p > 0.20$, for all ages).[3]

Finally, figure 6.1 shows that children's response to the other-reflection question about Mary's opinion about John's knowledge was as difficult to answer in the control condition as in the experimental condition. This difficulty came as a surprise, but can be explained within the framework of the mental-representation/theory view. It tells us something about the younger children's fall-back position. The open question is how children, who cannot yet mentally represent Mary's second-order belief, will answer the question. They have two plausible options. Instead of answering in terms of what Mary thinks about John's knowledge, they can answer either in terms of what John knows or in terms of what Mary knows. Their wrong answers in the control condition suggest that they answered in terms of Mary's knowledge.[4] Since in this condition Mary does not know where the chocolate is, they answered wrongly 'No' to the question. Had they answered in terms of John's actual knowledge they would have got the answer fortuitously right, because in that condition John does know where the chocolate is.

Children's difficulty with this question in the control condition also helps rule out a potentially interesting 'super-Cartesian' explanation of children's errors on the other questions. Children may assume with Descartes that the mind is transparent to itself, but they overdo it and assume that even the falseness of a belief is transparent, and furthermore that it is not just transparent to John's own mind but also to Mary's. This could explain children's errors on the reflective questions in the experimental condition. Since John holds a false belief in that condition children assume that both John and Mary would know that. And that's why they answer wrongly that John and Mary would say 'No! John does not know where the chocolate is.' However, if children were operating under such an overly Cartesian assumption then they should not make any errors on these questions in the control condition. Yet they do on the one about Mary.

4 Discussion

The central finding of this study is that the question about what John would say about his own knowledge was substantially more difficult to answer than the question about where John thinks the chocolate is. This difference is hard to explain if children worked out the answer by simulation, because once the child is simulating John's false belief by assuming, 'I think (am convinced) the chocolate is in the old place', the child is not only simulating the content of John's belief ('it's in the old place') but also his conviction that it is there ('I know it's in there'). The reason for this is that the child is presumably simulating a conscious belief, and the believer's reflective conviction that he is right is simply part and parcel of a conscious belief. In other words, our common-sense notion of belief entails the Cartesian notion of transparency of mind.

But, one might ask, would it not be possible that children simulate a different belief, or only the non-reflective part of it. This suggestion can be pursued in two different directions, both of which turn out to be implausible. One way to follow up this suggestion is to assume that children's beliefs are different from adults' in that they lack the self-reflective component, i.e. when children believe that an object is in a particular place they do not think they know where the object is. This, however, is unlikely. In fact, we know that three-year-olds (e.g. Wimmer, Hogrefe and Perner, 1988), though they may not know much about the origin of their knowledge, have no problem deciding whether they do or do not know where something is.

The other possibility is that children set the initial parameters for their simulation not quite in the right way. This is a particularly interesting possibility because it can be used to defend the simulation theory against the examples from Nisbett and Ross's (1980) book cited by Stich and Nichols (this volume, pp. 150–2). In these examples people's real-life reactions differ from what they think they were doing. This discrepancy, however, need not speak against the use of simulation as such, but can be explained by a mismatch between the actual conditions in which the real-life behaviour takes place and the assumptions made about these conditions (initial parameters) in the simulation. For instance, Stich and Nichols's first example (p. 151) revolves around people's strong spatial positional bias in their choices between goods of identical quality and their total lack of awareness of this bias. This lack of awareness can be explained by the simulation theory if people fail to take spatial position into account in their input parameters to the simulation (i.e. they do not encode their situation by a spatial visual image). If there is no spatial information in the input then the simulation cannot take it into account, and consequently, subjects are not aware of using that information in their real decisions.

A similar defence can be set up against the other examples given by Stich and Nichols, but it cannot so easily be raised against our data. The reason is that awareness of one's own mental state is, presumably, automatic and is not triggered by independent situational conditions which may or may not be included in the attempted simulation of the mental state. In other words, if children correctly simulate John's mental state that he thinks the chocolate is in the original location, then their simulation ought also to contain the information that John will be subjectively convinced that he knows where the chocolate is. So, the clear developmental gap between children understanding where John thinks something is and their understanding of John's insight in his belief is difficult to square with the simulation theory.

5 Other Relevant Developmental Data

Wimmer and Hartl (1991) attacked the Cartesian position, inherent in the simulation theory defended by Harris (1989), namely, that children have introspective insight in their own mental states which precedes and forms the basis for their understanding of other people's mental states. The basis for this attack is a series of recent experimental studies (Gopnik and Astington, 1988; Gopnik and Slaughter, 1991; Wimmer and Perner, 1990; Wimmer and Hartl, 1991) which found young children to have as much difficulty remembering their own false beliefs as they have inferring what another person thinks. And since both abilities emerge as children become able to explain the reasons for why they themselves or another person develop a false belief, the developmental evidence was taken as support for the 'theory view of mind', according to which the mind is understood as part of a causal system linking perceptions with action.

However Harris (in his letter of 12 November 1989 to Heinz Wimmer) argued in defence of his 'Cartesian' version of the simulation theory that such memory data do not challenge his position, since Cartesian transparency of mind applies only to present states of mind and allows for memory failure (as indeed does common sense). Hence, young children's failure to recall their false belief may attest to extremely short-lived memory of their own mental states rather than a lack of transparency or reflective insight into their current states of mind.

In fact, recent data by Mitchell and Lacohée (1991) seem to support such a theory of memory failure. They showed that children's usual problems of remembering what they had mistakenly thought could be largely alleviated with a little help. At the time of their mistaken statement (e.g. saying 'Smarties' when asked about an empty Smarties box) children were asked to post a card showing Smarties. This enabled most three-year-olds to answer correctly 'Smarties' when asked what they had thought was in the empty Smarties box.

However, we need to be cautious in concluding from children's correct memory of the content of their mental state ('Smarties in that box') that they fully understand the nature of their mental state with which they had held this content (e.g. whether it was a belief or pretence or knowledge). To probe into that understanding more directly Deborah Hutton (ongoing research) made children state what was in a container under three different conditions. That is, they said 'Smarties' either because they *knew*, because they *mistakenly thought*, or because they *pretended* that there were Smarties inside. After – depending on condition – confirming what they knew or correcting their mistaken assumption, they were asked about the reason for having said 'Smarties'. They were either given the choice: 'Did you say that because you *knew* there were Smarties in it or because you just *pretended* that there were Smarties in it?'; or they were asked: '. . . because you really *thought* . . . or because you just *pretended* . . .' Even at the age of three years children had little difficulty differentiating between knowledge and pretence; thus establishing that this method is adequate for assessing very young children's conceptual distinctions. However, even at the age of four years most children could not distinguish between pretence and false belief.

This inability to accurately identify their own mental state becomes relevant for present purposes if we assume that children remember the content of their belief in the original studies – as Harris claimed in his defence against Wimmer and Hartl – by simulation. Now, if children do use simulation in these tasks then their failure to identify their mental state correctly shows that simulation does not provide a conceptual understanding of mind. So, either children do not use simulation or their simulation is not transparent in Descartes's sense, because it does not make children understand which mental state they are simulating.

Stich and Nichols (this volume, (pp. 146–50)) review data by Wimmer et al. (1988) which are difficult to explain for the simulation theory. We would like to point out further aspects of these data which add to these difficulties. Perner (1991, pp. 269–70) pointed out that in these experiments two different conditions were used which should intuitively and by Harris's criteria (number of default parameters to be adjusted) pose quite different degrees of difficulty for children. But they don't. In one kind of task children knew that there was a toy car in a box and observed that the other person was prevented from looking inside the box. They had to judge whether the other person knew what was in the box. This should be relatively easy to simulate off-line, since imagining themselves staring at a closed box. their simulation should give the correct result, 'don't know', and hence 'other doesn't know'.

In the other condition children did not know what was in the box but observed the other person looking inside. Straight simulation should lead to the wrong answer because simply imagining themselves looking inside the box does not give a feeling of knowledge, since there is nothing in the simulating system that would provide an answer for the enquiring mind. Hence the answer would be, 'don't know', which generalized to the other person is the wrong answer to give. Correct simulation would require considerable hypothetical sophistication. The child would have to also provide an off-line assumption about a possible content and then simulate seeing that hypothetical content lying in the box when simulating having a look inside the box. This simulation should be noticeably more difficult to execute than the first case, where no such assumptions about a hypothetical content were required.

Unfortunately for the simulation theory, this apparent difference in simulation difficulty was not reflected in children's performances. In Experiment 2 by Wimmer et al. (1988), only 20 of 32 children answered correctly in the easy-to-simulate condition but 23 of 32 in the difficult-to-simulate condition. And in Experiment 3 these percentages were similar: 15 of 24 versus 14 of 24, respectively.

As a last thought we want to point out that for some mental states simulation is altogether impossible, namely for perceptual states. This is rather interesting, as the classic example for perspective taking in the developmental literature is Piaget and Inhelder's (1948/1956) Three-Mountain Problem. Children looking at a model of three Swiss mountains had to indicate how a doll viewing the same model from a different vantage point would see the mountains. It is difficult to see how children could arrive at the correct answer by 'perspective taking' in the sense of simulating the doll's view by imagining themselves sitting in the doll's place. All the information the child has for such an undertaking is a specification of the doll's position in relation to the three mountains. Left with this information as initial parameters for a visual simulation the child's visual apparatus cannot even be properly activated. To get an answer off the ground the child needs to have knowledge about vision, namely of how a person's vantage point relates to the relative position of objects within the visual field. Simulation cannot provide this knowledge.

Conclusion

Our last point above made clear that simulation can be used for only certain mental states. Furthermore, the developmental evidence that we reported and reviewed (see also Stich and Nichols, this volume; Perner, 1991, ch. 11) suggests that children do not use simulation even when it could be used in principle. In particular it is unlikely that children come to understand intentional/mental concepts by means of simulation (the Cartesian position defended by Harris). Experimental evidence suggests that these concepts have to be acquired by formation of the prerequisite mental representations. Whether these representations are part of a 'theory' or simply 'knowledge of the mind' cannot be decided on the basis of this evidence. The attraction of speaking of a 'theory of mind' comes – in our opinion – from the promise that the mysteries of concept formation can be best understood within the context of theory formation (Carey, 1985; Keil, 1989; Murphy and Medin, 1985).

Notes

The authors express their gratitude to the heads, teachers and pupils of McKee Public School and of Hollywood Public School in North York, Ontario for their friendly cooperation; to David Olson, who supervised the second author's Masters thesis; and to Paul Harris for his helpful comments on an earlier draft.

1   Stich and Nichols (this volume, ch. 5) are on occasion not clear on this point. For instance, in their reply to argument 1 of section 4 they say: 'The off-line simulation story makes no sense as an account of our ability to judge grammaticality.' But why should it? In our understanding of what simulation is supposed to achieve it is not intended to give such an account. It is intended as an account of how people figure out how the mind classifies sentences into grammatical and ungrammatical. What has to be kept separate here is people's ability to judge grammaticality (the mind as sentence cruncher, for which cognitive accounts are bad and which the simulation approach does not even attempt to explain) and people's account of this ability – typically in the form of making a prediction of how a set of sentences will be classified. The simulation theory only attempts to provide an explanation of how persons make these predictions, namely by observing the workings of their own mind as a paradigmatic sentence-classifying machine.

2   One could argue that in order to make this question more comparable to the other test questions we should have asked: 'If we ask John, 'Where is the chocolate?', what will John say?' Fortunately, Perner and Wimmer (1987) found that even younger children than tested in our experiment find both types of question equally easy. Even 4- to 5-year olds were 100% correct.

3   We would like to point out that the observed differences between the three questions are very reliable, as we have obtained comparable results in an earlier experiment with 69 4- to 8-year-olds (Howes, 1989).

4   Perner and Wimmer (1985) also reported evidence for the existence of this fall-back strategy (Experiment 3: more correct responses in belief-that-knew condition that in belief-that-thought condition).

References

Carey, S. 1985: *Conceptual Change*. Cambridge, MA: MIT Press.
Churchland, P. M. 1984: *Matter and Consciousness: A Contemporary Introduction to the Philosophy of Mind*. Cambridge, MA: MIT Press.
Coulter, J. 1979: *The Social Construction of Mind*. London: Macmillan.
Descartes, R. 1954: *Philosophical Writings*. Ed. and trans. E. Anscombe and P. T. Geach. Wokingham UK: Van Nostrand Reinhold.
Descartes, R. 1970: *Philosophical Letters*. Ed. and trans. A. Kenny. Oxford: Oxford University Press.
Eliot, J., Lovell, K., Dayton, C. M. and McGrady, B. F. 1979: A further investigation of children's understanding of recursive thinking. *Journal of Experimental Child Psychology*, 28, 149–57.
Feffer, M. H. 1959: The cognitive implications of role-taking behaviour. *Journal of Personality*, 27, 152–68.

Flavell, J., Botkin, P., Fry, C., Wright, J. and Jarvis, D. 1968: *The Development of Role-taking and Communication Skills in Children*. New York: Wiley.

Goldman, A. I. 1989: Interpretation psychologized. *Mind and Language*, 4, 161–85. Reprinted as ch. 3 in this volume.

Gopnik, A. and Astington, J. W. 1988: Children's understanding of representational change and its relation to the understanding of false belief and the appearance – reality distinction. *Child Development*, 59, 26–37.

Gopnik, A. and Slaughter, V. 1991: Young children's understanding of changes in their mental states. *Child Development*, 62, 98–110.

Gordon, R. M. 1986: Folk psychology as simulation. *Mind and Language*, 1, 158–71. Reprinted as ch. 2 in this volume.

Harris, P. L. 1989: *Children and Emotion: The Development of Psychological Understanding*. Oxford: Blackwell.

Harris, P. L. 1991: The work of the imagination. In A. Whiten (ed.), *Natural Theories of Mind: The Evolution, Development and Simulation of Everyday Mindreading*. Oxford: Blackwell.

Howes, D. L. 1989: Children's understanding of false beliefs as subjective attitudes. Unpublished M. A. thesis, University of Toronto, Ontario Institute of Studies in Education.

Johnson, C. N. 1988: Theory of mind and the structure of conscious experience. In J. W. Astington, P. L. Harris and D. R. Olson (eds), *Developing Theories of Mind*. New York: Cambridge University Press.

Keil, F. C. 1989: *Concepts, Kinds, and Cognitive Development*. Cambridge. MA: MIT Press.

Miller, P., Kessel, F. and Flavell, J. H. 1970: Thinking about people thinking about people thinking about . . . : A study of social cognitive development. *Child Development*, 41, 613–23.

Mitchell, P. and Lacohée, H. 1991: Children's early understanding of false belief. *Cognition*, 39, 107–29.

Murphy, G. L. and Medin, D. 1985: The role of theories in conceptual coherence *Psychological Review*, 92, 289–316.

Nisbett, R. E. and Ross, L. 1980: *Human Inference*. Englewood Cliffs, NJ: Prentice Hall.

Perner, J. 1991: *Understanding the Representational Mind*. Cambridge, MA: MIT Press.

Perner, J. and Wimmer, H. 1985: 'John thinks that Mary thinks that . . .': Attribution of second-order beliefs by 5- to 10-year-old children. *Journal of Experimental Child Psychology*, 39, 437–71.

Perner, J. and Wimmer, H. 1987: Young children's understanding of belief and communicative intention. *Pakistan Journal of Psychological Research*, 2, 17–40.

Piaget, J. and Inhelder, B. 1948/1956: *The Child's Conception of Space*. London: Routledge and Kegan Paul.

Shultz, T. R. and Cloghesy, K. 1981: Development of recursive awareness of intention. *Developmental Psychology*, 17, 465–71.

Wimmer, H. and Hartl, M. 1991: Against the Cartesian view on mind: Young children's difficulty with own false belief. *British Journal of Developmental Psychology*, 9, 125–38.

Wimmer, H., Hogrefe, G.-J. and Perner, J. 1988: Children's understanding of informational access as source of knowledge. *Child Development*, 59, 386–96.

Wimmer, H. and Perner, J. 1990: Children's memory for false statements. Unpublished manuscript, University of Sussex.

7

Reply to Stich and Nichols

ROBERT M. GORDON

In their vigorous, clear, and well-informed critique (ch. 5), Stich and Nichols tell us they are intrigued by the Simulation Theory, but skeptical. My aim in this reply is to answer their skeptical arguments and also, along the way, to show that the theory is even more intriguing than they suppose. In doing this I sharpen, strengthen, and build on what I wrote in the papers they cite.

1 Differences of Interpretation

Stich and Nichols have clearly tried to give a fair and accurate account of what they call 'the Gordon/Goldman proposal'. Still, there are some points at which my own view, at least, differs from the one they criticize.

They speak of the '*off-line* simulation theory'. This packs into the very name of the theory what I regard as an ancillary hypothesis: that when we simulate – that is, use our imagination to identify with others in order to explain or predict their behavior – many of the same cognitive systems that normally control our own behavior continue to run as if they were controlling our behavior, only they run off-line, with their normal output systems disconnected and their normal input systems usually modified to some degree. This hypothesis is very plausible, I believe, and I do take it for granted in some of my arguments, here and elsewhere. But I think the imaginative identification theory remains attractive even without the off-line hypothesis.

A second point is that I wouldn't want to characterize simulation as using oneself as a model. People gravitate toward this conception because extrapolation from a model is a familiar form of inference whose logical structure is fairly well understood. But to 'use oneself as a model', as I understand it, would be first to simulate *oneself* under counterfactual conditions – to ask what *I* in particular would do or feel – and then to extrapolate to someone else.

This is quite different, I have argued elsewhere, from simulating the other. Goldman and I evidently differ on this point. A related point – on which we also differ – is that simulation as I understand it doesn't demand that one already possess intentional concepts and be capable of applying them in one's own case. I have also advanced the far stronger suggestion – inspired in part by Stich's account of belief attribution (Stich, 1983) – that to ascribe to another individual x a belief that p is to assert that p within the context of a simulation of x (this volume, ch. 2).

Stich and Nichols offer two general objections to the simulation theory itself (ch. 5, section 5, 'In Defense of the Theory-Theory') and several objections to specific arguments for the theory (ch. 5, sec. 4, 'Arguments in Support of Simulation-Based Accounts'). I'll respond first to one of the general objections, the 'cognitive penetrability' argument. The other general objection I leave to the end, because it concerns developmental findings that remain much in dispute. As to the objections to specific arguments, I shall, given limitations of space, concentrate on those that appear to pose the most serious challenges to the simulation theory.

2 The 'Cognitive Penetrability' Argument

In their argument from 'cognitive penetrability', Stich and Nichols challenge us to predict the responses of subjects in certain experiments by imagining ourselves in the role of subject. The experiments uncovered little-known features of human psychology, reflected in generalizations such as the following: people tend to prefer the rightmost item in a display of merchandise, other things being equal. People who know nothing about the experiments and are ignorant of these generalizations tend to mispredict what they would do in such an experiment. This is just as one would expect if their predictions actually depended on their faulty knowledge of human psychology. If instead they arrived at their predictions by truly running their own behavior control systems off-line, then their ignorance should make no difference, Stich and Nichols argue. For, given that their own system is subject to the same bias toward the rightmost item – the 'position effect' – their simulation should *correctly* predict the findings.

Or should it? Consider an analogous use of imagination:

> I ask you to visualize two straight lines of equal length, one just above the other. One of the lines has a regular arrowhead at each end, the other has an inward-pointing arrowhead at each end. Now, *which line is longer?*

I have just tried to replicate the Müller–Lyer illusion, using only your visual imagination. There are two problems. One is *methodological*: It's silly to ask, 'Which line is longer?' because I stipulated that the two lines are *of equal length*. Suppose we ask, 'Which line *looks* longer?' There is still no reason to think we'll get the illusion going. That's because of the second problem, which may be called the problem of *imaginative impenetrability*: Even if visual imagery is a product of the visual-perception system running off-line, it is surely going to bypass some *stages* of visual processing, especially early stages–and the illusion may originate at one of these stages. In that case we will have failed to recreate the antecedent conditions for the illusion.

It's the same with trying to replicate the 'position effect' experiment. First, there is the methodological problem: unlike the subjects in the original experiment, the subject in the imagination experiment must be told that the items on display are identical (and thus of equal quality). Second, there is imaginative impenetrability. When we are actually viewing a display of identical items, position may generate illusory differences. But how can we generate illusory differences without actually viewing a display? As with visualizing the Müller–Lyer figure, visualizing a display evidently fails to 'penetrate' visual processing at the right place. That would explain why, as Stich and Nichols say (p. 151), 'most of us think we would report that the garments looked to be very similar, and then choose one randomly'.

The general problem is that for some types of psychological or psychophysical phenomena the difference between reality and imagined or simulated reality is crucial. To *imagine* drinking six martinis doesn't make one drunk, not even off-line. Here simulation is inherently inadequate, and an independent source of knowledge is indispensable. That's a shortcoming of *simulation*, but it isn't a shortcoming of the simulation *theory*. It is a *virtue* of the theory that simulation fails to predict phenomena that our common-sense belief-desire psychology fails to predict.

For Stich and Nichols's second example, predicting the results of the lottery ticket experiment, methodological inadequacy is the major problem. In the original experiment, subjects in one group were given a choice of tickets and those in the other group were sold tickets without a choice. Days later, on the morning of the lottery, they were asked to sell back their tickets, and the choice group demanded a much higher price than the no-choice group. Suppose a psychologist wanted to replicate the experiment. But suppose he is short of subjects. So he uses the same subjects over again, first in the no-choice condition and then in the choice condition. Any methodologist would tell us this is a bad experimental design. For one thing, a subject might be influenced on the second run by what he did on the first run. So we shouldn't be surprised if the subjects assigned the *same* price to the two tickets. But now suppose that the psychologist is also short of *time*. So he sells the two tickets only seconds apart; then, a second or two later, he proceeds to buy them back, instead of waiting several days, as in the original experiment. This of course makes the bad methodology far worse.

Finally, suppose that the psychologist is not only short of subjects and short of time, but also short of lottery tickets – or, more simply, suppose he is a philosopher. So he asks his subjects to *imagine* being sold two lottery tickets and then to *imagine* being asked to sell them back. I quote from Stich and Nichols (this volume, p. 151).

Now imagine yourself in both roles – first as a person who had been handed the ticket, second as a person who had been given a choice. What price would you ask in each case? Would there be any difference between the two cases?

What we now have is *simulation* harnessed to very bad methodology.

The third example offered by Stich and Nichols – the belief perseverance experiment – suffers from *both* a methodological problem and a problem of 'imaginative impenetrability'. One can't expect to replicate a belief perseverance experiment if subjects are *immediately* shown that they are getting false 'information'. And it is far from obvious that the mechanism responsible for the perseverance of *beliefs*, whatever it may be, must also be triggered by merely *feigned* beliefs.

Summing up so far: Stich and Nichols are wrong in saying that if we were simulating, then we would have correctly predicted the findings in these experiments. Contrary to what they suggest, simulation has its shortcomings, some inherent and some only when it's harnessed to bad methodology. And that is just as it should be, if the simulation theory is right.

3 The Comparison to Grammar

Stich and Nichols claim that two of the arguments Goldman and I advance against the theory-theory of folk psychology would apply to theory-theories in other domains where a theory-theory really is the only plausible account. Their chief example of such a domain is grammar. Replying to argument 1, that no one has been able to state the principles of common-sense psychology, they write (p. 134), 'It has proven enormously difficult to state the principles underlying a speaker's capacity to judge the grammaticality of sentences.' And in answer to the anomalous precocity argument (argument 3), they say that according to generative grammar (p. 136), 'the knowledge structures that underlie a child's linguistic ability are enormously complex'.

But there is a difference. Theory theorists generally assume that the laws of folk psychology can be formulated in terms of the common-sense mental vocabulary. They *must* assume this if they hold, as most seem to, that the common-sense theory implicitly *defines* these terms. Generative grammarians, on the other hand, have no such compunctions about introducing a technical vocabulary. They want to explain common-sense intuitions of grammaticality, but they are not constrained to do this by way of *a common-sense grammatical vocabulary*. The reason is simple. They don't claim that what explains our grammatical competence is *folk grammar* – the principles that underlie common-sense notions of grammar and common-sense explanations why one word string is grammatical and another is not. But theory theorists *do* generally make the corresponding claim: that what explains our competence in predicting behavior is *folk psychology* – the principles that underlie our mental attributions and explanations of behavior.

Why is this difference relevant? Well, for one thing, where there is no constraint on concepts – no requirement that the theory must be framed in terms of *the child's own concepts* – it isn't clear how a *precocity* issue could arise. Analogy: It's all right to say that to catch a ball children have to solve differential equations, as long as this doesn't entail that they have to *understand* differential equations.

What of the argument that no one has been able to state the principles? Actually it is Stephen Schiffer who argues most forcefully:

> But can anyone state so much as a single generalization that fills [the] bill? (Schiffer, 1987, p. 29; Schiffer's emphasis)

Schiffer's negative answer, argued at length in *Remnants of Meaning* (1987), makes him skeptical of the view that there is a

> system of law-like generalizations using the notions belief and desire that is known, or 'used', by plain folk who possess these concepts. (Schiffer, 1987, p. 29)

Yes, there remains serious disagreement about the computational mechanism underlying our grammatical competence: but *of course* that shouldn't lead us to think there is *no* computational mechanism that underlies our grammatical competence. These seem to be vastly different issues. But I won't argue the point. I have never made the complaint that no one has been able to state the principles. My charge has been that whatever common-sense laws and generalizations we may find, they are at best useful heuristics. We are much better predictors than our generalizations are, because *our own* decision-making system warns us when a generalization yields a crazy prediction: that is how we fill in the implicit *ceteris paribus* clause.

4 Simplicity

I turn now to Stich and Nichols's reply to argument 4 (pp. 137–8), that the simulation theory is simpler than a view that posits a special stock of laws corresponding to rules of logic and reason. Stich and Nichols ask: What about the investment in a special *control mechanism* for taking one's decision-making system off-line, feeding it pretend inputs, and interpreting its outputs as predictions of another's behavior? My answer is that it isn't special: we have to have it *anyway* if we're to do hypothetical and counterfactual reasoning. To judge whether a conditional statement is true or false would require (according to both the classical Ramsey account and Stalnaker's modified account) a belief generator that adds the antecedent to one's existing stock of beliefs. It would also require the capacity to use the modified stock of beliefs as a basis for deciding – *off-line*, of course – whether or not the *consequent* is true. Finally, it would require the capacity to interpret this output as a decision whether or not the *conditional* is true (Stalnaker, 1968). So, contrary to Stich and Nichols's claim, simulation gets its control system as well as its data base pretty much 'for free'.

But I agree with Stich and Nichols that greater precision is needed if the simplicity issue is to be given much weight – precision not only in formulating the theories to be compared but also in stating what the issue is. The general notion of theoretical simplicity isn't a clear one. Moreover, it isn't clear why nature should *answer* to it, that is, prefer the simpler theory. So I propose to put the notion aside altogether and talk instead of *code compression*. It's clear why nature would prefer a coding scheme that offers greater compression, other things being equal: Less code, therefore fewer synapses, therefore smaller brain, smaller energy demand, and so forth. Other things being equal, the more compression a scheme allows, the more probable it is that it's the scheme we've got.

I approach the topic by first considering an experienced Shakespearean actress, who has mastered a variety of roles: she can 'become' characters as diverse as Ophelia, Titania, and Lady Macbeth. How are these distinct characters represented in her brain? A very plausible answer, I think, is that for each character what is stored is not a set of *facts* about the character's mental life, such as an inventory of Lady Macbeth's mental states, processes, and tendencies; but rather a set of *operations*, namely the set of changes or adjustments the actress makes as she mentally prepares each evening to 'become' Lady Macbeth. Information about each character is stored as a procedure rather than in declarative form; and specifically, as a transformational procedure. Here is a partial analogy: video signals may be digitally transmitted or stored in compressed form by coding only the differences between each frame and its predecessor, rather than coding each frame in its entirety. Thus a frame is represented as a set of changes from the preceding frame – except for the initial frame, which would be coded in its entirety. One of the *dis*analogies is that in the case of the actress, the initial 'frame' – information about the actress herself – isn't coded at all. She needs no inventory of *her own* mental states, processes, and tendencies.

The simulation theory – together with the ancillary off-line hypothesis – tells a similar story about our common-sense knowledge of the mental lives of particular others. Such knowledge, insofar as we have it, is not a kind of speculative knowledge but rather a kind of know-how: it is knowing how to transform ourselves into the other. The various people we know are represented in their mental aspects as sets of transformational operations. But unlike the actress we aren't called upon to transform ourselves audibly or visibly; we keep it to ourselves. And whereas the actress transforms herself into characters in *fictional* worlds, we typically match these transformational operations with particular bodies in the actual world.

A theory, it is true, could gain some of the advantages of such a system by assigning *default values* to all parameters and then coding only *deviations* from those values. But the default values would have to come from somewhere. Even if they were just based on one's own case, the theory would have to be fed *information about one's own case*. In other words, the initial 'frame' would have to be coded. Simulation avoids altogether this initial investment in information acquisition and storage.

5 The Developmental Arguments

I have left the developmental arguments and counter-arguments to the end, because the findings on which they are based remain in dispute and there is a considerable amount of work in progress.

Stich and Nichols try to neutralize argument 6 (the 'Maxi' argument, pp. 141–4) by showing on the one hand that only one of several possible versions of the simulation theory predicts the experimental results, and on the other hand that a version of the theory-theory would make the same prediction. They also offer a developmental argument of their own, based on experimental results (Wimmer, Hogrefe and Sodian, 1988) which, they say, are readily explained by the theory-theory but not by the simulation theory. I shall argue that there is good reason not to trust the results Stich and Nichols cite in favor of the theory-theory, and further, that they are mistaken about the developmental implications of the two theories.

According to Wimmer et al. (1988), young children are much stingier in attributing knowledge to others than they are in attributing it to themselves. This seems at odds with the simulation theory, for 'the answer [the child] comes up with [as to whether the other knows] is *not* the one that she herself would come up with, were she in the subject's place'(Stich and Nichols, this volume, p. 150). But the result can be explained by a version of the theory-theory, according to Stich and Nichols.

Unlike the findings of Wimmer and Perner (1983), which have been replicated several times, this alleged disparity in first- and third-person attributions is by no means well established. (Indeed, it is in conflict with other recent findings, as Goldman shows in detail in this volume, ch. 9.) And there are independent reasons to distrust the finding. Whereas Wimmer and Perner (1983) were chiefly concerned with children's predictions of Maxi's behavior, Wimmer et al. (1988) ask children to say whether a particular individual 'knows' the answer to a certain question, namely, 'What is in the box?' And there are good reasons to be cautious in drawing inferences from children's applications of the predicate 'know' (or *wissen*, the term Wimmer et al., were working with). The verbal evidence appears to be too liberal a measure of attributions of knowledge to oneself and too conservative a measure of attributions of knowledge to others.

It is too liberal a measure of attributions to oneself because there is a cheap and easy procedure for giving generally plausible answers to questions about what one knows, namely, the 'answer check procedure' described by Wimmer et al.: to say whether one knows the answer to a question, simply check to see whether one has an answer to the question.[1] Virtually any speaker can be trained in this procedure, without any understanding of the sentence form 'x knows that p'. Likewise, a speaker may learn that it is optional to preface any assertion, such as, 'There's a pencil in the box', with the formula, 'I know that' or the formula, 'I believe that'. But from this it should not be inferred that the speaker is capable of meta-representation, that is, of believing that he knows or believes something.

On the other hand, the verbal evidence appears to be too conservative a measure of attributions of knowledge to others. Children about 5 years of age reportedly deny that another 'knows what is in the box', even after observing the other *looking* into the box or *being verbally informed* of its contents. Stich and Nichols infer that 'these children have not learned that people will come to know *that p* by seeing or being told *that p*'. But a more plausible account would be that the children haven't yet mastered the word 'know'. For there is a good deal of behavioral evidence that even four-year-olds are well aware that if one reports to X the fact that p, or if one makes the fact visually evident to X, then the fact that p becomes *accessible to X as a possible basis for action or emotion*. And if the fact that p is accessible to X as a possible basis for action or emotion, *then X knows that p*. Note, for example, that four-year-olds are reasonably skillful at hiding facts from others. If they don't want others to get angry or to tease them *about* something they did, they don't *tell* them they did it – much less *show* them, 'Look what I did!' And they ask others not to tell: 'Don't tell Bea I [had an "accident"]', my son at age $3\frac{1}{2}$ implored his mother, 'she'll tell *everybody*.'

I conclude that the alleged disparity between self-attributions and other-attributions is probably only a verbal disparity. Without supplementation by further research, the results reported in Wimmer et al. (1988) support *neither* the hypothesis that the subjects do recognize that *they themselves* can learn by seeing or being told nor the hypothesis that they fail to recognize that *others* can learn by seeing or being told. In short, there is reason to doubt that the developmental facts are as Stich and Nichols portray them.

Now consider what Stich and Nichols have to say about the developmental implications of the theory-theory and the simulation theory, respectively. They are right about two things. There is a possible version of the theory-theory that would explain the results of the Maxi experiment. And there is a possible version of the theory-theory that would explain the results of the ways-of-knowing experiments. But Stich and Nichols overlook a rather important point: these are *different* versions of the theory-theory; indeed, they are, or at least they appear to be, *incompatible* versions. I'll explain.

In chapter 2 of this volume, I argued that if it were by acquiring a *theory* that children develop the capacity to predict the behavior of others, the capacity to predict actions on the basis of the other's beliefs would develop, so to speak, as a single package: it should not matter whether a belief was true (in agreement with the child's own belief) or false (contrary to the child's own belief). And the Maxi experiment seems to show that in fact it does *not* develop as a single package. But as Stich and Nichols rightly point out, the theory-theory can accommodate the Maxi experiment by stipulating that (this volume, p.143):

[A]t a given stage of development, children have mastered the part of the theory that specifies how beliefs and desires lead to behavior, though they have not mastered the entire story about how beliefs are caused. At this stage, they might simply assume that beliefs are caused by the way the world is; they might attribute to everyone the same beliefs that they have. A child who has acquired this much of folk psychology would (incorrectly) attribute to Maxi the belief that the chocolate is in the cupboard.

Stich and Nichols argue that the theory-theory can also accommodate the ways-of-knowing experiments of Wimmer et al. (1988). It does this by stipulating that children acquire the fragment of folk psychology that associates knowledge or belief that *p* with its verbal expression, *saying* that *p*, while still in the dark to what causes knowledge or belief that *p*. Only later do they acquire the generalization that people will come to know or believe *that p* by seeing or being told *that p*, and later still the generalization that people acquire knowledge or belief by *inference* from what is perceived.

Both versions of the theory-theory, the one that accommodates the Maxi experiment and the one that accommodates the ways-of-knowing experiments, hold children to be initially naïve about the causes of knowledge or belief. *But they hold them to be naïve in exactly opposite ways!* According to the Maxi experiment version, the three-year-old folk psychologist is ultra-liberal about knowledge, ascribing it to others without asking whether the other has *access* to the facts, that is, a *way* of knowing what is the case. But to accommodate the ways-of-knowing experiments, the three- and four-year-old must be portrayed as ultra-conservative, ascribing knowledge only if there is a recognized way of knowing that would give the other access to the facts in question. The theory-theory can't have it both ways.

Moreover, each of these versions of the theory-theory is unattractive in itself. Especially bizarre is the *ultra-conservative* version, which implies that until age five children regard others, including their own care-givers, as presumptively windowless creatures, cut off from the world and consequently unresponsive to the environment. The problem facing the *ultra-liberal* version is this: If the initial supposition is that beliefs are never at variance with the facts, if they introduce no dimension of variability, then *why would children posit beliefs at all*? Is it that three-year-olds can't tolerate action at a distance and so must posit a proximate cause inside the head? Not likely.

It isn't surprising that for each of these experimental findings there is a possible version of the theory-theory that explains it. That is so because, as Stich and Nichols grant, the theory-theory 'is compatible with (but does not entail) lots of developmental patterns' (p. 144). Taken merely as the general claim that people use a theory to explain and predict behavior, the theory-theory is noncommittal as to whether people acquire the theory all at once or piecemeal, and if piecemeal, which pieces come first. But the simulation theory is not similarly neutral on these matters, contrary to what Stich and Nichols suggest. Try to devise a version of the simulation theory that would *conflict with* the finding that children predict behavior simply on the basis of the actual facts (the *actual* current position of the chocolate) before they develop the ability to consider the other's *beliefs* (for example, Maxi's belief that the chocolate is where he had left it). This is not just a matter of devising scenarios in which the capacity to generate 'pretend'-beliefs is developed before or simultaneously with the capacity for off-line decision-making. What is proposed is that from the start – from the very moment that the child begins to use off-line decision-making to predict the behavior of others – rather than naïvely projecting his own belief base to the other, he starts *making adjustments to it.* But if he doesn't at first naïvely project his own belief base and learn that this sometimes *leads to error*, what *reason* would he have to make adjustments? And how would he learn *when* to make adjustments? And how would he know *what* adjustments to make? Unable to learn any of this from his own experience, the child must either be innately equipped with the information and motivation or somehow acquire it from others. That is, children can skip the initial naïve stage and move directly into the sophisticated stage of the four-year-old, but only by using resources not derived from simulation. Left to simulation alone, they will do just as we actually find children doing in the Maxi experiment. The simulation theory is not neutral.

Conclusion

I have replied to what appear to be the most serious challenges posed by Stich and Nichols, and I believe I have successfully answered each challenge. But much has been gained from the dialectic. The 'cognitive impenetrability' argument has been rebutted, but we learned something about the *limits* of simulation. The simplicity argument has been made more precise with my sketch of a new account of the representation of other minds. The appeal to the Maxi experiment still stands, but it is now strengthened by a more careful contrast between the developmental implications of the simulation theory and those of the theory-theory. If Stich and Nichols's aim was to stimulate the development of the simulation theory – and I think it was, in part – then they have been successful, too.[2]

Notes

1 Actually, this is more appropriate to belief than to knowledge, as I argue in my 'Reply to Perner and Hower', this volume, ch. 8.
2 My thanks to John Barker and Russell Trenholme for helpful comments on an earlier draft of this reply.

References

Goldman, A. I. 1989: Intepretation psychologized. *Mind and Language*, 4, 161–85. Reprinted as ch. 3 in this volume.

Schiffer, S. 1987: *Remnants of Meaning*. Cambridge, MA: MIT Press.

Stalnaker, R. C. 1968: A theory of conditionals. In N. Rescher (ed.), *Studies in Logical Theory*. Oxford: Blackwell, APQ Monograph no. 2.

Stich, S. 1983: *From Folk Psychology to Cognitive Science: The Case Against Belief*. Cambridge, MA: MIT Press.

Wimmer, H., Hogrefe, J. and Sodian, B. 1988: A second stage in children's conception of mental life: Understanding informational access as origins of knowledge and belief. In J. Astington, P. Harris and D. Olson (eds), *Developing Theories of Mind*. Cambridge: Cambridge University Press.

Wimmer, H. and Perner, J. 1983: Beliefs about beliefs: Representation and constraining function of wrong beliefs in young children's understanding of deception. *Cognition*, 13, 103–28.

8

Reply to Perner and Howes

ROBERT M. GORDON

The simulation/theory debate has become an area of fruitful exchange between experimentalists and philosophers. Needless to say, there are misunderstandings. One of these is apparent in Perner and Howes's application of the label 'Cartesian.'

Perner and Howes correctly attribute to me the strong claim 'that simulation is *sufficient* for providing children with intentional concepts like belief, knowledge, desire, etc.' But then they go on to say that 'This strong claim is often referred to as "Cartesian"' (p. 161). I am not sure who characterizes it that way, but I want to make it very clear that it reflects a serious misunderstanding, at least of my position. According to the Cartesian doctrine, as they note, 'the mind knows what state it is in (i.e. must have the concept of what kind of state it is)'. But if mental concepts can – and, as I believe, do in fact – arise out of the procedure of *simulating others*, then it is *not* true that we already, independently, possess the concepts, much less that we already are capable of applying them in our own case, as the Cartesian doctrine would maintain. If we get our intentional concepts from simulating others, or if at least we *can* acquire them in that way, then we do not, or at least we *need* not, acquire them by some mysterious Cartesian self-awareness. These are in fact contrary, incompatible positions. It is true that some proponents of a simulation theory (Paul Harris, 1989, p. 57, for one), do seem to endorse some sort of Cartesianism. But in that case, they could not also hold, as I do, that mental concepts arise out of the procedure of simulating others.

The assumption that the Simulation Theory is Cartesian plays a large role in Perner and Howes's argument against the theory. For the relevance of their experimental data depends on whether the Simulation Theory would hold, as they suppose, that it is by *introspecting their own states* that their subjects decide, for example, whether John thinks he knows the answer to a question. But the focus of my discussion will be on a different assumption they make:

that introspection – specifically, a 'feeling of knowledge' – is our guide in attributing knowledge to ourselves.

1 Perner and Howes's Experiment

In Perner and Howes's experiment, children are told a story very similar to the 'Maxi' story of Wimmer and Perner (1983). In the experimental condition, but not in the control condition, the story includes information that is not available to the main character in the story. In this experiment, however, all the subjects were old enough (nearly five years and above) to take this lack of information into account in answering the question,

    Q1   Where does John think the chocolates are?

The children come up with the right answer both in the experimental condition, where the chocolates are relocated, and in the control condition, where they remain in the place where John had left them. But subjects were also asked:

    Q2   What if we . . . ask John: 'John, do you know where the chocolates are?' What will he say?

The correct answer to Q2 should be 'Yes' both in the control condition and in the experimental condition. Speaking for John, subjects should say, 'Yes, I know', whether or not from their own point of view John really does know. But in fact, for nearly 50 percent of the younger subjects (up to 5 years 8 months), the response varied according to *their own* belief as to whether John knows where the chocolates are. They described John as claiming to know, if and only if, by their own lights, John actually does know. So it would appear that their own point of view prejudiced what they said in the role of John.

Perner and Howes argue that the *representational* account explains why children would find Q2 more difficult to answer than Q1: Q2 concerns a second-order ('meta-') representation, a belief about a belief, which is a more difficult notion to master than the first-order representation Q1 is concerned with. They should therefore fare no better with Q2 than they do with Q3, which concerns *Mary's* second-order belief about whether John knows. The young *simulator*, on the other hand, needn't master the notion of a representation, much less that of a second-order representation. Perner and Howes consider and reject the parallel suggestion that answering Q2 would call for a comparably difficult simulation, namely a *simulation of a simulation*, as would be needed for Q3. There would be no need for this, they say, because 'it is part and parcel of a belief to be convinced that one knows where the object is' (p. 163). Hence, merely by simulating John's belief in order to answer Q1, the child ought to be in a position to answer Q2 correctly.

Crucial to Perner and Howes's argument are two assumptions:

1. It is by introspection that one answers the question, 'Do I know where the chocolates are?' or generically, 'Do I know [the answer to question Q]?'
2. Simulation (but not theorizing about representational mechanisms) enables us to identify the state another is in by introspection of our own states.

These assumptions are crucial to showing that simulation, but not representational theorizing, ought to get Q2 *right*. I believe that both of these assumptions are false. I have already said a few words that bear on assumption (2), but what I shall specifically contest here is assumption (1). Much more plausible than (1) – though not quite right, as we'll see – is the hypothesis of an 'answer check procedure' suggested in Wimmer et al. (1988), which I discuss in ch. 7 of this volume: If asked whether you know the answer to a question Q (for example, about the location of something), simply check to see if *you have* an answer to Q. To do this, you don't try to investigate your mental states: rather you just try to answer Q. Only, instead of presenting your answer aloud – instead of expressing your belief, in other words – you just say, 'Yes, I know'. And if you *fail* to answer Q (within a short time), then you say, 'No, I don't know', That's all there is to it.

Were this hypothesis correct as it stands, then in order to answer Q2, the child would have only to ask whether John *has an answer* to the question, 'Where are the chocolates?' According to the mental representation theory, this should be just a matter of determining whether John has a *first-order representation of the location of the chocolates*. This would in fact be a *less* difficult task than answering Q1, which requires that the child *state the content* of John's representation. In any case, to answer Q2, the child would have no need to picture John as having a *second*-order representation.

But the hypothesis is *not* correct as it stands. The answer check procedure would be appropriate for saying whether one has a *belief* as to the answer to a question, but not for saying whether one *knows* the answer.[1] The conditions for 'I know' are more restrictive than those for 'I have a belief'. I don't think what is required is introspection of what Perner and Howes call the 'feeling of knowledge'. The chief restriction is (roughly) that one shouldn't claim to know if one has an answer *A and also a reason to question whether A is the right answer* – that is, some other belief or beliefs that raise a doubt about *A*. For example, I have an answer to the question, 'Where is my briefcase?' but I also have a couple of reasons to question that answer, namely that I have often been wrong about where I left something, and in any case, my things sometimes get moved about by others in my house. Hence I wouldn't claim to *know* the answer. There is a reasonable doubt.

This further condition, I suggest, might trip up a substantial number of Perner and Howes's five-year-olds. On the matter of whether John would have reason to doubt his answer, reasons *of their own* come to mind that put John's answer into question. Because they themselves have reason to doubt that the chocolates are where John thinks they are, they impute such reasons to John. That is why their response to Q2 varies according *to their own* belief as to whether John knows where the chocolates are. It is true that they can successfully isolate the question, 'Where does John believe the chocolates to be?' from the question, 'Where are the chocolates?' and thus answer Q1 correctly. Yet is seems plausible that dealing with reasons for doubt – isolating the question 'Does John have reason for doubt?' from the question, 'Is there reason for doubt?' – would take cognitive development beyond that required for dealing with *facts*.

(A further possibility, though I don't think it is the main problem, is that some children attributed to John a justifiable skepticism, like mine about the location of my briefcase. John might reason, 'I forget where I put things; and besides, *Mom often moves them anyway*! So I don't *know*, at most I only *believe*.' True, there was no evidence of this in the *control* condition. But the relocation of the chocolates in the *experimental* condition could have suggested to the children that John had reason to be skeptical. That might explain why even some of the older children had John say, 'I don't know', in the experimental condition. Even so, this would account for only a small portion of the 50 percent of the younger subjects who got Q2 wrong in the experimental condition.)

If I am right in thinking that children's judgments as to whether John would have reason to doubt his answer are readily contaminated by their own reasons for doubt, then we should expect massive errors in answering Q2 whether the Simulation Theory is true or Perner and Howes's mental representation theory is true. If anything, the simulation theory comes out better, for it makes it easier to understand how one's own doubts might – by failing to be switched off in a simulation of John – lead one to attribute such doubts to John.

2 *A Prima Facie Case for Simulation*

In this last section, I offer two reasons for thinking that Perner and Howes's subjects produce their answers by simulating John. First, in Q2, one is asked, not to *predict* what John would say, but to *say* what John would say, which is a species of *doing as John would do*, or what might be called *behavioral simulation*. One is asked to employ one's own speech apparatus to give a direct quote, a *verbatim* copy, of the hypothetical verbal output of John's speech apparatus. But *behavioral* simulations are often generated by an underlying process of *mental* simulation. This seems especially true of explicit role play in which someone plays the part of a specific other person. One who wished to maintain that saying what another would say is generated in a radically *different* way at least owes us an explanation why this is so.

A second reason to think that Perner and Howes's subjects produce their answers by simulating John is that 'What would *x* say if ____ ?' questions sometimes dredge up, along with the verbal response, *unsolicited emotional accompaniments*. Consider the following simple experiment. Children are told the story of Emily, who loses her favorite doll and then, after much searching, finds it again. Then they are asked:

> What if we ask Emily, 'Emily, are you glad you found your doll?'
> What will she say, yes or no?

I suspect that a number of chilren of age four or five – let's say, at least 10 percent – will answer in an emphatically *glad* tone of voice – 'Yes!' – accompanied by an appropriate facial expression. (To rule out the possibility that they are just glad they know the answer,[2] they should also be asked if Emily would say she was *sad* when she lost her doll. I predict that some will answer 'Yes' with sadness in their voice. To get a scientifically respectable measure of these emotional accompaniments is of course no easy task.) Assuming that my suspicion is correct, how should we account for the unsolicited (yet appropriate) emotional response? If the children answered by mentally (not just behaviorally) playing the part of Emily – making the necessary adjustments if, for example, they themselves don't care about dolls – then we can easily explain the spontaneous, unsolicited emotionality. What alternative explanation may be given? Consider the following hypothesis, which might be offered by a mental representation theorist. The children picture Emily as having in her head or elsewhere a sort of 'desire box' containing a mental picture of her doll being held in her arms. They also picture a 'belief box': there she had a picture that showed her doll very far away, but that picture is now replaced by a picture of the doll being held in her arms. The children have learned that getting a picture in one's belief box that *matches* a picture in one's desire box tends to cause gladness. And they have learned that gladness tends to deposit in one's belief box a picture of oneself being glad. That explains why the children say 'Yes' when asked what Emily will say when asked if she is glad. But why would the children also produce an unsolicited expression of emotion? I have no idea, given this sort of account. The process that leads to their 'Yes' response is, after all, just *cool calculation*. Moreover, if such a process led to an unsolicited expression of emotion, the expression would be anything but *spontaneous*. It would be, quite literally, a calculated response, based on the children's general knowledge that gladness tends to produce certain vocal and muscular effects.

So those children who present unsolicited emotional accompaniments probably obtained their answer by simulation. What of the other children? The most economical hypothesis would be that some tend to be unexpressive even when *they themselves* are glad, and others are sophisticated enough to *suppress* emotional accompaniments when asked what Emily would say. It is of course possible that some children obtained their answer not by playing the part of Emily but in a radically different way, such as that sketched above. And it is also possible that matters are quite different for 'unemotional' questions, such as, 'Do you know where the chocolates are?' Finally, I may simply be wrong in thinking that there are unsolicited emotional accompaniments. I claim only to have given two *prima facie* reasons to think that Perner and Howes's subjects produce their answers by simulating John.

Notes

1   According to philosophers influenced by Moore's Paradox, this is the common procedure for determining what one knows or at least believes. As Gareth Evans wrote (Evans, 1982, p. 225):

> I get myself in position to answer the question whether I believe that *p* by putting into operation whatever procedure I have for answering the question whether *p*.

2   This possibility was suggested to me by Sharon Wilcox.

References

Evans, G. 1982: *The Varieties of Reference*. Oxford: Oxford University Press.
Harris, P. L. 1989: *Children and Emotion: The Development of Psychological Understanding*. Oxford: Blackwell.
Wimmer, H. and Perner, J. 1983: Beliefs about beliefs: Representation and constraining function of wrong beliefs in young children's understanding of deception. *Cognition*, 13, 103–28.

9
In Defense of the Simulation Theory

ALVIN I. GOLDMAN

1 Introduction

Stephen Stich and Shaun Nichols advance the debate over folk psychology with their vivid depiction of the contest between the simulation theory and the theory-theory (Stich and Nichols, this volume, ch. 5). At least two aspects of their presentation I find highly congenial. First, they give a generally fair characterization of the simulation theory, in some respects even improving its formulation. Though I have a few minor quarrels with their formulation, it is mostly quite faithful to the version which I have found attractive (Goldman, 1989, reprinted as ch. 3 in this volume). Second, I concur with Stich and Nichols in their assertion that the theory-theory and the simulation theory are the only two games in town. Where I disagree, of course, is in Stich and Nichols's contention that their arguments so dim the prospects of the simulation theory that it should no longer be taken seriously. On the contrary, I shall maintain, the simulation theory remains a very plausible contender, and should receive careful and respectful consideration in the continuing investigation.

The heart of the Stich and Nichols (henceforth: S&N) critique appears in their sections 4 and 5. Section 4 reviews seven arguments by Gordon (1986, reprinted as ch. 2 in this volume) and me (this volume, ch. 3) in support of the simulation theory, and tries to show that none are persuasive. Section 5 presents two arguments against the simulation theory. Before turning to these arguments, though, we must consider some stage-setting that occurs earlier in their paper and might loom as large in the debate as the material in sections 4 and 5.

2 Knowledge-rich vs. Knowledge-poor Paradigms

Briefly, S&N describe the 'dominant' explanatory strategy in cognitive science as a strategy that appeals to internally represented knowledge structures, typically a body of rules or principles or propositions. The theory-theory in folk psychology is a specimen of this sort of approach, whereas the simulation theory, as S&N portray it, fits a fundamentally different paradigm. The implication seems to be that opting for the simulation theory over the theory-theory would be an abandonment of the prevailing paradigm of cognitive science. And that sounds like mutiny.

In fact, choice of the simulation theory would not be a radical departure from familiar paradigms in cognitive science. It is true that a great deal of cognitive science fits the *knowledge-rich* paradigm stressed by S&N. But this is not the sole paradigm in cognitive science. There is also a substantial tradition that posits *knowledge-poor* procedures, i.e. processes or heuristics that are relatively simple or crude, and do not depend on quite so rich a set of rules or so complex a knowledge-base. The simulation theory fits this tradition fairly comfortably.

What are some examples of what I am calling 'knowledge-poor' procedures? A number of such examples are inferential heuristics proposed by Amos Tversky and Daniel Kahneman, e.g. the 'anchoring and adjustment' heuristic and the 'representativeness' heuristic. Instead of hypothesizing that naïve cognizers have rules or knowledge structures comparable in complexity and sophistication to the probability calculus, these psychologists conjecture that cognizers have simple procedures for making probability judgments. For example, people sometimes estimate a probability by starting with an initial, contextually determined, value (an anchor), and then adjusting this estimate upwards or downwards (Tversky and Kahneman, 1974). Another way of estimating the probability of an event is by assessing the degree to which it is representative of a population or class to which it belongs. When asked for the probability that a woman with a certain biographical profile is both a bank teller and a feminist, for example, subjects do not consult the conjunction rule of the probability calculus, but instead consider the degree to which the attribute of feminist bank teller is representative of the specified profile (Tversky and Kahneman, 1983).

In the case of vision, many researchers believe that the visual system is really a bundle of crude mechanisms, operating in parallel. V. S. Ramachandran (1990) describes the visual system as a 'bag of tricks', i.e. an assortment of relatively simple or 'dumb' heuristics that achieve efficiency by joint operation. He compares the system to a bunch of drunks staggering together toward a goal. It is easier for Nature, he conjectures, to evolve multiple crude mechanisms than a single, mathematically elegant algorithm. One component of the visual system, for example, constructs shape from shading with the help of a 'single light-source' constraint: it assumes that there is a single light-source, above the head, and constructs shape interpretations of images in accordance with this assumption. This is rather similar to the simulation heuristic, which assumes that other people are like oneself, and constructs mental interpretations of others on the basis of this assumption.

Moving closer to 'home' – the domain of interpersonal interpretation – there are simple heuristics in place that promote communication but do not involve sophisticated theory. I have in mind, for example, the heuristic of 'deictic gaze', or joint visual attention. The capacity for following the gaze of another is an extremely early accomplishment, as revealed in experiments by Butterworth and colleagues (Butterworth and Cochran, 1980; Butterworth, 1991; see also ch. 12). When a mother turns and visually inspects a target, her six-month-old baby will look to the correct side of the room the mother is attending to. The babies are accurate in locating the object referred to by the mother's change of gaze when the correct target is first along their path of scanning from the mother to the target; they are only at chance level, though, when the correct target is second along the scan path. So, at least in the earliest stage of joint visual attention, a fairly simple heuristic seems to be at work.

The point of these examples is simply to illustrate the fact that cognitive scientists quite commonly postulate rudimentary heuristics, which do not implicate any highly sophisticated theory in the head of the cognizer. To the extent that the simulation approach also postulates a comparatively crude and elementary heuristic, it does not violate any sacrosanct strategy of cognitive science. Knowledge-rich procedures may indeed be widely invoked, but they are not the only sort of procedure that can claim legitimacy under the banner of cognitive science.

3 Problems of Formulation and Acquisition

Let me turn now to the seven arguments by Gordon and Goldman (henceforth: G&G) which S&N (ch. 5) address in section 4, slightly permuting their order to facilitate discussion. I begin by grouping together arguments 1 and 3. Argument 1 is that nobody has been able to give an adequate formulation of the principles of the folk theory; and argument 3 is that the acquisition of such a theory would demand anomalous precocity.

There is an important background for these points that needs to be recalled. In the philosophical literature it has been widely assumed that it should be easy to formulate the principles of folk psychology because they are *platitudes*, i.e. truths that are obvious to everyone, much like 'All bachelors are unmarried'. Against this popular picture, it is worth stressing how difficult it has been to formulate such principles with accuracy. Of course, the theory-theorist may claim that the theory in question is *tacit*, no more accessible than internalized rules of grammar. But this is already a shift away from the original form of the theory-theory.

Another standard component of the theory-theory has been the assumption that folk-psychological platitudes are culturally produced and culturally transmitted. A typical statement of this idea is given by Paul Churchland (1988, p. 59): 'All of us learn [the folk-psychological] framework (at mother's knee, as we learn our language), and in so doing we acquire the common-sense conception of what conscious intelligence is . . . It embodies the accumulated wisdom of thousands of generations' attempts to understand how we humans work.' In response to this picture, it is highly germane to point out, as I did in chapter 3 of this volume, that the cultural transmission model is quite problematic. It is a non-starter if it implies that the platitudes themselves are learned from mother's formulations. Very few children have mothers that utter these platitudes. It is unclear, therefore, how the putative 'wisdom of thousands of generations' is supposed to be 'accumulated'. Perhaps children pick up clues from their elders' speech but generate the lawlike generalizations that constitute the platitudes by themselves. This leaves it questionable, though, whether they will generate the same platitudes as their elders.

Struck by problems of acquisition, a leading proponent of the theory-theory, Jerry Fodor, writes: 'there are, thus far, precisely no suggestions about how a child might acquire the apparatus of intentional explanation "from experience"' (Fodor, 1987, p. 133). He therefore postulates innate possession of the intentional apparatus. This hypothesis, however, would mark a major shift in the standard picture of folk psychology, for it would eliminate the image of an incremental accumulation of wisdom by thousands of generations of theorizers.

If Fodor's hypothesis seems too radical, we must ask how the child generates and accepts its 'theory of mind'. The old view carried the implication that the standard methods of scientific theory-generation and theory-acceptance are employed (whatever exactly these are). In normal cases of hypothesis construction, however, different scientists come up with different theories (especially when they work independently); whereas here we are told that all children arrive at essentially the same theory. That is indeed anomalous. S&N respond to this challenge by granting that 'it is implausible to suppose that the swift acquisition of folk psychology is subserved by the same learning mechanism that the child uses to learn history or chemistry or astronomy'. This is an important concession, again moving the discussion some distance from the usual perspective of philosophers of mind.

S&N call attention to other cases in which the child's accomplishment is comparably impressive and comparably swift: the cases of grammar acquisition and the acquisition of 'folk physics'. They are certainly right to cite these cases as possible analogues, and I agree that such analogues show that the theory-theory cannot be ruled out by the mystery of acquisition. At the same time, we see that there are difficulties for the standard 'cultural creation and transmission' model of folk psychology, and this is significant. Second, there seems to be convergence on the idea that we should be looking for some sort of 'special purpose' component, perhaps some kind of cognitive module. This could take the form of an innate knowledge structure or a special-purpose learning mechanism. But it could also take the form of a special type of heuristic: the off-line simulation heuristic. I agree, then, that G&G's first and third arguments are not knock-down refutations of the theory-theory. As S&N remark, knock-down refutations are hard to come by in cognitive science. But these arguments do cast doubt on some popular variations of the theory-theory theme, and highlight the difficulties that must be met by any detailed development of the theory-theory.

4 Simulation in Other Domains

I turn next to argument 2 of S&N's section 4. This argument points out that some cognitive scientists have endorsed the idea of mental simulation as a cognitive heuristic, though not in connection with determining the mental states of others. S&N reply that the 'other' so-called simulation models are really species of the theory-theory, properly classified under (D) in their figure 5.2 (p. 134), not instances of an off-line simulation heuristic.

To sort out this dispute, we need to discuss terminology a bit. By 'mental simulation', let us mean a mental process that is, or is intended to be, *isomorphic* in some relevant respects to the target process it is intended to mimic. If I mentally simulate the execution of a complex athletic maneuver, for example, the sequence of my mental representations corresponds step for step with the sequence of bodily contortions that constitute (or would constitute) an execution of this maneuver. Now a priori, it is an open question whether human beings use *any* mental simulation in their cognitive life. Thus, when someone conjectures that the task of assigning mental states to others is tackled by means of simulation, it is highly relevant to wonder whether mental simulation is used in *other* problem-solving tasks. If mental simulation is never utilized elsewhere, then postulation of it in *this* domain would be totally unparalleled, and to that extent dubious. It is therefore quite germane to the dispute to discover whether mental simulation in general is a prevalent sort of heuristic. In chapter 3 I cited two groups of cognitive scientists who endorse simulative activity in order to lend credence to its prevalence.

S&N are quite right, of course, in saying that *other* uses of the simulation heuristic would probably be special cases of the theory-theory because those uses would be subserved by a tacit theory of the domain in question. To reintroduce the terminology employed in chapter 3, those applications of simulation would be cases of *theory-driven* rather than *process-driven* simulation. Theory-driven simulation is simulation guided by a theory, whereas process-driven simulation is simulation guided only by the cognizer's natural mental processes (plus the inputs to the simulation, of course, which will commonly include beliefs). Since some mental simulation is undoubtedly theory-driven, we could not settle the present controversy against the theory-theory simply by establishing that third-person mental ascriptions are executed by simulations. It would also have to be shown that they are *process-driven* simulations. Nonetheless, it is a first step to show that third-person ascription proceeds (quite frequently, at any rate) by simulation; and this can be at least slightly supported by evidence that simulation occurs in other cognitive tasks.

5 Appeal to Introspection

Very similar remarks are in order in connection with S&N's discussion of argument 5 (pp. 138–41), which cites the introspective plausibility of the simulation idea. S&N dismiss the relevance of appeals to introspection by turning their attention to imagery. When asked how many windows there are in one's house, almost everyone introspectively reports that they imagine themselves walking from room to room, counting the windows as they go. But surely it does not follow, say S&N, that off-line simulation is involved (this volume, p. 140): 'The *only* way that people could possibly answer the question accurately is to tap into some internally represented store of knowledge about their house; it simply makes no sense to suppose that off-line simulation is being used here.'

In this context S&N seem to mean by 'off-line simulation' what I call *process-driven* simulation. This is an odd and unfortunate use of the phrase, since 'off-lineness' *per se* is quite a different matter from process-drivenness. (Even a theory-guided inferential process, for example, might be taken off-line, i.e. out of the normal sequence of behavior control.) Reading them this way, however, S&N are certainly right to point out that one cannot tell from introspection that a mental simulation is process-driven rather than theory-driven. But I did not intend the appeal to introspection to support the deployment of *process-driven* simulation, merely simulation *tout court*. When the dominant theoretical approaches do not mention the simulation heuristic at all, it is an essential first step to satisfy ourselves that simulation is a plausible hypothesis. The question of process-drivenness *versus* theory-drivenness then becomes a further item on the agenda, and it was indeed addressed later in my article.

For purposes of clarification it is worth pausing a moment longer over S&N's discussion of imagery. They consider the suggestion that the presence of imagery challenges the theory-theory when 'theory' is interpreted narrowly, on the grounds that imagery encodes information in a non-sentential or non-propositional format. This, I hasten to point out, is no facet of my argumentation. The simulation thesis need not take any particular stand on how the relevant information used in a simulation heuristic is represented, e.g. whether it is represented sententially or 'pictorially'. It is entirely compatible with the simulation idea that the entire process of generating pretend inputs, operating on them with practical reasoning, and then feeding the output of this reasoning into a belief box, is all accomplished by means of sentence-like representations. Nor does the assumption that sentential representations are used entail that the case is really an example of the theory-theory. The crucial characteristic of the theory-theory is its postulation of the possession and employment of *nomological* information, information about causal generalizations. Mere 'propositional' information, or sententially represented information, is not distinctive of the theory-theory, since the simulation theory can also claim that the prospects surveyed by a simulator can be propositionally expressed and sententially represented. On this point, it is unfortunate that S&N sometimes seem to regard 'propositional' status as sufficient for theory-hood, as when they describe a theoretical knowledge structure as 'a body of rules or principles *or propositions*' (p. 123; emphasis added). (Perhaps they mean this to be withdrawn, however, once they intro-duce the 'wide' sense of 'theory'.)

6 *The Question of Simplicity*

Argument 4 (pp. 137–8) claims that the off-line simulation theory is much simpler than the theory-theory. S&N reply that simplicity must be judged by comparing the theories in their entirety, not just at isolated parts. They grant that when we look at the data base, the theory-theory is 'strikingly unparsimonious', since it posits an elaborate system of internally represented generalizations or rules. The simulation theory, by contrast, uses the mind's own decision-making system as a surrogate for this data base, and this system has to be there on any theory. So the off-line simulation theory gets its data base for free. However, S&N continue, when we examine the other compo-nent of the competing theories, viz. the 'control mechanism', we find that the theory-theory gets its control mechanism for free. Since the mind makes many predictions about physical systems without using simulation, we know that the mind is going to have to have some mechanism for extracting infor-mation from internalized theories and applying it to particular cases. Any such mechanism that works for folk physics will presumably work for folk psychology as well. The simulation theory, however, must *add* a control mechanism above and beyond the ordinary decision-making system. For this theory needs to posit a capacity to take that system off-line: to feed in 'pre-tend' inputs and interpret its outputs as predictions about how someone else would behave. So the simulation theory is less parsimonious *vis-à-vis* the control mechanism.

What do S&N mean by saying that a theory gets a system 'for free'? Evidently they mean that the system in question must be posited in any case, no matter what side is chosen in the current dispute. I accept this construal for purposes of comparisons of parsimony. On that very criterion, however, the simulation theory also gets its crucial control mechanism for free, since the 'off-line' capacity must be posited in any case to handle other uncontroversial cognitive abilities!

Consider the activity of *conditional planning*. A group of us are trying to decide which restaurant to dine at this evening, and I am the designated driver. The two restaurants under consideration are both situated at distant and unfamiliar parts of town. Although our choice is yet to be made, I begin to plot which route I would take if we choose restaurant A, and which route I would take if we choose restaurant B. To make these conditional plans, I 'pretend' to have the goal of going to restaurant A, and deliberate on the best means to get there (shortest time, least traffic, or whatnot); and similarly for restaurant B. Since I haven't actually formed a goal or intention to drive to either restaurant, my decision-making system is operating off-line. The out-put from this process is not an actual decision to take the selected route but merely a conditional decision, viz. to take that route *if* we decide to go to that restaurant. Since this kind of deliberation must be accommodated by any theory, we are going to have to posit 'off-line' decision-making in any case. Thus, the simulation theory gets this control mechanism for free. The result is that the simulation theory gets *both* its 'data base' *and* its control mechanism for free, while the theory-theory gets only its control mechanism for free. Hence, the simulation theory is indeed more parsimonious.

7 *Evidence from Autism*

Arguments 6 and 7 (pp. 141–6) draw on some of the research in developmental psychology to support the case for the simulation theory. The first of these appeals to results in 'false-belief' experiments, and the second to the phenomenon of childhood autism. Unfortunately this developmental research is extremely difficult to interpret, and I am inclined to agree with S&N (in their section 4) that it cannot be used to support one theory over the other with any decisiveness. However, let me mention additional evidence about autism that does, I think, provide some support for the superiority of the simulation theory.

In one study of autistic children, Simon Baron-Cohen, Alan Leslie, and Uta Frith (1986) gave subjects scrambled pictures from comic strips which they were supposed to put in order to make up a story, with the first picture already in place. Second, the children had to tell the story in their own words. There were three types of stories: mechanical, behavioral, and mentalistic. All the autistic children ordered the pictures in the mechanical script correctly. They also used the right kind of language when telling the story, for instance: 'The balloon burst because it was pricked by the branch'. A behavioral script can be told without reference to mental states, for example: 'A girl goes to a shop to buy some sweets. She pays the shopkeeper and carries away her sweets.' This way of ordering and telling a social routine was also well within the competence of the autistic children. Not so, however, for the mentalistic stories. The vast majority of their autistic children just could not understand them. They put the pictures in a jumbled order, and told their 'stories' without the attribution of mental states.

The fact that autistic children do perfectly well on the mechanical and behavioral scripts suggests that they have no impairment in theorizing or making theoretical inferences. Their impairment is much more specific and localized. It is tempting to conclude that a different *sort* of deficit is present in autism, perhaps a deficit in imaginatively projecting oneself into the shoes of other people (or characters) so as to produce a mentalistic scenario. This explanation, of course, conforms to the simulation theory.

Theory-theorists, however, have a possible response here. Although these findings seem incompatible with the notion that autism involves an impairment of *general* theorizing capacities, it may be argued (as suggested earlier) that normal skills at mentalizing arise from a special module that contains the theory of mind, or from a special-purpose learning mechanism, dedicated to mentalizing. Such a module or learning mechanism may be the locus of impairment in autism.

However, other evidence about autism makes me doubt that the deficiency in autism is a *theoretical* deficiency. Frith (1989) relates two pertinent anecdotes about autistic people. The first is about an able autistic young man who despite suffering from autism is very helpful with household chores and errands. One day, as his mother was mixing a fruit cake, she said to him: 'I haven't got any cloves. Would you please go out and get me some.' The son came back a while later with a carrier bag full of girlish clothes, including underwear, from a High Street boutique. Clearly, the boy had misperceived the word 'cloves' as 'clothes'. But what normal young man would assume his mother asked him casually to buy her clothes, just like that? Now it seems to me that this autistic young man had a perfectly good grasp of the mentalistic notion of wanting. He understood that his mother wanted something, and her (misperceived) utterance was interpreted as stemming from that want. No deficiency in the concepts or relations of 'theory of mind' appear here. (See Harris, 1991, for further evidence that autistic children do not totally lack mentalistic understanding.) Nor does there appear to be any deficiency in 'meta-representational' capacity, as Leslie's (1987) theory postulates. What is striking is the son's attribution to his mother of an outlandish desire, which anybody else would reject immediately. This is naturally explainable as a failure to project himself into her shoes in an adequate way, and thereby eliminate the hypothesis of this particular desire. In short, it is a deficiency in simulation.

The same diagnosis seems apt for Frith's second anecdote. A ten-year-old autistic girl showed catastrophic anxiety when the nurse, about to do a simple blood test, said: 'Give me your hand; it won't hurt.' The girl calmed down immediately when another person said: 'Stretch out your index finger.' She had understood, at the first instruction, that she was to cut off her hand and give it to the nurse. Here again the autistic child understands that her interlocutor is expressing a desire; what is anomalous is the outlandishness of the desire she ascribes. This does not seem readily explainable as a lacuna in the child's theory of mind. But it does seem explainable as a deficiency in simulative capacity. A normal person would recognize the bizarreness of the interpretation because it would be difficult to simulate the nurse's whole sequence of behavior, including her casual request, if she did have the desire in question. Thus, if the autistic child's deficiency is the lack of a propensity to simulate, or a skill at simulation, this could explain her bizarre interpretation. The lack of such a propensity or skill at simulation also fits perfectly with two other well-known traits of autism: lack of pretend play and lack of empathy. Concerning the second trait, autistic people are noted for their indifference to other people's distress and their inability to offer comfort, even to receive comfort themselves (see Frith, 1989, pp. 154–5). This obviously could be associated with a deficiency in simulative propensities.

8 Acquiring Fragments of Folk Psychology?

Whereas S&N's section 4 is a defense of the theory-theory against arguments from simulation theorists, section 5 takes the 'offensive'. Here they present two kinds of findings in the psychological literature that can only be accommodated, they claim, by the theory-theory, not by the simulation theory.

The first set of findings is due to Wimmer, Hogrefe, and Sodian (1988) and concerns the ability of young children to infer the presence of beliefs in other people. A subject in these experiments was made aware of the informational conditions another child was exposed to concerning the contents of a box. The subject could see or hear whether or not the other child looked into the box and whether or not the experimenter told the other child what was in the box. The subject was then asked whether the other child knows what is in the box or does not know that. Older children (five-year-olds) gave uniformly correct answers, whereas younger children (three- and four-year-olds) did not. The most frequent error in the latter group was denial of the other child's knowledge when the other child had looked into the box or was informed by the experimenter. Following Wimmer et al. (1988), S&N conclude that the younger children have acquired only a fragment of folk psychology, but have not entirely mastered it. They have not learned, for example, how perceptual access leads to knowledge (or belief). This diagnosis seems borne out by further findings of Wimmer et al. (1988), where older children display 'inference neglect'. This is taken to show that older children have mastered the portion of the theory dealing with perceptual belief-formation but not inferential belief-formation. This gradual learning of the principles of folk psychology seems to be compatible with the theory-theory but not easily explained by the off-line simulation theory.

It turns out, however, that some of the main findings of the Wimmer et al. study are contradicted by other experiments, especially a set of experiments by Henry Wellman reported in Wellman (1990). First, if young children's difficulties in *inferring* belief in others are what account for their failure on traditional false-belief tasks, then three-year-olds should succeed on false-belief tasks where they are explicitly told what the protagonist believes (Wellman calls these *explicit* false-belief tasks). But in fact Wellman's three-year-olds did not succeed on these tasks, even when inference of belief was not at issue. Second, if three-year-olds are unable to infer knowledge (or belief) from perceptual access, then they should fail on what Wellman calls *inferred* belief tasks. A typical task of this kind is given as follows: 'This is Jane. This morning Jane saw her magic markers in the desk, not on the shelf. Now she wants her magic markers. Where will she look?' In fact, three-year-olds were highly successful on inferred belief tasks: 88 percent correct. Even more convincingly, three-year-olds were successful on so-called *inferred belief-control* tasks. Here stories were told of identical objects hidden in each of two locations, but only one of the objects was seen by the protagonist: 'There are magic markers in the desk, *and* there are magic markers on the shelf. This morning Jane saw the magic markers in the desk, but she did not see the magic markers on the shelf. Now Jane wants magic markers. Where will she look for magic markers?' Here too three-year-olds chose the correct location with 88 percent accuracy. Thus three-year-olds seemed to understand that the character's perception would lead to a belief, and they predicted the character's actions accordingly.

In these Wellman studies, unlike the Wimmer et al. studies, subjects were questioned about actions rather than about beliefs. But Pillow (1989) found that three-year-olds correctly understand the existence of a link between perception and belief even when queried directly about beliefs. This was further confirmed in research by Pratt and Bryant (1988; reported in Wellman, 1990), who may also have identified the critical factor that accounts for the differences between Wellman and Pillow's results versus Wimmer's results. Pratt and Bryant argue that Wimmer et al.'s question format was too complex. They asked children a double question: 'Does he know what is in the box, or does he not know that?' Pratt and Bryant found that even in a seemingly straightforward task about simple possession, children became confused with a double question, for example, 'Does he have the red counters, or does he not have them?' They therefore simplified the questioning procedures. One of their studies paralleled Wimmer et al.'s task almost exactly, except for the complexity of the question. Two children either saw or did not see into a box, and the subject was asked about the target child, 'Does she know what is in the box?' Seventy-five percent of the three-year-olds were correct with this procedure, whereas only 13 percent were correct with the double question in the Wimmer et al. research. Thus, it appears that three-year-olds do have a reasonable grasp of the fact that beliefs can arise from perception, contrary to Wimmer et al.'s studies.

There is another flaw in the Wimmer et al. studies that bears especially on the alleged phenomenon of 'inference neglect' among four- and five-year-olds. The trouble with their studies is that they asked the subjects whether a target child *knows* a certain fact, not whether she *believes* that fact. Knowledge is obviously a stronger epistemic attainment than mere belief, and it is distinctly possible that the four- and five-year-olds who refused to attribute knowledge did so because of requirements concerning knowledge as contrasted with belief. (Actually the Wimmer et al. experiments were done in German, using the verb *wissen* for the English *know*. But my point applies as well for the German verb.) In particular, these younger children may have thought that inference is not a sufficiently reliable or trustworthy mode of access to qualify as *knowledge*.

This hypothesis is directly supported by Wimmer et al.'s own discussion. Describing one experiment they write: 'Even when the other person gave evidence of his or her inferential knowledge by explicitly stating the conclusion, four-year-olds disregarded the other's inferential access and judged the conclusion *to be a guess*' (Wimmer et al., 1988, p. 180; emphasis added). This description makes it sound as if the subjects were aware that the target person *believed* the conclusion (especially where the person explicitly stated it), but just didn't think that the warrant or grounds for the belief were sufficient for knowing. Borrowing other terminology from Wimmer et al. themselves, the younger children may have a different appraisal of the *quality* of information sources than older children; in particular, the younger ones may not think that inference is a good enough source. (Of course, they credit themselves with knowledge even when their belief is based on inference; but they may not reflect on their own source of belief in quite the same critical fashion.) If this account is correct, it undercuts the supposition that four- and five-year-olds fail to appreciate that inference can lead to *belief*.

Even if future experiments should rectify this problem and suggest 'inference neglect' *vis-à-vis* belief (rather than knowledge), this will only tell against the simulation theory if it cannot accommodate such a result. But that is far from evident. As S&N themselves remark, getting the simulation 'control mechanism' to work smoothly is sure to be a very non-trivial task. One must feed it just the right pretend inputs, not allow its operation to be deflected by actual beliefs that should be suspended, and interpret its outputs as predictions about someone else's actions or states. There can be various levels of skill at this kind of operation, and success will vary with the task at hand (cf. Harris, 1991). Since we know from many experiments (including the Pratt and Bryant experiments cited above) that young children are easily confused, or overwhelmed by representational complexity, the simulation theory is in a position to avail itself of this fact in interpreting various findings.

To sum up this section, the Wimmer et al. (1988) studies simply do not provide firm, probative data that support the theory-theory in preference to the simulation theory.

9 Cognitive Penetrability

The second argument that S&N present against the simulation theory is that predictions of behavior should not be cognitively penetrable if the simulation theory is correct; but in fact they are cognitively penetrable. According to S&N, the simulation theory implies that if you use simulation to predict what you would do under certain hypothetical circumstances, then your prediction should be accurate even if there is something about your cognitive processes of which you are ignorant. This is because process-driven simulation just employs your actual cognitive operations, and makes no appeal to your knowledge or beliefs about them.

Let us not tarry over the definition of 'cognitive penetrability'. The crucial point is that the simulation theory implies accurate behavioral predictions only if two conditions are met: (1) the present inputs in the simulations *precisely* match the inputs in the actual cases, and (2) the cognitive processes deployed in the simulations operate on the pretend inputs in *precisely* the way the same processes operate on the actual inputs in the actual cases. If these conditions are not met, accuracy of simulation-based prediction is not guaranteed. These conditions are not likely to be met, however, in any of the cases S&N present.

In the product opinion survey case, it is very unlikely that a simulator who imagines herself examining an array of products in a mall will replicate all relevant aspects of the live situation. The simulated scene is unlikely to be as detailed as a real perceptual scene; one is unlikely to replicate the uncertainties of the live situation; and one is unlikely to simulate in detail the actual scanning and comparison operations. Thus, there is no reason to expect that a simulation would generate the same behavior as an actual incident. This is especially true when a simulation is guided by S&N's invitation to simulate, which tells you beforehand that 'you find no really significant differences among [the garments]' (p. 151). This bit of stage-setting probably tends to inhibit or deter a faithful simulation. For example, actual subjects in these experiments may think they detect minor differences between the garments, but the foregoing instruction tends to inhibit the imagining of any differences whatsoever. Hence, the simulation theory does not imply that a simulation-based prediction will be accurate.

In the second example, the lottery ticket example, it is improbable that you will simulate in sufficient detail the process of choosing a ticket from several that the seller has available. In a real case there would be tickets with actual numbers, and you would deliberately reflect on those numbers and possibly come up with some 'grounds' for preferring one of the numbers to the others. But if you casually imagine yourself in the situation, you would not exert the same deliberation and reflectiveness. This difference in the pretend inputs might well be enough to account for the discrepancy between the actual buy-back behavior and the expected buy-back behavior.

Finally, what about the belief perseverance example? What is undoubtedly crucial to the perseverance effect is that the subjects' initial beliefs about the evidence are allowed to pervade their whole network of beliefs and remain for a while in long-term memory prior to discrediting. These aspects of the real events are unlikely to be duplicated in a simulation. So once again, we cannot expect a simulation-based prediction to coincide with observed behavior. Discrepancies between such predictions and observed behavior do not provide evidence against the simulation theory.

10. Overview and Further Considerations

Where does the debate stand at this juncture? I have agreed that several of our (G&G's) original arguments against the theory-theory are not knock-down arguments; but they were not so conceived in the first place. I have also agreed that some of our arguments in favor of the simulation theory are not wholly decisive; but despite S&N's critique, these arguments still provide some measure of support. First, the argument from simplicity is still substantial. Second, we still have grounds, based at least on introspection, for thinking that *some* acts of prediction or interpretation utilize simulation. It has not been established that this simulation is process-driven rather than theory-driven; but the former remains a distinct possibility. Third, I have adduced new considerations from autism that support the simulation theory. What about S&N's two arguments *against* the simulation theory? These were found to be completely ineffective. The first rests on empirical work that is contradicted by other empirical findings or involves questionable interpretations. The second presupposes that the simulation theory makes certain incorrect predictions; but this presupposition was found to be mistaken. In sum, no unrefuted difficulties, either theoretical or empirical, have been presented for the simulation theory; and although the theory-theory has been given some plausible assistance, it still looks weaker on several counts than the simulation theory.

In closing, let me say a bit more about empathy and its relation to the simulation theory. A first point is that studies of empathy suggest a very important role for simulation, or 'role-playing', as it is often called in the literature. A second point is that empathic arousal provides a good example of process-driven simulation, and thereby lends some measure of support to the plausibility of process-driven simulation in the interpretation of mental states generally.

There are a number of modes or levels of empathic arousal, which can roughly be ordered developmentally. Hoffman (1984) identifies six such modes. The most elementary is the propensity of one- and two-day-old infants to cry in response to the sound of another infant's cry. This is not a simple imitative vocal response, but a vigorous, intense cry indistinguishable from the spontaneous cry of an infant in actual discomfort. At the highest level is what Hoffman calls 'role taking': the cognitive act of imagining oneself in another's place. The significance of role taking has been substantiated by Stotland (1969; reported in Hoffman, 1984). In one of Stotland's studies, subjects were instructed to imagine how they would feel and what sensations they would have in their hands if they were exposed to the same painful heat treatment that was being applied to another person. These subjects gave more evidence of empathic distress, both physiologically and verbally, than (a) subjects instructed to attend closely to the other person's physical movements and (b) subjects instructed to imagine how the other person felt when he or she was undergoing the treatment. The first finding indicates that imagining oneself in the other's place is more empathy arousing than observing another's movements. The second finding suggests, more specifically, that empathic affect is more likely to be generated when the focus of attention is not on the model's feeling but on the model's situation and how one would feel in that situation, i.e. if the stimuli were impinging on oneself. Corroborative results were reported in a study of six-year-olds by Meerum Terwogt, Schene and Harris (1986; summarized in Harris, 1989). The children listened to a story in which the main character had to say goodbye to a best friend. They were asked to listen to the story in one of three ways: to feel along with the story character; to remain detached; or to follow their own preferences. These instructions appeared to be effective: children asked to identify with the character were more likely to remember or even elaborate on the sad episodes in the story. Although these findings only support the importance of role taking in the arousal of emotion or affect, they are suggestive of the significance of role taking in general.

These studies also suggest, however, that the effects of role taking, or simulation, are not dependent on the possession of a theory. It seems unlikely that once a role-taking posture is adopted, its impact on affect arousal depends on the subject's *knowledge* about the psychological properties of affect arousal (or the like). On the contrary, it seems obvious that the process just 'runs off' by itself. Similarly, when we watch an absorbing film or play, or read a novel, genuine emotion can be triggered; and this does not seem to depend on the extent of our knowledge or belief about the psychology of emotion arousal. Again, in reading or viewing erotic materials, projection of oneself into the position of the characters can trigger genuine erotic arousal, with no apparent causal reliance on knowledge or belief about these psychological dispositions. *These* effects of simulation, then, are surely process-driven. It does not follow, of course, that all simulative activity involved in third-person interpretation is process-driven rather than theory-driven. But once the existence of process-driven simulation is granted, it may be easier to make the case for process-drivenness in the wider class of cases.

References

Baron-Cohen, S., Leslie, A. M. and Frith, U. 1986: Mechanical, behavioral and intentional understanding of picture stories in autistic children. *British Journal of Developmental Psychology*, 2, 113–25.

Butterworth, G. E. 1991: The ontogeny and phylogeny of joint visual attention. In A. Whiten (ed.), *Natural Theories of Mind*. Oxford: Blackwell.

Butterworth, G. E. and Cochran, E. 1980: Towards a mechanism of joint visual attention in human infancy. *International Journal of Behavioral Development*, 19, 253–72.

Churchland, P. M. 1988: *Matter and Consciousness*, rev. edn. Cambridge, MA: MIT Press.

Fodor, J. A. 1987: *Psychosemantics*. Cambridge, MA: MIT Press.

Frith, U. 1989: *Autism: Explaining the Enigma*. Oxford: Blackwell.

Goldman, A. I. 1989: Interpretation psychologized. *Mind and Language*, 4, 161–85. Reprinted as ch. 3 in this volume.

Gordon, R. M. 1986: Folk psychology as simulation. *Mind and Language*, 1, 158–71. Reprinted as ch. 2 in this volume.

Harris, P. L. 1989: *Children and Emotion: The Development of Psychological Understanding*. Oxford: Blackwell.

Harris, P. L. 1991: The work of the imagination. In A. Whiten (ed.), *Natural Theories of Mind*. Oxford: Blackwell.

Hoffman, M. L. 1984: Interaction of affect and cognition in empathy. In C. Izard, J. Kagan and R. Zajonc (eds), *Emotions, Cognition, and Behavior*. Cambridge: Cambridge University Press.

Leslie, A. M. 1987: Pretense and representation: The origins of 'theory of mind'. *Psychological Review*, 94, 412–26.

Meerum Terwogt, M., Schene, J. and Harris, P. L. 1986: Self-control of emotional reactions by young children. *Journal of Child Psychology and Psychiatry*, 27, 357–66.

Pillow, B. H. 1989: Early understanding of perception as a source of knowledge. *Journal of Experimental Child Psychology*, 47, 116–29.

Pratt, C. and Bryant, P. E. 1988: Young children understand that looking leads to knowing. Unpublished ms., Oxford University.

Ramachandran, V. S. 1990: Unpublished lecture, delivered at the University of Arizona Cognitive Science Program.

Stotland, E. 1969: Exploratory investigations of empathy. In L. Berkowitz (ed.), *Advances in Experimental Social Psychology, Volume 4*. New York: Academic Press.

Tversky, A. and Kahneman, D. 1974: Judgment under uncertainty: Heuristics and biases. *Science*, 185, 1124–31.

Tversky, A. and Kahneman, D. 1983: Extensional versus intuitive reasoning: The conjunction fallacy in probability judgment. *Psychological Review*, 90, 293–315.

Wellman, H. M., 1990: *The Child's Theory of Mind*. Cambridge, MA: MIT Press.

Wimmer, H., Hogrefe, J. and Sodian, B. 1988: A second stage in children's conception of mental life: Understanding informational accesses as origins of knowledge and belief. In J. W. Astington, P. L. Harris and D. R. Olson (eds), *Developing Theories of Mind*. Cambridge: Cambridge University Press.

10

From Simulation to Folk Psychology: The Case for Development

PAUL L. HARRIS

Research in developmental psychology suggests that young children are busy elaborating several, relatively autonomous, explanatory systems: by the age of four or five years, they have a good understanding of some of the basic principles underlying folk physics and folk psychology (Wellman and Gelman, 1992). More controversial is the strategy that they adopt in elaborating those diverse principles. The increasing recognition that children are simultaneously working on specialized domains makes it plausible to propose they use specialized tactics to handle the peculiarities of a given domain. Against that backdrop, I set out the psychological case, and more specifically the developmental case, for the proposal that children improve their grasp of folk psychology by means of a simulation process. To that end, I concentrate on describing and analyzing recent evidence on young children's ability to predict and explain mental states.

First, I ask whether a resolution of the debate between advocates of the simulation theory (ST) and the theory-theory (TT) has any implication for the status of the propositional attitudes.

1 ST, TT, and the Reality of the Attitudes

Part of Stich and Nichols's defence of TT (ch. 5) seems to be motivated by a belief that, were ST correct, the debate between eliminativists and their opponents would be otiose since it would have been shown that not even common sense subscribes to a folk psychology.

I think this conclusion is incorrect for most versions of ST. Let us suppose that a simulation allows the subject (S) to identify the particular emotion, desire or belief that another person (O) currently entertains. (I consider how this might work in more detail below.) According to this account, S would still make the kind of attributions that are routinely seen as the core of folk psychology: belief, desires, emotions, and so forth. In making such attributions, however, S need have no recourse to a general theory about the interrelationships among these mental states, even though S does operate with a conception of the states themselves. Stich and Nichols reach their conclusion, I think, because they are running together two separable claims about folk psychology: the TT claim that it is deployed by reference to a tacit theory that sets out generalizations in which beliefs, desires and so forth are interrelated, and the narrower claim that folk psychology calls for the attribution of propositional attitudes. In the version of ST that I try to develop below, I shall argue that the child does attribute propositional attitudes but not by virtue of subscribing to a theory. Of course, one might wish to claim that a simulation process allows S to dispense not just with a theory of the attitudes but with the attitudes themselves, but in my view such a position is untenable.[1]

One objection to my argument is that the propositional attitudes themselves are inescapably 'theoretical' precisely because their correct attribution depends on an integrated framework within which any particular attitude takes its place. This objection begs the psychological issue, however, of just how one comes to make appropriate attributions that are integrated with one another. The fact that the predictions and explanations that a child offers appear to conform to some theory-like version of folk psychology is not in itself proof that the child subscribes either explicitly or tacitly to that theory.

In short, eliminativists and their opponents may continue their debate about the reality of the attitudes unembarrassed: a resolution of the disagreement between ST and TT is not about to show that they have been wasting their time.

2 Some Historical Ironies

Investigations of the child's conception of mental states received an important stimulus from a paper by Premack and Woodruff (1978), who attempted to show that a chimpanzee can interpret the goal-directed behaviour of a human actor. For example, having watched a film of an actor trying (unsuccessfully) to reach for some bananas dangling overhead, the chimpanzee was asked to select between various pictures that depicted possible ensuing actions by the actor. The chimpanzee (Sarah) appropriately selected a picture of the actor's likely next move – for example, piling up crates beneath the bananas dangling overhead. The implication was that she had figured out the actor's goal and could predict what means he might adopt to attain it.

One might explain the chimpanzee's success by crediting her with some knowledge of Fodor's belief–desire–action law. (If X wants that P, and X believes that not-P unless Q, then X will try to bring it about that Q.) Some commentators on the data were reluctant to do so, not (I think) because they had Fodorean qualms about extending the attitudes beyond the human species, but because another plausible explanation remained in play, even though

Premack and Woodruff had attempted to rule it out. Specifically, the ape might well use a simulation strategy: being itself pretty good at crate-piling in pursuit of bananas (Kohler, 1957), it might imagine itself trying to reach for the bananas, note its own likely course of action, and project that onto the human actor.[2]

To obviate the use of this strategy, three commentators (Bennett, Dennett, and Harman) proposed a test that would drive a wedge between what the observing ape would do in the circumstances, and what the actor would do. They suggested variants of what has come to be known as the false-belief test: check whether the animal can predict an action (e.g. looking in Box A) that would be appropriate given the actor's (mistaken) belief (e.g. that Box A contains bananas), but which the ape itself would not engage in since it believes something different (e.g. it knows that the bananas have been surreptitiously moved to Box B). Wimmer and Perner (1983) developed a version of this task for children: the children had to predict where a puppet with a mistaken belief about the location of some chocolate would search. They reported a marked improvement between three and five years in the ability to take false beliefs into account. This important result was one of the first in what has become a very active area of developmental research.

I want to make two points about this bit of intellectual history. First, the false belief task was proposed to ensure that the ape's interpretive success could not be ascribed to its own beliefs about the problem facing the actor, but rather to its beliefs about the actor's beliefs. Children's success on the false-belief task might show, therefore, that under the special circumstances that it introduces, they go beyond a simulation strategy. (I shall argue below that it simply calls for a more elaborate simulation rather than an abandonment of simulation.) What it patently cannot show is that children never use that strategy outside those exacting circumstances.

This point needs emphasis in the light of what has happened since Wimmer and Perner's influential demonstration. Investigators have been tempted to erect the methodological proposals offered by Bennett, Dennett, and Harman into an inviolable canon: namely, test subjects in circumstances where their own beliefs and desires provide no clues for an appropriate attribution. Hence, there is a great deal of experimental evidence on children's ability to make appropriate attributions to someone whose beliefs they do not share. We know less about what attributions children make when they share the other's beliefs but diverge with respect to some other attitude, and even less about children's construal of their own, current mental states. Thus, the available evidence is skewed: it was deliberately designed to try to block the use of a simulation strategy.

This may explain, at least in part, the contemporary dominant interpretation of that evidence. Gordon and Goldman (this volume) both use developmental evidence to support the simulation model. Nonetheless, as the brief history above would suggest, it was not gathered by developmental psychologists with that view in mind. Rather, as Stich and Nichols correctly point out, the dominant interpretation has been of the TT variety: children are said to be acquiring a theory of mind. There are, of course, lively disagreements within the TT camp about where that theory comes from (from an innate module or from a quasi-theoretical insight into the representational function of mental states?) and its exact timetable (three-year-olds have no conception, a partial conception, or a fully-fledged conception of belief?). Yet, there is a widespread assumption that some version of TT is correct. In this respect, it is fair to point out that ST is as much a minority view among developmental psychologists as it is among philosophers. Nonetheless, I take comfort from the fact that developmental psychologists struggling to produce data that would support TT rather than a simulation or projection strategy have, despite themselves, produced data that philosophical advocates of ST find stimulating and congenial. Truly, cognitive science moves in mysterious ways.

In the concluding section, I discuss evidence that was not constrained by the proposals of Bennett, Dennett, and Harman. This evidence proves to be compatible with ST but inconsistent with current formulations of TT.

3 Simulation versus Theorizing?

It is pretty clear that we deploy both tacit theories and simulation in our folk-psychological attributions. Consider a member of the Azande tribe described in the classic ethnography by Evans-Pritchard (1937). The Azande have an elaborate system of beliefs concerning witchcraft, that includes tests (the use of poison oracles) for diagnosing who is and is not a witch, assumptions about the way that a witch transmits his or her malevolent intentions etc. It seems unlikely that members of the Azande seek to understand witch psychology by a process of simulation. Rather, they use their tacit 'theory' of witchcraft, and the answers supplied by the poison oracle to fill in gaps in the context of a particular accusation of witchcraft. To take a less exotic example,[3] consider the diagnosis of schizophrenia: psychiatry has slowly developed a classification system that sets out a check-list of symptoms. The clinician need not set about simulating paranoia when making a diagnosis.

Now consider the following thought experiment. I recruit your help, explaining that I am carrying out a two-part psycholinguistic study. I have presented English speakers with grammatical and ungrammatical sentences and they have made their judgments about which is which. I ask you to predict what decision most people came to about each sentence. Your hit rate turns out to be very high. In almost every case you can tell me whether the majority judged the sentence to be grammatical or ungrammatical. Moreover, when I ask you to explain your predictions you do so by indicating deviant constructions or morphemes in the ungrammatical sentences, something that speakers in the first part of the study also did. How are your predictions so accurate? The most plausible answer is that you read each sentence, asked yourself whether it sounded grammatical or not, and assumed that other English speakers would make the same judgements for the same reasons. The proposal that you have two distinct tacit representations of English grammar, a first-order representation that you deploy when making your own judgments, and a metarepresentation (i.e. a representation of other people's representations) that you deploy in predicting the judgements made by others, so designed as to yield equivalent judgements, strains both credulity and parsimony.

Again, consider the following conversation between two four-year-olds, each holding a toy telephone (Nelson and Gruendel, 1979, p. 76):

G: 'Who am I speaking to?'
D: 'Daniel. This is your Daddy. I need to speak to you.'
G: 'All right.'
D: 'When I come home tonight, we're gonna have . . . peanut butter and jelly sandwich, uh, at dinnertime.'

In generating his well-formed but make-believe paternal remarks, we can reasonably assume that D does not employ a tacit theory of the tacit theory of English grammar deployed by adults (or fathers). He simply takes the make-believe assumption that he is a father, and feeds that pretend input into the generative device that he himself uses in formulating English sentences. The output is a set of grammatical English sentences, whose content is adjusted in light of the pretend input.

The point of these examples is that we cannot adjudicate between TT and ST by attempting to show that either one of them is an implausible account of how we predict and explain other people's action or speech.

4 *The Centrality of Developmental Evidence*

Although children and adults may simulate or theorize depending on the context,[4] there remains the important issue of how children first acquire folk psychology. Here, a more specialized strategy, or family of strategies, might operate. Current evidence suggests that its acquisition has four features that are worth getting excited about. I list them in order, starting with the best-established: (1) there is an orderly elaboration with age in the kinds of predictive and explanatory strategies that children adopt; (2) some genetically based forms of pathology (e.g. autism but not mental retardation) are associated with a gross delay and/or deviation in that elaboration; (3) some of the simpler strategies have been observed in several species of primate, but the evidence is patchy or controversial for more complex strategies; (4) the elaboration is stable across marked variation in cultural milieu.[5]

This evidence suggests that we are dealing with the construction of a biologically constrained, pan-cultural knowledge system, whose development is disrupted in our species only by a specific, innate pathology. In the next section, I describe that orderly development in a bit more detail, before turning to a more explicit discussion of the ST and TT explanations.

5 *The Developmental Sequence*

Step 1: Toward the end of the first year,[6] children can begin to reproduce the intentional attitudes displayed by an adult. Specifically, they reproduce an adult's focus of attention or emotional stance. When an adult turns to look at an object, the infant will look toward that same object (Butterworth, 1991); when the adult looks at an object and simultaneously expresses an emotion toward it facially and/or vocally, the infant tends to adopt a similar emotional stance, avoiding it if the adult looks apprehensive, approaching it if the adult looks positive (Harris, 1989).

Step 2: Toward the end of the first year, and increasingly during the second year, the child begins to act on, rather than merely reproduce, another's current attitude. The child seeks to re-direct another's gaze by pointing at (Butterworth, 1991), showing, or giving an object of interest (Rheingold, Hay, and West, 1976). The child also seeks to alter another's current emotional state, by deliberate acts of teasing (e.g. removing a desired object) or comforting (e.g. proffering a desired object) (Harris, 1989).

Step 3: Three-year-olds (and to some extent two-year-olds) can anticipate or enact the reactions of people or toy characters whose current mental stance differs from their own. The other can diverge from the self with respect to the actual or potential objects or situations that he or she sees, wants, likes, expects, or knows (Harris, 1991; Wellman, 1990). For example, whereas the target X is currently seen or wanted by the self, the child can anticipate the fact that someone else currently sees or wants a different target.

Step 4: At around four years, and quite systematically by five years, one of the evident limitations of Step 3 is overcome. Children acknowledge that people can diverge not just with respect to the targets of their mental stance, they can also construe the very same target differently. They acknowledge that the beliefs, perceptual experiences, and emotions of two people may conflict with respect to the same situation; in addition, they acknowledge that the construal, and consequent attitudes of the same person with respect to a given situation, may conflict over time (Flavell, 1988; Perner, 1991). For example, they understand that whereas they see or believe that X is the case with respect to a given situation, another person – or they themselves at some earlier point in time – might see or believe that not-X is the case with respect to that situation.

The above description is a highly condensed summary of a large number of studies. It is intended to be theoretically neutral: a body of evidence, and a set of generalizations that the proponents of TT and ST alike would subscribe to. In the next two sections, I present the explanatory strategies of both camps.

6 *The Explanatory Strategy of TT*

A mere recitation of children's increasing appreciation of folk psychology, as set out in the preceding section, is clearly inadequate as an explanation of what is going on. We need some account of the process of change. Proponents of TT have been especially concerned with the transition from Step 3 to Step 4. (No one, of course, thinks that the developmental story stops at Step 4, but the evidence gets a lot more piecemeal.)

Most proponents of TT subscribe to the notion that the four- to five-year-old can, when required, think like a cognitive scientist. More specifically, the five-year-old subscribes to a representational theory of mind (RTM). Perner (1991) has articulated this view in its most explicit form. He argues that two- and three-year-olds are 'situation-theorists'. They think of people as being connected (by means of a variety of propositional attitudes) to actual or possible situations, but they do not think of people as mentally representing those situations. Thus, the three-year-old construes, for example, a person's desire as connecting that person to the target of their desire – some hitherto unrealized situation – but does not conceive of that unrealized target as being internally represented in the mind. The desire is like a mental homing device: it guides its bearer in a certain direction but carries no representation of the target – no photos of home, so to speak. Similarly, the three-year-old construes knowing as connecting someone to an external or upcoming situation but not as requiring a mental representation of the known situation.

The limitations of this 'situation-theorist' are highlighted by the sophistication of the older child. Perner argues that children of about four years of age achieve a crucial insight into the nature of representations. They realize that representations of various kinds (photos and models, as well as beliefs, mental images, and so forth) have both a referent and a content (or sense) which may or may not match one another. Applying this insight to the case of belief, the child is in a position to understand how someone might hold a false belief. The child grasps that although the referent of a belief is (typically) some aspect of current reality, the content of the belief may depict reality in a misleading or outdated fashion. This allows the child to further understand that the owner of the belief, unaware of this discrepancy, continues to regard the content of his or her belief as a useful guide to its referent, i.e. current reality. Hence, the owner is led into the various manifestations of a false belief, such as hunting in the wrong place and saying things that are not true.

This proposal has several things going for it. First, as a bit of theoretical knowledge about the mind it applies not just to the child's understanding of another's false belief but also to the child's understanding of his or her own false beliefs. The experimental evidence supports this prediction. Shown a closed Smarties box, three- and five-year-olds alike will claim that there are Smarties inside. Having discovered that, in fact, there are pencils inside but no Smarties, and then asked what they had originally thought was inside, three-year-olds typically insist that they thought there were pencils, whereas four- and five-year-olds admit that they thought there were Smarties (Astington and Gopnik, 1988; Wimmer and Hartl, 1991).

It provides an explanation for a parallel age change on a close cousin of the false-belief task: the reality–appearance task. For example, if five-year-olds are presented with a trick object – a fake rock that is made of sponge – they will admit after squeezing it that it is 'really a sponge – not a rock' although 'it looks like a rock not a sponge'. Three-year-olds, by contrast, tend to assimilate the appearance to the reality. They say that it is really a sponge and looks like one. The implication is that three-year-olds misconstrue the appearance question: asked to say what the object looks like they cannot conceptualise the gap between their initial perceptual representation of the object (as a rock) and the referent of that representation (the sponge that they now know it to be). Five-year-olds make the distinction and answer correctly (Flavell, 1988).

An improvement also occurs on a task less obviously allied to the false belief task: a visual perspective-taking task. If a three-year-old sits at a table looking at a picture lying on it, the child can correctly say whether the picture is upside-down or right way up. Asked, however, to say what view another person seated opposite has, the child fails to take account of the difference in perspective. Five-year-olds, however, acknowledge that what looks upright to them may look upside-down to the person opposite and vice versa. Here again, it can be argued that the three-year-old cannot grasp the distinction between content and referent. Asked whether the other person sees the picture upside-down or inverted, they construe the question as one that pertains to the picture itself, rather than to the way that the other sees it; and the 'picture itself' is, so far as they are concerned, oriented just as they see it (Flavell, 1988).

7 The Explanatory Strategy of ST

In this section I describe an alternative ST account of the body of data described above. This account is an extension of an earlier proposal (Harris, 1991) that focused on the transition from Step 3 to Step 4. The main addition is a more detailed discussion of Steps 1 and 2, as described above. My proposals with respect to these early stages elaborate on some of the points made by Goldman and Gordon (this volume). The gist of the account is that simulation is more or less difficult depending on the number of adjustments that have to be made to default settings. To facilitate exegesis, I go through the steps described above putting each one into the context of the proposals.

Step 1: Echoing another's intentional stance toward present targets. The child can drive his or her perceptual and/or emotional system by feeding into that system another person's currently attended visual target and/or the person's emotional stance toward that target. The result is that the child echoes the other person's attentional or emotional stance on-line; this on-line stance regulates the child's behavior toward the target in question. For example, the child inhibits or activates exploration of the target.

Step 2: Attributing an intentional stance toward present targets. The child now adopts the same procedure as at Step 1 but with an important refinement. The child continues to take as input another person's currently attended visual target and/or emotional stance toward a target, and simulates what the other is looking at or feeling. At this age, however, the simulation no longer regulates the child's behavior toward the target in a direct, on-line fashion. Instead, the child attributes the stance that is being simulated to the other person, effectively coding the other as 'looking at X' or 'liking/wanting Y'. This attribution provides a basis for simple interventions – actions intended to regulate the other's relationship to particular targets. For example, the child can try to change the other's direction of gaze by pointing at an alternative target[7] or to change the other's emotion by removing/proffering the targeted object or providing substitutes.

Step 3: Imagining an intentional stance. The child adopts the same procedure as at Step 2, but now in a fully fledged anticipatory or pretend fashion. The child no longer needs to emulate the other person by monitoring a visible target or the other person's current stance. The child can now set aside their own current intentional stance and simply imagine another person's. For example, they can anticipate or pretend that another person sees an object that is invisible to them, or wants an object that they themselves do not want.

Step 4: Imagining an intentional stance toward counterfactual targets. The child adopts the same procedure as at Step 3, but again with increased imaginative power. The child continues to drive the system off-line but now incorporates hypothetical situations that run counter to particular existing situations as intentional targets. Thus, the child can imagine someone believing or seeing a state of affairs that runs directly counter to what they currently take to be the case – as exemplified by the false-belief task, the reality–appearance task, and the visual perspective-taking task.

This developmental account has three features that should be made explicit. First, at Step 1, it is assumed that simulation processes are set in motion by special-purpose, inbuilt mechanisms for establishing joint attention and a joint emotional stance. Damage to those mechanisms would severely disrupt the developmental process that builds upon them, namely Steps 2–4. Supportive evidence for this claim comes from the study of autistic children. Concerning Step 1, they are poor at following another person's direction of gaze even when that direction is emphasized by a pointing gesture (Mundy, Sigman, Ungerer, and Sherman, 1986). Concerning Step 2, they are poor at taking measures (e.g. pointing and showing) to influence another's visual attention (Baron-Cohen, 1991a; Mundy and Sigman, 1989; Mundy, Sigman, and Kasari, 1993). Finally, concerning Steps 3 and 4, they show a variety of difficulties in talking about and diagnosing the mental states of others (Baron-Cohen, Tager-Flusberg, and Cohen, 1993; Frith, 1989; Harris; 1989).[8]

Second, the account implies that young children already start to 'interpret' other people's actions in the second year of life. The critical feature of Step 2 is that the child perceives the other as entering into intentional relations with visible targets. This provides a basis for the child's efforts to act on that intentional relationship – by enhancing it or blocking it. Examples of enhancement would be pointing at an object, but also showing it and giving it to the other person; examples of blocking would be removing a desired object, placing it out of reach, or calling attention to another target.

Third, once the 'interpretive' strategy is in place (at Step 2), subsequent developments involve improvements in the scope of its application rather than any dramatic change in the child's conception of mind. To be more precise, the changes described at Steps 3 and 4 stem from changes in the child's imaginative flexibility, rather than from a transformation in the child's so-called theory of mind. Thus, Step 3 allows the child to imagine intentional states that it does not currently entertain and in the absence of anyone else displaying those states. Strong evidence for exactly this kind of imaginative power is shown by studies of pretend play: two- and three-year-olds are adroit at investing toy dolls with pretend desires, perceptions and emotions, and causing them to act in accordance with those imagined states (Wolf, Rygh, and Altshuler, 1984).

Step 4 also involves an increment in imaginative power. It brings in the possibility of simulating someone's mental stance toward a counterfactual target. To conceptualize another's false belief, the child must imagine the other person holding a belief about a situation (e.g. that container A contains chocolate) which runs counter to the child's belief about that same situation (e.g. that container B, not A, contains chocolate). Similarly, to answer a question about the appearance of, for example, a fake rock, the child must imagine someone who sees it as a rock even though they now see it not as a rock, but as a sponge. Finally, to conceptualize a different visual perspective, the child must imagine someone who sees the picture or display in an orientation that is opposite (e.g. 'upside-down') to the orientation that is currently visible to them (e.g. 'right way up'). Thus, the important step taken between 3 and 5 years according to ST is not the discovery that the mind is a representational device, but rather the appreciation that mental states (notably seeing and believing) can be directed at situations which the child rules out as part of reality as it stands. This discovery is part of a more wide-ranging ability to think about and describe counterfactual substitutes for current reality. For example, children begin to produce counterfactual 'if–then' statements at around 4 years of age (Kuczaj and Daly, 1979).

Following this relatively global description, we may now make a more detailed comparison between the two accounts. I shall look closely at issues and at data that appear to create trouble for ST, and then turn to recent data that create trouble for TT.

8 Inaccuracies in Self-report

Critics have sometimes assumed that ST implies that understanding of the mental states of the self must inevitably be more accurate or more advanced than understanding of the mental states of another person. For example, Astington and Gopnik (1991, p. 24) argue that, for them at least, 'a central prediction of such a view would be that children's understanding of their own minds, of their own beliefs, desires, and so on, would consistently precede their understanding of the minds of others'. In attacking this prediction, they point out that three-year-olds are as inaccurate in reporting their own mental states as they are in diagnosing the mental states of others. This applies clearly to false-belief tasks where children's ability to state their own and another's mistaken belief has been systematically compared (Gopnik and Astington, 1988; Wimmer and Hartl, 1991).

However, the simulation account offers a straightforward explanation for children's difficulties in reporting their mistaken beliefs. In these tasks, children are not asked to state their current beliefs. They are asked about a belief that they once held, but now know to be false. To simulate such a belief, children must imagine the counterfactual state that they originally entertained – and took to be true. For example, they must imagine being shown a closed Smarties box, and while setting aside their current knowledge of its actual contents, they must report on its usual contents. The simulation account, far from being embarrassed by the difficulties that three-year-olds have in acknowledging an earlier false belief, explains them in exactly the same way as it explains three-year-olds' difficulties in working out another's false belief: the simulation is difficult because it calls for the imaginative construction of a counterfactual situation, as set out for Step 4 above.

9 Adult Errors

Astington and Gopnik (1991), like Stich and Nichols, also allude to a body of research suggesting that even adults are poor at interpreting their own actions or at anticipating those of other people. However, such inaccuracy does not in itself pose a problem for ST, which assumes that the simulation of a given psychological process may or may not lead to accurate results even among adults.

In general, we may distinguish between two different sources of error. First, using the helpful figure of Stich and Nichols (figure 5.1 on p. 128), it is necessary for the simulator to feed in pretend inputs that match in the relevant particulars the situation facing the agent whose actions are to be predicted or explained. Predictive errors will occur if inappropriate pretend inputs are fed in. Second, any simulation process assumes that an actor's behaviour is a faithful translation into action of a decision that is reached by the practical reasoning system. If that assumption is incorrect, the simulation will err.

Using this distinction, we may consider in more detail the three cases discussed by Stich and Nichols. In the case of belief perseverance, subjects in the experiments received two distinct and successive pieces of information. At first, they were given apparently veridical information about a particular trait or competence, and later they were given information that discredited that initial information. By contrast, anyone reading about such experiments and attempting to simulate their outcome is presented with a single, integrated account of both the trait information and its disconfirmation. They can judge

218 Paul L. Harris

the trait information for what it is worth as soon as they read about it. Under these circumstances, a reader will find it difficult to reproduce the naïve, unsuspecting commitment to the initial information that is entertained by participants in the experiments. Nisbett and Ross (1980, p. 192) themselves emphasize the important role of sequence effects in producing belief perseverance: 'People do not observe the "commutativity" rule in response to sequentially presented evidence. Instead, early-presented evidence seems to create theories which are not revised sufficiently in response to later-presented, conflicting evidence.' Thus, the fact that a simulator presented with both sources of information at the same time does not reproduce the belief perseverance phenomenon is exactly what would be expected according to ST. The simulator feeds in the pretend inputs in a different way from a naïve, experimental subject.

A similar analysis can be applied to the lottery experiments. Here, a reader needs to simulate the vacillation and eventual commitment of the free-choice subjects. Moreover, in making that simulation they must also set aside the tacit reminder embedded in a narrative that juxtaposes the two groups of subjects, namely that any lottery ticket whether selected or allocated, has the same likelihood of winning. Subjects in the experiment who were offered a free choice had no knowledge of the other group, and by implication no such tacit reminder.

In sum, the belief perseverance and lottery experiments highlight the fact that our folk psychology leads us to be surprised at the outcome of some psychological experiments. Our surprise occurs precisely because we do engage in a simulation process but one that misses some of the critical features of actual participation.

We may now consider the shopping-mall experiment which, I suspect, involves the second source of difficulty identified above: faulty assumptions about what causes the actor's behaviour rather than an inappropriate choice of pretend inputs. Scrutiny of the results described by Nisbett and Ross actually reveals two surprises. First, there is the unexpected behaviour of the subjects in the experiment: their biased selection of right-most items. In addition, however, there is the type of explanation given by the subjects: they denied any such position influence when questioned by the experimenter.

Stich and Nichols argue that if ST were true, then a person reading about this experiment should be able to feed in the relevant pretend input (choosing from among an array of identical items) and anticipate the position bias. I happily concede that the experiment illustrates an interesting case where readers would probably make inaccurate predictions about their likely behaviour and where participants offered incorrect explanations of their actual behaviour. However, I draw a different moral. I conclude simply that simulators and participants sometimes make faulty assumptions about the way that an action is caused. To make this argument I need to go over some earlier ground.

Stich and Nichols reasonably suppose that actors typically reach decisions on the basis of beliefs and desires about what to do next. For example, wanting a glass of milk, and knowing that there is milk in the refrigerator, they feed this input into a practical reasoning or decision-making system. This system comes up with a decision, e.g. to go to the refrigerator. This decision is then passed on to the action control system (cf. figure 5.1 on p. 128) and they head off in the direction of the refrigerator. If we intercept them at the refrigerator and ask them what they are doing, they can interpret their action for us – they can explain that they are about to look in the refrigerator for some milk.

Consider, however, the position bias described by Nisbett and Ross (1980). One possibility is that once subjects have scanned the items on offer, that information is fed into the system, and yields a decision, such as 'choose the right-most item'. Subjects pass this on to the action-control system and act accordingly. There is a problem with this account, however. If we ask subjects what they have done, they do not interpret their action in terms of choosing the right-most item. Maybe they formulate a position-based decision, act on it, and then for some reason, lose track of what they are up to (just as we occasionally open the refrigerator, and find that we cannot remember what we went there for). However, it seems unlikely that subjects uniformly forget their decision in this way. A more plausible explanation is that subjects' action of choosing the right-most item is not governed by the decision-making system at all. In terms of figure 5.1 (p. 128) we need a supplementary route that allows perceptual input to gain access to the action-control system without passing through the conscious decision-making system. Perhaps the right visual field exerts an unconscious dominance over the motor system. Whatever the explanation, it is not one that engages the decision-making system in the usual way, and not surprisingly, subjects do not mention it in explaining their actions. Instead, having selected a particular item, they distort what has actually happened by imagining various features of the item that might have triggered that decision. Thus, Stich and Nichols's example shows that there are limits to the accuracy of the simulation process, limits which no amount of developmental change can overcome. This is a welcome outcome for psychologists since it guarantees them employment in discovering responses that would not be anticipated by simulation alone.

Yet the existence of such a constraint does not call into question the possibility that actions that are guided by the decision-making system can be anticipated via simulation. Nor does the constraint show that people who read about such experiments, or participate in them, make incorrect predictions by virtue of an inadequate theory. An equally plausible explanation is that actors and readers alike try to reconstruct what has happened by engaging in a misguided simulation: they try to simulate the choice of the right-most item as if it were guided by the normal decision-making process.

More generally, the shopping-mall experiment provides a simple example of a pervasive phenomenon: our folk psychology works unevenly. It does a good job of predicting and explaining what we might dub 'kitchen pragmatics'. If we know the layout of someone's kitchen, and we know what they want to cook, we can predict a lot of their actions. Introduce some complicating factors – for example, they are paranoid, or depressed – and our predictive accuracy will slide rapidly. Yet, my assumption is that when faced with unexpected or deviant actions, adults either continue to try to interpret them via simulation and do so inaccurately, or they elaborate special-purpose theories to deal with such anomalies: Western psychiatry or Azande witchcraft beliefs.

Finally, it is worth noting that developmental psychologists are lingering for good reason in the kitchen. We have been asking children where a story character will look for his chocolate after his mother put it back in the wrong cupboard. We want to know whether children can understand and predict Maxi's pragmatic (albeit misguided) actions: their grasp of his more bizarre responses (e.g. a right-most position bias) are not part of the immediate agenda.

10 Knowledge Assessment

Stich and Nichols review two sets of interesting experiments reported by Wimmer, Hogrefe, and Sodian (1988) concerned with children's knowledge assessment. The experiments looked at children's understanding of the causal link between seeing and knowing, and between inference and knowing. I shall consider each in turn.

10.1 Seeing, Telling, and Knowing

Wimmer and his colleagues claim that an understanding of the way that seeing (or telling) leads to knowing emerges between three and five years. When children in this age range assess whether they themselves know something (e.g. the contents of a closed box), they do not consider whether they have looked in the box (or been told about its contents). Instead, they simply carry out an 'answer check procedure': they perform a mental check to see whether they can come up with an answer to a question about the contents of the box.

Three-year-olds attempt a similar check when evaluating another person's knowledge. Inevitably, they are unable to make that same evaluation with respect to another person who has not yet stated whether he or she knows the contents, so that they make errors. They frequently deny that the other person knows what is in the box, neglecting what the other person has seen (or been told). By contrast, older children aged five years consistently adopt a different and more accurate procedure in assessing what the other person knows: they carry out an 'access check procedure' by evaluating the other person's access, visual or verbal, to information about the contents of the box.

Like Wimmer and his colleagues, Stich and Nichols attribute this alleged developmental change to an improvement in children's theory of mind. They conclude that (this volume, p. 148): 'a very natural way to describe the situation is that while the younger children know that people who say *that p* typically believe or know *that p*, these children have not learned that people will come to know *that p,* by seeing or being told *that p.* The younger children have acquired a fragment of folk psychology, while the older children have acquired a more substantial part of the theory.'

There are two difficulties that stand in the way of this conclusion. First, any claim about the child's alleged theory ought to be consistent with other well-known findings. For example, one of the most robust findings about three-year-olds is that they often perform poorly on false belief tasks, attributing to the false believer knowledge that he or she can have had no access to. However, if three-year-olds were to use the 'answer-check procedure' in the false belief task, they should insist that the returning puppet does not know the new location – since he has offered no overt sign of knowing it. Alternatively, they should make him re-exhibit behaviour he exhibited earlier, namely approach to the old location, on the grounds that his earlier overt action at that location (i.e. placing the object there) is consistent with a belief that the object is to be found there. What three-year-olds patently should not do is credit the returning puppet with knowledge he has, as yet, shown no sign of possessing, namely that the object has been moved to a new location.

The second problem with Stich and Nichols's conclusion is that it rests on data that have proved difficult to replicate. As Goldman points out in his commentary, subsequent research has shown that three-year-olds do quite well when they are asked to say which of two people will know what is in a box, when one has looked inside and the other has merely lifted the box (Pratt and Bryant, 1990). This accuracy is consistent with what would be expected according to Step 3 described earlier: children can imagine themselves looking inside the box, and simulate seeing the contents (irrespective of whether they themselves have looked in the box).

10.2 Inference Assessment

In a further series of experiments, Wimmer and his colleagues discuss the issue of so-called 'inference neglect'. Most four- and six-year-olds realized that if a container contained only a certain type of item, chocolate nuts for example, and if they learn that someone has shifted one of the items out of the container and into a bag, then the bag must now, by inference, contain a chocolate nut. On the other hand, four- but not six-year-olds had difficulty in crediting another person with such inferential knowledge even though they were well aware that the other person, like themselves, had seen chocolate nuts in the original container, and had been told about the transfer of an item from the container into the bag. Wimmer and his colleagues argue that four-year-olds apply the 'access check' described above, and noticing that the other person has not looked in the bag, conclude that he or she cannot know what is in it. By contrast, six-year-olds carry out a further check, asking themselves in effect whether the other could infer even without looking in it that the bag now contains a chocolate nut.

Stich and Nichols take this to be a strong piece of evidence against ST. They point out that four-year-olds do not credit the other person with an inference that they themselves make, even though they would appear to be well aware that the other person fulfils two critical conditions for making the inference, i.e. knowing what is in the container, and that a transfer from container to bag has been made. Stich and Nichols find the notion of 'inference neglect' congenial because it fits their general claim that children are gradually acquiring more and more 'theoretical' knowledge about the way the mind works: four-year-olds do not grasp the role of inference (despite being capable of inference) whereas six-year-olds both engage in and understand the use of inference.

Again, however, the line of explanation favoured by Stich and Nichols (and by Wimmer and his colleagues) flies in the face of other well-established findings. Consider the well-known Smarties box experiment. The child is shown that a box of Smarties contains pencils rather than Smarties. The lid is replaced, and the child is asked to predict what another person will say is inside the box before opening it: four-year-olds predict that the other person will say 'Smarties' even though they themselves know that the box actually contains pencils rather than Smarties; three-year-olds, by contrast, predict that the other person will say 'pencils'.

Suppose, now, in line with the explanation proposed by Wimmer and his colleagues, that four-year-olds suffer from inference neglect but do perform an 'access check': they assess whether or not the other has looked inside the Smarties box. On this basis, they should conclude that the other person, being unable to see inside the Smarties box, will have no idea what is inside it. The four-year-olds do not do this, however. They correctly anticipate the other person's answer, and that answer calls for a simple inference from the familiar external appearance of the Smarties box to its likely contents. Thus, the notion of 'inference neglect' while offering a seductive explanation of findings in the chocolate nuts experiment cannot handle the well-established results of the Smarties box experiment.

What kind of explanation might ST offer? As noted earlier, the child's simulation depends on an appropriate choice of pretend inputs. In the case of the chocolate nuts experiment, the child must set aside what they do or do not know and feed in two pretend inputs: first, the other person's visual inspection of the chocolate nuts in the container, and second the other person's verbal information in the absence of visual access – concerning the transfer of an item from container to bag. Consider, however, what would happen if their simulation is incomplete: they merely feed in the second and more recent pretend input. They imagine what the other person might conclude from simply being told about the transfer of an item without seeing the item in question being transferred into the bag, but they do not feed in the person's inspection of the container and their ensuing knowledge of the identity of the to-be-transferred items. This should lead them to anticipate that the other person will know that 'something' has been transferred but will not know what precisely has been transferred; this was essentially the pattern of results obtained for the four-year-olds. By implication, six-year-olds engage in a more exhaustive simulation of the other, feeding in both of the successively presented inputs in a pretend fashion, and arriving at a simulated output that includes information about both the identity of the items in the container, and the transfer of one of those items into the bag.

Why should four-year-olds fail to engage in an exhaustive simulation? One possibility is that they have developed a 'conservative' simulation strategy: in trying to answer questions about what another will say, know or do with respect to a particular box or bag, they feed in as pretend input the visual or verbal information that has been supplied to the other person concerning that particular receptacle, and then work out their own hypothetical decision on the basis of that pretend information. In the inference neglect experiment, children are questioned about the other person's knowledge of the contents of the bag. Hence, they feed in the fact that the other person has been told that something has been transferrd into the bag, but has not seen the transfer of a specific, identifiable object into the bag.

In the standard false belief task, they use as pretend input the fact that the puppet has seen the chocolate placed at one hiding place but has not seen the transfer to the new hiding place. In the Smarties box task, they use as pretend input the visible exterior of the Smarties box, and not its invisible contents. In each of these two cases, therefore, they correctly anticipate the other person's mistaken response. Note that this interpretation, unlike the 'inference neglect' hypothesis, is not embarrassed by the fact that children credit the other with an inference-based answer in the Smarties box experiment while failing to do so in the chocolate nut experiment. Children can infer what is inside a closed Smarties box from its familiar exterior, and they can presumably imagine another person doing the same. By contrast, the bag used in the chocolate nuts experiment provides no external clues as to its contents.

More generally, this discussion has helped to bring out a general difference between TT and ST which will help in future comparisons of their relative explanatory strength. TT is inclined to assume that children are acquiring successive insights into epistemic categories such as 'false belief' or 'inference' or 'informational access'. It predicts increments in predictive power as these categories are incorporated into the pre-existing theory of mind. By contrast, ST predicts that such increments, if they occur, will result from a more exhaustive and accurate simulation of the starting conditions that face the person being simulated. Increments in predictive accuracy are unlikely to fall into any tidy epistemological category.

11 Problems for TT

In discussing the recent historical background to research on the child's conception of mind, I pointed out that the methodological proposals made by Bennett, Dennett, and Harman have had an important influence on its direction. A great deal of the initial research focused on the child's understanding of other people's false beliefs. The field has since expanded in two ways. First, the initial emphasis on belief has gradually expanded to include desire and intention. Second, the initial emphasis on the diagnosis of other people has been expanded to include the child's diagnosis of his or her previous mental states, be they earlier beliefs, or desires or perceptions. Despite this two-fold expansion, typical experiments continue to require the child to diagnose a mental state that is not currently their own: they are required to diagnose a mental state that belongs to another person or one that they did entertain, but no longer.

As a result of this restriction, we have very little understanding of children's ability to report their current mental states. What would such an investigation produce? The TT approach has no obvious warrant for predicting more accurate reports of current mental states of the self, whether in comparison with current mental states of other people or with past mental states of the self. For example, when Perner and Astington (1992) discuss the way in which mental terms might acquire their meaning, they advocate the 'folk-theory' position according to which:

> mental terms of our language do not get meaning through introspection but as theoretical concepts which are part of a theory for explaining and predicting behaviour. Mental states have the status of hypothetical constructs. They are not directly observable, need to be inferred, and provide advantages for predicting behaviour.

Advocates of TT have gone on to emphasize that when children are asked about their own mental states they gain no advantage from any privileged access. For example, Wimmer and Hartl (1991) and Astington and Gopnik (1991) cite evidence showing that children have similar difficulties whether they are asked to state their own beliefs or another person's.

The simulation model, on the other hand, makes a different prediction: in general, young children should be quite accurate in answering questions about what they currently think, know, pretend, want, or see because privileged access can be used in applying those terms to the self. It can inform them about the current object or target of experience, and their current attitude toward that target. Thus, a child knows whether she is wanting some juice that is in the cup, or pretending that there is juice in the cup. Accordingly if we create conditions in which three-year-olds do or do not want something, do or do not think something, and ask them about their desires or thoughts, it is likely that they will be able to give an accurate report, so long as they understand the terms of the question. Moreover, they should be able to do this despite their frequent inaccuracies in diagnosing other people's thoughts and desires, or their own previous thoughts and desires.

The developmental evidence supports this claim. For example, Gopnik and Slaughter (1991; experiment 1) report that three-year-old children gave appropriate replies (as judged by the situation and/or their behavior) to questions about what they were currently pretending, seeing, wanting, thinking, and intending. Subjects did not always reply accurately to questions about their previous mental states; errors were especially likely to occur for reports of previous desires, thoughts, and intentions.

Similar results were obtained by Baron-Cohen (1991b), who tested three- and four-year-old normal children, autistic children, and mentally handicapped children. They were again asked to report what they were currently thinking, pretending, seeing, wanting, or thinking of (i.e. visualizing). In all three groups, children typically answered two such questions with respect to their current mental state without difficulty.[9] They were less accurate in reporting past mental states, especially in the autistic group.

Gopnik and Slaughter (1991) and Baron-Cohen (1991b) direct their attention almost exclusively to the errors in reporting past mental states, ignoring the important question of how subjects achieve such high accuracy in reporting their current mental states. One possible explanation is that the figures reported are spuriously high because they contain false positives. More specifically, when subjects are shown a milk carton and asked: 'What do you think is inside this?', they might ignore the mental verb and simply gloss the questions as an enquiry about current reality: 'What . . . is inside this?' However, this interpretation cannot be the whole story. On the pretend task, children were asked: 'What are you pretending is in the cup?' Mental verb deletion in this case would yield the question: 'What . . . is inside the cup?' Similarly, in the imagination task, children (having been asked to form a mental image) were asked: 'What are you thinking of?' Mental verb deletion in this case would lead to an uninterpretable: 'What . . . of?'

Accepting that subjects understood the questions in the form in which they were stated, and that their high scores are genuine, one might still deny that their reports called for any privileged access. Recall once more the 'answer-check' procedure postulated by Wimmer et al. (1988). Maybe subjects take the question about their mental state to refer to an overt or even a covert response tendency. For example, when they are shown a milk carton and asked: 'What do you think is inside it?' they assume that the experimenter is asking them what they would be disposed to say is inside the carton. Again, this account becomes strained as soon as we examine the other tasks. In the pretending task, children were asked: 'What are you pretending is inside the cup?' Clearly, children would reply incorrectly if they glossed this as a question about what they would be disposed to say as being inside the cup. Admittedly, they would be more accurate if they interpreted it as a question about their make-believe action *vis-à-vis* the cup. However, a focus on action alone (e.g. pretend drinking) would also lead to error since children were required to pretend first that orange juice and then that milk was inside the cup. Presumably, the pretend actions in these two cases are highly similar. Indeed, Gopnik and Slaughter comment on the observed similarity.

In sum, it is hard to see how normal, retarded, or autistic children could achieve such high accuracy if (a) they do not benefit from privileged access to their own current mental states, and (b) do not construe the experimenter's questions as calling for replies based upon that privileged access.[10] Such accuracy is consistent with the claim that privileged access is an important feature of our mental lives. It makes uncomfortable reading for those adherents of the theory-theory who have ignored the role of privileged access and the importance of current self-report, asserting instead the apparent equivalence in accuracy of first- and third-person reports.

12 Conclusions

I have tried to correct some misconceptions about the simulation approach. As I see it, there is no reason to doubt that adults resort to theories, be they tacit or explicit, in explaining and predicting behaviour. The more interesting and important question is how we should explain the orderly development that we see among children in their grasp of folk psychology. The simulation approach is not embarrassed by the fact that children and adults often make inaccurate predictions. The accuracy of any simulation depends (1) on feeding in the relevant pretend inputs, and (2) on the target behavior being guided by the decision-making system. If these twin assumptions are not met, inaccurate predictions are likely. In the course of development, children become increasingly proficient at feeding in the appropriate pretend inputs. Much of that advance is constrained by increments in imaginative power.

Historically, research on the child's theory of mind was stimulated by commentaries and experiments aimed at blocking the use of a simulation strategy. Paradoxically, that stimulus has led to several findings that simulation theorists find quite congenial. Nonetheless, the direction that developmental research has taken is not unproblematic. Efforts to block the simulation strategy have led to a neglect of children's accuracy in reporting their current mental states. Even when such accuracy is observed it is left unanalyzed. It would be a nice irony if careful empirical scrutiny of children's utterances about their current mental states led us to a re-examination of the conceptual problem of privileged access.

Notes

I thank Simon Baron-Cohen, Alison Denham, Carl Johnson and Andrew Woodfield for their constructive criticism of this manuscript.

1   In describing and explaining the actions of themselves and other people, children produce well-formed utterances in which they refer quite appropriately and explicitly to what the person in question 'wants', 'thinks', 'knows', 'feels', and so forth (Bretherton and Beeghly, 1982; Harris, 1989; Shatz, Wellman, and Silber, 1983; Wellman, 1990).

2   Premack and Woodruff (1978) took two precautions against the use of a simulation strategy. First, in a follow-up task they asked Sarah to choose the next move with respect to a disliked rather than a liked actor. She often chose pictures showing a possible mishap or accident that might

befall the actor in those circumstances (e.g. the actor falling over a box). These choices presumably did not reflect her own preferred or likely course of action. This precaution, however, simply shows that she did not approach the disliked actor with empathy; she still may have used an empathic or simulation strategy in choosing with respect to the liked actor. Premack and Woodruff's second strategy was to present Sarah with problems that she, personally, never faced or resolved. For example, she appropriately chose a lit paper wick rather than an unlit or burnt out one, as a next move for a shivering actor trying to light a heater. Yet, this merely shows that Sarah was capable of observational diagnosis of cause and effect sequences. She still might use a simulation strategy to understand or predict their utilization by an actor.

3   Exotic, I mean, only from our point of view. Evans-Pritchard found the 'theory' quite serviceable during his field-work. 'I found this as satisfactory a way of running my home and affairs as any other I know of', he remarks drily.

4   It is tempting to argue that although ST can work well for the attribution of grammatical judgement, TT will be required for the attribution of beliefs, because beliefs unlike grammatical rules need not be 'shared'. However, this argument ignores the important distinction between process and product. So long as the process by which beliefs are generated is shared, a simulator can engage that process off-line to generate a belief that he or she does not share.

5   For (1) see six recent books, Astington, Harris, and Olson (1988), Butterworth, Harris, Leslie, and Wellman (1991), Frye and Moore (1991), Harris (1989), Perner (1991), Wellman (1990). For (2) see Frith (1989) and Baron-Cohen et al. (1993). For (3) see Whiten (1991). For (4) see Avis and Harris (1991) and Flavell, Zhang, Zou, Dong, and Qi (1983).

6   Developmental psychologists get exercised about exactly what abilities emerge when. The ages I give are not very precise. My intention is to describe a developmental sequence rather than to be exact about the age at which each transition occurs.

7   In line with the limitations operating at Step 2, the child finds it difficult to imagine the other looking at an object he or she cannot see. In showing an object such as a picture to another person, therefore, 18-month-olds orient it so that they can still see it. This restriction disappears as the child moves into Step 3 at around two years (Lempers, Flavell, and Flavell, 1977).

8   It is important to note that high-functioning autistic children show a selective rather than a total impairment in their understanding of mental states. For example, if we take a normal three-year-old, he or she can understand that another person may differ from the self in what he or she *wants, sees, knows*. Current evidence suggests that high-functioning autistics are as good as normal three-year-olds in their understanding of *seeing* and *wanting* (Hobson, 1984; Tager-Flusberg, 1993; Tan and Harris,

228 Paul L. Harris

1991). Yet they show little understanding of cognitive states such as *knowing* (Tager-Flusberg, 1993). The simulation account that I have described does not explain this selective preservation for *seeing* and *wanting*. The results for autistic children suggest that the development of simulation processes may be less monolithic than I have allowed. This is a matter for future research. One important step would be to take a task that involves *seeing* and *knowing* (e.g. Pratt and Bryant, 1990) and to find out exactly which components autistic children do and do not understand. Goodhart and Baron-Cohen (1991) have begun to do this.

9 Some subjects did have difficulty on the pretence task which involved pretending that there was orange juice or milk inside a cup, until they were prompted to enact (rather than simply imagine) pretend drinking. In addition, four autistic subjects claimed that they were unable to see (i.e. visualize) anything with their eyes closed.

10 One might object to my conclusion by arguing that children possess the concept of thinking or seeing if and only if they can as readily conceive of others, as well as themselves, engaged in thinking or seeing. Hence, any asymmetry between reports on the self and reports on others must be spurious. However, this objection collapses two different conceptual tasks: (a) the recognition that others can, in principle, entertain mental attitudes equivalent to those enertained by the self, and (b) the diagnostic procedures for making attributions to the self as compared with others. Children might display an asymmetry with respect to (b) but not (a).

References

Astington, J. W. and Gopnik, A. 1991: Theoretical explanations of children's understanding of the mind. *British Journal of Developmental Psychology*, 9, 7–31.

Astington, J. W. and Gopnik, A. 1988: Knowing you've changed your mind: Children's understanding of representational change. In J. W. Astington, P. L. Harris and D. R. Olson (eds), *Developing Theories of Mind*. New York: Cambridge University Press.

Astington, J. W., Harris, P. L. and Olson, D. R. 1988: *Developing Theories of Mind*. New York: Cambridge University Press.

Avis, J. and Harris, P. L. 1991: Belief–desire reasoning among Baka children: Evidence for a universal conception of mind. *Child Development*, 62, 460–7.

Baron-Cohen, S. 1991a: Precursors to a theory of mind: Understanding attention in others. In A. Whiten (ed.), *Natural Theories of Mind*. Oxford: Blackwell.

Baron-Cohen, S. 1991b: The development of a theory of mind in autism: Deviance or delay. *Psychiatric Clinics of North America*, 14, 33–51.

Baron-Cohen, S., Tager-Flusberg, H. and Cohen, D. (eds) 1993: *Understanding Other Minds: Perspectives from Autism*. Oxford: Oxford University Press.

Bennett, J. 1978: Some remarks about concepts. *Behavioral and Brain Sciences*, 1, 557–60.

Bretherton, I. and Beeghly, M. 1982: Talking about internal states: The acquisition of an explicit theory of mind. *Developmental Psychology*, 18, 906–21.

Butterworth, G. E. 1991: The ontogeny and phylogeny of joint visual attention. In A. Whiten (ed.), *Natural Theories of Mind*. Oxford: Blackwell.

Butterworth, G. E., Harris, P. L., Leslie, A. M. and Wellman, H. M. 1991: *Perspectives on the Child's Theory of Mind*. Oxford: Oxford University Press.

Dennett, D. C. 1978: Beliefs about beliefs. *Behavioral and Brain Sciences*, 1, 558–70.

Evans-Pritchard, E. E. 1937: *Witchcraft, Oracles and Magic among the Azande*. Oxford: Oxford University Press.

Flavell, J. 1986: The development of children's knowledge about the appearance–reality distinction. *American Psychologist*, 41, 418–25.

Flavell, J. H. 1988: The development of children's knowledge about the mind: From cognitive connections to mental representations. In J. W. Astington, P. L. Harris and D. R. Olson (eds), *Developing Theories of Mind*. New York: Cambridge University Press.

Flavell, J. H., Zhang, X.-D., Zou, H., Dong, Q. and Qi, S. 1983: A comparison of the appearance–reality distinction in the People's Republic of China and the United States. *Cognitive Psychology*, 15, 459–66.

Frith, U. 1989: *Autism: Explaining the Enigma*. Oxford: Blackwell.

Frye, D. and Moore, C. 1991: *Children's Theories of Mind*. Hillsdale, NJ: Lawrence Erlbaum Associates.

Goodhart, F. and Baron-Cohen, S. 1991: The 'Seeing leads to knowing' principle in autism. Unpublished ms., Institute of Psychiatry, University of London.

Gopnik, A. and Astington, J. W. 1988: Children's understanding of representational change and its relation to the understanding of the appearance–reality distinction. *Child Development*, 59, 26–37.

Gopnik, A. and Slaughter, V. 1991: Young children's understanding of changes in their mental states. *Child Development*, 62, 98–110.

Harman, G. 1978: Studying the chimpanzee's theory of mind. *Behavioral and Brain Sciences*, 1, 576–7.

Harris, P. L. 1989: *Children and Emotion: The Development of Psychological Understanding*. Oxford: Blackwell.

Harris, P. L. 1991: The work of the imagination. In A. Whiten (ed.), *Natural Theories of Mind*. Oxford: Blackwell.

Hobson, P. R. 1984: Early childhood autism and the question of egocentrism. *Journal of Autism and Developmental Disorders*, 14, 85–104.

Kohler, W. 1957: *The Mentality of Apes*. Harmondsworth: Penguin.

Kuczaj, S. A. II and Daly, M. J. 1979: The development of hypothetical reference in the speech of young children. *Journal of Child Language*, 6, 563–79.

Lempers, J. D., Flavell, E. R. and Flavell, J. H. 1977: The development in very young children of tacit knowledge concerning visual perception. *Genetic Psychology Monographs*, 95, 3–53.

Mundy, P. and Sigman, M. 1989: The theoretical implications of joint-attention deficits in autism. *Development and Psychopathology*, 1, 173–83.

Mundy, P., Sigman, M. and Kasari, C. 1993: Theory of mind and joint-attention deficits in autism. In S. Baron-Cohen, H. Tager-Flusberg and D. Cohen (eds), *Understanding Other Minds: Perspectives from Autism*. Oxford: Oxford University Press.

Mundy, P., Sigman, M., Ungerer, J. and Sherman, T. 1986: Defining the social deficits of autism: The contribution of non-verbal communication measures. *Journal of Child Psychology and Psychiatry*, 27, 657–69.

Nelson, K. and Gruendel, J. 1979: At morning it's lunchtime: A scriptal view of children's dialogues. *Discourse Processes*, 2, 73–94.

Nisbett, R. and Ross, L. 1980: *Human Inference: Strategies and Shortcomings of Social Judgement*. Englewood Cliffs, NJ: Prentice-Hall.

Perner, J. 1991: *Understanding the Representational Mind*. Cambridge, MA: MIT Press.

Perner, J. and Astington, J. W. In press: The child's understanding of mental representation. In P. Pufall and H. Beilin (eds), *Piaget's Theory: Prospects and Possibilities*. Hillsdale, NJ: Erlbaum Associates.

Pratt, C. and Bryant, P. E. 1990: Young children understand that looking leads to knowing (so long as they are looking into a single barrel). *Child Development*, 61, 973–82.

Premack, D. and Woodruff, G. 1978: Does the chimpanzee have a theory of mind? *Behavioral and Brain Sciences*, 1, 515–26.

Rheingold, H. L., Hay, D. F. and West, M. J. 1976: Sharing in the second year of life. *Child Development*, 47, 1148–56.

Shatz, M., Wellman, H. M. and Silber, S. 1983: The acquisition of mental verbs: A systematic investigation of the child's first reference to mental state. *Cognition*, 14, 301–21.

Tager-Flusberg, H. 1993: What language reveals about the understanding of minds in children and autism. In S. Baron-Cohen, H. Tager-Flusberg and D. Cohen (eds), *Understanding Other Minds: Perspectives from Autism*. Oxford: Oxford University Press.

Tan, J. and Harris, P. L. 1991: Autistic children understand seeing and wanting. *Development and Psychopathology*, 3, 163–74.

Wellman, H. M. 1990: *The Child's Theory of Mind*. Cambridge, MA: MIT Press.

Wellman, H. M. and Gelman, S. A. 1992: Cognitive development: Foundational theories of core domains. *Annual Review of Psychology*, 43, 337–75.

Whiten, A. 1991: *Natural Theories of Mind*. Oxford: Blackwell.

Wimmer, H. and Hartl, M. 1991: Against the Cartesian view on mind: Young children's difficulty with own false belief. *British Journal of Developmental Psychology*, 9, 125–38.

Wimmer, H., Hogrefe, J. and Sodian, B. 1988: A second stage on children's conception of mental life: Understanding informational accesses as origins of knowledge and belief. In J. W. Astington, P. L. Harris and D. R. Olson (eds), *Developing Theories of Mind*. New York: Cambridge University Press.

Wimmer, H. and Perner, J. 1983: Beliefs about beliefs: Representations and constraining function of wrong beliefs in young children's understanding of deception. *Cognition*, 13, 103–28.

Wolf, D. P., Rygh, J. and Altshuler, J. 1984: Agency and experience: Actions and states in play narratives. In I. Bretherton (ed.), *Symbolic Play*. Orlando, Fla.: Academic Press.

11

Why the Child's Theory of Mind Really *Is* a Theory

ALISON GOPNIK AND HENRY M. WELLMAN

How do children (and indeed adults) understand the mind? In this paper we contrast two accounts. One is the view that the child's early understanding of mind is an implicit theory analogous to scientific theories, and changes in that understanding may be understood as theory changes. The second is the view that the child need not really understand the mind, in the sense of having some set of beliefs about it. She bypasses conceptual understanding by operating a working model of the mind and reading its output. Fortunately, the child has such a model easily available, as all humans do, namely her own mind. The child's task is to learn how to apply this model to predict and explain others' mental states and actions. This is accomplished by running simulations on her working model; that is, observing the output of her own mind, given certain inputs, and then applying the results to others.

The first position has a certain prominence; research on children's understanding of mind has come to be called "children's theory of mind". This position is linked to certain philosophers of mind such as Churchland (1984) and Stich (1983), who characterize ordinary understanding of mind, our mentalistic folk psychology, as a theory. It is also part of a recent tendency to describe cognitive development as analogous to theory change in science (Carey, 1985, 1988; Karmiloff-Smith and Inhelder, 1975; Wellman and Gelman, 1988; Keil, 1989; Gopnik, 1984, 1988). The second position, in a somewhat different form, has a venerable philosophical tradition, going back to Descartes. This is the tradition of emphasizing the special importance of the first-person case in understanding the mind. More recently Gordon and Goldman have advocated a "simulation theory" of mind (ST), and this position has been taken up in the developmental literature by Harris (1991, this volume) and Johnson (1988).

We do not believe that this is a dispute that can be settled on conceptual or a priori grounds. Rather it is a contest between two empirically testable hypotheses about the nature of "folk psychology". We believe that the child's understanding of mind is helpfully construed as a theory, and that changes in understanding may be thought of as theory changes. But we believe this because such an account provides the best explanation for the currently available developmental evidence.

In spite of the prominence of the "theory theory" (TT), the exact nature of such folk-psychological theories has rarely been spelt out in much detail, and in fact, this is often raised as an objection to this view. What exactly are the theoretical entites and laws that are involved in this theory? How is it constructed from the available evidence? We will first attempt to provide some of this detailed exposition. When the full story is told, we believe, a theory of early developments is compelling indeed. Second, we will argue that a contrasting simulation account fails to fit the data in key places and fails more generally to provide as comprehensive a view of development.

1 The Theory Theory

The question of what distinguishes a theory from other types of conceptual schemas is, of course, an enormous and difficult one. Nevertheless, it seems to us that there are characteristic features of both theories and theory change that can be outlined in very broad and simplified terms.

Theoretical constructs are abstract entities postulated, or recruited from elsewhere, to provide a separate causal-explanatory level of analysis that accounts for evidential phenomena. Gravity is not itself two bodies moving in relation to one another, it is postulated to explain such phenomena. Such theoretical constructs are typically phrased in a vocabulary that is quite different from the evidential vocabulary. For example, Kepler's theory of the planets includes ideas about elliptical orbits that are notoriously not visible when we look at the stars' motions in the sky. Theories in biology postulate unseen entities, like viruses and bacteria, with distinctive properties some of which are implicated in transmission of disease. Theoretical constructs need not be definitively unobservable, but they must be appeals to a set of entities removed from, and underlying, the evidential phenomena themselves. They are designed to explain (not merely type and generalize) those empirical phenomena. So, one characteristic of theories is their abstractness. They postulate entities and analyses that explain the data but are not simply restatements of the data.[1]

Theoretical constructs do not work independently, they work together in systems characterized by laws or structure. A second characteristic of theories is their coherence. The theoretical entities and terms postulated by a theory are closely, "lawfully", interrelated with one another.

The coherence and abstractness of theories together give them a characteristic explanatory force.[2] These features of theories also give them a very characteristic sort of predictiveness. To put it crudely, we can map a bit of evidence on to one part of the theory, grind through the intratheoretic relations, come out at a very different place in the theory and then map back from that part of the theory to some new piece of evidence. In this way, the set of abstract entities encompass a wide range of events, events that might not even seem comparable at the evidential level of description. A theory not only makes predictions, it makes predictions about a wide variety of evidence, including evidence that played no role in the theory's initial construction. Kepler's account allows one to predict the behavior of new celestial objects, moons for example, which were quite unknown at the time the theory was formulated. Theories in biology allow us to predict that antibiotics will inhibit many bacterial infections, including some, like scarlet fever, that present none of the symptoms of an infected wound, or some, like Legionnaire's disease, that were unknown when the theory was formulated. They also allow us to predict that such drugs will be useless against viral infections, even when the symptoms of the viral infection are identical to those of a bacterial one.

Some of these predictions will be correct, they will accurately predict future events described at the evidential level, and will do so in ways that no mere empirical generalization could capture. Others will be incorrect. Since theories go beyond the evidence, and since theories are never completely right, some of their predictions will be falsified. In still other cases the theory will make no prediction at all. In fact, the theory may in some circumstances have less predictive power than a large set of empirical observations. This is because explanatory depth and force do not simply equate with predictive accuracy. We can make predictions about events without explaining them: Kepler's theory still leaves many of Tycho Brahe's observations unexplained. The differences in cases of theoretical prediction are twofold. First, a few theoretical entities and laws can lead to a wide variety of unexpected predictions. Second, in the case of a theory, prediction is intimately tied to explanation.

An additional characteristic of theories, related to this central function of explanation, is that they produce interpretations of evidence, not simply descriptions of evidence and generalizations about it. Indeed theories influence which pieces of evidence we consider salient or important. In modern medicine, for example, similar sets of symptoms do not necessarily yield the same disease diagnosis. An empirical typology of similar symptoms is overriden by deeper, more theoretic biological explanations. The interpretive effects of theories may be stronger still: it is notoriously true that theoretical preconceptions may lead a scientist to dismiss some kinds of evidence as simply noise, or the result of methodological failures. Nor is this simply prejudice. On the contrary, deciding which evidence to ignore is crucial to the effective conduct of a scientific research program.

All these characteristics of theories ought also to apply to children's understanding of mind, if such understandings are theories of mind. That is, such theories should involve appeal to abstract unobservable entites, with coherent relations among them. Theories should invoke characteristic explanations phrased in terms of these abstract entities and laws. They should also lead to characteristic patterns of predictions, including extensions to new types of evidence and false predictions, not just to more empirically accurate prediction. Finally, theories should lead to distinctive interpretations of evidence; a child with one theory should interpret even fundamental facts and experiences differently than a child with a different theory.

So far we have been talking mostly about the static features of theories, the features that might distinguish them from other cognitive structures such as typologies or schemas. But a most important thing about theories is their defeasibility. Theories are open to defeat via evidence, and because of this theories change. In fact, a tenet of modern epistemology is that any aspect of a theory, even the most central ones, may change. The dynamic features of theories, the processes involved in theory formation and change, are equally characteristic and perhaps even more important from a developmental point of view.

While any very precise specification, any algorithm, for theory change may elude us, there are certainly substantive things to be said about how it typically takes place. There are characteristic intermediate processes involved in the transition from one theory to another. One particularly critical factor is the accumulation of counter-evidence to the theory. The initial reaction, as it were, of a theory to counter-evidence may be a kind of denial. The interpretive mechanisms of the theory may treat the counter-evidence as noise, mess, not worth attending to. At a slightly later stage the theory may develop *ad hoc* auxiliary hypotheses designed to account specifically for such counter-evidence. Auxiliary hypotheses may also be helpful because they phrase the counter-evidence in the accepted vocabulary of the earlier theory. Such auxiliary hypotheses, however, often appear, over time, to undermine the coherence that is one of a theory's strengths. The theory gets ugly and messy instead of being beautiful and simple.

A final step requires the availability or formulation of some alternative model to the original theory. A theory may limp along for some time under the weight of its auxiliary hypotheses if no alternative way of making progress is available. But the fertility of the alternative idea itself may not be recognized immediately. Initially it may only be applied to the problematic cases. We may see only later on that the new idea also provides an explanation for the evidence that was explained by the earlier theory.

The development of the heliocentric theory of the planets provides some good examples of these processes. Auxiliary hypotheses involving more and more complex arrangements of epicycles were initially invoked to deal with counter-evidence. Later heliocentrism was introduced by Copernicus. It is worth noting though that Copernicus's theory fails to apply the central heliocentric idea very widely. In many respects Copernicus's account is more like the Ptolemaic ones, than, say, Tycho Brahe's account. It includes epicycles, for example. Brahe's account acknowledges many of the flaws of the Ptolemaic ones, and uses the idea of heliocentrism to deal with them (other planets revolve around the sun which revolves around the earth). But Brahe fails to accept the central idea that the earth itself goes round the sun. Only with Kepler is there a really coherent heliocentric account that deals both with the anomalies and with the earlier data itself.

We propose that these same dynamic features should be apparent in children's transition from one theory to a later one, and specifically from one view of the mind to another. Children should ignore certain kinds of counter-evidence initially, then account for them by auxiliary hypotheses, then use the new theoretical idea in limited contexts, and only finally reorganize their knowledge so that new theoretical entities play a central role.

2 The Child's Theories of Mind

We propose that there is a change from one mentalistic psychological theory to another somewhere between ages two and a half and around four. The change is not a simple all-or-none one, but rather involves a more gradual transition from one view of the mind to another. Indeed this change manifests the tell-tale intermediate processes that are characteristic of theory change. Two-year-olds have an early theory that is incorrect in that it does not posit the existence of mental representational states, prototypically beliefs. In three-year-olds there is an intermediate phase where children demonstrate an understanding of the existence of representational states, at times, but only as auxiliary hypotheses. That is, children in this phase can acknowledge that representational states of mind exist, if forced to do so in certain ways, but this realization is peripheral to their central explanatory theory. In a third phase, beginning around age four, children reorganize their central explanatory theory, it becomes properly a belief–desire psychology. Children begin to realize that what the actor thinks – his or her representation of the world rather than the world itself – inevitably determines actions.

2.1 The Two-year-old Theory

The two-year-old is clearly a mentalist and not a behaviorist. Indeed, it seems unlikely to us that there is ever a time when normal children are behaviorists. Even in infancy, children seem to have some notions, however vague, of internal states as evidenced in early primary intersubjectivity (Trevarthen and Hubley, 1978) and imitation (Meltzoff and Moore, 1977; Meltzoff and Gopnik, 1993) and later, more clearly, in social referencing and joint attention behaviors (e.g. Wellman, 1993). It seems plausible that mentalism is the starting state of psychological knowledge. But such primary mentalism, whenever it first appears, does not include all the sorts of mental states that we as adults recognize. More specifically, even at two years psychological knowledge seems to be structured largely in terms of two types of internal states: desires on the one hand, and perceptions on the other. However, this knowledge excludes any understanding of representation.

Desire and perception alone provide examples of the two basic categories of explanatory entities in folk psychology – the two types of theoretical constructs that Searle calls "world-to-mind" and "mind-to-world" states (Searle,

1983). An understanding of desire encompasses an early knowledge that what's in the mind can change what's in the world. An understanding of perception, on the other hand, encompasses an early knowledge that what's in the mind depends on what's in the world. Moreover, both desire and perception, as theoretical constructs, work to explain action but may also be divorced from any particular actions that an agent may perform.

Importantly, however, desire and perception can be, and at first are, understood in non-representational terms. Desires at first are conceived simply as drives towards objects (Wellman and Woolley, 1990). Perceptions are at first understood simply as awareness of objects (Flavell, 1988). In neither case need the child conceive of a complex propositional or representational relationship between these mental states and the world. Instead, these very young children seem to treat desire and perception as fairly simple causal links between the mind and the world. Given that an agent desires an object, the agent will act to obtain it. Given that an object is within a viewer's line of sight, the viewer will see it. These causal constructs are simple, but they have considerable predictive power. In particular, together they allow the first form of "the practical syllogism": "If an agent desires X, and sees it exists, he will do things to get it." Even that form of the practical syllogism is a powerful inferential folk-psychological law. It allows children to infer for example, that if John wants a cookie and sees one in the cookie jar, he will go there for it. If he doesn't want it, or doesn't see it, he won't.

2.2 The Three-year-old Theory

By three, children begin to show signs of a more elaborate mental ontology. Given the difficulties of testing children younger than three, the earliest emergence of this aspect of the theory is difficult to document. While two-year-olds' successes on desire and perception tasks are striking, their failures on other tasks are more difficult to interpret. However, natural language can provide us with one avenue for exploring these abilities. Before three, children make extensive and appropriate use of terms for desire and perception (Bretherton and Beeghly, 1982). More cognitive mental terms (think, know, remember, make-believe, dream) only begin to emerge at around the third birthday (Shatz, Wellman, and Silber, 1983).

There is further evidence that at three children begin to have a more general notion of belief and also of such representational but "not real" mental states as pretenses, dreams, and images (e.g. Wellman and Estes, 1986). When these concepts first appear, however, they have an interesting character, framed by the child's larger theory which is still a desire–perception theory. This manifests itself in two ways. First, understanding of belief appears to be initially modelled on a non-representational understanding; that is, modelled on an earlier understanding of desire and especially perception. Second, even when the notion of belief, as a representation, appears, it first plays little if any role in the child's explanations of behavior. In these respects the child's first conception of belief seems to be a conceptual construction based on reworking earlier theoretical constructs. Moreover, even the more advanced representational notion initially functions like an auxiliary hypothesis rather than a central theoretical construct.

To elaborate, three-year-olds' first understanding of belief seems like their earlier understanding of perception in that it shares something of that construct's non-representational character. Specifically, belief does not at first easily encompass a sense of misrepresentation. On this view, belief, like perception and desire, involves rather direct causal links between objects and believers. This view has variously been called a "copy theory" (Wellman, 1990), a "Gibsonian theory" (Astington and Gopnik, 1991a), a "situation theory" (Perner, 1991), or a "cognitive connection"(Flavell, 1988) theory of belief. The similar idea in all these accounts is that belief contents directly reflect the world. The introduction of a notion of belief promises an important additional complexity to the child's theory of mind. Initially, however, the notion seems to be quite strongly embedded in the non-representational desire–perception framework of the earlier theory.

At times, however, at least as the fourth year progresses, three-year-olds are able to recognize the existence of beliefs that clearly misrepresent. They can explain already completed, ineffective actions as indicating a false belief by the actor, and can at times even acknowledge the presence of mistaken, wrong beliefs (e.g. Siegal and Beattie, 1991; Moses, 1990). However, these same children do not often construe actions as stemming from false beliefs. When predicting action they typically, consistently, resistantly act as if the actor's desire along with the objective facts determine action, ignoring a role for false belief in influencing action (e.g. Gopnik and Astington, 1988; Perner, Leekham, and Wimmer, 1987; Wellman and Bartsch, 1988). Similarly, when asked the contents of a person's belief, they consistently, resistantly cite the facts (e.g. Perner et al., 1987; Moses and Flavell, 1990). In short, when predicting action and when diagnosing belief contents, three-year-olds evidence largely a non-representational desire–perception understanding.

What about "non-real" mental states, such as pretences, dreams, and images? There is evidence that children actually have such fictional mental states as young as 18 months (e.g. Leslie, 1987). Evidence that they understand such states, however, is much less clear. By the third birthday, however, children have some conceptual knowledge of these aspects of mental life (e.g. Wellman and Estes, 1986; Harris, Brown, Marriot, Whittall, and Harmer, 1991). Moreover, they may distinguish such imaginary or hypothetical states from the states of desire and perception. However, these states appear to play little role in children's explanation of ordinary behavior. More significantly, these states have little causal connection to objects (that, in fact, is what is distinctive about them). While children see desires as states that modify the world, and perceptions as states that are modified by the world, pretences, images and dreams, on their view, bear no causal relation to the world at all. It is possible that postulating these states, which are representational but divorced from reality, also plays a role in the eventual development of the full representational theory.

In summary, mental representations exist for three-year-olds, but only as a relatively isolated auxiliary hypothesis necessary to explain certain (to them) peripheral mental phenomena – the odd infrequent misrepresentation and explanatorily impotent fictional representations.

2.3 The Five-year-old View

By four or five, children, at least in our culture, have developed a quite different view of the mind, one that we have called a "representational model of mind" (Forguson and Gopnik, 1988). On this view almost all psychological functioning is mediated by representations. Desires, perceptions, beliefs, pretences, and images all involve the same fundamental structure, a structure sometimes described in terms of propositional attitudes and propositional contents. These mental states all involve representations of reality, rather than realities themselves. In philosophical terms, the child's view of the mind becomes fully "intentional". To use Dretske's terminology, perceiving becomes perceiving that, and desiring becomes desiring that; we might even add, that believing becomes believing that (Dretske, 1981). This new view provides a kind of Copernican, or better Keplerian, revolution in the child's view of the mind. In addition to distinguishing different types of mental states with different relations to a real world of objects, the child sees that all mental life partakes of the same representational character. Many characteristics of all mental states, such as their diversity, and their tendency to change, can be explained by the properties of representations. This newly unified view not only provides new predictions, explanations, and interpretations; it also provides a new view of the very evidence that was accounted for earlier by the desire–perception theory.

3 The Child's Theory as Theory

What evidence do we have for thinking that these understandings are theoretical in the sense that we have been outlining so far? The following: The child's understanding involves general constructs about the mind that go beyond the focal evidential phenomena. These constructs feature importantly in explanation. They allow children to make predictions about behavior in a wide variety of circumstances, including predictions about behavior they have never actually experienced and incorrect predictions. Finally, they lead to distinctive interpretations of evidence.

3.1 Explanations

Children's explanations of actions show a characteristic theory-like pattern. In open-ended explanation tasks (Bartsch and Wellman, 1989; Wellman and Banerjee, 1991) children are simply presented with an action or reaction ("Jane is looking for her kitty under the piano") and asked to explain it ("Why is she doing that?"). There are many mental states that might be associated with such situations. Yet three- and four-year-old children's answers to such open-ended questions are organized around beliefs and desires just as adults' are ("she wants the kitty"; "she thinks it's under the piano"). Moreover, there is a shift in explanatory type between two and five. Two-year-olds' explanations almost always mention desires, but not beliefs. Asked why the girl looks for her doll under the bed they will talk about the fact that she wants the doll, but not the fact that she believes the doll is there. Three-year-olds invoke beliefs and desires, and some three- and most four- and five-year-olds consistently refer to the representational character of these states, explaining failure in terms of falsity. These same trends can be seen in the explanations children give in their spontaneous speech (Bartsch and Wellman, 1990).

3.2 Predictions

Consider the desire-perception theory. Even that early theory allows children to make a variety of predictions about actions and perceptions, both their own and others. For example, they should be able to predict that desires may differ, and that, given a desire, an actor will try to fulfil that desire. They should know that desires may not be fulfilled. They should predict that fulfilled desires will lead to happiness, while unfulfilled desires will lead to sadness (Wellman and Woolley, 1990). And there is evidence that, in fact, all these kinds of predictions are made by very young children (e.g. Wellman and Woolley, 1990; Yuill, 1984; Astington and Gopnik, 1991b). Similarly, a child with the desire-perception theory should be able to predict the perceptions of others in a wide variety of circumstances, including those in which the perceptions are different from their own. Such very early activities as shared attention and social referencing behaviors already indicate some capacity to understand the perception of others (Wellman, 1993). Other aspects of this understanding quickly develop. By two and a half years these Level-1 under-standings, as Flavell calls them, are firmly and reliably in place (Flavell, 1988). At this age children can reliably predict when an agent will or will not see (and hear and touch) an object (e.g. Flavell, Everett, Croft, and Flavell, 1981). They can also predict how seeing an object will lead to later actions. However, they are unable to make predictions about representational aspects of perception, what Flavell calls Level-2 understanding. They fail to predict, for ex-ample, that an object that is clearly seen by both parties can look one way to one viewer and another way to another.

These predictions may seem so transparent to adults that we think of them not as predictions at all but simply as empirical facts. A little reflection, however, should make us realize that the notion of desire or perception used by these very young children is theoretically broad and powerful. Children can use the notion of desire appropriately and make the correct predictions when the desired objects are objects, or events, or states of affairs. They can attribute desires to themselves and others even when they do not act to fulfil the desires and when the desires are not in fact fulfilled. Similarly, children seem to make accurate predictions about perception across a wide range of events, involving factors as different as screens, blindfolds, and visual angles, and do so across different perceptual modalities. Again, they may do so even when the perceptions do not lead to any immediate observable actions. Moreover, given novel and unfamiliar information about an agent's desires and perceptions, children will make quite accurate predictions about the agent's actions.

More significantly, however, these children also make incorrect predictions in cases where the desire-perception theory breaks down. Both desires and perceptions, on the two-year-old view, involve simple non-representational causal links between the world and the mind. Even the early non-representational notions of belief have this quality. This theory cannot handle cases of misrepresentation. Presented with such cases it makes the wrong predictions. The theory also cannot handle other problems that require an understanding of the complexity of the representational relations between mind and world. For example, the theory breaks down when one must consider the fact that the same belief may come from different sources, or that there may be different degrees of certainty of beliefs.

The most well-known instance of such an incorrect prediction is, of course, the false-belief error in three-year-olds (Wimmer and Perner, 1983; Perner et al., 1987). The focus on false-belief tasks may, however, be somewhat unfortunate since it has promoted a mind-set in which any ability to perform "correctly" on a false-belief task is taken as evidence that the child has a representational theory of the mind. As we will see, there are cases in which three-year-olds indicate some understanding of false belief. However, to begin with it is worth pointing out the much greater ubiquity and generality of the incorrect false-belief predictions. Three-year-olds make erroneous predictions, not only in the "classic" tasks but also in many other cases involving beliefs about location, identity, number and properties. They make incorrect predictions for "real" others, for puppets, for children, and for hypothetical story characters. Incorrect predictions are made when the question is phrased in terms of what the other thinks, what the other will say and what the other will do, and across a wide range of syntactic frames. They are made by North American (Gopnik and Astington, 1988), British (Perner et al., 1987), and Austrian (Wimmer and Perner, 1983) children, and recently by Baka children of the Cameroons (Avis and Harris, 1991).

Moreover, and more significantly from the point of view of the theory theory, these incorrect belief predictions are mirrored in three-year-olds' performance on a wide range of other tasks. A brief inventory would include (a) appearance–reality tasks, which themselves have proved robust across many variations of culture, question, and material (Flavell, Green, and Flavell, 1986), (b) questions about the sources of belief (Gopnik and Graf, 1988) and the understanding of subjective probability (Moore, Pure, and Furrow, 1990), and (c) the understanding of pictorial representational systems (Zaitchek, 1990). In some of these tasks the desire-perception theory makes incorrect predictions, and children consistently give the same wrong answer. In others, it makes no predictions at all and the children respond at random. On any information-processing account these tasks would require quite different kinds of competences. Moreover, the standard methodology of these studies has included control tasks, involving similar or identical information-processing demands, which children seem entirely capable of answering. Nor do any dimensions of familiarity, at least in any simple terms, seem to underlie the difference between tasks at which children succeed and fail.

3.3 Interpretations

In these cases children are clearly using belief and desire to make predictions – one of the central functions of theoretical constructs. In addition to the explanatory and predictive effects, children also show strong interpretive effects. Suppose we present the child with counter-evidence to the theory? If the child is simply reporting her empirical experience we might expect that she will report that evidence correctly. In fact, however, children consistently misreport and misinterpret evidence when it conflicts with their theoretical preconceptions. Flavell and his colleagues have some provocative but simple demonstrations of evidential misinterpretation (Flavell, Flavell, Green, and Moses, 1990). A child sees a blue cup, agrees that it is blue and not white, and sees the cup hidden behind a screen. At this point another adult comes into the room, and she says "I cannot see the cup. Hmm, I think it is white." Then the child is asked what color he thinks the cup is and what color the adult thinks it is. To be correct the child need only report the adult's actual words, but three-year-olds err by attributing to the character a true belief. Even if corrected, "well actually she really thinks it's white", three-year-olds continue to insist the adult has a factually correct belief: "She thinks it's blue." Moreover, as we will see, three-year-old children consistently misreport their own immediately past mental states.

3.4 Transitional Phenomena

In developmental psychology we are often better at describing the states at two points in development than at describing changes from one state to another. Nevertheless, recent evidence suggests that during the period from three to four many children are in a state of transition between the two theories, similar, say, to the fifty years between the publication of *De Revolutionibus* and Kepler's discovery of elliptical orbits. This is rather bad luck for developmentalists since this period has been the focus of much of our investigation. But it also means that we may have some intriguing evidence about the mechanisms that lead from one theory to another.

We have already seen in our discussion of interpretation how children with the earlier theory begin by simply denying the existence of the counter-evidence. Johnny and I really did think and act as if there were pencils in the box when we first saw it. We have also seen that at around three children develop a first non-representational account of belief, which extends their original desire-perception psychology. We can also ask where the first signs of an understanding of misrepresentation, the centerpiece of the five-year-old theory, begin to appear. Recall that we suggested, in the scientific case, that in a transitional period the crucial idea of the new theory may appear as an auxiliary hypothesis couched in the vocabulary of the original theory, or be used in order to deal with particularly salient types of counter-evidence, but may not be widely applied. There is evidence for both these phenomena in the period from three to four. Children seem to us to initially develop the idea of misrepresentation in familiar contexts like those of desire and perception, without extending the idea more generally. They also initially apply the idea only when they are forced to by counter-evidence.

There is evidence that by placing the misrepresentation questions in the context of the earlier theory we can begin to see (or perhaps, in fact, induce) glimmerings of the later theory. Desire and perception may be construed either non-representationally, or representationally. In fact, in the adult theory, desire and perception are as representational as belief. What we want and see (by and large) is not the thing itself but the thing as represented. Understanding some aspects of desire and perception requires this sort of representational understanding. When we are satiated with something we no longer desire it, but the object itself has not changed. When different types of people have different tastes or values, their desires differ but the objects of desire remain the same (Flavell et al., 1990). There is evidence that these representational aspects of desire are understood earlier than equivalently representational aspects of belief (Gopnik and Slaughter, 1991). However, three-year-old children still do not perform as well on these tasks as they do on simple non-representational desire tasks. Similarly, while non-representational aspects of perception are understood by two and a half, representational ones, what Flavell calls Level-2-perspective-taking, are only understood later (Flavell et al., 1981; Flavell et al., 1986; Masangkay, McCluskey, McIntyre, Sims-Knight, Vaughn, and Flavell, 1974). However, there is evidence that these aspects of perception are understood before corresponding aspects of belief. Both in Flavell's earlier studies and in a recent study we conducted (Gopnik and Slaughter, 1992), children were better at misrepresentation tasks involving perception than they were at similar appearance–reality and false-belief tasks.

We have suggested that for the two-year-old the central theoretical constructs are non-representational desires and perceptions while for the five-year-old they are representational beliefs. Three-year-old precursors seem to include both non-representational accounts of belief and representational accounts of desire and perception. This is reminiscent of the way that Copernicus and Tycho Brahe mix epicycles and heliocentrism.

There is also evidence that early signs of an understanding of misrepresentation may come when children are forced to consider counter-evidence to their theory. In particular, Bartsch and Wellman (1989) found, as others had, that three-year-old children continued to make incorrect false-belief predictions even given counter-evidence. However, if children were asked to explain the counter-evidence, at least some of them began to talk about misrepresentation as a way of doing so. Making the counter-evidence particularly salient seemed to help to induce the application of the theory in this transitional age group. Similarly, in a recent study, Mitchell and Lacohée (1991) found that children in a representational change task who selected an explicit physical token of their earlier belief (a picture of what they thought was in the box) were better able to avoid later misrepresentation of that belief. That is, these children seemed to recognize the contradiction between the action they had just performed (picking a picture of candies) which was well within the scope of their memory, and their theoretical prediction about their past belief. Some evidence from natural language may also be relevant. Before age three (or slightly earlier) we simply do not find genuine references to belief. At about three, however, we begin to see such references, and also to see beginnings of contrastive uses of belief terms (Bartsch and Wellman, 1990). These uses may occur in contexts in which some particularly salient piece of counter-evidence to the earlier theory takes place. During the following year, however, the use of these terms increases drastically.

In short, children seem to first understand both belief and representation as small extensions of the original non-representational desire-perception theory, essentially as auxiliary hypotheses. This stage appears to be an intermediate one between a fully non-representational and a fully representational theory of mental states.

Do three-year-olds really understand false belief then? Did Copernicus really understand planetary movement? The answer in both cases is that the question is a bad one. One of the strengths of the theory theory is that it makes such questions otiose. 'Understanding' false belief, or developing an idea of representation, involves the development of a coherent, widely applicable theory. It may be possible to have some elements of that theory, or to apply them in some cases, without operating with the full predictive power of the theory, particularly in a transitional state.

We argue therefore, that the transition from two and a half to five shows all the signs of being a theory change. While initially the theory protects itself from counter-evidence, the force of such counter-evidence eventually begins to push the theory in the direction of change. The first signs of the theory shift may emerge when counter-evidence is made particularly salient. Moreover, the theory initially deals with such counter-evidence by making relatively small adjustments to concepts that are already well-entrenched, such as desire and perception. Finally, by four or five the new theory has more completely taken over from the old. The predictions are widely and readily applicable to a range of cases.

4 Simulation Theory

In the theory theory, to predict someone's behavior we have recourse to theoretical constructs such as beliefs and desires. Explaining someone's behavior involves more than empirical generalization (X has always done this in similar situations in the past). It involves appeal to constructs at a very different level of vocabulary – X wants Y and believes Z. A distinction between a phenomenal description and a theoretical explanation is crucial.

On the simulation theory, however, the child's (and adult's) understanding of mind is more closely linked to the phenomenal than to the theoretical. Understanding states of mind involves empirically discovering the states or results of a model. Consider again an understanding of the planets. An appeal to theoretical notions such as heavenly bodies revolving around one another can be contrasted to use of a planetarium model to predict the star's appearance. (Here we want to be careful to focus on a user of a planetarium who has no deeper understanding of its workings and not focus on the planetarium's creator, for example, who presumably understood something theoretical about planetary motion in order to build a successful device.) The user need only see, empirically, that the planetarium's behavior mimics the stars, then the user can make predictions by 'running' the planetarium rather than waiting for the actual events. And the user can achieve a sort of explanation, explanation-by-demonstration, as well. Let's say the user experiences a real eclipse for the first time, noting that in the middle of the day it very uncharacteristically gets dark, although there are no clouds in sight. 'Why?', he asks himself. Is this a breakdown in all his empirical generalizations about the system; is it to be expected again; what happened? By running the planetarium under appropriate conditions the user can 'see' the phenomenon again, see that it occurs regularly, in the model; see that it is a natural although infrequent empirical fact. If asked by someone else 'What was that (eclipse)?' or 'Why did that happen?' the user can explain-by-demonstrating: 'Look, it (the eclipse) was one of these (demonstrate the model's state). It happens when the other stars are like this.'

The simulation theory contends that our prediction and explanation of mental phenomena is like that of the planetarium user. The child (or adult) doesn't need and doesn't appeal to a theory of mind, a conceptual understanding of mental states, to predict behavior or understand others. Instead she simply runs a perfect working model of a mind, her own mind. By considering the output of her own mind she can predict the mental states and resultant behaviors of others. And to explain curious or unexpected actions she can run her model, find a suitable simulated demonstration of the phenomena, and then explain it as 'look, it's one of these'.

Consider, for example, the classic false-belief task. The child sees a candy box, finds out that it is full of pencils, and then is asked what another person will think is inside it. Simulation theorists contend that the child need not have anything like a theoretical construct of belief (or desire) to solve this task. She simply has access to her own first-hand mental system and uses that. When asked what the character 'thinks', she need not understand beliefs as something like a representational construct, she simply simulates the experience and reports her own specific resulting state – 'Oh, I (she) think's there is candy in the box.' The earlier failure to solve this task, on this view, reflects a failure of simulation, rather than a failure of knowledge. It is not that the younger child fails to understand beliefs as states of misrepresentation, as we described it earlier, it is just that the younger child makes an egocentric simulation, projecting her own current mental states onto the other, rather than adjusting the simulation to the other's particular condition.

The simulation view has a number of telling empirical consequences; we will focus on two. The first concerns the centrality of your own mind in any understanding of the minds of others. To answer questions about others, according to ST, you must conduct a simulation on a model, and that model is your own mind. On the simulation view, therefore, the outputs of your own mental system are particularly central to all discourse about the mind. Moreover, these outputs must be easily and transparently accessible. This must be true in order for the simulation account to work at all in the case of other people. A presupposition of the account is that it is possible to read off and report the output of your own mental states, and to use them in explanation, prediction, and inference. Moreover, access to your own states requires no inference or interpretation, no conceptual intermediaries, no theorizing; you simply read them off. A consequence of this view is that one cannot erroneously misinterpret, or misconceive, one's own mental state. You could of course run a bad simulation, in the sense that you entered the wrong inputs. But given those inputs, the output must be accurate. It must accurately reflect what your mind would actually do in that situation, because it *is* what your mind actually does in that situation.

On the theory view, in contrast, erroneous self-interpretations are not only possible, they are to be expected. One typical characteristic of theories, after all, is that they allow and often even force interpretation of the evidence. If the theoretical prediction and evidence are in conflict it is often the evidence rather than the theory which is reinterpreted. Equally, on the theory theory psychological constructs, such as beliefs and desires, are generically applicable to the self or to others. If you possess a faulty conception of some mental state, say belief, then you will incorrectly attribute that mental state to others, and you should make parallel incorrect attributions to yourself. In short, on the simulation theory false interpretations of your own mental states should not occur. On the theory theory such false interpretations should occur whenever your theoretical constructs are faulty.

A second empirical consequence, related to this first one, concerns how development should proceed. For both TT and ST we can predict that there will be development: children should first be good at predicting/explaining 'easy' states and then later 'hard' ones. But the notions of easy and hard should differ dramatically between these two theories. For ST the critical difference should be between states that are difficult or easy to simulate. Presumably, the metric for such ease and difficulty must be intimately related to the similarity of the states to the child's own states. In this sense the simulation theory is in another long and honorable tradition, the tradition of 'perspective-taking' views in development. Several of the simulation theorists in this volume, for example, presume that young children's errors are 'egocentric'. That is, the child's early errors consist of not correctly adjusting their simulation to the other person's condition. Note that on this theory there is no reason to expect that different mental states should be easier or harder to attribute to others. Take beliefs and desires. Both beliefs and desires are equally available to the child as states of her own mind. At a young age we could predict that reading off one's own beliefs and desires should be equally easy, and attributing conflicting beliefs and desires to someone else should be equally difficult.

In contrast, for the theory theory the critical metric concerns states that are easy or difficult to conceive of. Earlier we described what we take to be a succession of changes in the child's conceptions of mental states, as the child develops and replaces a succession of theories. Especially important is a difference between an early non-representational understanding of mind and a later more representational understanding. Early on children have a relatively adequate understanding of non-representational desire-perception states. Later they develop an understanding of the representational state of belief, specifically, and a representational understanding of mind more generally (including a representational understanding of certain aspects of perception and desire). Theoretical conceptions of the sort we have described are equally applicable to the self and others. If a theory has formulated a particular theoretical construct, such as the concept of false representations, it should in principle be able to use this concept equally to explain the child's own behavior and the behavior of others. If the theory does not include this construct, it should not be so applicable to either the self or others. In short, for the theory theory it will not be so important whether the mental states to be reasoned about are those of self or other. What is important is the relevant conceptions of mental states that the child must bring to bear. Thus, we find different developmental predictions from the two theories.

We want to describe several empirical findings based on these two main issues that tell against the simulation account. (1) Three-year-old children make false attributions to themselves, that exactly parallel their false attributions to others. (2) Three-year-old children make correct non-egocentric attributions to themselves and others for some mental states. (3) Children refer to only some mental states in their explanations, and refer to different mental states at different stages of their development. (4) Children's understanding of other psychological phenomena changes in parallel with their understanding of false belief. Understanding these phenomena does not require simulation, but it does require a representational theory of the mind.

The first set of findings concern children's ability to understand and report their own mental states. For example, children not only fail to understand that other's beliefs can misrepresent; they also fail to understand that their own beliefs can. In our original experiment (Gopnik and Astington, 1988) we used an analogue of the 'false-belief' task. We presented children with a variety of deceptive objects, such as the candy box full of pencils, and allowed them to discover the true nature of the objects. We then asked the children the standard false-belief question, 'What will Nicky (another child) think is inside the box?' But we also asked children about their own false beliefs about the box: 'When you first saw the box, before we opened it, what did you think was inside it?' The pattern of results for self and for other was very similar. Three-year-olds tend to say that Nicky will think what is true. But they also report that they themselves thought what was true, that they had originally thought there were pencils in the box. Children's ability to answer the false-belief question about their own belief was significantly correlated to their ability to answer the question about the others' belief, even with age controlled, a result recently replicated by Moore et al. (1990). Children who could not answer the question about the other, also could not answer it about themselves.

The children also received an additional control task. They saw a closed container (a toy house) with one object inside it, then the house was opened, the object was removed and a different object was placed inside. Children were asked 'When you first saw the house, before we opened it, what was inside it?'. This question had the same form as the belief question. However, it asked about the past physical state of the house rather than asking about a past mental state. Children were only included in the experiment if they answered this question correctly, and so demonstrated that they could understand that the question referred to the past and that they could remember the past state of affairs. Several different syntactic forms of the question were asked to further ensure that the problem was not a linguistic one. Recently, this experiment has been replicated, with additional controls, by Wimmer and Hartl (1991).

In more recent experiments we have investigated whether children could understand changes in mental states other than belief (Gopnik and Slaughter, 1991). A crucial comparison is to desires and perceptions. In three different tasks we presented children with situations in which their desires were satiated and so changed. For example, initially the child desired one of two short books. That one was read to him and the child said he now desired the other book. The test question was just like the one for past beliefs: 'When you first saw the books, before we read one, which one did you want?' In these tasks three-year-old children were considerably better at reporting past now-changed desires than past now-changed beliefs. Similarly, we presented children with situations in which their perception was changed. Children saw an object on one side of a screen and they were then moved to the other side of the screen where they saw a different object. We asked 'When you first sat on the chair, before we moved over here, what did you see on the table?' Children were completely able to report their past perceptions.

These experiments concern the child's report of their own mental states, beliefs, desires, and perceptions. From a simulation point of view, why do the children make errors when they are simply reading off their own mental states? And why do they make errors for one state but not the other? Perhaps the trouble is that the questions require not a report of current mental states, but a memory of past states. Two things need to be kept in mind in considering this objection. First, the span of time we are talking about is very brief, at the most one or two minutes and often much shorter. At least for adults such experiences are well within the immediate introspective span. If I were to report the output of my mental system in such a situation, I would report the change in my belief that comes with the new discovery, with all its attendant phenomenological vividness and detail. The very psychological experience of the change in belief depends on the fact that I continue to remember the previous belief. A simulation account must presuppose some ability to report immediately past states (after all, any state will be past by the time it is reported).

Second, and perhaps more crucially, is the difference between belief and other states such as desire and perception. The data suggest that even these young children can report some mental states that are just immediately past. The poor performance for beliefs therefore cannot be simply a problem of poor memory or lost access. This finding presents a paradox for simulation accounts. If reporting these immediately past states requires simulation, then three-year-olds are perfectly good simulators of their past desires and perceptions: why not beliefs? If reporting past states does not require simulation, because these states are just read off, then why do the three-year-olds have so much trouble reporting past beliefs?

In essence, children find some sorts of mental state attributions to be difficult and some to be easy. But the difference between the easy and hard attributions is not clearly related to the distinction between self and other, as expected from ST. The distinction is related to the ability to conceive of and interpret some types of mental states and not others, for self and for other. From a theory point of view this makes sense. Even your own mental states come in several conceptual varieties, such as beliefs, desires, and perceptions, and you could be correct at reporting one variety and erroneous at another depending on your conceptual understanding of that state.

A second difficulty concerns whether children are at first generally egocentric about the mind and then overcome this by learning they must adjust their simulations for others. In Gordon's terms, is there evidence for a stage of early 'total projection'? The developmental data do not fit this general mold; there is evidence for non-egocentric understanding quite early for some states. We have already described one such task, the early 'Level-1' perspective-taking task, in which children can predict that the other child will not see what they see themselves. Similarly quite young children can predict that someone else will have a desire different from their own (Wellman and Woolley, 1990). One issue for simulation theory therefore must be to explain why children who can obviously 'adjust their simulations' for some states do not do so for others, say beliefs. Indeed, even for belief itself, the data do not suggest that children's main difficulty involves mis-attributing their own beliefs to others. Instead, it involves a failure to understand that beliefs can misrepresent.

This is only one example of many results that suggest that young children's errors at understanding the mind are not properly termed 'egocentric'. Even very young children are quite able to attribute to others mental states different from their own. Instead, they err by sometimes misunderstanding what certain mental states are really like.

A third empirical problem is that the simulation theory has difficulty explaining the structure of the explanations that children offer. It is commonplace to say that the child's theory is not, of course, an explicit theory but rather an implicit one, which may have to be inferred from behavior rather than being openly stated. However, in examining children's natural language and particularly their explanations for aberrant actions, we can see many explicit explanatory appeals to beliefs and desires and relations between them. One example comes from open-ended explanation tasks. In these (Wellman and Bartsch, 1989; Wellman and Banerjee, 1991) children are simply presented an action or reaction ('Jane is looking for her kitty under the piano') and asked to explain it ('Why is she doing that?'). Consider a task in which the child is asked to explain why Jane is looking for the kitty. In such an actual situation the child herself would be and should be experiencing many mental states – a fear that the kitten is lost, a creak in her back from bending down, a sensation that it is dark and not very visible under the piano, a fear the kitty will scratch, a belief the kitty is under there, a desire to find the kitty, a fantasy the kitty is a small tiger, and more. Yet children's answers to such open-ended questions are organized predominantly around beliefs and desires just as adults' are. On a simulation account why would the child answer with beliefs and desires more than fears and fantasies, pains and sensations or any of a vast number of experientially available mental states? On a simulation account there is no principled reason for the child to organize mental experiences into beliefs and desires and report those appropriately. Other empirical categories seem more compelling for categorizing and reporting first-hand mental experience (e.g. pains and sensations). On a theory-theory account, in contrast, there is a good reason why such explanations predominantly appeal to beliefs and desires. These are the theoretical constructs that structure the child's understanding of mental states.

More important is the shift in explanatory type between two and five, to which we have already referred. Two-year-olds' explanations almost always mention desires, but never beliefs. Asked why the girl looks for her doll under the bed they will talk about the fact that she wants the doll, but not the fact that she believes the doll is there. Three-year-olds invoke beliefs and desires, and some three- and most four- and five-year-olds consistently refer to the representational character of these states, explaining failure in terms of falsity. These same trends can be seen in the explanations children give in their spontaneous speech (Bartsch and Wellman, 1990).

From an ST point of view, the child's own mind, even at the very youngest ages, is a device that itself contains states like beliefs as well as desires. The child's model outputs both beliefs and desires. Why should children's explanations and predictions first privilege desires over beliefs? There is no reason to expect this if the child is simply running simulations and reporting their outcomes. From TT there is a good reason why children's explanations and predictions at first ignore beliefs and especially false beliefs or misrepresentations. Young children have yet to come to a theoretical conception of belief as an explanatory psychological construct.

A fourth difficulty involves the predictive scope of the simulation theory versus the theory theory. The simulation theory provides a good account of one particular type of deficit, perspective-taking difficulties, when they occur (although as mentioned earlier ST seems to mischaracterize the nature and the developmental progression of egocentric errors). However, ST fails to account for other related difficulties. For example, we (Gopnik and Graf, 1988) investigated children's ability to identify the sources of their beliefs, elaborating on a question first posed by Wimmer, Hogrefe, and Perner (1988). As noted in Goldman's and Stich and Nichols's papers (this volume, ch. 9 and ch. 5), there was originally some evidence suggesting that children had difficulty understanding how perceptual access leads to knowledge. More recently, however, other studies have suggested that children can indeed understand that people who see an object will know about it, while those who do not see the object will not. However, there still appear to be important limits on children's understanding of sources. For example, O'Neill, Astington, and Flavell (1992) found that three-year-old children could not differentiate which source a particular piece of information might come from. They claimed for example that someone who had simply felt an object would know its color, or someone who had seen an object would know its weight.

In our experiments, we tested children's understanding of the sources of their own beliefs. Children found out about objects that were placed in a drawer in one of three ways, either they saw the objects, they were told about them, or they figured them out from a simple clue. Then we asked 'What's in the drawer?' and all the children answered correctly. Immediately after this question we asked about the source of the child's knowledge 'How do you know there's an *x* in the drawer? Did you see it, did I tell you about it, or did you figure it out from a clue?' Again three-year-olds made frequent errors on this task. While they knew what the objects were, they could not say how they knew. They might say, for example, that we had told them about an object when they had actually seen it. Their performance was at better than chance levels, but was still significantly worse than the performance of four-year-olds, who were near ceiling. In a follow-up experiment (O'Neill and Gopnik, 1991) we added a condition with different and simpler source contrasts (tell, see and feel) and presented children with only two alternative possibilities at a time. We also included a control task which ensured that the children understood the meaning of 'tell', 'see', and 'feel'. Despite these simplifications of the task, the performance of the three-year-olds was similar to their performance in the original experiment. These experiments provide another striking example of the child's failure to accurately report his own mental states when they conflict with his theoretical preconceptions, and of the parallels between attributions to the self and to others.

Similarly, there is evidence for deficits in children's understanding of subjective probability. Moore et al. (1990) found that three-year-olds were unable to determine that a person who knew about an object was a more reliable source of information than one who merely guessed or thought. Similarly, three-year-olds, in contrast to four-year-olds, showed no preference for getting information from someone who was certain they knew what was in a box rather than someone who expressed uncertaintly about their knowledge. These children seemed to divide cognitive states into full knowledge or total ignorance, they did not appreciate that belief could admit of degrees.

We believe that understanding sources and subjective probability is difficult for young children because these notions involve an understanding of the causal structure of the representational system. These aspects of the mind are not particularly different for the child and the other. However, they do require a complex causal account of the origins of beliefs. This account is at the heart of the causal-explanatory framework that eventually allows children to fully understand the representational character of the mind. These tasks should be difficult if children have not yet worked out a representational theory of mind, as we suggest, and thus should be related in development to false-belief errors. ST offers no explanation for their appearance or their relation to false-belief errors. Understanding sources and subjective probability does not seem to require complex simulation abilities, especially not when the child's own states are being reported.

In sum, the developmental pattern of children's errors and accuracies is not consistent with the view that the outputs of your own mind are simply and directly accessible, and that these outputs are attributed to others through a process of simulation. If such an account were correct, children's errors should differ between self and other in some clear fashion over development. Instead the errors divide between certain theoretical construals of inner mental states, such as beliefs versus desires, for both the self and the other. The child's understanding of mind is filtered through a coherent conceptual understanding of the mind; a theory. The theory organizes their interpretation of the phenomena of mental life and provides a causal-explanatory understanding of how the world informs the mind and mind guides behavior.

5 Precocity and Theory Formation

We would like to end by considering an argument that Gordon, Goldman, and Stich and Nichols share. This is the claim that children's folk-psychological abilities are intellectually precocious. Children could not develop an elaborate psychological theory in a mere three or four years. Gordon and Goldman use this as an argument for simulation; children need not develop a theory of the mind, they only need to develop a mind, and run simulations on it. Stich and Nichols reply that this is an indication that important aspects of the theory are innate. We think the assumptions behind both of these arguments are ill-founded. In particular they rest on the idea that we have some a priori way of measuring the temporal course of conceptual change, of saying what is slow or fast or easy or difficult.

Even in the case of scientific theory change, this seems a dubious claim. How long does it take to make a theory? If we measure change sociologically it may, of course, take years or even centuries. But how long does an individual theory change take? How long did Kepler take to formulate the heliocentric theory? How long does it take a current-day student immersed in a culture that has assimilated heliocentrism to appreciate and internalize it? Days, weeks, months?

Claiming that three or four years is insufficient time for substantial theory development seems even more dubious when we consider the general cognitive achievements of young children. Developing a theory of mind is indeed an impressive achievement, but it may seem less unique if one considers parallel developments in a variety of domains. While there may be innate abilities that play a role in these achievements, there is much evidence that a great deal of abstract and complex knowledge is also learned in this period. For example, no matter how powerful the universal constraints on grammar may be, there is still an enormous amount of language-specific structure that varies sharply from one language to another. Young children quickly master these language-specific principles as well as manifesting mastery of universals (Slobin, 1981; Maratsos, 1983). More relevantly to the present case, children acquire large amounts of physical knowledge in this period. While some aspects of children's 'folk physics' are innately given, others, such as their appreciation of gravity and support, appear to be learned in months or weeks, even during infancy itself (Spelke, 1991). By four or five children also seem to have an initial understanding of biological kinds. They recognize, for example, that membership in such a kind depends on an animal's internal state, and even on its reproductive potential (Gelman and Coley, 1992).

These achievements are certainly impressive. But as we consider them it is well to remember the general intensity of the child's cognitive life. Naturalistic language data, for example, suggest that the three-year-old child may be working on the theory of mind virtually all his waking hours. And quite possibly many of his sleeping ones as well. Who knows what adults could accomplish in three years of similarly concentrated intellectual labor?

It is certainly true that there are some innately given kinds of psychological knowledge. However, it seems to us that these are most likely to be 'starting state' theories, initial conceptions of the mind that are themselves subject to radical revision in the face of evidence. They do not function as constraints on the final possibilities, in the way that, say, a Chomskyan account would propose. Moreover, it seems very unlikely that we can determine, a priori, which aspects of psychological knowledge are likely to be innate and which are likely to be learned. Children, for example, seem to start out as mentalists, though they must learn to be representationalists.

The evidence of developmental psychology, and indeed the evidence of common observation, suggests that young children have learning capacities (and we would claim theory formation abilities) far in excess of anything we might imagine in our daily cognitively stodgy experience as adults. Indeed we would say, not that children are little scientists but that scientists are big, and relatively slow, children. The historical progress of science is based on cognitive abilities that are first seen in very young children.

We might end by telling an evolutionary just-so story to this effect. The long immaturity of human children is a notable and distinctive feature of human beings. It seems plausible that the cognitive plasticity that is also characteristic of human beings is related to this immaturity. Human beings, unlike other species, have unique cognitive capacities to adjust their behavior to what they find out about the world. A long period of protected immaturity, the story might go, plus powerful theory-formation abilities, enable children to learn about the specific cultural and physical features of their world. These capacities typically go into abeyance once ordinary adults have learned most of what they need to know. Still, their continued existence makes specialized scientific investigation possible. Science, on this view, might be a sort of spandrel, parasitic on cognitive development itself. Young children may not only really be theorizers, they may well be better ones than we are.

Notes

A. G. was supported by NSF grant BNS-8919916 during the preparation of this paper. H. W. was supported by a fellowship from the Center for Advanced Study in the Behavioral Sciences and grant HD-22149 from NICHD. We are grateful to Andrew Meltzoff, Clark Glymour, Chuck Kalish, and Doug Medin, who commented on an earlier version of this paper.

1   It is important to be as clear as possible about the way in which we take theoretical constructs to be abstract, unobservable, and postulated. We mean abstract in the sense of 'thought of apart from' observable particularities, we do not mean abstruse or merely ideal. By unobservable we mean not obviously a part of the evidential phenomena to-be-explained; not that theoretical entities are necessarily incapable of being observed in any fashion whatsoever. Thus, we could postulate that genes control inherited features such as eye color and height, in order to provide a theoretical account, and still fully expect that genes are observable in some fashion. It is simply that genes are not directly evident in, observable in, the phenomena of eye color and height themselves. Similarly, postulated does not mean conjured out of thin air, it means recruited for explanatory purposes from outside the evidential phenomena themselves. Thus (natural) selection can be postulated to account for the origin of species but at the same time selection can be fully concrete and observable, in the realm of human animal breeding for example. It is the recruitment of selection to account for natural speciation that is postulational, selection itself is not a mere postulated entity.

2   On the theory theory, the ages of development are not crucial. In fact we would expect to find, as indeed we do, wide variation in the ages at which successive theories develop. We would expect to find similar sequences of development, however. We will use ages as a rough way of referring to successive theories.

References

Astington, J. W. and Gopnik, A. 1991a: Developing understanding of desire and intention. In A. Whiten (ed.), *Natural Theories of Mind*. Oxford: Blackwell.

Astington, J. W. and Gopnik, A. 1991b: Theoretical explanations of children's understanding of the mind. *British Journal of Developmental Psychology*, 9, 7–31.

Avis, J. and Harris, P. L. 1991: Belief–desire reasoning among Baka children. *Child Development*, 62, 460–7.

Bartsch, K. and Wellman, H. M. 1989: Young children's attribution of action to beliefs and desires. *Child Development*, 60, 946–64.

Bartsch, K. and Wellman, H. M. 1990: Everyday talk about beliefs and desires: Evidence of children's developing theory of mind. Paper presented at the meeting of the Piaget Society, Philadelphia, PA.

Bretherton, I. and Beeghly, M. 1982: Talking about internal states: The acquisition of an explicit theory of mind. *Developmental Psychology*, 18, 906–21.

Carey, S. 1985: *Conceptual Change in Childhood*. Cambridge, MA: MIT Press.

Carey, S. 1988: Conceptual differences between children and adults. *Mind and Language*, 3, 167–81.

Churchland, P. M. 1984: *Matter and Consciousness: A Contemporary Introduction to the Philosophy of Mind*. Cambridge, MA: MIT Press.

Dretske, F. 1981: *Knowledge and the Flow of Information*. Cambridge, MA: MIT Press.

Estes, D., Wellman, H. M. and Woolley, J. D. 1989: Children's understanding of mental phenomena. In H. Reese (ed.), *Advances in Child Development and Behavior*. New York: Academic Press.

Flavell, J. H. 1988: The development of children's knowledge about the mind: From cognitive connections to mental representations. In J. Astington, P. Harris and D. R. Olson (eds), *Developing Theories of Mind*. New York: Cambridge University Press.

Flavell, J. H., Everett, B. A., Croft, K. and Flavell, E. R. 1981: Young children's knowledge about visual perception: Further evidence for the level 1–level 2 distinction. *Developmental Psychology*, 17, 99–103.

Flavell, J. H., Flavell, E. R. and Green, F. L. 1987: Young children's knowledge about apparent-real and pretend-real distinctions. *Developmental Psychology*, 23, 816–22.

Flavell, J. H., Flavell, E. R., Green, F. L., and Moses, L. J. 1990: Young children's understanding of fact beliefs versus value beliefs. *Child Development*, 61, 915–28.

Flavell, J. H., Green, F. L., and Flavell, E. R. 1986: Development of knowledge about the appearance–reality distinction. *Monographs of the Society for Research in Child Development*, 51 (serial no. 212).

Forguson, L. and Gopnik, A. 1988: The ontogeny of common sense. In

J. Astington, P. Harris and D. R. Olson (eds), *Developing Theories of Mind*. New York: Cambridge University Press.

Gelman, S. A. and Coley, J. D. 1992: Language and categorization: The acquisition of natural kind terms. In S. A. Gelman and J. P. Byrnes (eds), *Perspectives on Languages and Thought*. Cambridge: Cambridge University Press.

Gopnik, A. 1984: Conceptual and semantic change in scientists and children: Why there are no semantic universals. *Linguistics*, 20, 163–79.

Gopnik, A. 1988: Conceptual and semantic development as theory change. *Mind and Language*, 3, 197–217.

Gopnik, A. and Astington, J. W. 1988: Children's understanding of representational change and its relation to the understanding of false belief and the appearance–reality distinction. *Child Development*, 59, 26–37.

Gopnik, A. and Graf, P. 1988: Knowing how you know: Young children's ability to identify and remember the sources of their beliefs. *Child Development*, 59, 1366–71.

Gopnik, A. and Slaughter, V. 1991: Young children's understanding of changes in their mental states. *Child Development*, 62, 98–110.

Gopnik, A. and Slaughter, V. 1992: Children's understanding of perception and belief. Unpublished ms.

Harris, P. L. 1991: The work of the imagination. In A. Whiten (ed.), *Natural Theories of Mind*. Oxford: Blackwell.

Harris, P. L., Brown, E., Marriot, C., Whittal, S. and Harmer, S. 1991: Monsters, ghosts and witches: Testing the limits of the fantasy–reality distinction in young children. *British Journal of Developmental Psychology*, 9, 105–23.

Johnson, C. N. 1988: Theory of mind and the structure of conscious experience. In J. Astington, P. Harris and D. R. Olson (eds), *Developing Theories of Mind*. New York: Cambridge University Press.

Karmiloff-Smith, A. and Inhelder, B. 1975: If you want to get ahead, get a theory. *Cognition*, 3, 195–212.

Keil, F. C. 1989: *Concepts, Kinds, and Cognitive Development*. Cambridge, MA: MIT Press.

Leslie, A. M. 1987: Pretence and representation: The origins of theory of mind'. *Psychological Review*, 94, 412–26.

Maratsos, M. 1983: Some current issues in the study of the acquisition of grammar. In J. H. Flavell and E. M. Markman (eds), *Handbook of Child Psychology, Volume 3: Cognitive Development*. New York: Wiley, 707–86.

Masangkay, Z. S., McCluskey, K. A., McIntyre, C. W., Sims-Knight, J., Vaughn, B. E. and Flavell, J. H. 1974: The early development of inferences about the visual percepts of others. *Child Development*, 45, 357–66.

Meltzoff, A. N. and Gopnik, A. 1993: The role of imitation in understanding persons and developing theories of mind. In S. Baron-Cohen, H. Tager-Flusberg and D. J. Cohen (eds), *Understanding Other Minds: Perspectives from Autism*. New York: Cambridge University Press.

Meltzoff, A. N. and Moore, M. K. 1977: Imitation of facial and manual gestures by human neonates. *Science*, 198, 75–8.

Mitchell, P. and Lacohee, H. 1991: Children's early understanding of false belief. *Cognition*, 39, 107–29.

Moore, C., Pure, K. and Furrow, P. 1990: Children's understanding of the modal expression of certainty and uncertainty and its relation to the development of a representational theory of mind. *Child Development*, 61, 722–30.

Moses, L. J. 1990: Young children's understanding of intention and belief. Unpublished Ph.D. dissertation, Stanford University.

Moses, L. J. and Flavell, J. H. 1990: Inferring false beliefs from actions and reactions. *Child Development*, 61, 929–45.

O'Neill, D. K., Astington, J. W. and Flavell, J. H. 1992: Young children's understanding of the role that sensory experiences play in knowledge acquisition. *Child Development*, 63, 474–90.

O'Neill, D. K. and Gopnik, A. 1991: Young children's ability to identify the sources of their beliefs. *Developmental Psychology*, 27, 390–9.

Perner, J. 1991: *Understanding the Representational Mind*. Cambridge, MA: MIT Press.

Perner, J., Leekam, S. R. and Wimmer, H. 1987: Three-year-olds' difficulty with false belief. *British Journal of Developmental Psychology*, 5, 125–37.

Searle, J. R. 1983: *Intentionality*. New York: Cambridge University Press.

Shatz, M., Wellman, H. M. and Silber, S. 1983: The acquisition of mental verbs: A systematic investigation of first references to mental state. *Cognition*, 14, 301–21.

Siegal, M. and Beattie, K. 1991: Where to look first for children's understanding of false beliefs. *Cognition*, 38, 1–12.

Slobin, D. I. 1981: The origin of grammatical encoding of events. In W. Deutsch (ed.), *The Child's Construction of Language*. New York: Academic Press.

Spelke, E. S. 1991: Physical knowledge in infancy. In S. Carey and R. Gelman (eds), *The Epigenesis of Mind: Essays on Biology and Cognition*. Hillsdale NJ: Lawrence Erlbaum Associates.

Stich, S. 1983: *From Folk Psychology to Cognitive Science: The Case Against Belief*. Cambridge, MA: MIT Press.

Trevarthen, C. and Hubley, P. 1978: Secondary intersubjectivity: Confidence, confiders, and acts of meaning in the first year of life. In A. Lock (ed.), *Before Speech: The Beginning of Interpersonal Communication*. New York: Academic Press.

Wellman, H. M. 1990: *The Child's Theory of Mind*. Cambridge MA: MIT Press.

Wellman, H. M. and Banerjee, M. 1991: Mind and emotion: Children's understanding of the emotional consequences of beliefs and desires. *British Journal of Developmental Psychology*, 9, 191–224.

Wellman, H. M. and Bartsch, K. 1988: Young children's reasoning about beliefs. *Cognition*, 30, 239–77.

Wellman, H. M. and Estes, D. 1986: Early understanding of mental entities: A reexamination of childhood realism. *Child Development*, 57, 910–23.

Wellman, H. M. and Gelman, S. 1988: Children's understanding of the nonobvious. In R. J. Sternberg (ed.), *Advances in the Psychology of Intelligence, Volume 4*. Hillsdale, NJ: Lawrence Erlbaum Associates.

Wellman, H. M. and Gelman, S. A. 1992: Cognitive development: Foundational theories of core domains. *Annual Review of Psychology*, 43, 337–75.

Wellman, H. M. and Woolley, J. D. 1990: From simple desires to ordinary beliefs: The early development of everyday psychology. *Cognition*, 35, 245–75.

Wellman, W. H. 1993: Early understanding of mind: The normal case. In S. Baron-Cohen, H. Tager-Flusberg, and D. J. Cohen, (eds), *Understanding Other Minds: Perspectives From Autism*. Oxford: Oxford University Press.

Wimmer, H. and Hartl, M. 1991: Against the Cartesian view on mind: Young children's difficulty with own false beliefs. *British Journal of Developmental Psychology*, 9, 125–38.

Wimmer, H., Hogrefe, J. and Perner, J. 1988: Children's understanding of information access as source of knowledge. *Child Development*, 59, 386–96.

Wimmer, H. and Perner, J. 1983: Beliefs about beliefs: Representation and constraining function of wrong beliefs in young children's understanding of deception. *Cognition*, 13, 103–28.

Yuill, N. 1984: Young children's coordination of motive and outcome in judgments of satisfaction and morality. *British Journal of Developmental Psychology*, 2, 73–81.

Zaitchek, D. 1990: When representations conflict with reality: The preschooler's problem with false beliefs and 'false' photographs. *Cognition*, 35, 41–68.

12

Reading the Eyes: Evidence for the Role of Perception in the Development of a Theory of Mind

SIMON BARON-COHEN AND PIPPA CROSS

Efforts at explaining how we understand other minds have thrown up two main rival theories: the theory theory (e.g. Perner and Howes, this volume, ch. 6) and the simulation theory (e.g. Gordon, 1986, reprinted as ch. 2 in this volume). The theory theory suggests that we reason what someone else might think, desire or intend (etc.) by virtue of our ability to represent their mental representation of the world, and by using our theory of how mental states relate to behaviour. The simulation theory argues that we reason what someone else might think, desire or intend (etc.) by using privileged access to our own mental states as a model for theirs, simply imagining what we would think if we were 'in their shoes'. In this paper, we do not attempt to test these theories against each other. Rather, we present data from young normal children which show how a correct account of how we understand other minds must be constrained in new ways that neither of these two theories has considered. Specifically, we present evidence for the role of *perception* in the use of our theory of mind.[1] Perceptual input has been largely ignored in this debate, yet the data to be presented suggest it does play an important role.

1 Eye Direction as Symptoms and Criteria

In what follows, we will focus on perceptual input derived from face-processing. More particularly, we will focus on the role of a special class of information, namely *eye direction*. Might much information play a role in judging another person's mental states, and if so, how?

These questions can be considered in relation to two broad types of mental state: perceptual and cognitive. How do we succeed in judging someone's visual *perceptual* experience? One highly reliable way seems to be by checking their eye direction, and then computing what could lie in their line of regard. Lempers, Flavell and Flavell (1977) showed that young two-year-old normal children understood this, and Scaife and Bruner (1975) suggested that most nine-month-olds were sensitive to such cues and used them meaningfully (see also Butterworth and Jarrett, 1991).[2] This suggests that eye direction is *criterial* for judging someone else's visual perceptual experience.

In judging someone's *cognitive* mental state it is not usually assumed that we make use of any kind of specific perceptual input.[3] The argument goes something like this: since cognitive mental states (like thoughts) are unobservable, it follows that there can be no outward signs that a person is currently involved in such mental activity. Of course, such an argument contains a simple error: if x is unobservable, this in no way implies that x has no outward manifestation. An example will serve to reject this argument firmly: The heart is unobservable (to all but surgeons), yet has some outward signs (e.g. the pulse, or rosy cheeks, after exercise in the gym). Could thinking also have some outward sign? And if so, might we use such perceptual data in reasoning about mental states?

Here we argue that Wittgenstein's (1958) distinction between *symptoms* and *criteria*[4] might be useful. Thus, for perception, eye direction necessarily specifies a person's visual focus, whereas for thought, it seems implausible that there will be anything as simple as criteria, but there may nevertheless be some outward symptoms that a person is thinking. A far-fetched example of such a symptom in the realm of action would be the 'thinker' pose, made famous by Rodin. Such an example obviously lacks any ecological validity, since in the real world people rarely adopt such poses. A more plausible class of information that we might well use to infer that a person is thinking could, once again, be eye direction, but this time eye direction of a very specific kind. When people are asked to solve problems they usually look towards one of the upper quadrants of their visual field, at nothing in particular (Kinsbourne, 1972; Gur, Gur and Harris, 1975). It struck us that such eye behaviour cues might provide important scaffolding for constraining when and to whom a novice 'mentalizer' (Morton, 1989) might apply his or her theory of mind.

We have, then, the possibility that a certain class of perceptual information, namely, eye direction, is used not only to judge what another person can see, but also to judge when another person is thinking. If one thinks of what eye direction could be taken to cue, it makes good sense that eye direction should be read as playing this dual role. Thus, if the eyes are taken as indicating a person's focus of attention, then monitoring a person's eye direction will tell you either that a person's attention is directed *outward* (at an external object or event, i.e. that they are *perceiving*) or, in the absence of any particular external object, *inward* (at an intentional object, i.e. that they are *thinking*).

The idea that eye direction might convey important information about an individual's mental state has been discussed elsewhere (Baron-Cohen, in press). The notion that perception may be important in the development of a theory of mind can be found in Hobson's (1990) theory.[5] In this paper, we specifically examine the role of eye-direction information. We report two experiments. In the first, in order to confirm that children do understand the criterial role eye direction plays in diagnosing someone else's visual perceptual focus, we tested if normal three- and four-year-olds could make fine discriminations based *solely* on eye direction in photos of faces, to judge when another child was looking at *them*. In our second experiment, we tested if these children also made use of eye direction as symptoms of when someone else was thinking.

Before turning to our experiments, it is worth briefly reviewing what is known about the processing of eye direction. Gaze has been the subject of a long tradition of social psychological research (Argyle, 1972; Rutter, 1984) which has identified various interpersonal functions of eye contact. Following another's gaze seems to be a very basic and evolutionarily old ability, judging from research in human infancy (Scaife and Bruner, 1975) and non-human primates (Whiten, 1991). Animal research has located cells specifically sensitive to this information in the superior temporal sulcus of the cortex (Perrett et al., 1985). Evolution thus appears to have ensured that the brain is able to detect eye direction, though it is only recently that the adaptive function of this has been explored (Whiten, 1991; Perrett, 1991; Baron-Cohen, in press). Secondly, neuropsychological studies have demonstrated that some patients with prosopagnosia, as well as monkeys with specific lesions in the temporal cortex, can be selectively impaired in eye-direction detection (Campbell et al., 1990; Cowey and Heywood, 1991; De Haan and Campbell, 1991), whilst being relatively unimpaired in other face-processing tasks. Such dissociation provides tempting evidence for the existence of a specialized eye-direction detector (or EDD) mechanism (Baron-Cohen, in press). To trace the development of this ability therefore seemed to us to be an important exercise. The current experiments begin such an endeavour.

2 Experiment 1: Which Child is Looking at You?

2.1 Subjects

We tested two groups of children, three-year-olds (mean chronological age (CA): 3 years 6 months, sd = 0.3) and four-year-olds (mean CA: 4 years 4 months, sd = 0.3). They all attended nursery schools in Inner London. There were 15 children in each of these two age groups. The sex ratio was approximately equal in each age group.

2.2 Materials

We used 20 pairs of photographs of children's faces, comprising an equal number of male and female models, of different ethnic groups. The models were all children or teenagers, on the grounds that to young children, faces of other children might be both more interesting and more familiar than faces of adults. In each pair, one of the photographs was of a face looking directly forward. The other in the pair was looking either to the right, or to the left. In these off-centre gazes, in 10 instances (condition 1) the nose faced directly forward (see illustration 1a), whilst in the remaining 10 instances (condition 2) the nose faced in the same direction as the eyes, leaving the face as a three-quarter pose (see illustration 1b). This allowed us to test whether children were specifically using eye-direction information, or simply face-direction information. The photos were 3 inches square, black and white, and were reproduced from The Fairburn System of Visual References (1978). The expression of the mouth was either neutral or smiling.

2.3 Method

The experimenter placed each pair of photographs down on the table, in front of the subject, randomizing the position of each with respect to left or right. She then asked 'Which child is looking at you?' The subject simply had to point to one or the other.

2.4 Results

Table 12.1 shows the mean score of each group. As is clear, both groups performed significantly above chance (Binomial, $P < 0.02$), the four-year-olds performing significantly better than the three-year-olds ($t = 2.92$, 28df, $p < 0.025$). Errors, when they did occur, tended to occur equally in each condition. Indeed, an Age by Condition ANOVA showed a significant effect of group (F 5.8, df (56,3), $p < 0.02$) but no significant effect of condition.

Table 12.1   Mean scores of each group on Experiment 1 (maximum = 20)

Group	mean	sd
3-year-olds	15.1*	4.0
4-year-olds	18.5	2.0

*3 × 4-year-olds, $p < 0.025$

2.5 Discussion

This first experiment confirms earlier findings (Butterworth and Jarrett, 1991) that young children are sensitive to other people's gaze direction. It also extends these by using a new technique involving photographic stimuli, and by testing if eye direction is *the* critical information being used. Both three- and four-year-olds use eye direction to detect where someone is looking, and

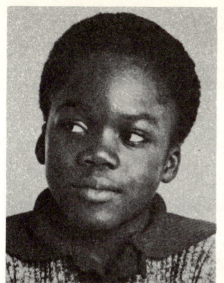

Figure 1(a)

Figure 1(b)

Illustration 1   *Examples of photographs used in Experiment 1: 'Which one is looking at you?' (a) Eye-direction cue only; (b) Eye- and face-direction cues available*

it is clear that they do not simply rely on a coarse level of information, such as face direction. There is some developmental improvement between these ages, but essentially both groups performed well. In this respect they resemble adults in their level of competence at this (Cowey and Heywood, 1991). In the next study we explored if children of the same age also make use of eye direction (of a slightly different kind) to judge if a person is *thinking*.

3 Experiment 2: Which Child is Thinking?

3.1 Subjects

The same children took part in this experiment as had participated in Experiment 1.

3.2 Methods and Materials

Once again, we used stimuli from the Fairburn System of Visual References, as in Experiment 1. However, this time we used 10 pairs of photographs, one of which was looking to one side and in an *upwards* direction, and the other of which was looking directly forwards, at the camera. The photos in which the child was looking away were all judged (by two independent raters) to depict 'thinking'. An example is shown in illustration 2. Again, the mouth in all photographs was either neutral or smiling. The subject was simply asked 'Which one is thinking?', as the experimenter laid out each pair of photographs, randomizing which was on the left or right.

3.3 Results

Table 12.2 shows the mean score of each group. Again, the four-year-olds performed significantly better than the three-year-olds (t = 2.64, 28df, p < 0.025). As a group, the four-year-olds scored significantly above chance (Binomial Test, p < 0.05), whilst the three-year-olds did not. However, analysing each subject's score, 30 per cent of the three-year-olds did score significantly above chance (>8 out of 10), and these were among the oldest three-year-olds in the sample (youngest CA = 3 years 5 months).

Errors in Experiment 2 could have occurred for one of two reasons: either failing to detect that the eyes were directed upward, or failing to understand that this signifies that a person is thinking. In order to isolate the proportion of subjects who were failing on Experiment 2 simply for the first of these reasons, we carried out a correction analysis.[6] This entailed scoring each subject for the number of errors in Experiment 2, minus the number of errors on the 10 nose-forward pairs from Experiment 1. This allowed for a tighter test of group differences on 'thought-detection' ability. Building in this correc-

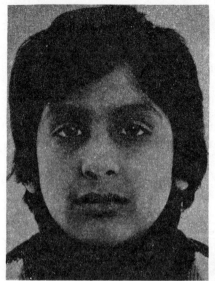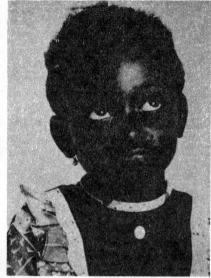

Illustration 2 *Examples of photographs used in Experiment 2: 'Which one is thinking?'*

Table 12.2 Mean scores of each group on Experiment 2 (maximum = 10)

Group	mean	sd
3-year-olds	7.4*	1.9
4-year-olds	9.0	1.4

*3 × 4-year-olds, p < 0.025

tion factor eliminated the group difference (t = 0.66, 28 df, p > 0.05) on Experiment 2, both groups now performing above chance.

3.4 Discussion

Children in both age groups showed that they judge if a person is thinking by where the eyes are pointing – away and in an upwards direction from the viewer. In terms of mean group scores, only the four-year-olds were significantly above chance on this task, though in terms of individual scores, 30 per cent of three-year-olds were also above chance, these being children older than three and a half years old. After correcting for errors in Experiment 2 that were a result of errors in eye-direction detection rather than thought-detection, most of the older three-year-olds were above chance on Experiment 2. This suggests that for children above 3 years and 5 months old, eye direction provides information not only about another person's perceptual experience, but also about their cognitive mental state (whether they are thinking). That even the three-year-olds were clearly above chance on this test is consistent with findings from other tasks showing that they possess the concept of thinking (Wellman and Estes, 1981; Baron-Cohen, 1989; Perner, 1991). The present study demonstrates not only that they *possess* this concept, but also that they map eye-direction information on to it. In the final section of this paper, we turn to consider the implications of these data.

4 General Discussion

Our experiments show that both three- and four-year-old normal children used eye direction to judge a person's visual *perceptual* state and to judge if a person is *thinking* or not. In doing this, three- and four-year-olds – like adults – reveal that they *do* make use of physical cues in the face in attributing cognitive mental states. As far as we are aware, this is the first such demonstration.[7] Such data provide some ammunition for the notion that the development of a theory of mind may to some extent make use of perceptual input (Hobson, 1990; Baron-Cohen, in press). In the remainder of this paper we consider some of the different possible roles such perceptual input might play.

First, should this data be taken to support the Gibsonian 'direct-perception' theory (Butterworth, 1990; Loveland, 1991) of how we understand mental states? The strong Gibsonian account would presumably insist that the necessary information for reading a person's mental state is specified in the perceptual array. Consider how one proponent of this theory expresses it:

> it is crucial to question whether the capacity to imagine other people's mental states is ultimately derived from the direct perception of the expression of such mental states . . . According to Gibson (1966), knowing is an extension of perceiving – acquiring knowledge of mental states is therefore to be understood as a natural extension of the process of perception . . . Can the mind be read from behaviour? Is there information available which is consistent with there being other minds in the world? (Butterworth, 1990, pp. 136–7)

Gibsonians will certainly find our data consistent with their claim, but in so far as eye direction is only a symptom (and not criterial) for indicating that a person is thinking – that is, it is possible for a person to be thinking whilst manifesting *any* pose they care to choose – the notion that perceptual information is all you need in order to read minds is not supported.[8]

Secondly, should our data be taken to refute the notion that attribution of mental states is all theory driven (Premack and Woodruff, 1978), or 'top down'? Clearly, in so far as both children and adults can attribute mental states to objects that lack anything even remotely resembling eye-direction information, such as the wind (Piaget, 1930), thermostats or computers (Dennett, 1978), a theory of mind is unlikely to *require* perceptual input for its functioning.[9] Rather, a theory of mind is likely to be theory driven.

However, it may still be the case that objects which manifest certain kinds of eye-direction information are more likely to be seen as perceiving and thinking objects. Such a possibility is testable. If supported, it would suggest that eye direction may function as a perceptual *constraint* guiding the toddler to attribute mental states to a particular class of objects (those with eyes) under particular conditions. Such a constraint might be expressed as follows: a *system with eyes is thinking when its eyes are looking away, but not at any external object in particular.*[10] We assume that cartoonists exploit such psychological truths in succeeding at conveying Disney-type fantasy characters as intentional systems.[11]

Thirdly, given that children seem to use different kinds of eye direction in both tasks, might it be that their understanding of cognitive mental states such as thoughts is developmentally related to their understanding of simple perception? This possibility is both attractive and plausible, for two reasons: Given that thinking is an abstract activity, if children initially recognize this through concrete symptoms, this might greatly facilitate the acquisition process.[12] Furthermore, the idea that children use eye direction for understanding perception and thought may help account for how toddlers acquire the notion of mental states with *intentionality* (Brentano, 1874). To clarify, visual perception possesses intentionality: it is always *about* something. Eye direction signals this intentionality by specifying the *target* of visual perception: what perception is about. This might serve as the toddler's first lesson in intentionality, making it only a small (but important) step to extend this to mental states such as thoughts.

It remains possible that there might be other external, observable symptoms of mental states. Certainly, adults (cross-culturally) appear to use facial information to distinguish such mental states as *regret*, *scheme* and *worry* (Baron-Cohen, Rivière and Cross, 1992), and toddlers from as young as 9–18 months use eye information (probably eye direction) to identify a person's *goal* behind an ambiguous action (Philips, Baron-Cohen and Rutter, 1992; Baron-Cohen, 1993). The search for the facial symptoms of mental states is likely to reveal the complexity of information we use in employing our theory of mind.

Let us now turn to the question running through the papers in this volume. If we do use perceptual input in employing a theory of mind, what bearing does this have on the debate between the theory theory and the simulation theory? At the outset of this paper we suggested that both camps might incorporate such findings without undue concern. Consider, for example, this suggestion from simulation theory (Gordon, this volume, p. 70; some italics added):

268   *Simon Baron-Cohen and Pippa Cross*

One interesting possibility is that the readiness for practical simulation is a prepackaged 'module' called upon automatically in the *perception* of other human beings. One might even speculate that such a module makes its first appearance in the useful tendency many mammals have of turning their eyes towards the target of another's *gaze*. Thus, the very *sight of human eyes* might *require* us to simulate at least their spatial perspective and to this extent, at least, to put ourselves in the other's shoes.

This quotation stands as a virtual prediction of the results presented in this paper. On the other hand, the theory theory scores some points too, in that while such observable features as eye direction may serve as cues to what a person is perceiving, at best such cues can only index *that* a person is thinking – not *what* that person is thinking *about*. To go 'the extra mile' and reason about the *content* of someone's thoughts is likely to require the use of a *theory* about the relationships between perception, cognitive mental states and action (Wellman, 1990; Perner, 1991). In this paper, we inject new data into the white heat of this debate not in order to refute either the simulation theory or the theory theory, but rather to draw attention to one possible meeting point of these two theories – in the role of face processing in mental state understanding.

In closing, we would like to touch on the relevance of this approach for understanding children with autism. Our earlier studies have revealed significant impairments in such children's development of a theory of mind (Baron-Cohen, Leslie and Frith, 1985; see Baron-Cohen, 1993, for a review). Other studies show that, whilst older children with autism can judge a person's perceptual experience under controlled laboratory conditions and when specifically instructed to do so (Baron-Cohen, 1989), they do not engage in joint-attention behaviours spontaneously (Mundy, Sigman and Kasari, 1993). In addition, younger children with autism are relatively insensitive to the significance of another person's gaze direction (Mundy et al., 1993), and also appear not to monitor eye direction to clarify an actor's *goal* (Phillips et al., 1992). It therefore seemed logical to test them on the 'Which one is thinking?' task described here. In a recent study of this (Baron-Cohen, Campbell and Walker, 1992), children with autism, as predicted, showed severe impairments on this task, and this was dissociated from performance on other face-processing tasks. Further studies are needed in order to throw light not only on the development of autism, but also on the development of a theory of mind, and on the nature of what Magnus (1885) called 'eye language'.[13]

Notes

This paper was written whilst the first author was supported by grants from the Mental Health Foundation, the British Council and the Medical Research Council. We would like to thank the staff at Camberwell Day Nursery, and

Helena Day Nursery for their cooperation with this research. Illustrations 1 and 2 were originally published in the 'Fairburn System of Visual References' (1978). Efforts at tracing this publisher have been unsuccessful, but their source is gratefully acknowledged. We are grateful to Paul Harris, George Butterworth, Ruth Campbell, Andy Whiten, Helen Tager-Flusberg, Alison Gopnik, and Dave Perrett for their comments on the first draft of this paper. We apologise to Peter Hobson for the error in our discussion of his work, in the original version of this article. We are fortunate that this volume provides us with an opportunity to correct this.

1 We use the term 'theory of mind' to refer to the ability to reason about one's own or someone else's mental states. In this article, we do not intend this to be coterminous with the theory theory. 'Theory of mind' has simply become convenient shorthand. Whether our theory of mind really is theory-like is a question that, as this volume suggests, is up for grabs.

2 In fact, the youngest infants in Scaife and Bruner's (1975) study who showed gaze-following were 3 months, but these were a minority of the sample overall.

3 The exception to this is informational access in the case of attributing knowledge; though this hardly counts as a 'specific perceptual input', given the range of forms this can take.

4 We are grateful to Angel Rivière for drawing our attention to this distinction.

5 In the original version of this article, we stated that Hobson (1990) restricts his discussion to the perception of emotional expression in the face. This was not correct. Hobson has emphasized the importance of perceiving the directedness of a person's mental attitudes in that person's bodily orientation, and has stressed how 'the observable directedness of behaviour might complement the observed "expressiveness" of bodies in providing a child with pointers towards the directed quality of mental states' (Hobson, 1991, p. 51). He has also highlighted the role of a child's experience of 'visual co-orientation' with others in acquiring an understanding of people's intentional mental states. This notion leads Hobson to predict that children with perceptual problems, such as the congenitally blind, should show abnormalities in the development of a theory of mind.

6 We are very grateful to Paul Harris for suggesting this correction analysis.

7 After we had completed these experiments, George Butterworth drew our attention to a paper by Gibson and Pick (1962). This used a similar technique to ours, to test adult's competence at judging when someone is looking at them. Reading eye direction to infer when someone is thinking has not been tested before. We are grateful to George Butterworth for guiding us to this.

8 Gibson himself did not make such a strong claim. Our data will hopefully sound a cautionary note to those Gibsonians who do.

9   Inagaki and Hatano (1987) suggest that young children ascribe mental states to a range of phenomena they do not understand, as a strategy for rendering them understandable. Such personification suggests that the child's theory plays a more crucial role than perception.

10   Dave Perrett (personal communication) pointed out that a further test of this idea would come from an experiment in which the child observes a person in an environment of objects. The person could then either look directly at an object, or at no object in particular. The child would then be asked to judge when the person was thinking.

11   Clearly, there may be other such constraints (such as motion) that guide children in the application of their newly acquired theory of mind (Mandler, 1991).

12   It may be, then, that Hobson is correct to predict that blind children will be delayed in the acquisition of a theory of mind (ToM), though we will have to wait for the critical experiments to be done. If blind children were found to be delayed in the development of ToM, we would suggest the explanation for this lay in their inability to see and make use of eye direction. Hobson discusses this in terms of the blind child being delayed in coming to understand mental states, through being deprived of the experience of 'visual co-orientation'. Such a handicap would, we predict, at worst only *slow down* the acquisition of a ToM, but not prevent its emergence at all. We make this latter claim on the grounds that whilst perception of information like eye direction may facilitate the acquisition of a ToM, ToM is likely to be a central process which can function independently of perceptual input (Leslie and Sellars, 1990; Baron-Cohen, in press). And certainly, the normal social skills and social under-standing of blind *adults* suggests that even if there are delays in ToM development during childhood, these have no long-term effect on their eventual attainment of a ToM.

   Similarly we would predict that children with prosopagnosia – even prosopagnosia involving impairments in eye-direction detection – would at worst be slowed down in their acquisition of a theory of mind, but not prevented from acquiring one. Young and Ellis (1989) report what we think is the only data relevant to this, of an 8-year-old girl with prosopagnosia who passed a false belief test. The critical test would be to assess such cases at 4 years old.

13   In this paper we have not explored the role of *learning* in the acquisition of 'eye language'. There are of course several interesting possibilities here. First, toddlers may learn that gaze directed away from themselves is associated with the person attending to something else ('not-me') and that that something else may be external (a percept, if something is indeed present) or internal (a thought). Such learning could proceed without any teaching, though this would assume prior possession of the concept of thinking.

   On the other hand, some eye language may be 'taught' through some non-verbal form of motherese. The skyward look in order to convey scepticism about someone's sanity, or the wink in order to convey being a co-conspirator, are clear instances of eye language that might well be taught explicity. We would argue for a distinction between the parts of eye language that are explicitly taught and are culture specific versus other parts of eye language that are not taught and are universals. Our testable prediction is that eye-direction detection of the sort described in both experiments in this paper will fall into the universal category.

We end this paper with an invitation to play a game. Sit opposite a friend. Now, without vocalizing or moving any other part of your body except your eyes, try 'catching' your friend's eye to get him or her to look at a particular spot in the room. We expect that you will have done the following: (a) Made pronounced eye contact; (b) rolled your eyes sideways until you are looking at the spot in question; (c) returned your gaze to remake eye contact; (d) finally, repeated this sequence, perhaps with a small embellishment of eye widening or eyebrow raising. Furthermore, we expect that this is what you would do irrespective of either your or your friend's culture. And that it works. That's what we mean by the universality claim.

References

Argyle, M. 1972: *The Psychology of Interpersonal Behaviour*. London: Penguin.
Baldwin, J. 1905: *The Dictionary of Philosophy and Psychology*. London: Macmillan.
Baron-Cohen, S. 1989: Are autistic children behaviourists? An examination of their mental–physical and appearance–reality distinctions. *Journal of Autism and Developmental Disorders*, 19, 579–600.
Baron-Cohen, S. 1993: From attention–goal psychology to belief–desire psychology: The development of a theory of mind and its dysfunction. In S. Baron-Cohen, H. Tager-Flusberg and D. J. Cohen (eds), *Understanding Other Minds: Perspectives from Autism*. Oxford: Oxford University Press.
Baron-Cohen, S. In press: Theory of mind and face-processing: How do they interact in development and psychopathology? In D. Cicchetti and D. J. Cohen (eds), *Manual of Developmental Psychopathology*. New York: Wiley.
Baron-Cohen, S., Campbell, R. and Walker, J. 1992: Are children with autism blind to the significance of the eyes? Unpublished ms. Institute of Psychiatry, University of London.
Baron-Cohen, S., Leslie, A. M. and Frith, U. 1985: Does the autistic child have a 'theory of mind'? *Cognition*, 21, 37–46.
Baron-Cohen, S., Rivière, A. and Cross, P. 1992: Reading mental states in faces: A cross-cultural study. Unpublished ms., Institute of Psychiatry, University of London.
Brentano, F. von 1874/1970: *Psychology From an Empirical Standpoint*, ed. O. Kraus, trans. L. L. MacAllister. London: Routledge and Kegan Paul.
Butterworth, G. 1990: Review of J. Astington, P. Harris and D. Olson (eds),

Developing Theories of Mind (Cambridge: Cambridge University Press). *Perception*, 19, 135–8.

Butterworth, G. and Jarrett, N. 1991: What minds have in common is space: Spatial mechanisms serving joint visual attention in infancy. *British Journal of Developmental Psychology*, 9, 55–72.

Campbell, R., Garwood, J., Franklin, S., Howard, D., Landis, T. and Regard, M. 1990: Neuropsychological studies of auditory–visual fusion illusions: Four case studies and their implications. *Neuropsychologia*, 28, 1123–42.

Cowey, A. and Heywood, C. 1991: The role of 'face-cell' areas in the discrimination and recognition of faces in monkeys. Paper presented at the Meeting of the Royal Society on Processing the Facial Image, July 1991.

Dennett, D. 1978: *Brainstorms: Philosophical Essays on Mind and Psychology*. Cambridge, MA: MIT Press.

De Haan, E. and Campbell, R. 1991: A 15 year follow-up of a case of developmental prosopagnosia. *Cortex*, 27, 1–21.

Fairburn System of Visual References 1978: Fairburn Publications Ltd.

Gibson, J. 1966: *The Ecological Approach to Visual Perception*. Boston: Houghton Mifflin.

Gibson, J. and Pick, A. 1962: Perception of another person's looking behavior. *American Journal of Psychology*, 76, 386–94.

Gordon, R. 1986: Folk psychology as simulation. *Mind and Language*, 1, 158–71. Reprinted as ch. 2 in this volume.

Gur, R., Gur, R. and Harris, L. 1975: Cerebral activation, as measured by subjects' lateral eye movements, is influenced by experimenter location. *Neuropsychologia*, 13; 35–44.

Hobson, R. P. 1990: On acquiring knowledge about people and the capacity to pretend: Response to Leslie (1987). *Psychological Review*, 97, 114–21.

Hobson, R. P. 1991: Against the theory of 'theory of mind'. *British Journal of Developmental Psychology*, 9, 33–51.

Inagaki, K. and Hatano, G. 1987: Young children's spontaneous personification as analogy. *Child Development*, 58, 1013–20.

Kinsbourne, M. 1972: Eye and head turning cerebral lateralization. *Science*, 176, 539–41.

Lempers, J. D., Flavell, E. R. and Flavell, J. H. 1977: The development in very young children of tacit knowledge concerning visual perception. *Genetic Psychology Monographs*, 95, 3–53.

Leslie, A. M. and Sellars, C. 1990: The deaf child's theory of mind. Unpublished ms., MRC Cognitive Development Unit, 17 Gordon St, London, WC1.

Loveland, K. 1991: Social affordances and interaction II: Autism and affordances of the human environment. *Ecological Psychology*, 3, 99–119.

Magnus, H. 1885: *Die Sprache der Augen*. Wiesbaden. Quoted in Hess, E. and Petrovich, S. (1987) Pupillary behaviour in communication. In A. Siegman and S. Feldstein (eds), *Nonverbal Behaviour and Communication*. London: Lawrence Erlbaum Associates.

Mandler, J. 1991: Prelinguistic primitives. Paper presented at the SRCD Conference, Seattle, April.

Morton, J. 1989: The origins of autism. *New Scientist*, 1694, 44–7.

Mundy, P., Sigman, M. and Kasari, C. 1993: Theory of mind and joint attention deficits in autism. In S. Baron-Cohen, H. Tager-Flusberg and D. J. Cohen (eds), *Understanding Other Minds: Perspectives from Autism*. Oxford: Oxford University Press.

Perner, J. 1991: *Understanding the Representational Mind*. Cambridge, MA: MIT Press.

Perrett, D. 1991: Organization and function of cells responsive to faces in the temporal cortex. Paper presented at the Meeting of the Royal Society on Processing the Facial Image, July 1991.

Perrett, D., Smith, P., Potter, D., Mistlin, A., Head, A., Milner, A. and Jeeves, M. 1985: Visual cells in the temporal cortex sensitive to face view and gaze direction. *Proceedings of the Royal Society of London*, B223, 293–317.

Phillips, W., Baron-Cohen, S. and Rutter, M. 1992: The role of eye-contact in goal-detection: Evidence from normal toddlers, and children with mental handicap or autism. Unpublished ms., Institute of Psychiatry, University of London.

Piaget, J. 1930: *The Child's Conception of Causality*. London: Kegan Paul.

Premack, D. and Woodruff, G. 1978: Does the chimpanzee have a 'theory of mind'? *Behavior and Brain Sciences*, 4, 515–26.

Rutter, D. 1984: *Looking and Seeing: The Role of Visual Communication in Social Interaction*. Chichester: John Wiley and Sons.

Scaife, M. and Bruner, J. 1975: The capacity for joint visual attention in the infant. *Nature*, 253, 265–6.

Wellman, H. 1990: *The Child's Theory of Mind*. Cambridge, MA: MIT Press.

Wellman, H. and Estes, D. 1986: Early understanding of mental entities: A reexamination of childhood realism. *Child Development*, 57, 910–23.

Whiten, A. 1991: *Natural Theories of Mind*. Oxford: Blackwell.

Wittgenstein, L. 1958: *Philosophical Investigations*. Oxford: Blackwell.

Young, A. and Ellis, H. 1989: Childhood prosopagnosia. *Brain and Cognition*, 9, 16–47.

13
Theory, Observation and Drama

SIMON BLACKBURN

There are two familiar suggestions and one less familiar about understanding the sayings and doings of others. The first suggestion is that their meanings are manifest in their utterances and perceptible by suitably tuned observers. Call this the observational approach. The second, yet more familiar, is that the interpretations we arrive at are theoretical beliefs, arrived at by the tacit use of a 'folk theory' or rough set of principles that take us from observed behavior, thought of as evidence, to one particular attribution of belief and meaning. The third suggestion is that we attribute meaning by a process of reenactment: a dramatic projection or entering into the position of another, seeing for ourselves what must have been in his mind for things to have fallen out as they did – for him to have said or written or done what he did. In the Anglo-American tradition the main proponent of this alternative was R. G. Collingwood, whose forceful advocacy never managed to make the theory popular. But more recently it has been explicitly endorsed under the title of the 'replicating strategy' by Jane Heal, and as 'simulation theory' or the theory that understanding others is generated by 'off-line simulation' in other recent writers (Heal, 1986; Gordon, 1986; Goldman, 1989; reprinted as chs 1, 2 and 3 in this volume). And it is at least a cousin of the suggestion that propositional attitude psychology constitutes an 'essentially dramatic idiom' or that it is better seen as the taking up of a stance than as an act of theory, although one might be attracted to those ideas without making much of the idea of replication or simulation (Dennett, 1982, p. 79).

There are many difficulties in assessing these views. It is not clear whether they compete, or whether they offer compatible elements that may or may not be present on an individual occasion. It is not clear how each of them is best formulated, in particular to do justice to the apparent absence of observation, or theorizing, or drama on many routine occasions of understanding. It is, above all, not clear to what extent they ought to be taken simply as empirical hypotheses, debated primarily on evidence derived from developmental studies, or whether they have deeper roots in the philosophy of mind. I have no settled view on the empirical issues, but it is this last possibility that I wish to explore.

Part of the difficulty is the Protean concept of a theory, often used so that any activity that ends up with a belief counts as forming it by a process of theorizing. If we are good at something, on this view, then we can be thought of as making tacit (very tacit) use of some set of principles that could, in principle, provide a description of a device, or possibly a recipe for the construction of a device, that is also good at it. This will be true whether the skill is understanding others, recognizing syntactic correctness, perceiving spatial objects, or riding a bicycle. If this conception of theory is on offer, then it will be difficult to avoid describing our understanding of others as theoretical, although it will not necessarily be we who theorize. The existence of theoretical principles, thought of like this, is simply a consequence first of the skill, and secondly of the possibility of describing a device that has it in these terms. (It will be an option for theory-theorists whether they put further conditions on one set of tacit principles amongst many that could deliver the same result, in order to award them superior 'psychological reality' (Davies, 1987). In this paper I am not concerned with the option.) On this promiscuous theory of theories, the theoretical nature of our capacity is obviously quite compatible with each of the observational, and the dramatic proposals. But the question will remain whether a more interesting conception of theory fares so well, and I shall argue that it does not.

1 A Historical Interlude

A full history of the '*Verstehen*' tradition would be a large document. It would certainly need to include early writing on the communication of emotion, and the mechanism of sympathy as a necessary condition of understanding the emotions of others, and eventually of taking up altruistic and ethical stances (Hume, 1739). But I shall content myself with mentioning Collingwood, the most vociferous English champion of the notion this century. For Collingwood the 'mind–body' problem is purely one of two different epistemologies: the way we know about peoples' thoughts, as opposed to the way we know other things about them. The only serious question is the relationship between the sciences of matter – physics, chemistry and physiology – and knowledge of mind, which in Collingwood means history. To understand mind and its place in nature means understanding mind and its place in mind. He is quite clear that what he calls history and we would call 'folk psychology' is not only concerned with the remote past (Collingwood, 1946, p. 219):

> If it is by historical thinking that we re-think and so rediscover the thought of Hammurabi or Solon, it is in the same way that we discover the thought of a friend who writes us a letter, or a stranger who crosses the street

– and, he adds, our own thoughts of ten years or five minutes ago.

The twist is that history is autonomous, so that properly speaking there is not and can never be a science of content, although there can be sciences of non-intentional mental events. As I understand him Collingwood had three interlocking reasons for this doctrine. The first is that to study persons' mental features is to study their own self-understanding, and that means the concepts under which they put themselves and their actions: the concepts that determine their plans, activities and thoughts. At least for anything more than a very primitive intentional system, deployment of concepts involves understanding oneself to be deploying concepts; this understanding and rational control of what one is doing (somehow) prevents what one is doing from being thought of as a natural, law-governed event. The argument here is at best enthymematic, and the second thought may be a way of providing missing premises in the first. It is that understanding the concepts with which a self-conscious agent is thinking is not an atomistic project, a matter of finding individual elements of a person, perhaps written in the brain, connected by scientific law with other elements. It is an essentially holistic enterprise that needs to draw on indefinitely wide knowledge of the person's human context: like many since, Collingwood thinks that holism stands in the way of reductive naturalism. The similarity between two people who think the same is invisible to science: they need not use the same words, since they may speak different languages; they need not behave the same, since they may have different beliefs and desires; they need not have the same images, or the same neural organization. In the theory of thought there is no unmoved mover – no method except rethinking the same thought for understanding this common property. Most contemporary writers would associate these themes with Wittgenstein or Davidson, although I shall argue later that Collingwood's insight goes beyond the way that these writers tend to get taken. But it is his third reason that brings us to the topic of this volume. It sees psychological understanding as akin to deliberation, so that just as when I deliberate I am not in the business of simply predicting my future behaviour, so when I come to understand why you acted as you did I am not concerned to place you in any kind of lawlike causal network, but to see the point of your doings. Understanding you is a distinct activity, not reducible to seeing your behaviour just as part of what generally happens, part of a scientifically repeatable pattern. Understanding you is like deliberating what to do in projected situations, which I do by 'recentring' myself, imagining the situation and responding from within it. The suggestion then is that:

> Deliberation stands to Predicting my own future behaviour *as* Off-Line Deliberation stands to Off-Line Self Prediction, *which is as* Interpretation stands to Putting your behaviour into a lawlike pattern.

If putting your behaviour into a lawlike framework is thought of as the goal of theory, then understanding is not theory. It stands to it only in whatever way deliberation stands to prediction.

There is a further element in Collingwood's picture of these things that also needs highlighting. It is sometimes suggested that a simulation model gives improper privilege to the first person, even involving a 'Cartesian' transparency of the mind to itself. Collingwood had no patience with Cartesian transparency, and his forthright declaration of the relation between mental life and social life is as strong as anyone's (Collingwood, 1938, p. 248):

> the child's discovery of itself as a person is also its discovery of itself as a member of a world of persons . . . The discovery of myself as a person is the discovery that I can speak, and am thus a persona or speaker; in speaking I am both speaker and hearer; and since the discovery of myself as a person is also the discovery of other persons around me, it is the discovery of speakers and hearers other than myself.

This means that there is no irremovable first-person privilege in the theory of understanding. It takes 'historical' thinking to understand myself just as much as it does to understand you: in my thinking I am both speaker and hearer. Of course, as speaker, my relationship to my own words is indeed special: I have made them my own. But what happens when I do this? Do my words come 'dead', ready to be animated only by some meta-activity of theorizing? Certainly not in general (if only because the words of the meta-activity would then need to be self-animating). My home words can sound alien only on occasion, and when they do other words fill their place. I take it that what Collingwood has hit upon is not only the fundamental role of this home reliance, but the need *not* to think of that as essentially private: the home case includes other *personae* amongst whom I am only one. Hearing my words is relevantly like hearing yours.

I think this last element puts Collingwood ahead of much of the contemporary debate. The process of *Verstehen* has been identified, and attacked, as a process of using myself as a 'model' for understanding others. The image brought to mind is that I think what I would do in some situation, then presume that you are relevantly similar to me, and conclude that this is what you would do (perhaps factoring in known differences between me and you). On this 'model model' there is an element of stepping outside my own skin, as if I *observe* my own reactions, and then you, antecedently to imputing my reactions or something like them to you, as I might observe what happens in the wind tunnel, before imputing the same results to the system that is being modelled. And this picture is wide open to the charge made, for instance, by Paul Churchland, that it takes theory to justify the supposed similarity between the modelled and the modeller (Churchland, 1989). But this is not how it happens. I could do *that* in an alienated spirit: knowing that these words will come to my mind I might predict that they will come to yours, but still not have made the words my own. As Heal puts it, this 'misdescribes the direction of gaze' of the replicator (this volume, p. 48; see also Gordon, this volume, p. 102). What I do is to 'recenter' my situation as yours, or change my 'egocentric map' and think about the world as it appears from that point of view. I gaze neither at me, nor at my words, nor at you, but at the situation as I take it to have been for you. This will include an element of 'laying off' for your position and your background beliefs and passions, and we may be more or less good at that, which is why the advice to put yourself in others' shoes is often needed (Gordon, this volume, p. 101). I do what I can, and then the thinking (or emotions) I then imagine I impute to you.

2 War or Peace?

If observation, theory and drama are the three suggestions on the table, which should we choose? Perhaps we do not have to choose – perhaps they are after all compatible. Or, perhaps they divide the field. We might suggest that the observational paradigm is best fitted to direct uncomplicated cases – conversation with a friend, say, where understanding is immediate and certain. Theory is more in place when complicating factors such as historical distance enter: we theorize about possible uses of the term 'idea' in Locke or 'eudaimonia' in Aristotle, for example. And dramatic reenactment is empirically an occasional process, best suited to cases where it is actually difficult to see the point of someone's doings, and an element of 'seeing the situation from his point of view' or projecting oneself into his situation is one heuristic for overcoming the difficulty. But the issues go deeper.

To appreciate the difficulty of arguing with the 'theory-theory', consider first the possible choice between the observational and the theoretical model. As I have said, while the promiscuous theory of theories rules, it is impossible to make much of that. But suppose we try a slightly thicker notion of a theory, and in particular one that has implications for the semantics of various terms (the promiscuous theory has none, for it allows our sub-doxastic systems to theorize without we ourselves using any terms at all). Suppose we agree with Patricia Churchland, who endorses the claim that Sellarsian and Quinean directions in the theory of knowledge should have us think that all empirical and perceptual knowledge is theoretical (Churchland, 1986):

> Whether a term is theoretical, on this more recent view, is a matter of its being semantically embedded in a network of corrigible assumptions. And whether a term is observational, on this more recent view, is a matter of whether the speaker who uses it has learned to make spontaneous but reliable applications of it in response to appropriate perceptual circumstances. A term can clearly meet both of these criteria, and it is also a consistent assertion that every instance of the latter is an instance of the former.

Churchland is surely right: spontaneous or uninferred and reliable judgments can be highly theoretical in her sense. And if this is the last word on the alleged observation/theory boundary there is still no point whatever in contending about it. Obviously we say that we see or hear what people mean, just as we see the light of intelligence in their eyes, or the knavery in their countenances. And such judgments are made spontaneously, and unless we are eliminativists or error theorists we will suppose them reliable. But this is compatible with there being a theory or 'network of corrigible assumptions' that in fact govern the attribution of meaning, whether or not they do so implicitly or tacitly, behind the scenes of the observer's consciousness. In like manner an astronomer may observe what he calls the passage of a comet, but it may have taken a great deal of theory for him to learn to make that judgment spontaneously, and more still to provide a justification of its reliability. Theory here plays an explanatory role, not a phenomenological one. It is not that the astronomer or the listener finds himself making an inference or indulging a train of reasoning. Obviously no such conscious process occurs: this is what makes the judgment spontaneous. But it may nevertheless be true that there exist principles to take us from evidence to interpretation; that these principles can be cited when dispute or demand for justification arises; that it was necessary to 'internalize' those principles to become a trained or well-tuned observer; and that one learned they form a 'network of corrigible assumptions', or in short a theory.

Is there any more meat to be got out of the observation/theory distinction? It can go one more round, for there ought to be a stronger notion of observation to be identified. Consider that I may spontaneously and reliably judge what has happened or will happen on the basis of present experience. Yet there should be a sense in which I do not now observe either the past or the future (and even when I see the knavery in your face, I do not thereby observe your knavery). The natural suggestion for a more restrictive notion of an observation would be this. We all agree now that the senses do a great deal of organizing for us: we have no acquaintance with raw data, uncontaminated by work of selection and synthesis. In particular, we suppose that our perceptual systems select some features for us, and discard others. A language user does not hear the same as the outsider. His experience is itself different. It comes, we might say, synthesized as a succession of distinct words, and is different from any experience not so synthesized. This means that there is no neutral ground between someone so hearing and someone not so hearing: if a problem arises about what went on, they cannot agree on what was heard. We can say that an experience intrinsically bears a content if there is no independent characterization of it, as there is no independent characterization of the experience of hearing spoken words, or of my current visual experience in non-spatial terms. Now suppose someone disposed to a judgment because his experience intrinsically bears that content: the best, final account the subject can give of why he is disposed to that judgment, is that this is the way it appeared. Then, plausibly, there is no neutral ground between him and a companion whose experience did not come like that: no identification of what was seen or heard independently of the interpretation. If disagreement arises there is no retreat to what can be agreed to have been seen or heard: instead one of the disputants simply has to query the provenance of the experience altogether, supposing that one of them not only misinterpreted what he saw, but was the victim of imagination or illusion in seeing as he did in the first place. The judgment itself is in the last ditch, with no retreat to a neutral 'given' open.

Now not all spontaneous and reliable judgments made on the basis of experience have this last-ditch character. Judgments of the past and future spontaneously made, and many judgments of the identity of objects do not: I may spontaneously and reliably suppose that it has rained, or will rain, or that I am looking at Jupiter through my telescope. But in case of challenge I can retreat to describing what I see neutrally: the wet pavements or dark clouds, or light source of some trajectory in the visual plane of the instrument. We can then agree on the experience without agreeing on the interpretation, however spontaneously it arose.

We can now ask whether judgments of the meaning or beliefs of others are observational not only in the spontaneous, but in the stronger, last-ditch sense. Unfortunately for anyone seeking to rehabilitate the interest of the distinction, the answers to both questions seem to be either indeterminate or negative. Firstly, when a question arises about how to understand someone's sayings and doings, we do not typically have no retreat. We do not have to suppose ourselves the victims of imagination or illusion in seeing or hearing as we did, but are frequently well able to characterize the experience neutrally. Typically we can agree, or attempt to agree, on the words used or the movements made. Of course, at a later time we may forget the words used in favor of the message they conveyed, just as we forget the movements in favor of remembering an action under its more interesting intentional description. But further characterization was at the time available and could have been drawn upon in case of doubt or dispute.

There will be cases where there is no retreat. A good example is heard intonation: I may have no retreat from characterizing in illocutionary terms the tone in which I heard you say something: ironically, condescendingly and so on, just as I may have no retreat from seeing your countenance as knavish. A theoretician may have a retreat, enabling her to say what it is about the tone or the face that prompts the judgment. But even if we imagine that a meaning is simply witnessed in a last-ditch gestalt by a particularly well-tuned observer, theory theorists need not care. For, relying on the promiscuous theory of theory, they will say that it goes like this. The well-tuned observer is so in virtue of having internalized tacit principles of interpretation, giving him spontaneous understanding of the sayings of another. But being like this can have consequences for the way experience is synthesized, that is, for the way in which those other sayings are experienced in the first place. There will be a pre-conscious filtering or massaging of the flow of information so that what is eventually seen or heard carries the attributed content in its own nature. In which case Churchland's position remains correct: the observation of meaning, even in the strong, no-retreat sense, is quite compatible with its theoretical status.

I should mention in passing that this point has more general application. It suggests that very few philosophical disputes over the status of a particular concept – say that of causation, or temporal passage, or spatial distance – are well conducted by first determining what we 'strictly and literally' perceive. For our perceptions could apparently be influenced as much as we like by a tacit inclination to apply or withhold some concept, and that will tell us nothing about the status of the concept or the nature of that inclination. So, for instance, when disputants about causation take up ground on whether we can strictly and literally perceive causal relations, or whether a Humean reduction of what we actually observe is better, we may query whether the ground has any general interest. For, even if the former camp were correct, it could be that this is because a Humean story has already done its work, transposing experience itself into a causal key.

So the attempt to make anything of the observation/theory borderline founders. But the real problem with the observational approach is not highlighted if we leave it at that. The real problem must be that it seeks to model the *transparency* of my own words to myself on the intimacy of observation, as if by being directly confronted with a word I thereby made it my own. But when we are trying to understand thinking, this model is useless. The transparency of acquaintance is not what we want. Here Collingwood triumphs: *using* a word is not observing it; it is not a question of knowing it by acquaintance. In fact, there is an irony in that while the transparency of others to me is billed as an *anti*-Cartesian move, as long as it is modelled on observation the essence of a Cartesian theory of mind remains. This is the modelling of thought upon vision, so that if something is clear and distinct *in the way that* perceived objects are, it counts as understood. This has to be rejected.

Should we conclude that we might as well allow that knowledge of the meaning of others is indeed theoretical? We have not been presented with any evidence of the tacit network of corrigible principles akin to those of a scientific theory, governing the use of intentional terms in our lives. It is just that the view that such a network exists is compatible with any stress on observation that might have hoped to unseat it.

If observation fails to find a stronghold from which to do battle with the theoretical option, the same may be true of simulation. Suppose it is true that when I understand you I do so by re-enacting what I would think, or what I would have thought, or perhaps what was to be thought, and therefore must have been thought, in order to say or act as you did. This reenactment shares three immediate features with the alleged tacit use of theory. First, it is typically spontaneous and pre-conscious. Secondly, it is involved in the same way with the 'last-ditch' factor: insofar as there lacks any independent characterization of the experience prompting us to theorize, so equally there lacks any independent characterization of the situation in which we perform our reenactment. The reenacting, like the theorizing, must be conceived as having been done for us before the synthesis of the experience. But thirdly, the reenactment must be constrained. It too is something of a skill, for not just any old dramatic reconstruction of a chain of events leading to your doings and sayings will do. And then there is a real threat that the principles constraining a plausible reenactment just turn out to be the principles governing attribution of theoretical terms according to the second option. Suppose, for instance, it is true that a good chess player visualizes the board from her opponent's point of view. Then her skill may be described and 'modelled' by a programme for just such a display, and the principles governing its construction maintain the same right to being thought of as a 'tacit theory' of how to achieve the result. Again the attempt to set up a rival stall has foundered.

To assess this further, I think we should distinguish two options for the theory-theorist. The one option may be resolutely modelled on method in science. It acknowledges no interesting difference between theorizing in terms of belief and desire, to describe what people normally do, and theorizing in terms of force and mass to describe what objects normally do. We can call this the functionalist option: the theoretical terms of psychology are held in place by a network of tacit assumptions about what normally causes what, just as those of mechanics are.

The other option is to acknowledge that there is something special about the normativity of psychological attribution. In one way or another the fact that we need to theorize under a 'principle of rationality', or to see a proper point in peoples' doings in order to understand them, marks off this kind of theorizing from anything found in the natural sciences. Pressing, on behalf of this model, we can point out that the alleged causal laws of the functionalist are few, doubtful, and gain what credibility they have by reflection of rationality, coming out as versions of 'people tend to avoid inconsistency'.

It will be particularly evident that this option is disturbingly close to the dramatic reenactment model. For on this option the theorist aims for a theory of what best rationalizes these sayings and doings in the light of our best knowledge of the subject's position. And the dramatist presents his drama as a reconstruction of what would (have to) have been thought in the subject's position, to behave as he did. And the difference between these, if it exists, seems to be exceedingly small.

We can see how small, but potentially how important, by returning to Collingwood's analogy with the deliberation/prediction distinction. This distinction too might seem small, if we reflect as follows. A good way, and often the only way, of predicting what I shall do is this: recognize what my situation will be, and then think how to act in that situation; then predict that I shall do what I have just 'off-line' decided to do. I predict how I should behave on hearing a burglar in the cellar by imagining myself hearing one, and finding thoughts and feelings going through my head. This minimizes the prediction/deliberation distinction, but by making prediction hinge on off-line deliberation. Still, the prediction is in principle a different thing, as we can see if we imagine it produced by other routes. In particular I may predict something of myself or others without being at one with any reasoning that would issue in the action predicted. I can make what I shall call an alienated prediction.

It is not difficult to understand an alienated *functional* prediction. Deliberating what to think in some situation, I come up with some result. But credible science tells me I will do something different. Wondering how to behave in some version of Milgram's notorious experiments, I envisage myself refusing the experimenter's orders. But (conceivably) excellent inductive evidence tells me that I will do what the others do. I may be told that great detail about my functional 'architecture' makes this prediction just about certain: I have no option but to accept it. Notice, however, that this need have no tendency to make the behavior of Milgram's subjects intelligible. I might still feel quite baffled, both by them, and if I am like them, by me. Or, to give a different example, consider that there is no very sensible process of deliberating how to spend my retirement: it is too far away for me to know what interests and abilities I will retain by then. But I might, more or less reluctantly, be forced to recognize likely predictions: that I shall not do as much mountaineering as I often think I will, for instance.

These cases show the space between a theoretical stance towards my future self, when the theory is conceived along 'functional' lines, and an attitude informed by my taking on the deliberative posture of my future self. And it accords with one motivation for the dramatic option, which is that I should not think of my relations to others as detached, and scientific in spirit, where that means that total predictive and instrumental success could be achieved while their reasoning processes yet remained 'foreign' to me.[1] But what if the theory is conceived along normative, Davidsonian lines? Can we get a similarly alienated normative prediction? Here, again, deliberating what to think in some projected situation, I come up with some result. But credible normative principles of rationality tell that one ought to do something different; a predictor using that theory tells me that I shall do something different. The difficulty is apparent. Why am I to believe this prediction? If I accept the normative theory, I must at the same time recognize a defect in my deliberation. Then, either of two things happens. I move to erase the defect, rethinking what to do, and coming up with the preferred answer. Or, I shrug my shoulders, and plead a kind of akrasia, acknowledging a gap between how I decide these things, and how they should be decided. In the first case, I close the gap, and in the second case I do not accept the prediction. What we do not get is the analogue of the gap that is open on the functionalist model, where I retain my initial reasoning, and also retain the prediction, but in an alienated spirit. In other words, if there is a gap between predicting according to the second, normative theory and deliberating, it is not brought out in this way.

Yet if the above remarks about direction of gaze are right, there should be a difference. Theorizing under a normative umbrella is still *theorizing*. It could, it seems, be done quite externally, in the light of a sufficient stock of principles telling what it would be right or wrong to think or feel in some situation, and then coming up with the best balance of right things to have thought or felt that rationalizes what was said or done. Replication is different to this, for the replicator needs no explicit or tacit theory of rationality. He *uses* his rationality; he does not gaze at it, in the hope of extracting principles that are first genuine principles of rationality, second ones that he instances, and third ones that the other person instances.

Of course, we are relentlessly self-conscious. What is used at one moment can be itself an object of reflection at another. We can reflect about a particular exercise of projection or reenactment, and wonder if we did it well or badly. But if we do decide it was done badly, this is just because another exercise of thought or rationality has stepped into the breach, just as you use your vision even if what you are looking at is your own eye.

3 The Home Case

I said above that Collingwood got something right about the home case, by seizing both on the foundational place of reliance on our own words, and the necessity of avoiding a Cartesian theory of it. In this section I try to develop this insight by relating it to contemporary sources of skepticism about meaning.

First let us remember Quine's problems, both of the inscrutability of reference, and of the indeterminacy of radical translation. The upshot is, briefly, that Quine suggests that in the scenario of radical translation there is no fact of the matter whether the native means (say) rabbit, or undetached rabbit part, by the term 'gavagai'. And because analytical hypotheses can be adjusted without end to accommodate either decision, and for reasons connected with the underdetermination of theory by experience, there ends up being no fact of the matter whether the native means one thing or another by whole sentences of his language.

Secondly remember Kripke's problem with the meaning of functors and predicates. The upshot, again, is that there is no fact of the matter whether some subject means one function or another by his mathematical sign, or whether a predicate has one range of correct application or another in his mouth.

These problems are not supposed to arise only in relation to 'outsiders'. If they did, we could rest secure in our own understanding, and lament our inability to remove indeterminacies in our understanding of others. We would have, in the case of meaning, what traditional Cartesian philosophy had in the case of sensation: subjects individually certain of their meanings, but clinging to faith or analogy to assure them that others mean the same, or indeed anything at all. But of course this is not the intended upshot, for the arguments are supposed to infect 'the home case', and therefore the very fact of reference or predication or meaning itself. So taken, they naturally generate a puzzle; and it is one, I shall argue, that forces us to acknowledge the difference between understanding and (mere) theorizing.

The puzzle is this. Consider the natural situation of someone attending to Quine's or Kripke's argument. The form of those arguments (at a level of generality that encompasses them both) is this:

(1) There are two (and more, but we need only two) rival hypotheses A and B about what is being meant or understood by some saying.

(2) No facts that can properly be identified or even conceived of – no facts from physics or from the totality of verbal and non-verbal behavior – make it true that A or that B.

(3) So there is no fact of the matter whether A or B is true.

I shall refer to this as the master argument. I am not here endorsing it, for far too much hinges on whether (2) is true and what the authority of physical and behavioral facts is supposed to depend upon. My concern, rather, is with the logic of positions that do accept the master argument, or, more widely, think of the area of interpretation in terms that invite the master argument (theory-theories).

The crucial question is: are we to assume we understand the master argument? If so, then we are relying in our own case on our meaning one thing when we identify hypothesis A and another when we identify B. When I say, for instance, that some functor could be taken to mean plus, or could be taken to mean quus, I need to rely on my own understanding of the difference. I rely on my own understanding of the difference between a term referring to rabbits, and one referring to undetached rabbit parts as I read Quine. Otherwise I cannot understand the argument, for no two different hypotheses have been presented, and no argument. This first-person reliance is necessary to follow the argument. But it is itself undermined by the argument. For if the argument is good it cannot be so that I, determinately, succeed in taking a word to mean rabbits at one point in the argument, and rabbit parts at another, or a functor to mean addition at one point and quaddition at another. *This would be a success that the conclusion of the argument rules out.*

How are we to respond to this puzzle? One way is to distinguish first-person reliance from anything the arguments show. They show at best that in any third person case – whether the subject of interpretation is an alien, as in Quine's starting point, or whether it is the 'home' case of my understanding of fellow English speakers, indeterminacy arises. I can remain secure in the bunker of my own determinate understanding, and lament the lack of fact in the case of others. This is to return to the Cartesian model. I shall take it that it is quite unacceptable (following Collingwood, amongst others). Indeed, it would be particularly ironic if the right response to arguments from indeterminacy were to be to retreat to irremovable first-person privilege, for it would mean that we could only make sense of Quine's argument by adopting something very close to one of its targets – a myth of the museum, or source of determinate first-person understanding that transcends the public and the behavioral. Because without surreptitious reliance on some such myth, it would be impossible to sustain the privilege demanded.

If we do not go this way, what other responses to the puzzle are open? One might try to downplay it, urging that the situation is no worse than that of a standard *reductio ad absurdum*. The thinker rehearsing the argument starts off confident that he understands the difference between A and B; but as it proceeds that confidence is undermined. At the end, he knows that he never did, or at least there was no fact of the matter that he ever did. This is a possible form of argument. On this suggestion, the puzzle feeds on the notion that you must rely on the difference between A and B to follow the master argument. Whereas really you only need to hypothesize a difference, en route to showing that the hypothesis is false, as the supposed difference evaporates.

But the situation is not like this. In a standard *reductio* one can review every step of the argument from the point of view of the final understanding. There is no premise of which we have to say that it now means nothing; there are only premises of which we have to say that they are false. Yet it is essential to the master argument that it presents two different hypotheses about meaning. To understand the master argument I must pose the question of whether, in someone's mouth, a term means plus or quus, for example. To understand the argument we rely on being able to think that under the one hypothesis, the right answer to some problem is 125, whereas under the other it is 5, or that it is one thing to refer to rabbits, and another to refer to rabbit parts. Someone who cannot themselves understand the difference cannot understand the argument, and this is indeed the initial position of many pupils, who need the unfamiliar function or unfamiliar principle for sorting things explained to them. Only once this understanding is achieved can the argument be intelligible, and anyone supposing that Quine or Kripke has presented an argument supposes that they have that understanding. This first person reliance is non-negotiable – a condition of engaging the issue at all. And the puzzle is that Quine or a skeptic following Kripke uses the master argument to undermine that understanding.

First-person reliance on the meanings of my own words or the contents of my own thoughts is not to be confused with incorrigibility. I can focus my thoughts on the issue of whether some particular act of thinking was all I took it to be – whether I really knew what I meant, or meant something different, or meant anything at all. But of course, as I do this, I will be relying on an understanding expressed in yet further terms. The point is only that if the content of one piece of thinking becomes 'theoretical' for me, it will be investigated relying on concepts that for the moment are not. I need other words in order to think about my potential betrayal by one word. The general fact that I have such understanding, using determinate concepts with determinate standards of correctness, is not a theoretical option amongst others, but a presupposition of any piece of theory, thought and deliberation in the first place.

We now seem subject to a real problem. Rejecting irremovable first-person privilege seemed to mean that my own thinking is simply one piece of thinking of a person in the home community. The immediate community and I are of one mind: any indeterminacy or theoretical jeopardy their thinking suffers, mine suffers too. But first-person reliance puts a non-negotiable stop in front of consistently supposing that my own understanding is thus jeopardized by some version of the master argument.

Quine famously halts the 'decline into the abyss' whereby thought disappears altogether with the observation that in practice we 'acquiesce' in a home language (Quine, 1960). But this is an evasion, and does nothing to halt the decline. It is no good saying that we can be happy at home, if there is no place for home to be. The trouble is that acquiescence in a language is not something that I can actually do, given the conclusion of the argument. Consider a language L in which 'rabbit' means rabbit, and a language L* in which it means proxy-rabbit; or a language L in which '+' means plus, and a language L* in which it means quus. Can I acquiesce in L as opposed to L*? To understand the master argument, I have to do so, but if its conclusion is correct, then I cannot do so. For there can be no truth that I speak L or L*. Either conforms equally well to physics, or to the whole pattern of my linguistic and non-linguistic behavior, or to anything else that makes up the non-intentional world.

Can this problem be evaded by suggesting that it depends upon a pre-Quinean, primitive notion of what understanding must be, so that the proper moral is that once we accept the master argument, we see that we understand it only in a new, Quine-friendly sense (perhaps we learn that our understanding is 'immanent' or 'internal')? This is, I think, the usual way of reacting to the issue by Quineans, their position being that an old, misconceived determinacy – a Cartesian or primitive hyper-determinacy – has been swept away and replaced by a naturalized determinacy, relativized and internal to a scheme or language. But what is on offer? Is this homely determinacy guaranteed by the way we coordinate our *verbal* assurances, when we chorus together disquotational sentences of which the following are samples: 'by "rabbit" I mean rabbit, and by "+" I mean plus'; '"X is a rabbit" is true iff X is a rabbit', and '"X + Y = Z" is true iff X plus Y = Z'? These sentences have no special talismanic force. They would be issued in exactly the same way and with the same confidence if we spoke L and if we spoke L*. It is, of course, true that in its second occurrence in each of these sentences the word 'rabbit' or the word '+' is used, not mentioned, but this is not to the point: the conclusion of the master argument was that this use cannot determinately be to refer to rabbits, as opposed to rabbit parts, or to the function plus as opposed to the function quus, any more than any other use can be. As far as that goes, it is just another use, and if there is no truth that the alien, or the home speaker, or I myself mean some determinate one of the options on any occasion of use, then there is no truth that I mean anything determinate within these options by voicing variations on T-sentences either. If I do, then determinacy within these options exists in my case, and therefore, rejecting first-person privilege, in the home case as well. If I do not, then there is no understanding the master argument.

Or is the homely determinacy created by non-verbal as well as verbal behavior? But how is even the totality of behavior supposed to generate a homely determinacy, when the master argument tells us that it cannot capture what we stared out looking for – namely, the truth that we mean rabbits, not rabbit parts, and plus rather than quus? It was not, on the face of it, that we had any exalted conception of what that determinacy had to consist in. Rather, the master argument supposedly left us with *nothing* for it to consist in – nothing at all to make a difference between speaking L and speaking L*.

Why do followers of Quine not see the difficulty of their position? I think one can be lulled into complacency by a vague thought that relativized determinacy is somehow alright; that together and at home we can generate a kind of conventional determinacy, where physics and behavior failed to generate a metaphysical, external one (Putnam, 1981). But the solace is empty, blown away in a moment by revisiting the crucial premise of the master argument. Unless, together and at home, we generate more than a physically and behaviorally determinate world, we fail to make any kind of determinacy whatsoever. And if we do generate more, then the master argument indeed fails, but only because, somewhere, there is a metaphysically determinate fact not fixed by the totality of physics and behavior.

4 The Upshot

Determinacy of my own meaning has not only a non-negotiable status, but it has a non-theoretical one. That is, whilst I can on occasion make my own meaning into an object of theorizing, if I do so the terms in which I conduct this theory take up the uncontestable status in their turn. Here is another way of making the point. Consider a term with which I am absolutely at home: 'rabbit', say. Then deliberating whether something marginal is a rabbit is nothing different from deliberating whether the word 'rabbit' applies. There is no use/mention confusion here, because the contingency that opens up that distinction, that 'rabbit' might not have meant what it does, is not in play. I know what the word means, which is why rolling it around in my mind as applicable, is exactly the same as wondering whether the object is a rabbit. I know that it would not be for someone else, brought up to a language in which the term means something different. But my difference from such a person is *not* theoretical for me. It is not subject to a network of corrigible assumptions, because it could not have been learned by any process of internalizing such assumptions. There is nothing else that I can access to reassure myself of my difference from such a person. I cannot look over my shoulder, to reassure myself that by 'rabbit' I reliably mean rabbit. This is not a piece of theory for me – or if it is, because I am told and believe of some special dysfunction, say with that particular term – then terms with which I then start to think about what the dysfunction might have done attain the forfeited status.

But by rejecting first-person privilege, we reap the consequence that the same is true of my relations with those with whom I am at home. So their meaning is not simply theoretical for me either.

Of course, we have moved from the promiscuous theory of theories by insisting that if a body of knowledge counts as theoretical there must be a possible stance from which the body is considered, and assessed in the light of independent thoughts and principles of inference. It is this that the non-negotiable reliance on first-person understanding, coupled with the absence of first-person privilege, blocks. If someone contends that it is not criterial of a body of opinion being theoretical that this condition is met, then I think we are back to the promiscuous theory of theories, and we can throw away the term: the consequence will be that any process of belief formation counts as theoretical, but the reason for counting that interesting will be lost. The dramatic option then reformulates as the view that understanding others is, like everything else, theoretical, but it consists in something else special as well, something whose essence must include the non-theoretical status of my own deliberations for me, and the place of the first-person stance in my understanding of others (or of myself at different times).

My argument has been very simple. If other persons' understandings were merely theoretical, then space always opens for Quinean or Kripkean skepticism; this space is not open in my own case; my own case cannot be regarded as privileged above those in my home community; hence my understanding of other persons is not merely theoretical. Now it is true that this is not directly a defence of a replication or simulation approach, for we learn what understanding others is not, rather than what it is. But the attractions of that approach as an alternative now derive from its emphasis on the right fact, the fact that blocks application of Quinean or Krikpean skepticism in my own case, which is that my own functioning as a thinker has a non-negotiable, and non-theoretical, and foundational role in any account of my relations with others.

Note

1 A curious aspect of Stich and Nichols (this volume, ch. 5) is that they suppose that 'off-line simulation' theory should enable us to predict (find intelligible?) quirks of belief and choice described in the cognitive dysfunction literature. But this is exactly wrong, if the process is as Collingwood intends. When I replicate learning that the evidence that someone is good at detecting fake suicide notes was fraudulent, I do not think 'so, better go on believing that they are good at it'. My behavior, if I do in fact go on believing it, is as alien to me as that of others.

References

Churchland, P. S. 1986: Replies to comments. *Inquiry*, 29, 241–73.
Churchland, P. M. 1989: Folk psychology and the explanation of human behaviour. In J. Tomberlin (ed.), *Philosophical Perspectives, Volume* 3. Atascadero, Calif.: Ridgeview Publishing Co.
Collingwood, R. G. 1938: *The Principles of Art*. Oxford: Oxford University Press.
Collingwood, R. G. 1946: *The Idea of History*. Oxford: Oxford University Press.

Davies, M. 1987: Tacit knowledge and semantic theory: Can a five per cent difference matter?. *Mind*, 96, 441–62.

Dennett, D. 1982: Making sense of ourselves. In J. Biro and R. Shahan (eds), *Mind, Brain and Function*. Brighton: Harvester Press.

Goldman, A. I. 1989: Interpretation psychologized. *Mind and Language*, 4, 161–85. Reprinted as ch. 3 in this volume.

Gordon, R. M. 1986: Folk psychology as simulation, *Mind and Language*, 1, 158–71. Reprinted as ch. 2 in this volume.

Heal, J. 1986: Replication and functionalism. In J. Butterfield (ed.), *Language, Mind and Logic*. Cambridge: Cambridge University Press. Reprinted as ch. 1 in this volume.

Hume, D. 1739: *A Treatise of Human Nature*. London.

Putnam, H. 1981: *Reason, Truth and History*. Cambridge: Cambridge University Press.

Quine, W. V. 1960: *Word and Object*. Cambridge, MA: MIT Press.

Index of Authors

Altshuler, J.   216
Anderson, J.   95
Argyle, M.   261
Astington, J. W.   124, 168, 213, 216–17, 224, 227, 238, 240, 241, 247–8, 251
Avis, J.   227, 241

Bach, K.   55
Banerjee, M.   239, 250
Baron-Cohen, S.   39, 42, 70, 86, 87, 155, 198, 215, 225, 227, 228, 259–71
Bartsch, K.   238, 239, 240, 243–4, 250
Beattie, K.   238
Beeghly, M.   226, 237
Bennett, J.   209, 223–4
Bever, T.   123
Blackburn, S.   8, 10, 29, 274–89
Block, N.   94
Brentano, F. von   267
Bretherton, I.   226, 237
Brown, E.   238
Bruner, J.   260, 261
Bryant, P. E.   201, 202, 221
Butterworth, G.   193, 212, 227, 260, 266, 269

Campbell, R.   261, 268
Carey, S.   170, 232
Cheney, D. L.   120
Cherniak, C.   78
Chomsky, N.   123

Churchland, P. M.   7, 10, 11, 26, 71, 88, 93, 100, 114–15, 116, 118, 120–1, 124, 161, 193, 232, 277
Churchland, P. S.   278
Cloghesy, K.   162
Cochran, E.   193
Cohen, D.   215
Cohen, L. J.   78
Coley, J. D.   253
Collingwood, R. G.   64, 96, 117, 274, 275–7, 281, 282
Cooper, L.   86
Coulter, J.   160
Cowey, A.   261, 264
Croft, K.   240
Cross, P.   259–71
Cummins, R.   123
Currie, G.   42

Daly, M. J.   216
D'Andrade, R.   124
Davidson, D.   46, 68, 75–6, 91, 102–3, 117, 121
Davies, M.   1–42, 275
De Haan, E.   261
Dennett, D. C.   18, 19, 49, 76, 84–5, 95, 101, 118, 123, 140, 209, 223–4, 267, 274
Descartes, R.   161
Doyle, A. Conan   63–4
Dretske, F.   95, 239
Dummett, M.   7

Eliot, J.   162
Ellis, H.   270
Estes, D.   237, 238, 266
Evans, G.   190
Evans-Pritchard, E. E.   210, 227
Everett, B. A.   240

Fairburn System of Visual References
    262, 264
Field, H.   46, 55, 58–9, 95
Flavell, E. R.   227, 240, 241, 242, 260
Flavell, J. H.   159, 212, 214, 227, 237,
    238, 240, 241, 242, 243, 251, 260
Fodor, J. A.   11, 22, 55, 56, 80–1, 95,
    106, 123, 124, 140, 154, 194
Forguson, L.   239
Frith, U.   39, 70, 86, 87, 155, 198–9,
    215, 268
Frye, D.   227
Furrow, P.   241

Gärdenfors, P.   95
Garon, J.   133
Garrett, M.   123
Gelman, S. A.   207, 232, 253
Gibson, J.   269
Goldman, A.   I. 18–19, 21, 25, 74–96,
    100, 103, 104, 124–5, 128–40, 145,
    154–5, 159, 161, 180, 191–205, 252,
    274
Goodhart, F.   228
Gopnik, A.   27–9, 42, 168, 213, 216–
    17, 224–5, 232–54
Gordon, R. M.   15, 16, 20, 25, 42, 60–
    73, 81, 82, 87, 100–21, 124–5, 128–37,
    138–45, 154–5, 159, 161, 174–90, 191,
    252, 268, 274, 277, 278
Graf, P.   241, 251
Grandy, R.   68, 81
Green, F. L.   241, 242
Greeno, J.   123
Gregory, R. L.   39, 123
Gruendel, J.   211
Gur, R. and R.   260

Harman, G.   46, 209, 223–4
Harmer, S.   238
Harris, L.   260
Harris, P. L.   29, 30–2, 38, 42, 87, 100,
    159, 161, 162, 168, 179, 199, 202, 204,
    207–28, 227, 232, 238, 241
Hartl, M.   161, 168, 169, 213, 217, 224,
    248
Hatano, G.   270
Hay, D. F.   212
Hayes, P.   123
Heal, J.   19, 20, 21, 24, 45–58, 96, 124,
    274, 277
Heywood, C.   261, 264
Hinton, G.   86
Hobson, R. P.   228, 260, 266, 269, 270
Hoffman, M. L.   204
Hogrefe, J.   167, 180, 200, 220, 251
Horgan, T.   116
Howes, D.   32–3, 159–71, 185–90
Hubley, P.   236
Hume, D.   275

Inagaki, K.   270
Inhelder, B.   159, 170, 232

Jarrett, N.   260
Johnson, C. N.   96, 232
Johnson-Laird, P.   133

Kahneman, D.   17–18, 77, 83, 86, 135,
    192
Karmiloff-Smith, A.   232
Kasari, C.   215, 268
Keil, F. C.   170, 232
Kinsbourne, M.   260
Kohler, W.   209
Kosslyn, S.   86, 140
Kripke, S.   96, 284–6
Kuczaj, S. A. II   216

Lacohée, H.   168, 244
Leekam, S. R.   238
Lempers, J. D.   227, 260
Leslie, A. M.   38–42, 70, 86, 87, 124,
    145–6, 155, 156, 198, 199, 227, 238,
    268, 270
Levi, I.   95
Lewis, D.   9–10, 46, 76, 79, 90, 96
Loar, B.   96
Loveland, K.   266
Lycan, W.   123

Magnus, H.   268
Mandler, J.   270

Maratsos, M.   253
Marr, D.   123
Marriot, C.   238
Masangkay, Z. S.   243
McClelland, J.   86
McCloskey, M.   123
McCluskey, K. A.   243
McDowell, J.   48, 55
McGinn, C.   55, 56, 58–9, 76
McIntyre, C. W.   243
Medin, D.   170
Meerum Terwogt, M.   204
Meltzoff, A. N.   236
Miller, P.   162
Millikan, R.   95
Mitchell, P.   168, 244
Montgomery, R.   96, 124
Moore, C.   227, 236, 241, 248, 251–2
Moore, M. K.   236
Morton, A.   72, 81, 82
Morton, J.   260
Moses, L. J.   238, 242
Mundy, P.   215, 268
Murphy, G. L.   170

Nelson, K.   211
Newell, A.   145
Nichols, S.   8, 13, 22, 23, 26, 123–56,
    174–83, 191–204, 207–8, 217–19, 220–
    1, 222, 252
Nisbett, R. E.   95, 105, 151, 152, 167,
    218, 219
Nozick, R.   72, 96, 118–19

Olson, D.   124, 227
O'Neill, D. K.   251

Perner, J.   2, 29, 30, 31–7, 41, 42, 69,
    86–7, 110, 145, 155–6, 159–71, 180,
    185–90, 209, 212, 213, 224, 227, 238,
    241, 251, 266, 268
Perrett, D.   261
Phillips, W.   267, 268
Piaget, J.   159, 170, 267
Pick, A.   269
Pillow, B. H.   201
Pinker, S.   123
Pollock, J.   78
Pratt, C.   201, 202, 221
Premack, D.   1, 72, 208–9, 226–7, 267

Pure, K.   241
Putnam, H.   46, 67, 96, 288
Pylyshyn, Z.   22, 140

Quine, W. V. O.   46, 67, 68, 72, 81, 89,
    284–7

Ramachandran, V. S.   192
Ramsey, W.   133
Rheingold, H. L.   212
Ripstein, A.   96, 124, 153–4
Rivière, A.   267
Rock, I.   123
Rosch, E.   91
Ross, L.   105, 151, 152, 167, 218, 219
Roth, D.   41
Rumelhart, D.   86, 135
Rutter, D.   261
Rutter, M.   267
Rygh, J.   216

Sahlin, N. E.   95
Scaife, M.   260, 261
Schene, J.   204
Schiffer, S.   79, 96, 178
Schutz, A.   64
Searle, J. R.   71, 236–7
Sellars, C.   270
Sellars, W.   124
Seyfarth, R. M.   120
Shatz, M.   226, 237
Shepard, R.   86
Sherman, T.   215
Shultz, T. R.   162
Siegal, M.   238
Sigman, M.   215, 268
Silber, S.   226, 237
Sims-Knight, J.   243
Slaughter, V.   168, 224–5, 243, 248
Slobin, D. I.   253
Smolensky, P.   86
Sodian, B.   180, 200, 220
Spelke, E. S.   253
Sperber, D.   84
Stalnaker, R. C.   178–9
Stich, S.   8, 13, 22, 23, 26, 45, 49, 67–8,
    72, 81–2, 83, 123–56, 133, 174–83,
    191–204, 207–8, 217–19, 220–1, 222,
    232, 252
Stone, T.   1–42

Stotland, E.   204
Strawson, P. F.   117

Tager-Flusberg, H.   215, 228
Tan, J.   228
Thagard, P.   95
Thaiss, L.   40, 41, 42
Tiensen, J.   116
Trevarthen, C.   236
Tversky, A.   17–18, 77, 83, 86, 135, 192

Ungerer, J.   215

Van Fraassen, B.   89
Vaughn, B. E.   243
Vendler, Z.   119–20

Walker, J.   268
Wellman, H. M.   12–13, 27, 28–9, 42, 200–1, 207, 212, 226, 227, 232–54, 266, 268

Wellman, W. H.   236
West, M. J.   212
Whiten, A.   227, 261
Whittal, S.   238
Wilson, D.   84
Wilson, E. O.   120
Wimmer, H.   2, 69, 86–7, 145, 147, 148, 149, 161, 162, 167, 168, 169, 170, 171, 180, 182, 200, 201–2, 209, 217, 220, 222, 224, 238, 241, 248, 251
Wittgenstein, L.   260
Wolf, D. P.   216
Woodfield, A.   52
Woodruff, G.   1, 72, 208–9, 226–7, 267
Woolley, J. D.   237, 240, 249
Von Wright, G. H.   64

Young, A.   270
Yuill, N.   240

Zaitchek, D.   241
Zaitchik, D.   41

Index of Subjects

access check procedure 148, 220, 221, 222
aerodynamics analogy 115, 116, 117–18, 125–7
animal models, behavior interpretation 208–9
answer check procedure 148, 180–1, 187, 220, 221
autistic children
  blood test anecdote 199
  comic strip experiment 198
  developmental sequence 215
  eye direction 268
  Goldman's case for simulation theory 70, 87, 145, 198–9
  Gordon's case 70, 87, 144–5
  information processing 39–42
  pretend play 39–41, 70, 87, 144–6, 155
  self-reporting accuracy 225
  shopping anecdote 199
Azande tribe, witchcraft 210

behavioral laws, simulation theory and 105–6
beliefs and belief attribution 2–6, 24–5
  five-year-old theory 239
  functionalism or replication 45–7, 48–51, 56, 58–9
  Goldman's case 25, 74–82, 85–7, 90–1, 92–3, 200–2: Stich and Nichols and 130–2, 201–2

Gordon's case 25, 66–71: autistic children 70, 87, 144–5; behavioral laws 106; projection 103, 104–5; reply to Perner and Howes 186–9; Stich and Nichols and 130–2, 141–4, 145–6, 155, 180–3
inferred belief tasks 200–1
knowledge assessment 221–3
link with perception 201, 214, 248–50
make-believe belief 49–50, 211
misrepresentation 247–9
moving from belief to prediction 21–2
observation and drama 274–89
Perner and Howes's case 161–70: behavioral simulation 188; emotional responses 189–90; Gordon's reply 186–9; memory failure 168–9; second-order simulation 162–3, 186
privileged access to mental states 224–6
psychological concepts in simulation theory 25–6
self-reporting accuracy 217, 224–5, 246–7, 249, 251
sources of 251, 252
Stich and Nichols's case: belief perseverance 152, 177, 203, 217–18; eliminativism 124–5; Goldman and 130–2, 201–2;

Gordon and 130–2, 141–4, 145–6,
155, 180–3; Harris's reply 217–18,
222; inference 148–50, 155–6, 222;
mechanisms outlined 127
subjective probability
understanding 251–2
theory change process 213–14, 240
three-year-old theory 237–8
transitional phenomena 243–4
see also false belief task
blindness, theory of mind acquisition
270

Cartesian introspectionism 45, 57, 161,
166–7, 168–9, 185–6
categorization 90–1
cause and effect
connections between 116
developmental evidence 252
functionalism 54–5
see also explanation
ceteris paribus clauses 67, 76, 79
charity principle 68, 75–6
child development
adult experimental errors 217–20
autistic children: blood test
anecdote 199; comic strip
experiment 198; developmental
sequence 215; eye direction
268; information processing 39–
42; pretend play 39–41, 70, 87,
144–6, 155; self-reporting accuracy
225; shopping anecdote 199
centrality of evidence on 211
concepts of mind 27–8
desire 27–8, 213, 224–5, 236–9, 240–
3, 248–50
eye direction signals 261–7, 268
Gopnik and Wellman's account 27–
9, 232–54
grammar 136–7, 194, 211, 253
Harris's case 207–26
imitative mechanisms 113–14, 193,
204, 212, 214–15
inference 148–50, 155–6, 200–2,
221–3
interpretation: animal models 208–
9; Goldman's case 78–9, 80–1, 86–
7, 136, 193; Gopnik and Wellman
242; Gordon 141–2; Harris's view

214–16; Stich and Nichols's case
136–7, 141–4
kinship-preserving substitutions
110–11
knowledge and pretence
differentiated 169
perception 201, 214, 236–9, 240–3,
248–50, 267
Perner and Howes 159–70, 185–90
perspective-taking tasks 170, 214,
216, 251
precocity 80–1, 136–7, 193–4, 252–4
pretend play: autistic children 39–
41, 70, 87, 144–6, 155;
developmental sequence 216;
grammar acquisition 211; mental
state representation 87
reality of attitudes 207–8
representation 28–37, 39–41, 213:
Gopnik and Wellman's
description 236, 237–9, 240, 241,
242–4, 247–8, 252; meta-
representational theory 29–37,
159–70, 185–90; meta-
representations 40–1, 146, 199
sequence of 212: explanation 239–
40; five-year old theory 239;
interpretation 242; knowledge
assessment 220–3; prediction
240–2; privileged access to mental
states 223–6; self-reporting
accuracy 216–17, 224–5, 246–7,
249, 251; simulation/theory
theory explanation 212–16; three-
year-old theory 237–9;
transitional phenomena 242–4;
two-year-old theory 236–7
theory change 4, 7, 27–9, 212–16,
235–54
see also beliefs and belief attribution;
false belief task; prediction
Chomskyan linguistics 8–9
code compression 179–80
cognitive competence, functionalism
and replication 52–4, 57–8
cognitive penetrability 22–4, 150–2,
175–7, 202–3
cognitive science, use of simulation
models 86, 135–6, 192–3, 195
common-sense theories

precocity and 136–7
scientific theories and 11, 12–13
communication
   deductive inference 84
   intonation and judgment 280
   see also perceptual inputs
conditional planning, simulation/
   theory theory simplicity 197–8
connectionism, theory theory 133, 135
content attributions, simulation
   theory 89–92

decision-making processes
   belief attribution 67–71, 141–4, 145–
      6, 155–6
   cognitive penetrability 23–4, 150–2,
      175–7
   direction-of-gaze 20–1
   functionalism and replication 53–4
   knowledge and pretence
      differentiated 169
   off-line simulation outlined 127
   position effect experiment 218–19
   practical reasoning 62–6, 68–71, 100,
      129, 154–5
   self-prediction 16, 62
   simplicity debate 138, 178–9, 197–8
desire
   developmental approach 27–8, 213,
      224–5, 236–9, 240–3, 248–50
   eliminativism 124–5
   functionalism 45–7
   simulation 127, 130–1
determinacy, skepticism about
   meaning 284–8
developmental evidence *see* child
   development
dominant explanatory strategy 8–9,
   38–9, 124, 191–3
drama, meaning through reenactment
   274–89

eliminativism 93, 124–5, 207–8
empathetic understanding 116–19,
   204–5
entification 90–1
experience, basing judgments on
   279–80
explanation
   deductive structure 11

dominant explanatory strategy 8–9,
   38–9, 124, 191–3
Gopnik and Wellman,
   developmental sequence 234,
   236–8, 239–40, 250, 252
Gordon's case for simulation theory
   88–9, 100–1: behavioral laws 105–
   6; introspection 114–20;
   projection 102–5, 106–12
reality of attitudes 208
referential and non-referential 54–7
Stich and Nichols's case 124, 129–
   52, 154–5: Goldman's reply
   191–202
eye direction 20–1, 48, 259–71
   attribution of mental states 267
   development and perception 267
   experiments 261–6
   gaze mimicry 113, 193, 212, 214–15
   Gibsonian direct-perception theory
      266
   Gordon's view 70–1
   as symptoms and criteria 259–61

fallibilism 54, 56–7
false belief task 2–6
   animal models 209
   answer check procedure and 221
   autistic children 39–41, 70, 145–6,
      198
   developmental sequence 213–14,
      216, 238, 241–2, 243–4, 245–6,
      247–8
   explicit type 200
   false belief or memory failure 168–
      9, 244, 249
   reason for use of 209
   representation and 29–32, 35–6
   self-reporting inaccuracy 217
first-person reliance, skepticism about
   meaning 285–6, 288–9
functionalism 45–59
   alienated predictions 282–3
   beliefs and desire 45–7
   Goldman's case for interpretation
      theories and 75, 79–81, 93, 94, 95
   replication and 47–58, 274, 283:
      compatibility 51–4; concepts and
      modes of explanation in 54–8;
      make-believe belief 49–50; setting

up replication state 48–9;
thinking sequences 50–1
see also simulation/theory theory
debate

gaze
direction of *see* eye direction
mimicry of 113, 193, 212, 214–15
generalizations 11
behavioral laws 105–6
belief attribution 66–7
cause and effect connections 116
hypothetico-practical reasoning 66
inductively based 21–2, 80–1, 83, 88
simplicity argument 137–8, 178–80,
197–8
Gestalt principles, entification 91
Gibsonian theory 238, 266
grammar *see* linguistics

hiker scenario 20–1, 102–5, 107–9,
111–12, 116–17
historical reenactment, Collingwood
64, 275–6, 277
home case, skepticism about meaning
284–8
humanity principle 68, 81
humor, making others laugh 84
hypothetico-practical reasoning 64–6,
131

'I', rigid designator 119–20
imagination
developmental sequence 215–16
imaginative impenetrability 176,
177
imitative mechanisms 113–14, 204,
215
information processing 37–8
make-believe belief 49–50
Model Model 118–19, 120, 277
projection 21, 102–5, 106–12, 120
psychological concepts in
simulation theory 26
Stich and Nichols's case 23, 126–7,
140–1, 151: Goldman's reply 196,
202–3; Gordon's reply 175–7
see also introspection; meta-
representational theory
imitative mechanisms 113–14, 193,

204, 212, 214–15
inductively based generalizations 21–
2, 80–1, 83, 88
inference 84, 148–50, 155–6, 200–2,
221–3
information processing 4–5, 6, 37–42
innateness, of folk theory 80–1, 194
intentional descriptions 76, 124,
129–32
see also interpretation
interpretation
animal models 208–9
Goldman's case 74–94: charity
theories 75–6; content attributions
89–92; cultural transmission
model 194; deictic gaze 193;
rationality 75, 76–9, 83, 84;
simulation approach 75, 81–9, 92–
4; theory theory 75, 79–81, 93, 94;
uniformity 89–92
Gopnik and Wellman's
developmental approach 242
Gordon's reply to Stich and Nichols
174–5
Harris's explanation 214–16
Stich and Nichols's case 131, 132–
52, 154–5
intonation, judgment and 280
introspection
Cartesian 45, 57, 161, 166–7, 168–9,
185–6
Goldman 87–8, 138–40, 195–6
Gordon 63–4, 101–2, 114–20, 138–9,
140: projection and 113; reply to
Perner and Howes 185–8; reply
to Stich and Nichols 174–5
Perner and Howes's case 161–70,
185–8
Stich and Nichols 138–41, 174–5,
195–6

kinship-preserving substitutions
110–11
knowledge
code compression 179–80
dominant explanatory strategy 8–9,
38–9, 124, 191–3
functionalism and replication 57
link between theories and concepts
14–15

Perner and Howes's case 161–70:
Gordon's reply 185–8
recentring and 21, 48, 57
Stich and Nichols's case 13, 123,
147–9, 155–6: Goldman's reply
191–3, 196, 201–2, 205; Gordon's
reply 180–3; Harris's reply 220–3
tacit 8–9, 11–12, 13, 123
theory- or process-driven
simulation 18

least pretending principle 65, 68, 181
linguistics
analogy to theory theory 8–9, 10,
11–12, 13
children's acquisition of grammar
136–7, 194, 211, 253
Goldman's case for grammar 89
grammaticality judgments 134–5,
171, 177–8
prediction experiment 210–11
logical consistency, rationality 76–7,
83
lottery scenario, predictions 151–2,
176–7, 203, 218

make-believe belief 49–50, 211
Maxi experiment 69, 141–4, 145–6,
180–3
meaning, skepticism about 284–9
memory failure, or false belief 168–9,
244, 249
meta-representational theory 29–37,
159–70, 185–90
meta-representations 40–1, 146, 199
mimicry 113–14, 193, 204, 212, 214–15
Model Model, simulation 117–19, 120,
277
modus ponens law 106

non-referential content, functionalism
and replication 55–7

observation, understanding through
274–89
off-line simulation 18
Stich and Nichols's description
127–9, 132, 174, 196
see also simulation/theory theory
debate

patched projection 21, 106–12
perception, developmental change
201, 214, 236–9, 240–3, 248–50, 267
perceptual inputs
deductive inference 84
eye direction: development 267;
experiments 261–6; mental states
attribution 267; as symptoms and
criteria 259–61
intonation and judgment 280
selectivity 279–81
simulation theory 79, 82, 131
perspective-taking tasks 170, 214, 216,
251
platitudes, in theory theory 9–10, 79–
80, 134, 193–4
play *see* pretend play
position effect experiment, quality
rating 23, 151, 167, 175, 176, 202–
3, 218–20
practical reasoning 62–6, 68–71, 127,
129, 130–1, 154–5
precocity 80–1, 136–7, 193–4, 252–4
prediction 15–18, 22
alienated type 282–3
cognitive penetrability 22–4, 150–2,
175–7, 202–3
connectionist models 133
developmental sequence: Gopnik
and Wellman 233–6, 240–2, 250–
1; Harris 208, 210–11, 217–23
functionalism 47–8
gaze-direction 20–1
Goldman's case 82–3, 84–6, 89–90,
191–205
Gordon's case 61–4: behavioral
laws 105–6; belief attribution
67–71, 141–2; direction-of-gaze
20–1; hypothetico-practical
reasoning 65–6; introspection
114–20; projection 102–5, 106–12;
reply to Perner and Howes 186–8;
reply to Stich and Nichols 175–7,
180–3; self-prediction 16, 61–3
knowledge and pretence
differentiated 169
Perner and Howes's case 161–8,
186–8
psycholinguistic experiment 210–11
self-prediction 15–16, 22–3, 61–3

Stich and Nichols 23, 125–9, 130, 131, 132–52, 154–6: Goldman's reply 191–205; Gordon's reply 175–7, 180–3; Harris's reply 217–23
Verstehen 275–8
pretence 16
    belief attribution 67–71, 142–3, 145–6, 155
    burglar in basement example 16, 62, 128
    developmental sequence 215, 216, 238–9
    differentiation between knowledge and 169, 222–3, 224–5
    direction-of-gaze 20–1
    Goldman's case 85–6
    Harris's reply to Stich and Nichols 217–20
    hypothetico-practical reasoning 65–6, 131
    'I' as rigid designator 119–20
    in projection 109–10
    Tees/Crane experiment 18
pretend play
    autistic children 39–41, 70, 87, 144–6, 155
    developmental sequence 216
    grammar acquisition 211
    mental state representation 87
principles, simulation/theory theory debate 133–5, 193–4
probabilistic coherence, rationality 76, 77, 83, 192
process-driven simulation 18–19, 85, 195, 196, 204, 267
professional science
    analogy with theory theory 9–11, 12–15
    theory change in 4, 7, 28–9, 36–7, 235–6, 245
projection 21, 102–5, 106–12, 113, 120, 249
promiscuous theory theory 7, 275, 288–9
prosopagnosia 270
psychological concepts
    children 27–8
    link with psychological theories 12, 14–15

simulation theory and 24–6
theory theory and 11–15
psychological theories
    psychological concepts link 12, 14–15
    for setting up simulation 21–2
    theory and simulation in 26–9: information processing accounts 37–42; representation 28, 29–37

rationality
    empathetic understanding 116–17
    functionalism and replication 52–4, 57–8, 282–3
    interpretation theories 75, 76–9, 83, 84
    projection and 104–5
    see also practical reasoning
reality–appearance task 213–14, 216
recentring 21, 48, 57, 277–8
referential relations, functionalism and replication 54–7, 58–9
reliabilism 93, 108, 112
replication theory *see* functionalism, replication and; simulation/theory theory debate
representation 28–37
    autistic children 39–41
    Gopnik and Wellman's description 236, 237–9, 240, 241, 242–4, 247–8, 252
    Harris's view 213
    meta-representational theory 29–37, 159–70, 185–90
    meta-representations 40–1, 146, 199
role-taking
    empathic arousal 204–5
    see also simulation/theory theory debate
rule-based models, theory theory 133, 135, 192, 196

science
    analogy with theory theory 9–11, 12–15
    theory change in 4, 7, 28–9, 36–7, 235–6, 245
selection processor (SP) 41
self-prediction 15–16, 22–3, 61–3
semantic properties

observational and theoretical
models 278–9
psychological states, functionalism
and replication 54–7
sentence-based models, theory theory
133, 135, 192, 196
shopping-mall experiment, position
effect 23, 151, 167, 175, 176, 202–
3, 218–20
simplicity argument, simulation/
theory theory debate 137–8, 178–
80, 197–8
simulation/theory theory debate 3–26
developmental approaches 6:
Gopnik and Wellman's account
232–54; Harris's case 207–26;
Perner and Howes 159–70,
185–90
eye direction 259–71
Goldman's case 17–19, 74–94, 191–
205
Gordon's case 15–16, 20–1, 25, 60–
73, 100–20, 174–83, 185–90
linguistics analogy 8–9, 11–12, 13,
177–8
observation and drama 274–89
professional science analogy 9–11,
12–15
psychological concepts and 12–15,
24–6
psychological theories and 26–9:
information processing 37–42;
representation 28, 29–37
replication and functionalism 45–59
Stich and Nichols's case 13–14, 123–
53: defense of theory theory 146–
52; Goldman's reply 191–205;
Gordon's reply 174–83; Harris's
reply 217–20; intentional
explanations 129–32; predicting
behavior 22–4, 125–9; for
simulation theory 132–46;
terminology 132–3, 174–5, 196;
theory- or process-driven
simulation 18–19, 85, 195, 196,
204, 267

Slavic waiter scenario, hypothetico-
practical reasoning 64–5, 130
Smarties box experiment 168–9, 213,
222, 223, 247–8
suspension bridge analogy 18–19, 49–
50, 84–5

tacit knowledge
or generic notion of knowledge 13,
123
linguistics and 8–9, 11–12
tacit theory 7, 29, 275, 281–2
see also simulation/theory theory
debate
Tees/Crane experiment 17–18, 83
term-introducing theory 9–11, 79
theory, sense of 7–8, 275
theory change, child development 4,
7, 27–9, 36–7, 212–16, 235–54
theory of mind module (ToMM) 40–1
theory theories, terminology and
distinctions between 133
see also simulation/theory theory
debate
theory-driven simulation 18–19, 85,
195, 196, 204, 267
Three-Mountain Problem 170
total projection 21, 102–12, 113, 120,
249
trivialization, theory theory
challenged 7, 8–12, 36–7
truth
perceptual inputs 79
referential relations and 56, 58–9
truthfulness principle 76

uniformity, interpretation theories
89–92

Verstehen 64, 81, 118–19, 275–8
vision, mechanisms of 192
see also eye direction

wind tunnel scenario 115, 116, 117–18,
125–7
witchcraft *see* Azande tribe